THE CLARKE PAPERS

FURTHER SELECTIONS FROM THE PAPERS OF WILLIAM CLARKE

THE CLARKE PAPERS

FURTHER SELECTIONS FROM THE PAPERS OF WILLIAM CLARKE

Secretary to the Council of the Army 1647–1649, and to General Monck and the Commanders of the Army in Scotland, 1651–1660

edited by
FRANCES HENDERSON

CAMDEN FIFTH SERIES
Volume 27

CAMBRIDGE
UNIVERSITY PRESS

FOR THE ROYAL HISTORICAL SOCIETY
University College London, Gower Street, London WC1 6BT
2005

Published by the Press Syndicate of the University of Cambridge
The Edinburgh Building, Cambridge CB2 2RU, United Kingdom
40 West 20th Street, New York, NY 10011–4211, USA
477 Williamstown Road, Port Melbourne, VIC 3207, Australia
Ruiz de Alarcón 13, 28014 Madrid, Spain
Dock House, The Waterfront, Cape Town 8001, South Africa

First published 2005

A catalogue record for this book is available from the British Library
Library of Congress Cataloging-in-Publication Data applied for

ISBN 0 521 86267 1 hardback

SUBSCRIPTIONS. The serial publications of the Royal Historical Society, *Royal Historical Society Transactions* (ISSN 0080–4401) and Camden Fifth Series (ISSN 0960–1163), volumes may be purchased together on annual subscription. The 2005 subscription price which includes print and electronic access (but not VAT) is £77 (US $124 in the USA, Canada and Mexico) and includes Camden Fifth Series, volumes 26 and 27 (published in July and December) and Transactions Sixth Series, volume 15 (published in December). Japanese prices are available from Kinokuniya Company Ltd, P.O. Box 55, Chitose, Tokyo 156, Japan. EU subscribers (outside the UK) who are not registered for VAT should add VAT at their country's rate. VAT registered subscribers should provide their VAT registration number. Prices include delivery by air.

Subscription orders, which must be accompanied by payment, may be sent to a bookseller, subscription agent or direct to the publisher: Cambridge University Press, The Edinburgh Building, Shaftesbury Road, Cambridge CB2 2RU, UK; or in the USA, Canada and Mexico; Cambridge University Press, Journals Fulfillment Department, 100 Brook Hill Drive, West Nyack, New York, 10994–2133, USA.

SINGLE VOLUMES AND BACK VOLUMES. A list of Royal Historical Society volumes available from Cambridge University Press may be obtained from the Humanities Marketing Department at the address above.

Printed and bound in the United Kingdom at the University Press, Cambridge

CONTENTS

[1] Clarke's notebooks were not allocated these numbers until, many years after his death, they had become the property of Worcester College, Oxford. Clarke himself seems to have arranged his working notebooks by size and date. There is no shorthand in Notebooks XXI and XXIII. Dates refer to the time-span of the selected documents presented in this volume, and not to the coverage of each entire notebook.

PREFACE AND ACKNOWLEDGEMENTS

It is now more than a hundred years since Sir Charles Firth's edition of four volumes of *Clarke Papers* was published by the Camden Society; it is a particular pleasure to be able to contribute a fifth. This volume offers a selection from the large number of documents which William Clarke left to us only in shorthand, unread by Firth and indeed – so far as I am aware – unread by anyone except myself since Clarke's own day.

The transcription and analysis of almost a quarter of a million words of Clarke's shorthand has been a lengthy and demanding process, and one during which I have incurred many debts of gratitude. Foremost among them must be that to Professor Blair Worden, supervisor of the doctoral thesis from which this volume springs. To him I wish to express my warmest thanks for his wise guidance and unfailing vigilance and encouragement.

The late Dr Anne Whiteman offered greatly valued counsel during the early stages of a project which without her might never have begun. I also owe much to the perceptive and constructive comments of the two examiners of my Oxford thesis, Professor John Morrill and the late Dr Gerald Aylmer, and also to those of the late Professor Austin Woolrych.

I have greatly benefited from the support of my two colleges in Oxford, New College and Worcester College. Without it the project might never have been completed. In 1996 Worcester College expressed confidence in my research by electing me to a Research Associateship. A Visiting Fellowship at the Huntington Library, San Marino, California, during October 2000 provided access to the richness of their seventeenth-century collections. To them all I extend my sincere gratitude.

I wish also to thank the many librarians on whose help I have relied during this undertaking, particularly those of my two Oxford colleges, of Duke Humfrey's library, and of the History Faculty library in Oxford. At Worcester College, Dr Joanna Parker has been especially helpful in providing speedy access to innumerable books and manuscripts. I am most grateful to the Provost and Fellows of Worcester College, Oxford, for kind permission to reproduce excerpts from William Clarke's papers which appear here; also to the British Library and Hull City Archives for permission to quote from manuscripts in their care, and to Oxford University Press for permission to quote from my article in volume 105 of the *English Historical Review*.

Others I particularly wish to thank are Lord Briggs of Lewes, Professor James Campbell, Mr Eric Christiansen, Mr Timothy Clayton, Dr Frances Dow, Dr Paul Hardacre, Dr Anne Laurence, Mrs Elspeth Lemmon, Mr Keith Lemmon, Dr Daniel Lunn, Professor Michael Mendle, Professor Tony Nuttall, Mr David Palfreyman, the late Dr Saul Rose, Mr Stuart Sharp, Mr Laurence Weeks, and Dr Penry Williams. The late Dr Eric Sams was typically generous with his support in introducing a new recruit to the somewhat *recherché* field of seventeenth-century shorthand. The help of those who have kindly furnished me with information on particular points is gratefully acknowledged in the relevant footnotes. Without the introduction which the then Librarian of Worcester College, Miss Lesley Montgomery (now Mrs Le Claire), effected between myself and William Clarke, it goes without saying that there would be no occasion for me to write this preface. To her also I wish to express my most grateful thanks.

I have been conscious throughout this exercise of following circumspectly in the majestic footsteps of Sir Charles Firth, whose achievement in producing exemplary editions of such a large part of Clarke's archive will remain one of the great contributions to seventeenth-century scholarship. The new material which I have retrieved has occasionally allowed me to make small adjustments to his readings and confirm, clarify, or correct some of his deductions. If I have been able to amplify his work in any useful way, then I shall more than have attained my goal.

EDITORIAL PRACTICE

Within the transcript, text which appears in the original in longhand is italicized.[2] Text deleted in the original is struck through. Editorial interventions are signalled by square brackets, as are uncertain readings; where more than one reading is possible, the alternatives are enclosed within square brackets, each separated by a solidus. Three points within square brackets indicate one illegible word; four denote more than one illegible word. Round brackets imitate parentheses in the original. Angled brackets are used to enclose insertions. In transcriptions from longhand, abbreviations have been silently expanded and the thorn rendered as 'th'. Dates are in all but a very few cases given in Old Style, with the year taken to begin on 1 January; where they occasionally appear in New Style (usually as an aid to identification for those wishing to check the shorthand), that is signalled in a footnote.

The volume is arranged in 12 chapters, each corresponding to one of Clarke's notebooks. Thus the length of each chapter varies according to the amount of relevant shorthand in each particular notebook; that covering Notebook XXVI, for example, with 140 documents, is much longer than Notebook XXIX with only 4.

Document headings have been supplied from Clarke's own notes; discrepancies between those and information in the relevant documents are signalled in footnotes. Dates or names which are missing in the original but can be securely inferred from internal evidence are enclosed within square brackets. Both in the headings and elsewhere in the supporting commentary the term 'newsletter' is used to indicate that an entire document is written in shorthand, 'news' describes shorthand passages which form only part of a longer newsletter otherwise written in longhand; 'newsbook' denotes printed news-sheets.[3] 'Memorandum' refers to documents which do not appear to form part of a letter.

[2] This is possible as Clarke always used longhand for the foreign words and phrases which would normally so be indicated.

[3] In citing a few newsbooks where confusion might arise between closely similar titles or aberrant numbering, I have provided the serial numbers allocated by C. Nelson and M. Seccombe (comps), *British Newspapers and Periodicals: 1641–1600* (New York, 1987).

Punctuation

In Clarke's shorthand, there are virtually no punctuation marks, divisions by paragraph, or indications of upper case; his notes usually run on without a break. I have provided these where I judged them to be appropriate; doubtful cases are footnoted.[4] The wary reader will, however, always bear in mind that almost all punctuation was imposed upon the text by the editor.

Orthography

The conversion of a contracted and partly phonetic writing system into conventional longhand cannot always accurately reflect the orthography which the writer would have visualized. I have as a rule adopted modern spelling except where the shorthand unequivocally follows a characteristically seventeenth-century form, where I have provided as faithful a transliteration as possible within the confines of the medium, not so much to convey an early modern 'feel' as to demonstrate how such outlines were formed and so have been read by me.[5] The words 'hath' and 'has' are indistinguishable in Clarke's shorthand and are rendered throughout as 'has'.

Duplicated material

Duplicates of a number of the documents occur in other easily accessible sources. In such cases I have noted all but the most minor variations in footnotes but have restricted commentary on their subject matter.

Appendices

The volume ends with three appendices. Appendix A lists correspondents identified by Clarke in shorthand in a document

[4] It has occasionally been virtually impossible to judge whether certain phrases should be attached to the end of the preceding sentence or the beginning of the succeeding one.

[5] For example in the words 'heroick' and 'governour', for which both outlines are clear.

otherwise written *en clair.* As many of them appear in Sir Charles Firth's edition of *The Clarke Papers* I have cited their location there. Clarke's shorthand record of Colonel Edmund Sexby's trial of June 1651 can be compared with the much shorter account which Clarke wrote in longhand, reproduced as Appendix B. Appendix C provides a short description of the development and usage of shorthand in seventeenth-century England.

ABBREVIATIONS

A&O	C.H. Firth and R.S. Rait (eds), *Acts and Ordinances of the Interregnum 1642–1660*, 3 vols (London, 1911).
Abbott	W.C. Abbott, *The Writings and Speeches of Oliver Cromwell*, 4 vols (Oxford, 1937–1947).
Baker, *Chronicle*	Sir Richard Baker, *A Chronicle of the Kings of England from the Time of the Romans Government unto the Death of King James . . . whereunto is now added the Reign of King Charles the I and the first thirteen years of King Charles the II* (London, 1670).
Bayley	A.R. Bayley, *The Great Civil War in Dorset 1642–1664* (Taunton, 1910).
Beinecke	Beinecke Rare Book and Manuscript Library, Yale University, New Haven, USA.
BL	British Library, London.
Bodl.	Bodleian Library, Oxford.
Burton, *Diary*	J.T. Rutt (ed.), *The Diary of Thomas Burton Esq. Member in the Parliaments of Oliver and Richard Cromwell, from 1656 to 1659 . . .*, 4 vols (London, 1828).
C&P	S.R. Gardiner, *History of the Commonwealth and Protectorate 1649–1660*, 3rd edn, 3 vols (London etc., 1901).
CClarSP	W.D. Macray and H.O. Coxe (eds), *Calendar of the Clarendon State Papers preserved in the Bodleian Library*, 6 vols (Oxford, 1869–1976).
Chequers	Chequers Court, Buckinghamshire.
CJ	*Journals of the House of Commons*, VI (London, 1803), VII (London, 1813).
CP	C.H. Firth (ed.), *The Clarke Papers: Selections from the Papers of William Clarke*, 4 vols (Camden Society, N.S., XLIX, LIV, LX, LXXII, 1891–1901). Vols I–II reprinted with a new introduction by A. Woolrych (London, 1992).
CSPD	*Calendar of State Papers, Domestic Series*
CSPV	*Calendar of State Papers, Venetian*

Davies, *Restoration*	G. Davies, *The Restoration of Charles II 1658–1660* (San Marino, 1955).
DBR	R.L. Greaves and R. Zaller (eds), *Biographical Dictionary of British Radicals in the Seventeenth Century*, 3 vols (Brighton, 1982–1984).
DNB	*Dictionary of National Biography*, 63 vols (London, 1885–1900).
F&D	Sir Charles Firth and G. Davies, *The Regimental History of Cromwell's Army*, 2 vols (Oxford, 1940).
Folger	Folger Shakespeare Library, Washington, DC.
HMC	Historical Manuscripts Commission.
Hull CRO	Hull City Archives, Kingston upon Hull.
Hutton, *Restoration*	R. Hutton, *The Restoration: A Political and Religious History of England and Wales 1658–1667* (Oxford, 1985).
K&C	E. Kitson and E.K. Clark, 'Some Civil War accounts, 1647–1650' (Thoresby Society, 11, 1904), pp. 137–235.
L-P	Historical Manuscripts Commission, *Report on the Manuscripts of F.W. Leyborne-Popham, Esq. of Littlecote, Co. Wilts* (Norwich, 1899).
LRHO	J.Y. Akerman (ed.), *Letters from Roundhead Officers written from Scotland and Chiefly Addressed to Captain Adam Baynes, July MDCL–June MDCLX* (Bannatyne Club, XIV, 1856).
Ludlow, *Memoirs*	C.H. Firth (ed.), *The Memoirs of Edmund Ludlow Lieutenant-General of the Horse in the Army of the Commonwealth of England, 1625–1672*, 2 vols (Oxford, 1894).
LYP	C.H. Firth, *The Last Years of the Protectorate 1656–1658*, 2 vols (London, 1909).
N&S	C. Nelson and M. Seccombe (comps), *British Newspapers and Periodicals 1641–1700*, (New York, 1987).
OPH	*The Parliamentary or Constitutional History of England; Being a Faithful Account Of all the Most remarkable Transactions in Parliament, From the earliest Times, to the Restoration of King Charles II* (London, 1760).
OxDNB	*Oxford Dictionary of National Biography*, 60 vols (Oxford, 2004).
OED	*The Oxford English Dictionary*, 2nd edn, 20 vols (Oxford, 1989).

PRO	The National Archives (Public Record Office), London.
S&C	C.H. Firth (ed.), *Scotland and the Commonwealth* (Scottish History Society, XVIII, 1895).
S&P	C.H. Firth (ed.), *Scotland and the Protectorate* (Scottish History Society, XXXI, 1899).
SS	G.E. Aylmer, *The State's Servants: The Civil Service of the English Republic 1649–1660* (London and Boston, 1973).
Terry	C.S. Terry (ed.), *The Cromwellian Union* (Scottish History Society, XL, 1902).
Thoresby	Library of the Thoresby Society, Leeds.
TSP	T. Birch (ed.), *A Collection of the State Papers of John Thurloe Esq*, 7 vols (London, 1742).
Wariston, *Diary*	J.D. Ogilvie (ed.), *Diary of Sir Archibald Johnston of Wariston*, III, 1655–1660 (Scottish History Society, 3rd ser., XXIV, 1940).
Whitelock, *Memorials*	B. Whitelock, *Memorials of the English Affairs from the Beginning of the Reign of Charles the First to the Happy Restoration of King Charles the Second*, 4 vols (Oxford 1853).
Woolrych, *C–P*	A. Woolrych, *Commonwealth to Protectorate* (Oxford, 1982).
Worc.	Worcester College, Oxford.
Worden, *Rump*	B. Worden, *The Rump Parliament 1648–1653* (Cambridge, 1977 edn).

INTRODUCTION

The legacy of Sir William Clarke

The Clarke Papers, the working papers of Sir William Clarke (1623/4–1666) now at Worcester College, Oxford, need no introduction to students of the English civil wars and Interregnum. Since their discovery and publication by Sir Charles Firth in the late nineteenth century, they have constituted one of the most comprehensive and important primary sources for the period.[1] Firth's editions took no account, however, of the substantial quantity of Clarke's notes found only in shorthand, which consequently – and erroneously, as can now be seen – have since that time tended to be dismissed as containing little of importance.

From 1645, and perhaps earlier, Clarke was one of the civilian secretaries attached to the headquarters of the parliamentarian army. His career began as an assistant to John Rushworth, secretary to the commander-in-chief of the New Model Army, Sir Thomas Fairfax.[2] From 1647–1650 Clarke acted as secretary to the Council of Officers and by 1650 he had become principal assistant to Rushworth as Fairfax's military secretary.[3] In June of that year Fairfax resigned his command in protest over the Commonwealth's plans to invade Scotland in order to forestall a serious royalist/Scottish insurrection. He was succeeded by Oliver Cromwell, newly returned from his victorious campaign in Ireland, and it was as part of Cromwell's

[1] Several collections from the manuscripts have been published, principally C.H. Firth (ed.), *The Clarke Papers: Selections from the Papers of William Clarke . . .*, 4 vols (Camden Society, N.S. XLIX, LIV, LX, LXII, 1891–1901); *idem* (ed.), *Scotland and the Commonwealth* (Scottish History Society, XVIII, 1895); *idem* (ed.), *Scotland and the Protectorate* (Scottish History Society, XXXI, 1899); A.S.P. Woodhouse (ed.), *Puritanism and Liberty* (London, 1938; 2nd edn, 1974); G. Davies (ed.), *Dundee Court Martial Records 1651*, (Scottish History Society, 2nd ser., XIX, 1919). Vols I–II of the original edition of *The Clarke Papers* were reprinted by the Royal Historical Society in 1992 with a new introduction by Austin Woolrych. Before Firth discovered Clarke's papers they were described in H.O. Coxe's *Catalogus Codicum MSS*, 2 vols (Oxford, 1852) and had been cited by at least one previous scholar, J.B. Deane in *The Life of Richard Deane . . .* (London, 1870), pp. 495–496. For Clarke's life and career see *The Oxford Dictionary of National Biography*, 60 vols (Oxford, 2004).

[2] Clarke may already have been acting in some similar capacity when the New Model Army was formed in 1645.

[3] Fairfax was by now Lord General of the Commonwealth and had succeeded to his family title as 3rd Baron Fairfax of Cameron.

entourage that Clarke accompanied the invading army when it entered Scotland in July 1650.

There he was to remain, principally in and around Edinburgh, for the next ten years as secretary to successive commanders-in-chief of the English army of occupation.[4] For most of that time the post was held by George Monck, whose actions in 1659 and 1660 paved the way for the reinstatement of the Stuart monarchy in May 1660; Clarke's loyalty to Monck earned him many rewards and honours during the Restoration, including a knighthood. His new-found prosperity was short-lived, however, as in June 1666 he was killed in action during one of the fiercest battles of the second Anglo-Dutch war.[5]

Throughout his career, his official position guaranteed Clarke a privileged viewpoint from which to witness and to record many of the foremost military and political events of his day. Perhaps best remembered now for his detailed record of the army debates which took place at Putney in October–November 1647, he was also present on the scaffold during the execution of Charles I, one of three clerks appointed to record in shorthand the king's final words.[6] He carefully preserved his working papers of the 1640s and 1650s, and at the time of his death was systematically engaged in putting them in order, making fair copies of those he wished to keep and discarding those he did not. They eventually passed to his only surviving son George Clarke (1661–1736) who in turn bequeathed them to Worcester College, where for the most part they remain.[7]

The collection, comprising fifty-one volumes of official correspondence, memoranda, accounts, and orders, most of them still in their original calf or vellum bindings, together with a considerable quantity of unbound material,[8] first became widely known with Sir

[4] They are listed in G.E. Aylmer, *The State's Servants : The Civil Service of the English Republic 1649–1660* (London and Boston, 1973), p. 38.

[5] BL, Additional MS 14286, fo. 41^{r}.

[6] G.E. Aylmer (ed.), *Sir William Clarke Manuscripts 1640–1664* (Brighton, 1979), p. 11; *England's Black Tribunall* (London, 1703), p. 47. Clarke's fair copy of the Putney debates survives at Worcester College (Worc. MS LXV), but not his written record of the king's speech.

[7] Some of Clarke's papers found their way to Littlecote House in Wiltshire. Worcester College was eventually able to acquire some of these while a few went to the British Library; others have now disappeared. Those which remained at Littlecote in 1899 (although by then some had already been sold) are described in the Historical Manuscript Commission's *Report on the Manuscripts of F.W. Leyborne-Popham Esq.* (Norwich, 1899). There are isolated volumes in the National Library of Scotland, the library of the Thoresby Society, Leeds, and at Chequers Court, Buckinghamshire. For George Clarke see *OxDNB*.

[8] There is no printed catalogue, but the best summary of their contents is found in Aylmer, *Sir William Clarke Manuscripts.* A more detailed listing of the unbound papers is held by the National Register of Archives.

Charles Firth's editions for the Camden Society and Scottish History Society in the 1890s and 1900s.[9] It is not always realized, however, that these did not include any of the documents which Clarke recorded in a contemporary shorthand.[10] Now known to amount to some 230,000 words, most of them are to be found in a series of small working notebooks, some 14.5 × 19.5 cm in size, which Clarke used between May 1651 and early 1660 during his time in Scotland.[11] In these, shorthand notes alternate with the longhand passages which were found and published by Firth. Presumably Clarke had already worked through and disposed of similar volumes from the earlier part of his career when he met his unforeseen death.[12] The shorthand had apparently not been read since Clarke's own lifetime when, in 1973, Worcester College sought the help of an expert cryptographer, Dr Eric Sams, who established that Clarke had used Thomas Shelton's *Tachygraphy* (1635), one of the most popular of some dozen or so systems then available.[13]

Despite this breakthrough, the shorthand remained unread until I began my own transcription in the mid-1980s. Now that this is complete, I am able to say that the notes fall into three distinct but unequal categories. The largest of these relates, predictably, to the administration of the army in Scotland during the 1650s. Secondly, there is a small collection of Clarke's own personal letters and memoranda, the only such known to survive. A third component, of more than 400 documents, relates to the English (and, to a lesser extent, European) political and military intelligence which was being sent from England to army headquarters in Scotland, and occasionally vice versa. It is this category which forms the basis of the present volume.[14]

[9] See above, p. 1n.

[10] It appears that, despite a considerable scholarly interest in early shorthands at the time when he was producing his editions, Firth made no attempt to have Clarke's shorthand deciphered. I have discussed the possible reasons for this in F. Henderson, 'The hidden hand of William Clarke', *Worcester College Record*, (1998), pp. 70–73.

[11] Worc. MSS XIX, XX, XXII, XXIV–XXXII. The last section of MS XXXII was begun by Clarke during his return to London from Scotland in early 1660. There is also a small amount of shorthand in a later, post-Restoration notebook (Worc. MS XXXIII), not included in the present volume.

[12] None of the original notebooks which Clarke processed in this way survive. A note on the fair copy of the Putney debates tells us that Clarke began that in 1662 (Worc. MS LXV, flyleaf).

[13] E. Sams in Aylmer, *Sir William Clarke Manuscripts*, pp. 29–34. I am much indebted to Dr Sams who, with characteristic scholarly generosity, made available to me not only the original notes on his sample decryptment but much helpful advice in the early stages of my work.

[14] Editions of the other two categories are in preparation.

The historical background[15]

The decade which Clarke spent in Scotland was unlike any other period in British history – a decade which followed revolution and regicide, when the country was without a king and was often governed by nothing less than crisis management.[16] While it may have seemed to the republic's principal architects, political and religious radicals and army activists alike, that they had permanently changed the course of British history, the reality was that the constitutional stability which they strove to establish was never truly within their grasp. Throughout the 1650s, as the abrupt termination of one parliament after another demonstrated, there were irreconcilable conflicts of interest between civil and military leaders. In a nation where the majority of the population would have welcomed a return of the monarchy – if not necessarily a Stuart monarchy – its successive parliaments were obliged to maintain a substantial military force in order for the regime to survive. The army in its turn was dependent upon parliamentary legislation for even such inadequate funding as it was able to acquire; the two bodies found that they could live neither with nor without each other.

After the death in 1658 of Oliver Cromwell, who had governed the country as Lord Protector since December 1653, and a brief interlude during which his civilian elder son and successor Richard faced escalating confrontation with both army and republican civilian leaders, the Protectorate collapsed during the spring of 1659. The near anarchy which followed saw the most serious split yet to occur within senior army ranks, and it was George Monck, based in Scotland and commanding an army paid up to date and rigorously disciplined, who took control by marching to London in early 1660, and in doing so paved the way for the restoration of the Stuart monarchy a few months later. By now Clarke had earned the position of one of Monck's most trusted advisers, rebuffing an attempt by his former commander, Robert Lilburne, to lure him over to the side of the military junto in England.[17] It was his loyalty to Monck at this stage which would earn Clarke such rich rewards during the reign of Charles II.

These dramatic events provide the backdrop to Clarke's papers, whether in longhand or in shorthand, most often in the 1650s

[15] The course of the English Interregnum is traced here in only the briefest detail. Introductions provided at the beginning of each notebook describe more fully the background to the documents to be found there.

[16] There are many detailed accounts of the Interregnum, from S.R. Gardiner, *History of the Commonwealth and Protectorate*, 3 vols (London, 1886–1891) to Austin Woolrych, *Britain in Revolution 1625–1660* (Oxford, 2002), pp. 434–702.

[17] Pp. 319, 324 below.

comprising his copies of London newsletters. It is easy to visualize how, at a time when even the fastest express from London took three days to reach Edinburgh, all news from the capital was eagerly received, passed round, and hoarded. When the large number of written newsletters to which we now know Clarke had access is added to his vast collection of printed newsbooks and pamphlets,[18] we realize just how well informed he was about affairs both inside and outside Scotland.

The value which he placed on such information is clear from the meticulous copies of most, if not all, of the incoming newsletters which are found in his working notebooks. Entered in strictly chronological order under their date of origin, many were copied in longhand, beginning in Clarke's own elegant hand and then taken up by another, presumably belonging to one of his clerks. Others, however, he preferred to write himself in shorthand, as he also did with certain memoranda and copies of official correspondence. We have to guess Clarke's reasons for doing so. Doubtless he used shorthand, at least on occasion, to save himself time, or space in his notebooks. But one of its main attractions – and one enthusiastically promoted by its early inventors – was its value for purposes of secrecy. There is no doubt that, for both Clarke and his colleagues in the army secretariat, this was one of its principal advantages.[19] While the sensitive nature of some of the documents which Clarke copied in 'tachygraphy' is self-evident,[20] his criteria for deciding which passages he wished to protect in this way are not always so readily apparent.

Although Clarke's shorthand notes conceal much that is new to us and much that is of interest, the value of the unexplored information which they provide is cumulative. There is no sensational new dimension of Interregnum politics (although that realization will itself be important to scholars who have long wondered what secrets Clarke's shorthand might contain); sometimes the gains in understanding are slight. As we read through the documents, however, we undoubtedly acquire a richer sense both of the world of army intelligence within which Clarke moved and of the broader picture of national events. Of particular interest are the fresh details which emerge concerning two episodes: the court martial at Edinburgh in June 1651 of Colonel Edward Sexby, of which Clarke kept a full, but hitherto unknown, record; and the part played by George Monck in the events preceding the Restoration, an issue which has

[18] Clarke's collection of printed material is now also at Worcester College.

[19] See below, Appendix C, pp. 378–379, 382.

[20] For example, much of the material relating to the 'Overton plot' in Notebook XXVII, and the unsuccessful royalist approaches to George Monck of 1658 (pp. 268–270).

always tantalized historians and on which Clarke gives us crucial new evidence.[21]

The transcript

The documents reproduced below vary considerably not only in content but in frequency, and the number written in shorthand during periods of intense political activity is strikingly higher than at other times. In the last three months of 1659, for example, during Monck's clash with the army commanders in London, the number of shorthand items averages sixteen per month, whereas there are only four from the whole of 1657.[22] Similarly, in the notebook covering 1654 – the year of Glencairn's Rising – almost every page is written in shorthand.[23] While Clarke's shorthand includes both memoranda and copies of official correspondence, most are incoming newsletters. Of these nearly three-quarters (some 72 per cent) originated in London, while the rest came from correspondents in a wide range of locations, from important intelligence gathering centres near the English-Scottish border such as Newcastle and Carlisle, to those on the Continent and particularly in Holland.[24]

Out of a total of 403 documents, some 31 are more or less exact copies of documents known from other sources, either in manuscript or print, although none is an exact duplicate.[25] In manuscript, these include 14 written also in longhand among Clarke's own papers,[26] and 5 among the newsletters which Gilbert Mabbott sent to the mayor and aldermen of Hull,[27] while a few others are found in the British Library.[28] Of those duplicated in print, some are copies of pamphlets

[21] Pp. 26–36, and Notebook XXXII *passim*.

[22] Notebooks XXXII and XXVII respectively.

[23] Notebook XXVI.

[24] Newcastle was also used as a centre from which to send Scottish news to London; *Mercurius Politicus*, 62 (7–14 Aug. 1651), pp. 988–989. In later 1659, when all Scottish post was being intercepted, Monck had letters from London directed to Newcastle, whence they were secretly carried to him in Scotland; T. Gumble, *The life of General Monck, Duke of Albemarle &c., with Remarks upon his Actions* (London, 1671), p. 170.

[25] A further six, all of them appearing in newsbooks, are sufficiently similar to suggest a direct connection (pp. 36, 62, 64, 69, 76, 89), and six others include short excerpts found elsewhere (pp. 26, 43, 117, 119, 307, 355).

[26] Pp. 47, 210, 231, 241, 245, 271, 272, 325, 328 which are at Worcester College; p. 159 in the Egerton MSS at the British Library. Longhand versions of documents on pp. 307, 349 and 355 now apparently lost but originally among Clarke's papers at Littlecote, Wiltshire, are calendared in *L-P*.

[27] Pp. 61, 71, 106, 107, 110, 157, 213.

[28] Pp. 21–24, 117, 119, 251, 253, 269.

printed during the political turmoil of 1659,[29] while several of Henry Walker's letters quote directly from the official journal of the House of Commons and/or the official newsbook of which he was an editor, *Severall Proceedings in Parliament*.[30] Other documents which originated in the Scottish headquarters appear subsequently in newsbooks such as the *Perfect Diurnall* or *Mercurius Politicus*.[31]

I have included transcripts of duplicated material for two principal reasons: first, in order that *all* shorthand passages can be identified and read by those consulting the original manuscript, whether or not they are familiar with Shelton's shorthand; second, because in almost every case there are minor but often important differences which the reader may wish to have the opportunity to assess.

Of the incoming newsletters reproduced below, by far the greatest number came from just two correspondents, the Scoutmaster-General, MP, and diplomat, George Downing, and Clarke's brother-in-law, the professional news impresario, Gilbert Mabbott, with sixty-one and sixty-two letters respectively.[32] Next in frequency are those from the newsbook editor Henry Walker (sixteen) and from John Thurloe (fifteen). Most of the seventy-four correspondents have army or private connections of some sort with Clarke and would have been personally known to him, and most of their names are familiar to us. There are several from Monck's brother-in-law Thomas Clarges (five), and from Clarke's old colleagues in the army secretariat, Richard Hatter (six), and John Rushworth (four), although relations between Clarke and Rushworth appear to have been cool in 1653.[33] Clarke's wife Dorothy, whom he married in September 1648 and who was with him during almost all of his time in Scotland, is among them;[34] there is also a letter from one John Milton writing from Westminster.[35]

From about 1657 Clarke identified most of his correspondents (and certainly all regular ones) by their initials only. In document headings, where I have felt that an identification was secure I have supplied it in

[29] Pp. 301, 312, 314, 316, 340.

[30] Pp. 62, 64, 69. Gilbert Mabbott also quoted directly from the journal of the House on occasion (p. 43–46).

[31] Pp. 36, 76, 83, 84, 89, 293.

[32] For Downing see *OxDNB*; J. Beresford, *The Godfather of Downing Street: Sir George Downing 1623–1684* (London, 1925). Mabbott, for whom also see *OxDNB*, was trusted as providing reliable information; T. Birch (ed.), *A Collection of the State Papers of John Thurloe Esq.*, 7 vols (London, 1742), VII, p. 377.

[33] P. 98.

[34] P. 271.

[35] P. 203. We cannot be sure which of several of the same name this particular John Milton is. There would have many opportunities for contact between Clarke and the poet and civil servant John Milton, who is perhaps the likeliest candidate. I am most grateful to Nicholas von Maltzahn for sharing his views on this question.

square brackets. For example, 'G.D.' writing from the Hague in 1659 is without doubt George Downing.[36]

Only rarely there is an indication within the text of whether the letters were addressed to the commander-in-chief, to the headquarters in general, or to Clarke himself.[37] Several items relating to the Leveller John Lilburne, including two eye-witness accounts of his trial in 1653, may have been intended for his brother Robert, acting commander-in-chief in Scotland from March 1653 to April 1654.[38] Sometimes where a letter is copied entirely in longhand, Clarke provided the writer's (or recipient's) name in shorthand.[39]

Many newsletters were probably provided on a reciprocal basis, as Clarke wrote regularly to both private individuals and public figures, a practice he recorded in a list of correspondents from late 1651 which survives among his papers.[40] Among those to whom he was sending weekly letters at that time were the Speaker, William Lenthall, George Downing, John Downes, John Rushworth, Richard Hatter, and his brothers-in-law Gilbert Mabbott and William Cary. From, unfortunately rare, copies which he made of his own letters, there are other clues that he was regularly sending news from Scotland; he actively promoted this service in letters to influential figures such as Oliver Cromwell in London or Robert Venables in Ireland.[41] On many occasions Clarke's letters to the Speaker appeared subsequently in the official *Severall Proceedings in Parliament*, edited by Henry Walker,[42] and Clarke may also have contributed directly to other newsbooks.[43]

Clarke seldom kept shorthand copies of official papers or correspondence, presumably because they needed to be accessible to others, although the number noticeably increased in the sensitive days of late 1659.[44] There are some copies of intercepted or confiscated

[36] P. 295.

[37] I have only provided such information when it is a certainty or (in square brackets) a near certainty. Mabbott, for example, sent letters both to Clarke and to Monck.

[38] Pp. 102, 103. News of John Lilburne featured in many of the London newsletters, and Clarke owned many pamphlets connected with him which he had bound into a single volume.

[39] These are listed in Appendix A and do not appear in the main transcript.

[40] Worc. MS CLXXXI, fo. 243^r.

[41] Pp. 34, 50, 53, 54, 91. One of Clarke's newsletters to William Lenthall is found at Bodl., MS Tanner LIII, fos 92–93.

[42] For example, a letter written on 25 September 1651 from Dundee; Worc. MS XIX fos 140^r–141^r; *Severall Proceedings*, 106 (2–9 Oct. 1651), pp. 1630–1631. Another, written by Clarke from Stirling Castle, is a compilation of his daily notes (in shorthand); *Severall Proceedings*, 100 (21–28 Aug. 1651), pp. [1545]–[1548]; Worc. MS XIX, *passim*.

[43] P. 36; *Perfect Diurnall*, 81 (23–30 June 1651), p. 1131.

[44] Out of a total of forty from the whole series, sixteen were written between October 1659 and January 1660.

papers, mostly associated with the Anglo-Dutch war, although one group concerns the discovery of the so-called 'Overton plot' in late 1654, and there is evidence that Monck was intercepting letters sent from London by Archibald Johnston of Wariston in late 1659.[45]

In addition to copies of written documents there are some rare records of oral material.[46] Foremost among these must rank Clarke's extensive notes of the court martial in Edinburgh in June 1651 of Colonel Edward Sexby.[47] There are also notes of two private conversations held with separate messengers sent from London immediately after the collapse of the Protectorate in May 1659,[48] and of an unidentified meeting of February 1660 at which there was violent criticism of Monck by leading radical political figures.[49]

Copies of twenty-one of Clarke's own official or semi-official letters provide some clues about Clarke himself and about his professional life.[50] Several suggest that, at least in the early years of the decade, his position was not a secure one. Its precarious nature is demonstrated by his unease in January 1652 on realizing that the English parliamentary commissioners had brought their own secretarial team with them.[51] Furthermore, with each new commander-in-chief, despite the high regard in which he was held, it appears to have been necessary for him to advance his claims for reappointment.[52] While promoting his own interests he did not forget those of others, for example his brothers-in-law Gilbert Mabbott and William Cary, both of whom were useful to him in maintaining close links with London,[53] and he also used his influence to secure the position of Nathaniel Mew, army postmaster first at Berwick and then at Leith.[54] Letters of introduction when the eccentric poet-turned-historian Payne Fisher (whom Clarke seems to have befriended during Fisher's time in Scotland) returned to London in 1653, earned him during the following year at least one newsletter in return.[55]

45 Pp. 83, 88, 94 (a translation from the Dutch apparently prepared at the headquarters), 231, 234, 242, 244, 349, 350.

46 These are not in the strictest sense verbatim accounts, but nonetheless provide full summaries of what was said.

47 Pp. 26–36.

48 Pp. 290–293.

49 P. 362.

50 Pp. 34, 49, 50, 77, 78, 80, 86, 91, 95, 96, 98, 104, 105, 117, 144, 153, 183, 240, 319, 324. These do not include many personal letters and memoranda of which Clarke kept shorthand copies, which are not included in the present edition.

51 P. 51, introduction to Notebook XXII.

52 Pp. 78, 80, 144.

53 Pp. 49, 144.

54 P. 47n, 86.

55 Pp. 104, 105, 180.

There is confirmation that in his professional life, Clarke was both careful and trustworthy. In February 1654 he turned down some kind of proposition from his colleague, the army treasurer George Bilton – wisely as it turned out, as Bilton was later discovered to have been engaging in embezzlement on a massive scale.[56] Clarke's loyalty and caution can be no better demonstrated than by the letters which he exchanged with Robert Lilburne in 1659.[57] When writing about his commanders, especially George Monck, Clarke was characteristically discreet, in Monck's case disguising potentially incriminating approaches from the ever-optimistic supporters of Charles Stuart by copying them in shorthand.[58] Nowhere even in these, however, is there the slightest hint that Monck might at any point have been tempted to join the royalist cause.

The shorthand of the Clarke manuscripts

Of the fifty-one volumes of William Clarke's papers now at Worcester College (some of them unbound), twenty-six include varying amounts of shorthand as follows:

In ten there are a few brief shorthand phrases, principally marginalia or other such short comments.[59]

Four have rather more shorthand, but fall outside the chronological limits or subject matter of this study.[60]

Twelve quarto leather-bound working notebooks, running consecutively from May 1651 to February 1660[61] contain substantial quantities of shorthand notes, all of them written by Clarke himself (some 230,000 words in all). These are scattered throughout longhand passages which are written in several different hands. It is from these volumes that the material reproduced below has been taken, although reference will be made to others in the collection. As I have noted above,[62] the proportion of shorthand to longhand varies considerably from volume to volume and from year to year.

56 Pp. 153, 264.

57 Pp. 319, 324.

58 Pp. 268, 269.

59 Worc. MSS XV, XLVI–LI, LXIX, LXXII, CX.

60 Worc. MSS XXXIII (1660–1665) and CXIV (1648–1649) fall outside the chronological limits; LXXXVI and CLXXXI contain only rough drafts and memoranda, many of them relating to internal matters in Scotland.

61 Worc. MSS XIX–XXXII, excluding XXI and XXIII.

62 P. 6.

The size of William Clarke's library of printed material (also at Worcester College) is such that it has not yet been possible to complete a systematic search for shorthand annotations. Such examples as I have seen either consist of personal memoranda or relate to the adjacent literary texts, and so do not qualify for inclusion in this study.[63]

The evaluation of texts which have reached us via the medium of seventeenth-century shorthand is greatly enhanced by an understanding of its history and context, its methodology, and its use for purposes of conciseness, speed, or concealment; these are discussed in Appendix C.

Most of the difficulties in producing this transcript have arisen from one of two causes: inherent weaknesses in Shelton's system, or its unclear, idiosyncratic, or hurried use by Clarke himself.[64] In the former category lie a number of ambiguous outlines which can be read in anything up to nine separate ways.[65] In most cases their intended meaning has been clear from their context. The absence of almost all signs denoting vowels in Shelton's system, in common with others of its time, can prove a particular problem in the transcription of proper names.[66] Where more than one reading was plausible I have offered the reader a choice of all likely equivalents. Initially, other obstacles arose from a number of personal symbols developed by Clarke. I have subsequently been able to establish equivalents for most of these by comparing such passages as are found in both shorthand and longhand.[67] Clarke's omission of virtually all punctuation marks has provided further difficulties; in order to clarify the reader's understanding of the text I have inserted these where I judged them to be appropriate, identifying any instances where I was in doubt about

[63] I am most grateful to Lesley Le Claire, Joanna Parker, Matthew Seccombe, and Laurence Weeks for drawing my attention to several of these. Clarke's library has been estimated to contain 7,000 items.

[64] The potential pitfalls were outlined by Eric Sams in his descriptive note on the shorthand in 1979; Aylmer, *Sir William Clarke Manuscripts*, p. 33. William Matthews has also drawn attention to the general difficulties in relation to the shorthand of Samuel Pepys, although Pepys's shorthand is more legible than most, and by no means all of Professor Matthews's comments apply in all cases; W. Matthews (ed.), T. Shelton, *A Tutor to Tachygraphy, or, Short-Writing* (Los Angeles, 1970), p. vii.

[65] As an example, in Clarke's shorthand the outline which resembles the Arabic numeral '2', apart from denoting 'to', 'two', 'too', and of course '2', can also, with or without the addition of a dot, represent 'upon', 'an', 'any' or the prefixes 'des-' or 'dis-'.

[66] For instance I found a printed reference to Nathaniel Mew, whose name I had transcribed as 'Maw' (p. 86). The same applies to place names; for example, 'Amiland' is indistinguishable from 'Holland'.

[67] In this way I was able to identify Clarke's idiosyncratic equivalent for 'cast': the symbol 'c' with a dot above, which he had adapted from Shelton's outline for 'fast' – symbol 'f' with a dot above; p. 252, *TSP*, IV, p. 745.

their correct position.[68] In a few cases ink-blots or modern rebinding have obliterated a whole word or phrase of shorthand where perhaps only a letter or two of longhand might have been lost.[69] Where an outline has proved illegible, the general meaning of the missing word or phrase will usually be clear to the reader from its context.[70]

As a general rule, because of the extremely abbreviated nature of shorthand outlines, the only person who is in a position to make an entirely dependable transcript of a document written in this medium (and not always then) is its author, who can draw on personal memory. No amount of editorial vigilance or skill can make up for that advantage. In making this transcription I have always been strongly aware that I was completing the task which William Clarke himself set out to perform. Where I have felt any doubt about the accuracy of a particular reading I have shown this in the way indicated in my note on editorical practice.[71] I hope that Clarke would have approved of the result.

[68] Comparison with *TSP*, IV, p. 745, was again helpful in establishing whether certain phrases should be placed at the end of one sentence or the beginning of the next.

[69] e.g. pp. 49, 246.

[70] e.g. p. 243.

[71] Above, p. IX.

THE CLARKE PAPERS

SELECTED TRANSCRIPTIONS FROM THE SHORTHAND

1. NOTEBOOK XIX

1 May–9 September 1651[1]

Introduction

By May 1651 William Clarke had been based in Scotland for almost a year. Having journeyed north as part of Cromwell's entourage in July 1650, he had witnessed the English triumph at the battle of Dunbar[2] and was now based at the English army headquarters in Edinburgh. Here Cromwell was poised to begin his final campaign against the largely Scottish army of Charles Stuart. Several documents in this volume demonstrate that, despite the ill health which had delayed the closing stages of the Scottish campaign, Cromwell was involved in several important external military and political matters.[3] He was, for example, in direct contact via Leith with the English ambassadors at the Hague during their important mission to explore a possible Anglo-Dutch alliance; on the precise day upon which (unknown to him) their negotiations had broken down, he again dispatched his usual courier to Holland.[4]

From some such issues Cromwell appears deliberately to have distanced himself. When in July 1651 Colonel Fortescue travelled from London to appeal to Cromwell in a vain attempt to save the Presbyterian minister Christopher Love from sentence of death for his part in a royalist plot, there were, as Clarke records, conflicting views among members of the council of war held to discuss the matter; their advice to Cromwell was to remain impartial, advice which he seems to have followed.[5]

Cromwell's intervention was also sought in a difficult case concerning the governorship of Poole both by the Council of State and, as we now learn, by the man dismissed from the post, Lieutenant-Colonel

[1] Worc. MS XIX.

[2] 3 September 1650.

[3] Cromwell's poor health was causing particular concern in London where it was rumoured that the royalist army in Scotland was about to invade England; *Mercurius Politicus*, 52 (29 May–5 June 1651), p. 846; p. 26 below.

[4] This was Captain Owen Cox of the *Constant Warrior*; p. 37 below.

[5] P. 46. Love's case is summarized in *C&P*, I, pp. 412–419, where this meeting is discussed; p. 419n.

John Reade.[6] On 1 May 1651 the Council had decided to report to its absent Lord General about this troublesome affair. Acting on articles laid against Reade 'and other informations against him', it had already on 15 April ordered his immediate replacement by a local man, Major George Skutt.[7] The incriminating articles, presumably enclosed with the Council's letter to Cromwell, were copied by Clarke into his notebook on 8 May.[8] Cromwell did not apparently respond, as on 20 May the Council ordered Major-General John Desborough, commander of the forces in the west of England, to appoint an interim replacement as governor until the matter was settled; this was not to be until well into June and possibly later.[9]

Clarke's notes also reveal that Reade provided sanctuary at Poole for John Radman, the fugitive leader of the abortive Leveller-inspired Oxford mutiny of September 1649.[10] While there were unsubstantiated stories that Radman had been arrested there, there is no evidence that he was ever tried or punished.[11] Reade was also accused of being absent from his garrison during the months of March and April 1649, that is, during the last serious Leveller-inspired army mutinies.[12] Again the evidence is lacking, but it may have been because of these dangerous associations that the Council was so eager to replace him as governor of one of the most strategically important garrisons in the south of England.[13] Reade flatly refused to relinquish the post, and in June 1651 appealed directly to Cromwell in Scotland, putting forward his side of the case and claiming that he had been treated less than fairly.[14]

[6] Pp. 21–26, 37–43. The case is described in detail in A.R. Bayley, *The Great Civil War in Dorset 1642–1660*, (Taunton, 1910), pp. 342–348, and the events when George Skutt turned up to take over Reade's command in BL, MS Stowe 189, fos 54^r–55^v.

[7] *Calendars of State Papers, Domestic Series, 1651*, pp. 149, 165, 173, 526.

[8] Pp. 21–26. They are already known from the closely similar copies in the British Library; BL, MS Stowe 189, fos 52^r–53^r, partially transcribed in Bayley, pp. 343–345. The Council may have enclosed copies of them in its letter to Cromwell of 1 May 1651. On the previous day it had ordered that copies be given to Reade himself; *CSPD 1651*, p. 171. Reade also sent copies of them to Cromwell (p. 37 below).

[9] *CSPD 1651*, pp. 211, 265. Reade had been finally 'outed' by late September 1651; *Mercurius Scoticus* (Leith), 10 (30 Sept–8 Oct. 1651), p. 81.

[10] P. 25. From the evidence available to him in 1981, H. M. Reece concluded that Reade had not sheltered Radman at Poole; 'The military presence in England 1649–1660', Oxford University D. Phil. thesis (1981), p. 170.

[11] C.H. Firth, 'The mutiny of Col. Ingoldsby's regiment at Oxford in September 1649', *Proceedings of the Oxford Architectural and Historical Society*, N.S. 4 (1884), p. 246. As a 'Sergeant Smith' was subsequently arrested and sent to London it is possible that some sleight of hand was used to prevent Radman's capture.

[12] P. 24.

[13] Even after Reade eventually died at the age of 97, he was still remembered as a 'violent Republican'; BL, Stowe MS 189, fo. 74^r.

[14] Pp. 37–43.

There is no evidence that Cromwell responded to Reade's appeal in any way. Why Clarke would wish to copy these papers can only be surmised; he and Reade were on friendly terms, at least in early 1648, and he may have done so purely out of personal interest.[15]

Cromwell did not attend the high-profile court martial of Colonel Edward Sexby, which took place in Edinburgh in June 1651, despite the fact that although not yet fully restored to health after his recent illness, he was evidently sufficiently well to conduct at least some official business on the days in question.[16]

Sexby had first risen to prominence as an agitator during 1647. Appointed governor of Portland in 1649, he was in the following year charged to raise a regiment of foot for service in Ireland, which was then diverted to Scotland where he arrived in September 1650.[17] His Edinburgh court martial and subsequent dismissal from the army have, despite the absence until now of any detailed corroboration, usually been interpreted as the result of a political frame-up,[18] and this is borne out by Clarke's comprehensive notes of the trial, at which he was apparently present.[19] One of his particular concerns was the potentially serious involvement in the case of his young cousin Captain James Staresmore, for whom he seems to have considered himself *in loco parentis*;[20] he would also have known Sexby well through their many contacts at army headquarters.[21]

Clarke's anxiety to extricate his cousin led him to write a long letter expanding upon his notes of the court martial.[22] Although he did not record the name of his correspondent, his reference to Staresmore's time of duty at Weymouth suggests that it may have

[15] BL, Stowe MS 189, fos 39–40; *L-P*, p. 16.

[16] *Perfect Account*, 25 (11–18 June 1651), p. 181; Beinecke, MS Osborn fb. 67/43; Bodl., MS Tanner LIV, fos 85–86.

[17] *CSPD 1650*, p. 341. For Sexby's career, see *OxDNB*, and R.L. Greaves and R. Zaller (eds), *Biographical Dictionary of British Radicals in the Seventeenth Century*, 3 vols (Brighton, 1982–1984); C. Firth and G. Davies (eds), *The Regimental History of Cromwell's Army*, 2 vols (Oxford, 1940), I, pp. 61–66; II, pp. 561–563.

[18] *DBR*, 'Sexby'; *SS*, pp. 155–156.

[19] Pp. 26–36. Until now the only known account of Sexby's court martial has been a short passage in longhand from the same notebook; Worc. MS XIX, fos 26^{r}–27^{r}. I have reproduced this in Appendix B to facilitate comparison with the documents recorded by Clarke in shorthand.

[20] Staresmore had been appointed captain in Major Rippon's dragoons at Weymouth in September 1650 but was now in Scotland, where he appears to have lodged with Clarke for part of the time; *CSPD 1650*, p. 334; Worc. MS XXIV, fo. 124^{r}, in shorthand.

[21] Contacts between Clarke and Sexby are extensively documented in both E. Kitson and E.K. Clark (eds), 'Some Civil War accounts, 1647–1650', (Thoresby Society, 11, 1904), pp. 137–235, and *CP*, I.

[22] P. 34.

been to the then governor, Colonel James Heane, that Clarke was writing.[23]

From both Clarke's record of the trial (as far as I am aware, the only detailed record of the proceedings of any court martial of a commissioned officer to survive from this period)[24] and his letter of 14 June,[25] it is evident that Sexby's downfall was brought about principally by Leveller sympathizers among the officers in his own regiment. Clarke's own critical opinion of this 'malicious crew of Levelling officers' is at the same time made unequivocally clear.[26]

The volume begins with a draft letter of attorney in the name of Captain Edmund Chillenden,[27] apparently framed by Clarke, who had some legal training.[28] Although it does not fall strictly within the guidelines of the present work, I have included it as an example of the way in which members of the army managed property taken in lieu of pay.[29] Clarke knew Chillenden well; as one of the original agitators for Edward Whalley's regiment he was one of those most active in publicizing the army's demands between 1647 and 1649, when he had regular dealings with and on behalf of the army headquarters.[30] Like Clarke, he was in Scotland during the 1650 campaign, and in April 1651 (just before the date of this document) had been paid £350 to raise and conduct recruits to Whalley's regiment there.[31] Chillenden took arrears of some £326 5s in the form of tenements and messuages in the London parish of Mary Le Savoy in the Strand in June 1650,[32] and we learn now that he also owned property in one

[23] Another (less influential and so perhaps less likely) candidate is Clarke's brother-in-law Kympton Hilliard, who served with the same regiment both in Weymouth and during the occupation of Jersey in October of the same year; *CP*, II, pp. 228–232.

[24] Unique records of courts martial set up by Monck at Dundee to deal promptly with breaches of discipline by the soldiery were recorded by Clarke in longhand; Davies, *Dundee Court Martial Records*, p. 6.

[25] P. 34.

[26] e.g. pp. 26, 34 below.

[27] See 'Chillenden', *OxDNB* and *DBR*. I have also benefited from discussions with Philip Baker about Chillenden.

[28] *OxDNB*, 'Clarke'.

[29] Among others who arranged their affairs in the same way was John Lambert; J.Y. Akerman (ed.), *Letters from Roundhead Officers written from Scotland and chiefly addressed to Captain Adam Baynes, July MDCL–June MDCLX*, (Bannatyne Club, XIV, 1856), p. 4.

[30] *L-P*, p. 102; many examples of contact between Chillenden and Clarke can be found in K&C and in *CP*, I–II.

[31] F&D, I, p. 224; *CSPD 1651*, p. 558. He was reported to be approaching Scotland in early May; *Perfect Account*, 17 (30 Apr.–7 May 1651), p. 136; 20 (21–28 May 1651), p. 159. Both Clarke and his brother-in-law Gilbert Mabbott were falsely mustered in Chillenden's troop, although it proved increasingly difficult for Chillenden to retain them; F&D, I, p. 196; *L-P*, pp. 104–105.

[32] BL, MS Harleian 427, fos 90^{r}, 93^{r}; I. Gentles, 'The sales of crown lands: a rejoinder', *Economic History Revview*, 29 (1976), p. 133n.

of the courts running north from Thames Street, in another part of the city.

The closely similar wording of a memorandum about the scandalous behaviour of the notorious duke of Buckingham to a later report in one of the printed newsbooks suggests that Clarke was its contributor.[33]

The volume ends with the receipt of the news of Cromwell's final victory over Charles Stuart and his Scottish army at Worcester on 3 September 1651.[34]

Draft letter of attorney, 1 May 1651

fo. [1]r

<London, May 1 1651>[35]

Form of a letter of attorney

Know all men by these presents that I Edmund Chillenden of the city of London esquire, have made, constituted and ordained and in my place have put my trusty and well-beloved friend Simon Cressy[36] of the city of London aforesaid girdler to be my true and lawful attorney in this behalf.

For me and in my name but to my only use to [ask], demand, receive, levy and recover of all and every of my tenants, occupiers and farmers of all or any of my lands and tenements sitewate and being in Three Tun Alley[37] in the parish of[38] London aforesaid, all such rent and arrearages of rent as are by them or any of them due and owing, and also to [ask], demand and receive their annuity or fee farm rent of the yearly rent of 53*l* issuing, going out and payable

[33] P. 36.

[34] P. 47. Even this important news took six days to reach the English garrison at Dundee.

[35] Marginated.

[36] Cressey, a modest investor in Irish land under the act of March 1642, was perhaps the man of this name who received payment for transporting soldiers from King's Lynn to Scotland in September 1651, and on 30 September 1653 was appointed a commissioner for accounts and public debts. Shortly after, the Irish investment was claimed by one L. Cressey, suggesting that the original holder may have died; K.S. Bottigheimer, *English Money and Irish Land* (Oxford, 1971), pp. 179, 201; *CSPD 1651*, p. 585; *Journals of the House of Commons*, VII, p. 326.

[37] Three Tun Alley (now built over) was one of the courts which ran north from Thames Street; H.A. Harben, *A Dictionary of London* (London, 1918), p. 582.

[38] Blank.

[of] and from the several farmers, occupiers and possessors of the lands and tenements at, being and belonging to the several wharfs or keys called or known by the several names of[39] in or near Thames Street London aforesaid giving and by these presents granting unto my said attorney my full whole power and authority in the presents all or any of the farmers, tenants and occupiers of any the lands and tenements aforesaid for non-payment of all such sum and sums of money [from] them or any [of] them due, to sue, arrest, attaint, distrain, [impede], imprison and out of prison again to deliver [the] acquittance or acquittances or any other discharge concerning the same to make, seal and deliver and also for non-payment of any the sums ~~aforesaid~~ so due as aforesaid in all and every of the lands and tenements aforesaid or any part thereof for and in the name of the whole to re-enter and repossess himself of all or any of the said lands and tenements and after such re-entry and possession had and made the same to [there set] and dispose to and for the best advantage of me, my executors and assigns and also for non-payment of the said yearly rent, annuity or fee farm rent of 53*l* aforesaid in any of the lands and tenements to re-enter and the goods and chattels of any person or persons upon any the lands and tenements out of which the said annuity or fee farm is due and payable aforesaid to take from their land and carry away and the same to detain and keep until the said rent and arrearages thereof be fully satisfied and paid and also one attorney or more under him to make, constitute and ordain and at his pleasure again to revoke ratifying, allowing, affirming and confirming all and every such act and acts, thing and things whatsoever as my said attorney or his sufficient deputy shall do or cause to be lawfully done in and about the premises aforesaid to be as lawfully done to all intents and purposes whatsoever as <[if]>[40] I myself did it and were personally present at the doing thereof.

In witness whereof I have hereunder set my hand and seal the[41] day of[42] in the year of our Lord God one thousand six hundred and fifty one.

Sealed and delivered in the presence of

[39] Blank.
[40] Interlined.
[41] Blank.
[42] Blank.

Copy of petition of 29 March 1651 from inhabitants of Poole and district to the Council of State, 8 May 1651[43]

fo. 5ʳ

To the Right Honourable the Council of State:

The humble petition of the well-affected and ingaged party of the eastern division of the county of Dorset inhabiting the town[44] and villages bordering on the garrison of Poole.

The humble petition of the well-affected and ingaged party etc.[45]

Sheweth

That your petitioners well weighing our native rights to which we are by a series of providence wonderfully set free, the words of our ingagement binding us to be true and faithful to the Commonwealth,[46] and considering that our silence under the exorbitant and arbitrary practices of men will not stand with either, and knowing that the irreligious and unjust practices of Lieutenant-Colonel Reade, governour of Poole, are a stumbling-block to us and[47] many others and a scandal to the State and army, we could no longer forbear but represent by this our petition [to] your honourable patriots[48] that the aforesaid governour not content with kinging it in his garrison has broken out on us the borderers by an unjust way of levying assessments by giving protection against law or overturning[49] men with threatening papers in point of civil right.

Whereas[50] we humbly pray your honours to take our cause and his actions[51] into serious considerations and do us justice on him by removing him out of our country and placing over us some religious, able and faithful countryman of our own if it[52] seem good unto you,

[43] Dates for this and the following two documents have been taken from the closely similar copies in the British Library; MS Stowe 189, fos 52–53. Variations between the two groups of manuscripts are noted in footnotes.

[44] BL, MS Stowe 189, fo. 52ᵛ reads 'townes' for 'town'.

[45] *Ibid.* omits this sentence.

[46] On 12 April 1649 the mayor, justices, burgesses, and other inhabitants of the town signed an engagement that they would 'unanimously, singly and voluntarily' support Reade, his garrison and the new Commonwealth; BL, MS Stowe 189, fos 43–44, printed in *The Moderate*, 40 (10–17 Apr. 1649), n.p.

[47] BL, MS Stowe 189, fo. 52ᵛ inserts 'to'.

[48] *Ibid.* reads 'to you (honourable patriots)'.

[49] *Ibid.* reads 'by outlawing' for 'or overturning'.

[50] *Ibid.* reads 'Wherefore' for 'Whereas'.

[51] *Ibid.* reads 'actings' for 'actions'.

[52] *Ibid.* inserts 'may'.

that so we may according to our principles comfortably go on to the end of our work, defend our country and assist that garrison if need be, that the great scandal that lieth on the state and army may be taken away and the stumbling[53] removed.

All which we[54] leave to your grave wisdoms to order as to your honours shall seem most meet and your petitioners shall daily pray etc.[55]

Copy of petition from the mayor, aldermen and burgesses of Poole to the Council of State. [8 May 1651][56]

fo. 5^r

To the Right Honourable the Council of State

The humble petition of the maior, aldermen and burgesses of the town and county of Poole on[57] the behalf of themselfs and the rest of the free people of the[58] town and county

Sheweth

That your petitioners in the beginning and through the heat of the late wars were guided and carried on by divine assistance to and with[59] the just cause so much owned by God and the representative of the people in which to the utmost of our abilities we acted faithfully and cheerfully even when all the country round about us was lost and deserted. The service then under the command of Colonel John Bingham a Member of the honourable House of Parliament whose principles[60] piety as they are well known to your honours, so [are] they our great comfort and incouragement.

But now so it is, may it please your Honours that since the[61] governour, Lieutenant-Colonel John Reade, was placed over us we

[53] *Ibid.* inserts 'block'.

[54] *Ibid.* inserts 'humbly'.

[55] *Ibid.* adds the names of the petitioners, perhaps an indication that Clarke's copies were of those sent by Reade, one of whose grievances was that he was not given the names of the deponents against him (below p. 38). However, see my comments above, p. 16.

[56] A shorter and much altered version of this document, taken from the closely similar text in the British Library, BL, MS Stowe 189, fo. 52^r, appears in Bayley, pp. 343–344.

[57] BL, MS Stowe 189, fo. 52^r reads 'in' for 'on'.

[58] *Ibid.* inserts 'said'.

[59] *Ibid.* reads 'in' for 'with'.

[60] *Ibid.* inserts '&'.

[61] *Ibid.* inserts 'present'.

walked on in the same cause with the same affection in the strength of our former principles. Yet we have[62] an insupportable burthen of grief on us by means of our present governour which causeth us[63] to address ourselfs unto[64] your Honours for how can it be otherwise when we see the sabboth ordinances and members of Jesus Christ.

fo. 5^{v}

publikely by the said governour slighted and condemned, the garrison the city and centre of refuge to exorbitant Levellers and Ranters, those grand enemies to just liberty, civility and godliness of[65] civil rights devoured by the power of his arbitrary sword with many other heart troubling oppositions.

Wherefore we humbly pray your Honours in these days of[66] and liberty to look down on us and ease us by calling off our said present governour and incourage us (that are but men)[67] by giving a call to and order that the said Colonel Bingham may be (as formerly he was)[68] our governour. All which we humbly leave to your grave wisdoms and will daily pray etc.

Robert Cleeve[69] *vic*
Lawrence Gigger
George Skutt[70]
Moses Durrell
John Polden[71]
Peter Hall
... Tho Cromwell

William Williams Maior
George Skutt senior
Aaron Derrell[72]
William Skutt
John Trottle[73]

[62] *Ibid.* transposes these two words, 'have we'.
[63] *Ibid.* inserts 'thus'.
[64] *Ibid.* reads 'to' for 'unto'.
[65] *Ibid.* reads 'our' for 'of'.
[66] Blank. *Ibid.* inserts 'reformation'.
[67] *Ibid.* omits these brackets.
[68] *Ibid.* omits these brackets.
[69] *Ibid.* reads 'Cleeves'
[70] Identified in Bayley, (p. 344) as George Skutt Jr. Either this man or his father was the Council of State's first choice as Reade's replacement although not in the event appointed (see below, pp. 37–42).
[71] Transcribed in Bayley as 'Pulson' (p. 344).
[72] BL MS Stowe 189, fo. 53^{r} reads 'Durell'.
[73] In Bayley, p. 344, '(Rev.) John Trottle (a Trier)'.

Copy of articles exhibited against Colonel John Reade by the town of Poole, [8 May 1651][74]

fo. 5^{v}

Articles exhibited against Lieutenant-Colonel John Reade governour of the town and county of Poole[75]:

<1>[76] That the said Lieutenant-Colonel John Reade, governour,[77] being disaffected to this present government has exceedingly countenanced and highly promoted the designs of the Levelling party against the State, not only within his command and government but also in the county of Dorset and elsewhere, *vizt.*

<1> That in the months of March and April 1648,[78] being a time of great danger when the Levellers were in actual arms against the State he, the said Lieutenant-Colonel John Reade, did absent himself from his charge and garrison of Poole aforesaid.

<2> That the said Lieutenant-Colonel John Reade upon his return to Poole after the defeat of the Levellers was angry and fell out with Captain Lilliston[79] (then a commander in the said garrison well affected to[80] the Commonwealth[ )] for apprehending some of the Levellers' party who had been active in the said design and fled to the said garrison of Poole[81] for protection.

<3> That the said Lieutenant-Colonel John Reade has from time to time made and still doth make the said garrison of Poole a shelter and receptacle for such of the Levellers as were notoriously disaffected to this State and present government and has taken them into service and advances them to places of great trust.

<4> That the said Lieutenant-Colonel John Reade in a time of eminent danger has disarmed the maior and other commissioners for the militia and the rest of the well affected inhabitants of the said garrison of Poole because they would not close with him in his Levelling designs.[82]

[74] A closely similar text (of which a shorter and much altered version appears in Bayley, pp. 344–345) in the British Library is dated 29 March 1651; MS Stowe 189, fo. 53^{r-v}.

[75] *Ibid.* adds 'March 29 1651'.

[76] All paragraph numbers in this document are marginated in Clarke's notebook.

[77] BL, MS Stowe 189, fo. 53^{r} omits 'governour'.

[78] i.e. 1649, the months of the army/Leveller mutinies which culminated at Burford on 14–15 May.

[79] *Ibid.* reads 'Lillingstone'.

[80] *Ibid.* inserts 'this present government and of knowne integrity to this state and'.

[81] *Ibid.* omits 'of Poole'.

[82] *Ibid.* reads 'design' for 'designs'.

<[3]>[83] That the said Lieutenant-Colonel John Reade has openly declared himself against the observation of the Lord's Day by favouring of the Ranters in opposition to the ministry and other public ordinances *vizt.*

<1>That the said Lieutenant-Colonel John Reade has cashiered out of the service of the said garrison of Poole such persons as were known to walk as visible saints and to be cordially affected to[84] this State and present government because they refused to joyn with him in his way of dipping but follow the ministry and other public ordinances.

fo. [6]^{r}

<2> That the said Lieutenant-Colonel John Reade has (to the great scandal of religion) entertained and countenanced such Ranters and dippers [( ]who hold and foment many[85] blasphemous opinions) as have been cashiered as well out of the said garrison of Poole as out of several other garrisons and preferred them to the utmost of his power.

<3> That the said Lieutenant-Colonel John Reade did protect and shelter Radman[86] the great Ranter and his companion after the Parliament has set forth an order for his apprehension.

<4> That the said Colonel John Reade endeavoured with an[87] high hand to impose one Gardiner, a soldier and dipper, to be pastor and lecturer of Poole aforesaid in opposition to such orthodox divines and well affected ministers as were provided by the magistracy of Poole aforesaid.

<[5]>[88] That the said Lieutenant-Colonel John Reade has contrived and indeavoured to make a dissension between the inhabitants of the garrison of Poole aforesaid and the soldiers therein by force, and has incroached upon the civil rights and privileges of the said town of Poole, *vizt.*

That the said Colonel John Reade by force caused William Williams, maior of Poole aforesaid, a man well affected to this state and present government, to be apprehended and brought before him as a delinquent in a disgraceful manner by a sergeant

[83] *Ibid.* reads '2', as clearly it should here.

[84] *Ibid.* reads 'with' for 'to'.

[85] *Ibid.* reads 'such' for 'many'.

[86] The shorthand 'Radman' is confirmed by a careful reading of BL, MS Stowe 189, fo. 53^{r}, transcribed as 'Rudman' in Bayley (p. 345). See my comments on Radman above (p. 16).

[87] BL, MS Stowe 189, fo. 53^{r} reads 'a' for 'an'.

[88] *Ibid.* reads '3'.

and 10 musketeers with lighted matches, which might have proved of dangerous consequence had not the maior quietly submitted himself and suffered the ignominious reproach and affront.

Newsletter from Whitehall, 7 June 1651

fo. [18]^r

Our news here is not much, depending much upon your northern motions which we hope will be to some purpose now the recovery of his Excellency [*sic*].[89] The rendition of Scilly totally to us I conceive will be communicated to you by a better hand with the articles of agreement, the substance whereof was shewn by Master Peters.[90] They are the largest [. . .] that have been given by any of our party and are for that cause much found fault with. All here toss though they will not be [. . .].

The French are setting forth a lusty navy to disarm us in these our coasts if they can catch us. They come forth from Brest.[91]

Whitehall, June 7, 1651.

Colonel Edward Sexby's court martial, Edinburgh, day 1, 10 June 1651

fo. 21^r

This day the court martial sat upon the trial of Colonel Sexby. They examined him upon the greatest part of the articles which [were/are] against him which [were/are] 16 in number, excepting only the 4th and 5th [~~of the~~ and] came to the 15th. The witnesses against the colonel carried themselfs with much bitterness and malice, and to spit their venom the more violent they accused Captain Staresmore[92]

[89] Cromwell had suffered two severe bouts of illness in the last three months, but by the date of this newsletter was well on the way to recovery; W. C. Abbott, *The Writings and Speeches of Oliver Cromwell*, 4 vols (Oxford, 1937–1947), II, p. 421.

[90] Presumably the army chaplain Hugh Peter or Peters (as Clarke, in common with many of his contemporaries, always calls him). The royalist Sir John Grenvile, who had been using the Scillies as a base for piracy against both the English and Dutch fleets, had formally surrendered the islands on 23 May, although they were not finally captured until 3 June; *C&P*, I, p. 364; B. Capp, *Cromwell's Navy* (Oxford, 1989), p. 67; *CSPD 1651*, p. 239.

[91] Although Brest was a notorious base for pirate ships (Capp, *Cromwell's Navy*, p. 70), I have not found any other reference to such an offensive at this time.

[92] Clarke's young cousin, James Staresmore, served as lieutenant at Weymouth in September 1647 alongside Sexby and several of the other witnesses at this court martial. Clarke's brother-in-law, Kympton Hilliard, also served there as captain; Worc. MS LXVII,

who was examined. The 2d witness for the colonel upon the 1st article, one ~~Captain~~ Mutloe, that had the name of a captain but the conditions[93] of a caitiff,[94] sent in word by the marshal general that he had some exceptions to make against ~~a~~ the[95] witness, and being sent for in said that he was twice cashiered the army, once out of the lieutenant-general's regiment, and next near cashiered at Weymouth for drunkenness upon the guard etc. Major Clobery was also called in and said something that he heard from Lieutenant-Colonel Pike[96] to that purpose who had about a week before signed a certificate on Captain Staresmore's behalf rendering him of a very pious and religious conversation, but it seems being sick and in distemper his fault was as violent in the relapse as it was formerly that made him mad, for he affected divers things that carried the face of untruth, as that all the garrisons in England were paid up to 3 days' pay, that Portland received wages equal with Weymouth, etc. The major-general required the [testimony] of Captain Staresmore and of one Tubben,[97] formerly lieutenant to Colonel Sexby, who was also accused by the Judge Advocate. The [accusation] against Tubben was for stealing a pair of gloves from his landlord and selling them for 2*s*.

Hereupon Colonel Sexby, since they began to fall upon his witnesses, recriminated upon theirs and charged one Captain George Everard,[98] a principal and very malicious witness against him who also swore several untruths against him, that he had been before cashiered the army for divers crimes.

In the procedure of the trial it was observed that there was more of malice than of matter in the articles. The colonel pleaded to all with much discretion and moderation, though his accusers and prosecutor shewed much violence and bitterness of spirit in their very appearances and countenances, and Major Clobery[99] was very

fo. 35^{v}. Sexby became governor of Portland in 1649. Staresmore was promoted to captain in Maj. Thomas Rippon's dragoons in September 1650, but apparently did not arrive in Scotland until just before the trial; *CSPD 1650*, p. 334; p. 35 below.

[93] 'Conditions' (now obs.) meaning personal qualities, morals, behaviour, temper, etc.; *The Oxford English Dictionary*, 2nd edn, 20 vols (Oxford, 1989).

[94] Despite Clarke's opinion of him, Capt. James Mutlow was to perform distinguished service in Scotland under Sexby's successor, Col Thomas Reade, and was promoted to lieutenant-colonel by General Monck in December 1659; F&D, II, pp. 564–567.

[95] '[T]he' superimposed on 'a'.

[96] Peter Pike was Sexby's lieutenant-colonel (*ibid.*, p. 562). Owing to illness he did not appear at the court martial until Friday 13 June; Worc. MS XIX, fo. 26^{r}; p. 35.

[97] Ensign Tulbin, serving at Weymouth garrison in September 1647, appears to have been still there in March 1650; Worc. MS LXVII, fo. 35^{r}; Bayley, p. 337.

[98] For the later career of Capt. George Everard see F&D, II, pp. 565–566, 569.

[99] John Clobery was major in Sexby's regiment, but is not recorded as having served at Weymouth (*ibid.*, p. 565).

pregnant[100] and more like to a prosecutor than witness, although the colonel had always carried himself with much consideration to him.

*fo. 21^v^*

The matter of about 12 articles was so trivial and the heart blood of his actions so squeezed out for matter of crime that Colonel Pride then present was pleased to say that if this were suffered they should have very few colonels left and that if he had such in his regiment he would cut them in pieces or knock them in the head or to that effect. Many of the colonels then present spake to that effect, although there appeared the hand of [. . . .] the hand of some grandees in it which gave occasion to some to think that it was set on foot by some great officers. The Major-General or Lieutenant-General Lambert then present, and Major-General Deane, carried themselves with a [structure] of wisdom and moderation towards both parties and nothing at all of bitterness appeared in them. Commissary-General Whalley, Colonel Thomlinson and the Comptroller[101] were very scrutinous upon every article and made many unnecessary queries and did what they could to find out something of [issue/ill] in his actions in which they were so frequently inquisitive and questionative that it was very apparent that they had a design rather to ruin him out of passion than out of justice and had rather aim prejudice to the person then to his actions.

Colonel Edward Sexby's court martial, Edinburgh, day 2, 11 June 1651

*fo. 22^r^*

At the court martial for the trial of Colonel Sexby

Present

~~Major~~ Lieutenant General Lambert	*Lieutenant Colonel*
Major General Deane	*Lieutenant Colonel Gough*
Lieutenant Generall Monke	*Lieutenant Colonel White*
Commissary General Whalley	*Lieutenant Colonel Mason*
Colonel Fairfax	*Major Berry*
Colonel Overton	*Major Packer*

100 'Imaginative, or inventive' (*OED*).

101 I take this to be the Comptroller of the Ordnance, by 1 May 1650 Solomon Saffery, who still held held the post in October 1654; Worc. MSS LXVII, fo. 27^r^; L, fo. 80^r^.

Colonel Okey *Major Knight*
Colonel Ashfeild *Major Cobbett*
Colonel Thomlinson *Major Keene*
Colonel Goffe *Major Butler*
Colonel Twistleton *Quarter Master Generall Moseley*
Colonel Fenwick *Comptroller*

This day the court proceeded upon the 3d and 4th articles[102] of the charge which it seems was remitted[103] the day before only a further foolish thing was read from Lieutenant-Colonel Pike to this effect, that Colonel Heane[104] had paid up all the forces under him or that none of the forces in the garrison of Colonel Heane were behind a <penny>[105] week's pay or that on his coming to this it was [. . .] that the colonel had [. . .] and [. . .] by several witnesses more that Major Rippon's[106] company were a week's pay behind.

Upon the 2 articles alledged, the one for receiving 500*l* for the repair of the castle at Portland and fortifications and not expending the same but leaving the same [. . . .],[107] the colonel made it appear that he has not received above 450*l* that he had a clear account to give [thereof] same

fo. 22^{v}

and had repaired the castle.[108] Major-General Deane gave a good account of what places of the castle were repairable [. . .] Commissary-General Whalley and others, upon the [witness's/witnesses'] testimony that Colonel White[109] had been there and had set out a platform for a new work to be made without, urged that he [must/should] have made that up [whereas] it appeared the strength of the castle lay in the walls or castle [. . .] which he had repaired.

[102] '3d and 4th articles' are underlined in the original.

[103] It is not clear whether 'remitted' is used in the sense of being referred for consideration, or fully pardoned.

[104] Governor of Weymouth in September 1647; Worc. MS LXVII, fo. 35^{r}. His career is summarized in F&D, II, pp. 718–719.

[105] Interlined.

[106] Thomas Rippon's rank was captain while serving at Weymouth; Bayley, p. 337.

[107] Lt-Col George Joyce was paid £200 for repairing Portland Castle in October 1650; *CSPD 1650*, pp. 386, 594.

[108] On 23 July 1649 the governor of Weymouth was paid £400 for repairing fortifications at Weymouth and Portland. Presumably it was out of this sum that Sexby had already been allowed £200 when the Ordnance Committee granted him a further £300 for more repairs on 24 November 1649; *CSPD 1649–1650*, pp. 581, 593, 405. By August 1650 Sexby's successor as governor, George Joyce, was requesting, and subsequently received, more money and timber for repairs; *CSPD 1650*, pp. 293, 386, 594.

[109] Probably Col J. White of the Ordnance Office, who was similarly involved in repairs at Portsmouth in December 1650; *ibid.*, pp. 195, 454, 462.

Only the great [recreation] was for making a dining room which few governors in any castle in England will be without.

After this they came to the article about the hanging of the soldier near Morpeth which the colonel confessed only that he had order from Sir Arthur Hesilrige. It was alledged that he was to be sent to the headquarters which was granted but that afterwards order was given to him to keep his men in [tow] upon a mutiny in Captain Gosnell's coming crying out money, money, no money, no march.[110] And Lieutenant-Colonel Mears[111] in his letter to the council [testifies] that after some discourse between Colonel Sexby and Sir Arthur, Sir Arthur bid him do what he would do with him.[112] Colonel Fenwick being there in that court martial at Newcastle and present here affirmed that he did not observe any such plea of the soldier as that he had leave from his captain, but that he was found clearly guilty of the articles and running away from his colours. It is also observable that a witness procured by the colonel did declare that a day after the execution of the man Captain Gosnell told him upon discourse together that he had observed a great providence of God in the execution of that man for that he was confident they should march into Scotland 200 men stronger for that execution. And because he denied it the ensign observed that at the same time he observed another providency,[113] that [money] should come up to that we listed when they were upon their march for Ireland[114] at such a time when they went not 2 mile out of the way to go for Scotland, and also that the money [must/should] again come not till they were out of Newcastle so that they could not go back but [must/should] go behind the town or else [. . . .]. That certainly God had some great work to do for that regiment which something convinced him that he could not deny it as true but said it was upon that account that he [thought] he had a better [order] of it than he had. But it seems that his [acting] since has not been answerable unto so great [providency/providences] of God which should rather lead him and the rest to acts of love and mercy then of hatred and malice, but their envy, [hatred] and malice and all [under honourable . . .] etc.

[110] A shorter version of this part of the proceedings is found in longhand in Clarke's notebook; Worc. MS XIX, fos 26^{r}–27^{r}, transcribed below, Appendix B.

[111] Or Mayers, lieutenant-colonel of Hesilrige's regiment, and deputy governor of Berwick.

[112] A letter rushed from Hesilrige testifying to this effect was read to the court in Sexby's absence on Friday 13 June; *ibid.*, fo. 26^{v}; below p. 33.

[113] A rare form of 'providence', first recorded in print in 1600 (*OED*).

[114] Sexby was originally ordered to raise a regiment for service in Ireland, but in September 1650 it was diverted to Scotland; F&D, II, p. 561.

*fo. [23]^r^*

After this they had squeezed in a 16 article which was that the colonel being desired to muster Captain Sumner's company in February last passed 3 of the company that were run away from their colours, to which the colonel, not having witnesses ready, replied that he did acknowledge he did muster the company but that he passed any that were not present upon sufficient [protestation]. He ordered not short. He had [. . . .] against the captain for drunkenness and other misdemeanours, whereby it was not [probable] that he would muster up 3 men to gratify him in any such indirect way.

The court adjourned till Friday next in the afternoon.

Colonel Edward Sexby's court martial, Edinburgh, day 3, 13 June 1651

*fo. 24^r^*

Major General L[ambert]
Major General D[eane]
Lieutenant General M[onck]
Commissary General [Whalley]
Colonel Thomlinson
Colonel Fairfax
Colonel Okey
Colonel Twisleton
Colonel Pride
Colonel Ashfeild
Colonel Berry
Colonel Overton
Colonel Goffe
Colonel Fenwick
Scoutmaster General Downing
Quarter Master General Moseley
Lieutenant Colonel Worsley
Lieutenant Colonel Mason
Lieutenant Colonel White
Lieutenant Colonel Goffe
Major Packer
Major Butler
Major Knight
Major Keene
Comptroller

At this court Colonel Sexby again appeared and gave in his answer to the 16th article denying to his best remembrance that he [. . .] any into the roll that were left out. Only he [joyned] one Richard Overton who upon Captain Andrews' importunity he permitted for to march along with the horse one march.[115] That he could have nothing of design in it of benefit to himself, being Captain Sumner's company, against

[115] This may well have been Richard Overton, the Leveller pamphleteer, about whose movements between 1649 and 1653 little is known, but who was implicated in Sexby's plotting in 1655–1656; *DBR*, 'Richard Overton'. I have been unable to identify Capt. Andrews.

the captain, whereof he had articles in his pocket at the very time when he mustered the men, but the unseasonableness of the weather might perhaps make him less careful in the muster then otherwise. But however he closed not the rolls.

Lieutenant-Colonel Pike, who was sick before, and so had 2 officers, *vizt* Major[116] and[117] sent to take his depositions, being very much [transported] with opposition,

fo. 24v

upon some reports he had of Captain Staresmore from Mutloe, Everard and other the malicious accusers of Colonel Sexby, adventured to come in person, and again asserted what he deposed upon the 1st article, adding further that to his knowledge not one that was in the garrison of Weymouth under Colonel Heane [missed] a day's pay all the time that he was there. Yet denied not but that Major Rippon's company might want pay when they came thither 1st, and that they did mutiny for pay.

He cleared the colonel as to the bottom that it was only mustered at Weymouth.[118]

He spake something concerning the execution of the man at Morpeth, that he knew nothing of it before the colonel gave command for the doing of it, but confessed the mutiny that was in Captain Gosnell's company, who cried, no money, no march, and though Captain Gosnell at 1st denied that it was the same day that he marched from Newcastle to Morpeth, yet afterwards he confessed it though before he said to the colonel, how dare you affirm this?[119]

After all, the colonel perceiving how things were like to go made his address unto the court, told them he had always manifested his faithfulness unto the interest of the Commonwealth, that there was a long charge against him to which he had made as good a defence as the shortness of his time and the want of witnesses who [were/are] in several places in England could admit, that he hoped as he had done all things in the integrity of his honour, and without any intentions of doing prejudice to the publike, so he hoped his faults would be interpreted and that if in any thing he had miscarried which to his knowledge he had not, it was through weakness and infirmity, and not through wilfulness or wickedness; that he should be ready to give in his accounts to the Parliament or any that should be appointed by them to receive the same; that it was his unhappiness that none of

[116] Blank.
[117] Blank.
[118] Clarke amplifies this in his letter of 14 June (below, p. 36).
[119] See above, p. 30.

his officers or any about him did at all manifest any dislike of these proceedings, nor did he know that they were discontented at them till the articles were exhibited against him.

After this Captain Gosnell seemed to [tend] off what he had said and to protest that what he had done was not out of malice, but for the satisfaction of his conscience, which now he had [attained]; that he had before told the colonel thereof, but that he refused to give any redress and something to that purpose.

After this both the colonel and his prosecutor were commanded to withdraw

fo. [25]r

and then 2 letters from Sir Arthur Hesilrige, one to Colonel Sexby and another to Major-General Lambert, were read. That to Colonel Sexby expressed that he had inclosed an answer to his letter, which if it gave not satisfaction he should indeavour to give it more fuller when he came [from] Newcastle, which would be very suddenly. In the letter to the major-general he gave a narrative of the proceedings against the soldier at Newcastle to his best remembrance. That my Lord General sent him a letter and orders for the punishing and execution of such soldiers as should come from the army, and that he could make some of them [exemplify] his order, upon which this soldier was condemned, being a [fellow][120] very inconsiderable. He said sometimes that he had a pass from his captain but lost it. Another time that he could get nothing but dry biskit and cheese and came away upon that. That he thereupon left him to Colonel Sexby either to carry along with him to the headquarters, or to execute him by the way to deter his regiment if he saw cause.

Another letter was read from Major Tolhurst,[121] wherein he gives an account that the soldier was condemned to die, but to be sent with a letter to the headquarters there to be proceeded against as the Lord General should see cause.

After some little debate and as I hear some heats amongst them, the court adjourned till the next day. Some say that some friends of the colonel's told others who[122] seemed [argued or/were highly] against them, and said that if that they should not [be called] directly against them they could withdraw that they might withdraw [*sic*], for they were a court without them.

It is [observable] that though there were about 15 or 16 colonels and general officers, and that divers lieutenant-colonels and majors

[120] In shorthand, 'follow'.
[121] Jeremiah Tolhurst, of Hesilrige's regiment; F&D, II, p. 459.
[122] Presumably the word 'it' is omitted here.

sat upon the trial, and the Comptroller,[123] who was no field officer and so might have been excepted against, yet the colonel did not at all challenge either one or the other, though he might have thereon [rooted/voted] out Major Packer and the Comptroller, who are grand enemies and it's thought contrivers of the charge against him. Also he might have excepted against Commissary-General Whalley, who had told him in the presence of the major-general not long before, Colonel Sexby you are now so high because you are a colonel, but it may be about a month hence we shall take you a pin lower.

Colonel Edward Sexby's court martial, Edinburgh, day 4, 14 June 1651

fo. 27ʳ

This day ~~Colonel~~ the court martial sat again upon the trial of Colonel Sexby and had debate [of/on] it from 9 in the morning to about 3 or 4 in the afternoon. They found him guilty of several articles *vizt.*[124]

[William Clarke] to an unidentified recipient, 14 June 1651

fo. 27ᵛ

Sir[125]

I have hitherto forborne to give you any account of our affairs here in regard I am [confident] you have them weekly from my brother Mabbott. Yet there being something [extraordinary] and unexpected happened in the trial of Colonel Sexby I desire to acquaint you therewith.

I doubt not but you are acquainted with the 16 articles exhibited against Colonel Sexby of which (I speak my heart freely) I did not think 3 of them proved against him but the contriving of them was by a malicious crew of Levelling officers (for the most part) which I know not how he raised up to pick as his own.

He has had 4 principal days of trial and behaved himself with much moderation and discretion though his opposites shewed much malice. His prosecutor was Captain Gosnell. The chief witnesses

123 Salomon Saffery.

124 Clarke does not attach the articles.

125 I have speculated upon the possible identity of the recipient of this letter above (pp. 17–18).

against him were Captain Everard, Captain Mutloe, Captain Yardley and Lieutenant Everard,[126] also Lieutenant-Colonel Pike and Major Clobery. The 1st article was for detaining a week's pay from his soldiers while he was in Portland, which how they could [reach] I leave to you to judge. Yet my cozen Staresmore being brought in as a witness to clear Colonel Sexby upon this account, that Major Rippon's company were a week's pay behind when in Weymouth, and Lieutenant-Colonel Pike hearing that he had deposed it and having with all some [misrepresentations] of him as 2 speeches by Colonel Sexby's prosecutors conceived it, was in opposition to him, who by reason of his dangerous sickness was examined by 2 officers upon a special commission and was so inraged at hearing a false report concerning Captain Staresmore that he said to some of them that Captain Staresmore had been either near cashiering or twice cashiered the army and instanced in the report of some troopers at Weymouth as also in that business which was urged against him (when there with you) by some of Major Rippon's company to you and then you referred to him. He now aggravates it in the highest terms that may be, of setting up drinking all night when he was in the watch, and then going the rounds after the [reveille] beaten and striking one of the sentinels. All which (upon the 1st day of trial) Major Clobery and Captain Mutloe had the confidence to attest before the whole court to Captain Staresmore's great disrepute, having about a fortnight before come into Scotland with me upon a very large testimony, subscribed by Colonel Sexby, Lieutenant-Colonel Pike and others had the command of a foot company in Colonel West's regiment conferred upon him.

fo. [28]ʳ

Now in regard that Lieutenant-Colonel Pike who came yesterday to the court martial as a witness in the business of Colonel Sexby, upon some rage spent between myself and him, was pleased to tell Captain Staresmore that he was by your direction forbidden to have any charge of a company or had any charge after that alledging you would be their captain, and that he never [exercised] them or did duty with them after that business brought against him (though the parties who then accused him to you being here deny it). I desire you will do me the favour as to certify in a line or 2 to me your best remembrance of those particulars that so I may in case of necessity be able to say something in vindication of Captain Staresmore or otherwise be silent, which I the rather earnestly importune in respect that I have observed very much goodness and sedulity in all the late carriage of my cozen Staresmore.

[126] I am grateful to George Southcombe for helping me to unravel some of the complexities of the Everards. The identification of this Lt Everard has however remained elusive.

<Besides he assures me that he was imployed as lieutenant on the coming away of Captain Rippon's company from Weymouth and was also after that pretended misbehaviour chosen agent for them and their garrison>[127] and did thereupon assist in procuring that reputation he now has wherein as I doubt not but he will perform with much diligence and faithfulness all such commands as shall be given. So I suppose you are not unacquainted with his abilities for the management of the same although this unhappy report will much prejudice him. Your clearing whereof will be much [dissatisfaction] to me, and I shall very highly prize your freedom in a few lines privately to myself and that you will keep secret what I now present to you.

And now I might give you a large relation of the charge and proceedings against the colonel which I know would be too tedious. One article was for receiving 500*l* for repair of the castle at Portland and not doing the same according to order. Another was the taking of the old lead and selling it and making the state pay for new. A 3d was that he had pay for a bottom but never had one, to the two former of which he gave answer that he had an account ready for the Council of State. And for the 3d, Lieutenant-Colonel Pike cleared him for that the bottom was [paid] at Weymouth. Most of the other particulars relate to him since his commanding the regiment, and therefore will not be so suitable to give you any hint of.

Upon the whole after 7 or 8 hours debate this day the court have voted Colonel Sexby to be cashiered chiefly upon the account of the 2d article, which was for the detaining of pay from 7 or 8 soldiers belonging to him at Portland who would not go with him for Ireland which (although he did in his intentions for the public service) yet now proved his greatest crime.

Memorandum, Edinburgh, 15 June 1651[128]

fo. 29^r

The duke of Buckingham[129] is very much taken notice of at court for whoring with all kind of women that come near the court and has

[127] Marginated.

[128] An amalgam of this snippet of gossip and the shorter version in longhand which follows it in Clarke's notebook appears in *Perfect Diurnall*, 81 (23–30 June 1651), p. 1131; Worc. MS XIX, fo. 31^{r-v}, suggesting that Clarke may have contributed it to this newsbook, which was edited by John Rushworth and Samuel Pecke.

[129] Buckingham, who had arrived in Scotland with Charles II the previous June, had recently been appointed commander-in-chief of English royalist forces there; *C&P*, I, p. 264; *OxDNB*, 'Villiers'.

already had a bastard given to him which he got since he came hither, so that if the Scots on the other side see a pretty child they call it Buckingham's bird with no heart, for he lay with their women one after another.

Memorandum, Edinburgh, 18 June 1651

fo. 33[r]

Yesterday Captain Owen Cox, <captain of the Constant Warwick>[130], had his despatch for Holland from his Excellency to the Lord Ambassador St John there and went out of Leith road this day bound for Holland.[131]

Colonel John Reade, Poole, to Oliver Cromwell, 18 June 1651[132]

fo. 38[r]

May it please your Excellency

I have inclosed the Council of State's order to Major-General Disbrowe of the 20th of May last[133] and the major-general having named Lieutenant-Colonel Joseph Hunkins,[134] I have inclosed the Council of State approbation with their authority to the said major-general of 26th ultim.[135] for his sending the said lieutenant-colonel to Poole and <there>[136] to take charge of that trust (until the matter referred unto him and his council of war should be heard and determined). Who came accordingly to Poole on Monday the 9th of June and the same day took possession of the garrison. But in the interim (*vizt*) before the said lieutenant-colonel came I obtained of the Council of State another letter to the major-general upon

[130] Interlined.

[131] Cox, a regular go-between, was returning with letters from Cromwell to the English ambassadors at The Hague, where negotiations with the Dutch had just broken down; *Perfect Diurnall*, 77 (26 May–2 June 1651), p. 1076; 81 (23–30 June 1651), p. 1132; *C&P*, I, p. 368.

[132] This and the following six documents were apparently sent by John Reade to Cromwell in support of his bid to retain the governorship of Poole (see also pp. 15 and 21–26 above).

[133] P. 40 below.

[134] Desborough recommended Hunkins on 23 May 1651 (*ibid.*).

[135] *Ibid.*

[136] Interlined.

my petition,[137] having seen some proceedings concerning me passing on some [actions] indirectly touching the examination of witnesses against me whilst Major Scutt remained in power as governor and before the said lieutenant-colonel came, which was the cause of my petition that the inclosed letter to the major-general of the 2d of June might be sent.[138] And yet for all this I could not prevent the same, for they had gotten their witnesses all examined at Wareham in Dorsetshire (before Colonel Heane and some 3 officers more) by a former order obtained from the major-general for the purpose) against me.[139] Before I could come down with the last letter above mentioned[140] and obtain the major-general's countermand thereupon, the place being 100 miles distant from London[141] and the major-general at Plymouth 100 miles beyond that, their witnesses were examined as I understand upon the 3d and 4th days of this instant June, and of all these depositions, copies were forthwith dispatched unto the major-general.[142]

fo. 38v

And about a week after this I did attend him at Blandford[143] (for he came up thither to meet his lady who at that place fell somewhat ill and stayed 4 nights and then went [. . .] till she recovered [and then] with her little ones gone with her husband unto Plymouth). But whilst the major-general stayed at Blandford I did humbly beseech him (because the articles which my opponents proffered were most of them in general heads, very few particulars being named and therefore impossible for me to know by the said articles (of which I sent your Excellency a copy) who those were which the deponents did mean) that the copies of the depositions might be granted me without the deponents' names, but that was denied although it was confessed no man could answer these things without other keys to unlock the meaning of them. Yet at last I got a few names of some of the persons which (as [is/then] said) [are/were] the men hinted at in the articles. And truly there is not so much [turn] given me as in reason [there/is] [ought/owed]. Yet instead of this mine accusers could obtain this inclosed order[144] to the muster-master who as soon

137 P. 41 below, which, as I explain there, I have assigned to 2 June.

138 *Ibid.* below.

139 The Council of State, in response to two petitions and a set of articles (presumably the documents found on pp. 21–26 above), had twice (on 30 April and on 12 May) authorized Desborough to hear the case at a court martial; *CSPD 1651*, pp. 171, 195.

140 P. 41 below.

141 Presumably Wareham, some five miles west of Poole.

142 It was not until 23 June 1651 that the Council of State ordered Desborough to appoint deputies to hear the court martial; *CSPD 1651*, p. 265.

143 Blandford Forum lies some fifteen miles to the north-west of Poole.

144 See p. 41 below, 15 June 1651.

as he had it came and shewed the same to me, at the sight of which I marvelled and presently took the muster-master and his order and ran to the major-general desiring to know whether that paper were his pleasure or no, whereupon he took it and read it again. And being just ready in the same place to take horse [. . . .] me, Major Skutt and the muster-master made the insuing legal order[145] and commanded the muster-master to muster accordingly. And therefore I am necessitated to inclose a copy of my commission[146] that you may see how I am relieved also of mine own company for want of 2 or 3 words in it nominating me captain and that before I am heard at a council of war notwithstanding my company has been twice established to me by the Parliament, (*vizt*) at the 1st, 100 private soldiers besides officers, and upon the 4th of May 1649, 80 private soldiers etc. And after this I did humbly crave to know the time when and the place where the council of war should be held for the determination of my business. The major-general answered I should know that a month hence and not before. Wherefore I humbly beseech your Excellency that a commission or an order may be granted unto me that I may be and remain captain of my own company at least until this case of mine be decided. At which time will appear, I am confident, a most deep design of the Scotified clergy in these parts to gain not only the power of Poole garrison into their hands but the command and interest of all this country,[147] if the proud armed enemy could any way prevail over you and your army whose heads [. . .] were high in the day of battle. And make all your hearts [stout] and valiant and hands strong to the overthrow of such as are implicitly set against the [ways] and saints of the most high God, the Lord Jehovah. What mine enemy have against me, I am fully satisfied already will vanish (as the thick mist) at the end of my trial they being mere scandals against me invented by the clergy because they could not cast [me] in their [Scottish/Skuttish] mould. But in the truth of the Lord I shall ever remain

your Excellency's and the Commonwealth's just and faithful servant

John Reade

Poole, June 18 1651

For his Excellency the Lord General Cromwell at the headquarters in Scotland.

[145] Reproduced below, p. 42.
[146] P. 43 below.
[147] i.e. county (of Dorset).

Copy of order of 20 May 1651 of the Council of State, [25 June 1651][148]

fo. 39v

For Major-General Desbrowe

Sir

We thought fit that some person should be appointed to the charge of the town of Poole until the business concerning Lieutenant-Colonel Reade and Major Skutt referred to your examination be heard and determined. We therefore desire you to think of some fit person for that purpose and to return his name unto this Council.

Signed in the name etc,

John Bradshaw, President

Whitehall 20th May 1651

Copy of letter of 26 May 1651 from the Council of State to Major-General Desborough [25 June 1651][149]

fo. 39v

To Major-General Desbrowe

Sir

We have received your letter of the 23th instant wherein you recommend Lieutenant-Colonel Joseph Hunkins as one you judge fit to the care of Poole as governour according to the order we formerly sent you, by which the business was referred to you concerning the late governour of that place. We have upon that your recommendation approved thereof, and desire you to commit that place to his care till you have determined that business [so/sir] as aforesaid referred which, when you have done, we desire you to certify the Council of your proceedings that further order may be taken for settling of that government.

Signed etc, John Bradshaw, President

Whitehall 26th May 1651

Copy

[148] *CSPD 1651*, p. 211. Clarke entered it under 25 June in his notebook.

[149] The Council's order for this letter is entered for the following day, 27 May 1651 (*ibid.*, p. 220). Clarke entered it under 25 June in his notebook.

Copy of letter of [2] June 1651 from the Council of State to Major-General Desborough, [25 June 1651][150]

fo. 40r

To Major-General Desbrowe

Sir

The inclosed petition of Lieutenant-Colonel Reade, late governour of Poole, being presented to the Council and there considered, we conceive it reasonable that the 3d person approved of by the Council to be governour of Poole[151] should be in the government thereof before any progress be made in the examination of that business, to the end that the proceedings may be therein with the more equality in regard the persons to be produced as witnesses live under the government of the said town. We therefore desire you not to proceed until such time as the 3d person shall be actually in the government and are to go on therein with all expedition and return an account according to former order.

Signed in the name and by the
order of the Council of State etc,

John Bradshaw, President

Whitehall 20th June 1651

Copy

Copy of order of 15 June 1651 from Major-General Desborough to Muster-master Eldred, [25 June 1651]

fo. 40r

Master Eldred

You are to muster Major George Skutt as governour of Poole and Brownsea Castle[152] and Lieutenant-Colonel Reade as captain of one of

[150] The instruction for this letter was issued on 2 June 1651; *ibid.*, p. 231, where it is found in draft. The date recorded in Clarke's notebook, 20 June, therefore appears to be an error. This would account for Reade's statement (p. 37 above) that the letter was written *before* Hunkins took over Poole garrison on 9 June 1651, and also explains the anomaly that one of Reade's enclosures appears to have been written later than his covering letter of 18 June (*ibid.*).

[151] i.e. Lt-Col Joseph Hunkins.

[152] On 27 May 1651 the Council of State had ordered Joseph Hunkins to be installed as governor at Desborough's own suggestion; *CSPD 1651*, p. 220.

the companies there, together with Master John Spence as chirurgeon, one of the aforesaid garrison. If Lieutenant-Colonel Reade has no commission as captain of it then you are to muster Major <Skutt>[153] as governour and captain, and for so doing this shall be your warrant.

Given under my hand at Blandford
this 15th of June 1651

John Desbrowe

Copy of Muster-master's order of 16 June 1651, [25 June 1651]

*fo. 40^r^*

Lieutenant-Colonel Reade upon sight of this order went to the major-general, who in the presence of him and Major George Skutt, gave me this larger order, *vizt*

Muster-master, you are notwithstanding this my order to take a letter of Lieutenant-Colonel Reade's commission and if he be [mentioned] there as captain then you are to muster him captain but if not yet you/shall

*fo. 40^v^*

shall not muster Major George Skutt as captain to that company, but let Lieutenant-Colonel Hunkins be mustered as captain to that company which was formerly Lieutenant-Colonel Reade's and the money to be deposited in our hands until the business be ended between Lieutenant-Colonel Reade and Major George Skutt.

Samuel Eldred, muster-master

This order was given me when the Major-General was taking horse at Blandford for Dorchester.

Samuel Eldred

June 16 1651

[153] Interlined.

Copy of commission of 11 November 1647 to Lieutenant-Colonel John Reade, [June 1651]

fo. 40[v]

Sir Thomas Fairfax, knight, commander-in-chief of all the land forces under the pay of the Parliament in the kingdom of England, dominion of Wales and in the island of Guernsey and Jersey in order to the security and peace of the kingdom, reducing of Ireland and [defending] such as shall be thought fit by both Houses.

To Lieutenant-Colonel John Reade, governour of Poole and Brownsea:

By the authority to me given by both Houses of Parliament I do hereby constitute and appoint you governour of Poole and Brownsea Castle in the county of Dorset and commander-in-chief of all the forces raised or to be raised for the defence of the same. These are therefore to will and require you to make your present repair to the said garrisons and take the same into your charge as governour with all the forts, towers and places of strength in and about the same, together with all the magazine, ordinance, arms and ammunition thereunto belonging. You are to keep and defend the same for the service of the Parliament and kingdom. And you are hereby required to exercise your inferior officers and soldiers of the said garrison in arms commanding them to obey you as their governour for the said service and you likewise to observe and follow such orders and directions as you shall receive from myself according to the discipline of war.

Given under my hand and seal this

11 of 9bris 1647

Thomas Fairfax

Gilbert Mabbott to Major-General Deane, 5 July 1651[154]

fo. 50[r]

Right Honourable

The Lord St John reported on Wednesday last the several transactions of himself and Master Strickland with the States General in order to

[154] This newsletter is largely confirmed by, and in places uses substantially the same wording as, the official journal of the House of Commons for 2–4 July 1651; *CJ*, VI, pp. 595–598. There are other examples of direct quotations from the journal in Mabbott's newsletters (e.g. Hull CRO, BRL 563).

the embassy delivered by them according to the order and commands of Parliament. The House hereupon approved of all proceedings and transactions and that they should have the thanks[155] of the House for their great and faithful service therein. The English gentlemen that attended their lordships were called in and had severally the thanks of the House given them. The House took notice of and well resented the respects and civilities performed by the Merchant Adventurers trading from Rotterdam and gave the Company thanks for the same. They ordered that all the proceedings of this treaty be entered into a book and that none but Members be permitted to see the same. It was resolved that the whole matter of this report and the several papers be referred to the Council of State to consider what is fit to be done therein for the best advantage of this Commonwealth, and report the same to the House, and that the Council of State do in some convenient time send back all the papers to the Clerk of the Parliament to be entered and kept as records of Parliament. The Parliament did declare that for anything pertaining to them in this report concerning Sir Walter Vaughan[156] and notwithstanding the letter and suspicion of him he the said Sir Walter Vaughan[157] may and is at liberty to resort into England as any other [person] beyond the seas and belonging to this Commonwealth may do. Yet ordered that an act shall be brought in to prohibit any public minister of this Commonwealth employed to any prince or state to receive or take any gratuity, gift or pension from any foreign state or prince, and a committee was appointed to prepare an act for that purpose. Thursday the House was divided upon the question whether leave should be given to speak to the vote formerly concerning the Lord Craven, and it was resolved in the negative. The House then ordered that a summons did issue forth for William, Lord Craven, requiring him to appear personally at such as the Parliament shall appoint, to answer such things as shall be observed[158] against him on the behalf of the Commonwealth of England. That the place of his appearance be at the Parliament, and day to be the 3d of 7bris next. A draught of the summons was read and agreed unto, the Sergeant-at-Arms being required to proclaim the same in Westminster Hall and printer to the House caused to print it and post it up at the Exchange and other places.[159] The Committee for Affairs of Ireland made a report to the House which is to be considered

[155] In shorthand, 'thinks'.

[156] *CJ*, VI, p. 595 reads 'Vane' for 'Vaughan'.

[157] *Ibid.* reads 'Vane' for 'Vaughan'.

[158] *Ibid.* reads 'objected' for 'observed'.

[159] See *Perfect Passages of Every Daies Intelligence*, 51 (4–11 July 1651), p. 363; *Weekly Intelligencer*, 28 (8–15 July 1651), p. 217.

Wednesday next. An act approved for allowing an 100*l* per annum to Master Hallowes, a Member of Parliament, out of delinquents' estates ordered for sale. Friday Lord Ambassadour St John[160] reported from the Council of State that the ~~that~~ Council[161] had received information of the scandalous carriage of divers ministers and condemning the acts and ordinances of Parliament whereby the peace

fo. 50v

of this nation is indangered. That the House be moved as preventing the like enemies for the future. That the said power may be given to some fit persons in the country as the Committee of Plundered Ministers have to receive information against such disaffected ministers and to place others in their stead, but the House agreed not. Therefore the petition of George Lilburne[162] was read, setting forth his former services and great sufferings for the Parliament, and that he is indangered to be sequestered by the Commission for Compounding for acts done in 1642 desiring by way of appeal that the Parliament would examine the same and give judgement therein. The House ordered that this petition be referred to the Commissioners for Compounding. That if nothing more appear against the petitioner then is contained in the petition that then the petitioner be discharged. The rest of the day was spent in debate of the act for sale of certain delinquents' estates and the report of the names of those persons to be imployed as trustees and contractors for sale of the said estates, the latter of which was ordered to be committed on Tuesday next. Master Love was brought this day to his trial when he received his sentence, *vizt* that his head should be severed from his body as a traitor for the several treasons he was found guilty of before the high court who had agreed unto it *nemine contradicente*.[163]

The Company of Porters, London presented a petition to the right honourable the Lord Maior, and the representatives of the city of London. There was much debate at the Common Council whether the petition should be read, being not directed to the Lord Maior, aldermen and Common Council of the city of London. Before this came to any result the Lord Maior withdrew with others. The rest of the court commanded them to stay, but they refused, 47 Common

160 *CJ*, VI, p. 595 reads 'Strickland' for 'St John'.

161 'Council' superimposed on 'that'.

162 The celebrated case involving George Lilburne (for whom see P. Gregg, *Free-born John; A Biography of John Lilburne* (London, 1961), *passim*) would eventually be used as the pretext for the banishment of his Leveller nephew, John Lilburne, in 1652; *Mercurius Politicus*, 85 (15–22 June 1652), pp. 1353–1358; *CJ*, VI, p. 598; *C&P*, II, pp. 7–8.

163 Army officers in Scotland were shortly to be asked to intervene in Love's case (below, p. 46).

Council men being left [besides/behind]. Colonel Rowe was called to the chair in the Lord Maior's place. The petition was then read and the petitioners received an answer.[164] This court then ordered that the lands and houses belonging to the city of London should be let for 99 years, whereby the city may be inabled to pay their debts to Morgan's widow and others that are in great [necessity] with the rest of those many debts that lie upon the city and that a declaration be drawn and presented with a petition to the Parliament to show wherein the Lord Maior and others of the court had acted contrary to their duty.[165]

We are in treaty for the render at Lerock.[166] Which is all present [*sic*] from

right honourable

your most faithful servant

Gilbert Mabbott

5th July 1651

For the Right Honourable Major-General Deane at the headquarters in Scotland these.

Memorandum, Burntisland, 29 July 1651

fo. 76[r]

This night there was a council of war held about the business of Master Love about which Colonel Fortescue with letters from several ministers and others of note about London. Colonel Goffe, Colonel Okey and others appeared tooth and nayle for him but Colonel Pride and others were as high against them upon the whole, to the mirth of

[164] The petition of London ticket porters first came before the Council on 28 March 1651; the court described here was held on 2 July 1651, but there is no formal record of proceedings after the withdrawal of the Lord Mayor and aldermen. It reappears briefly in the minutes of the court held on 8 July 1651; City of London Record Office, Common Council Journal XLI, fos 47[r], 55[r], 57[r].

[165] Mabbott may have included this detailed account of Common Council business as being of especial interest to Deane, who was probably a nephew or great-nephew of the Lord Mayor of London in 1628–1629 of the same name (*OxDNB*).

[166] I have been unable to find any evidence of negotiations concerning the siege of La Rochelle at this time, although Cromwell was reported to have been approached with such an offer during the following October; S.R. Gardiner, 'Cromwell and Mazarin in 1652', *English Historical Review*, 12 (1896), pp. 479–480; *C&P*, II, p. 91.

the Major-General Lambert and others. It was advised that my Lord should not at all ingage or write in the business for him.[167]

Memorandum, Dundee, 9 September 1651

fo. 124^{r}

This day we had the happy news of the rowting of the king's <of Scots'>[168] army on both sides Worcester by our men. 4,000 killed on the place etc.[169]

[167] This meeting was evidently held as a matter of urgency after Cromwell's arrival at Burntisland, captured by Lambert earlier on the same day. Clarke's record reveals details of divisions among the officers not reported in other accounts; *LRHO*, p. 37 (where Fortescue appears as 'Foskur'); *Mercurius Politicus*, 61 (31 July–7 Aug. 1651), p. 980.

[168] Interlined.

[169] Other contemporary accounts are in agreement that not more than 3,000 Royalists were killed at Worcester. There is an almost identical newsletter in longhand; Worc. MS CLXXXI, fo. 238^{v}, printed in *S&C*, p. 14. Nathaniel Mew, recently appointed army postmaster at Berwick at Cromwell's request, received a special payment from the army of £2 10s for conveying the news; Chequers, MS 782, fo. 22^{r}.

2. NOTEBOOK XX

December 1651[1]

Introduction

When, in early August 1651, Cromwell headed south in pursuit of Charles Stuart and his Scottish army, Clarke remained behind with Lieutenant-General George Monck, now in command of the remaining English force in Scotland. With the summoning of Dundee on 30 August, the last major pocket of Scottish resistance was wiped out. Here for the most part Clarke remained in his official capacity until he returned with Monck to Edinburgh in January 1652.[2]

Most of the shorthand items in this volume relate to army administration and there is little in the way of news from England, the single example having possibly been copied from a written newsletter.[3] In addition to his official duties, Clarke found time to promote both his own interests and those of his brother-in-law, Gilbert Mabbott.[4]

Memorandum, Dundee, 15 December 1651

fo. [73][r]

Intelligence that Prince Rupert's best ship was carried away near the Tircaria islands, that himself hardly escaped with not above 5 men and that about 300 or 360 men were drowned. Also that 2 other of his ships were then cast away.[5] 18 sayle of ship cast away near the Barbadoes, whereof 4 English, the rest Dutch, valued at 300,000*l.*

[1] Worc. MS XX.

[2] *S&C*, pp. 1–20, 31; Worc. MS XXII, fo. [9g][r]. Although Clarke's notebooks suggest that he remained at Dundee throughout the period, he travelled to Leith on at least one occasion, writing to the Speaker from there on 23 November 1651; *S&C*, pp. 20–21.

[3] Below Although the details are verified by the printed newsbooks, none gives an identical version.

[4] Pp. 49–50.

[5] Fully described in E. Warburton, *Memoirs of Prince Rupert, and the Cavaliers*, 3 vols (London, 1849), III, pp. 324–339, the incident was widely reported in e.g., *Faithfull Scout*, 46 (28 Nov.–5 Dec. 1651), pp. 347, 360; *Perfect Account*, 49 (3–10 Dec. 1651), p. 386.

The Janizaries have lately strangled the empress, whereon the Turks fell upon them and cut off [divers] of them. The Venetians have taken 2 ships of the Turks laden with ammunition going to Candy. Also taken a strong fort the Turks had there by storm.[6]

The Prince of Condé's party do not much increase in France yet they still maintain the tower of Saint Nicholas near Rochelle.[7]

[William Clarke], Dundee, to [a parliamentary commissioner], 15 December 1651[8]

fo. [73]ʳ

Sir

There being [~~. . . .~~] a [necessity], as we ~~humbly~~ conceive, for your self and the rest of the commissioners to have an agent to take care of the sending down from time to time of such orders and proceedings of Parliament and ~~such other things as shall be usual~~ during your being in Scotland and being well assured of the [~~obligation] of Master Gilbert Mabbott [. . .~~] [obligation] of Master Gilbert Mabbott who we suppose is not altogether unknown to you, we do hereby earnestly recommend him unto you, desiring you will please to <move the Lord St Johns and the rest of the honourable commissioners with you, that they will>[9] appoint him to that imployment and to allow him ~~such~~ like[10] consideration and incouragement as he has from the commissioners for the Parliament in Ireland to whom as he has been very serviceable,[11] so we doubt not but he will be to you and us here. We remain.

[6] Items in this paragraph were reported in e.g., *Faithfull Scout*, 48 (12–19 Dec. 1651), p. 373; *French Intelligencer*, 5 (16–23 Dec. 1651), p. 39.

[7] *Mercurius Scoticus* (Leith), 20 (9–16 Dec. 1651), p. 165, reported that the capture of the tower was the main priority of the Comte d'Harcourt 'and as yet no news of the taking of it'.

[8] This draft letter, probably written by Clarke himself, is clearly to one of the parliamentary commissioners appointed on 23 October 1651 to oversee the proposed union with Scotland. They convened at Dalkeith, near Edinburgh, on 15 January 1652. They were Oliver St John, Sir Henry Vane Jr, Maj. Richard Salwey, Col George Fenwick, Maj.-Gen. John Lambert, Maj.-Gen. Richard Deane, Alderman Robert Tichborne, and George Monck; C.S. Terry (ed.), *The Cromwellian Union* (Scottish History Society, XL, 1902), pp. xvii–xxiv.

[9] Interlined.

[10] '[L]ike' superimposed on 'such'.

[11] I have found no evidence that Clarke's recommendation was taken up, although in June 1653 Mabbott was to be appointed agent for Leith; *CSPD 1652–1653*, p. 376. In 1647 he had acted in this capacity for Cromwell; Folger, MS X.d 483/(197).

[William Clarke] to [Oliver Cromwell], [24] December 1651[12]

*fo. 76^v^*

May it please your Excellency

I have hitherto forborne to trouble your Excellency with any account of affairs here as from myself, knowing that you are furnished with it from better hands, but especially in regard that I wrote to the Scoutmaster-General[13] who I knew would impart what he had <from me from time to time>[14] to your Lordship. I have now presumed to ~~give your Excellency an account of affairs~~ present these lines to your letter, not as that they are worthy your perusal but only as a testimony of my duty, of which I humbly beseech your Honour's ~~receipt~~ favourable construct and remembrance.

[12] As with the previous document, the appearance of Clarke's draft suggests that he was himself the writer of this letter to Cromwell.

[13] George Downing.

[14] Interlined.

3. NOTEBOOK XXII

16 January–3 July 1652[1]

Introduction

In January 1652 the commissioners appointed by Parliament to settle the administration of Scotland and to pave the way for a formal union between England and Scotland began their deliberations at Dalkeith, some six miles from Edinburgh.[2] When Monck hurried back from Dundee in order to attend their first meeting, Clarke was able to return to his own quarters in Leith.

Now that the campaign against Charles Stuart and the subjugation of the Scots appeared to be all but over, Clarke's career prospects were presumably less certain, and he seems to have been exploring different openings.[3] This may account for his interest in the presence of the commissioners at Dalkeith and his attempts to see Oliver St John there at the earliest possible opportunity.[4] Clarke was apparently aggrieved that the commissioners had brought their own clerical staff,[5] depriving him not only of an opportunity for employment but, perhaps more important to him, inside knowledge of their discussions.[6]

Monck (who had still not recovered from a serious illness of the previous autumn) returned to England in mid-February 1652, followed only a few days later by John Lambert, who had been recalled in order to take up the post of commander-in-chief in Ireland.[7] This left Richard Deane as sole commander in Scotland, and Clarke became his secretary, accompanying him almost at once on official business

[1] Worc. MS XXII.

[2] *C-P*, II, pp. 65–66; Terry, pp. xv–xxxvii; the commissioners are listed above, p. 49n.

[3] P. 50.

[4] P. 53.

[5] Pp. 54–55. The commissioners' secretaries were John Phelps, assistant Clerk of Parliament, and Clement Baker (for whom see *SS*, pp. 277, 419n and pp. 99, 114; Terry, pp. 121, 117).

[6] Their situation outside Edinburgh and the secrecy surrounding their instructions would have made it difficult to gather any information about their proceedings; *ibid.*, p. xx; *Perfect Passages of Every Daies Intelligence*, [46] (12–19 Dec. 1651), p. 338. Clarke did his best to send what little news he could to the Speaker, William Lenthall; Bodl., MS Tanner LV, fos 135–136.

[7] *Ibid.*, fo. 135^{r}; *S&C.*, pp. xix, 14, 33, 323; *Nouvelles Ordinaires de Londres*, 67 (9/19–19/26 Oct. 1651), p. 268; *Perfect Diurnall*, 111 (19–26 Jan. 1652), p. 1628.

first to Dundee[8] and then to Dumbarton for secret negotiations held between Deane and Major Richard Salwey, both English commissioners, and the marquis of Argyle on 17–18 March.[9]

When the commissioners' work in Scotland was completed at the end of April, Clarke remained behind at army headquarters, retaining a close interest in events in London. The constitutional problems faced by the infant Commonwealth, many of them centring on the escalating struggles for political control between army and Parliament, are clear from a newsletter of early July 1652, written almost certainly to Clarke by his old friend and colleague, Richard Hatter, now secretary to the Council of Officers in London.[10] From it we learn that the meetings held during the summer of 1652 to discuss the army's forthcoming representation (submitted to Cromwell sometime before 10 August and in its final form to Parliament on 13 August) were more complex than has previously been thought.[11]

It is impossible to identify with certainty the 'ingagement' which Hatter reported had caused considerable controversy among the officers.[12] The subject of the army's engagements had long been a contentious one; the requirement to honour its own engagements of June 1647 had, for example, been hotly debated at Putney in the following October.[13] A further engagement, that requiring loyalty to the Commonwealth which was imposed by the Rump upon army officers (among others) on 12 October 1649, would still be an issue – although a less contentious one than it had been – in 1653; only after the establishment of the Protectorate would the engagement of 1649 be repealed.[14] However, as Hatter wrote that it was the '*word*' engagement rather than *a*[15] specific engagement which was in contention, he may possibly have been referring to a new engagement which was under

[8] P. 57.

[9] They set out from Edinburgh on 15 March 1652; *Mercurius Politicus*, 94 (18–25 Mar. 1652), pp. 1476, 1480; *LRHO*, p. 49. Strict secrecy was observed in the protracted negotiations with Argyle; Worc. MS XXII, fo. 80^{r-v}; *Faithfull Scout*, 63 (26 Mar.–2 Apr. 1652), p. 491.

[10] P. 57. I believe that my identification of Hatter is correct. I have found no other correspondent with the same initials, and the nature of this confidential army news makes it extremely likely that Hatter is the supplier.

[11] The draft presented by the officers to Cromwell does not survive, but was the subject of a contemporary pamphlet, *A Declaration of the Armie to his Excellency The Lord General Cromwel, for The dissolving of this present Parliament, and chusing of a new Representative* (London, 1652), which referred to the officers having had 'sundry Consultations and Conferences, touching the dissolving of this present Parliament, and electing of a new Representative . . . ' (p. 3). The background to these events is fully discussed in B. Worden, *The Rump Parliament 1648–1653* (Cambridge, 1977 edn), especially chs 13 and 14.

[12] P. 57.

[13] Gentles, *New Model Army*, pp. 205–207.

[14] Worden, *Rump*, pp. 227–232; A. Woolrych, *Commonwealth to Protectorate* (Oxford, 1982), p. 294.

[15] My emphases.

discussion, perhaps one to be placed upon future MPs. Whether or not such a proposal was being considered, there was no reference to it in the petition which the army finally placed before Parliament on 13 August.[16]

Hatter's closing gloomy prediction about the demand for the propagation of the gospel turned out to be correct.[17] When in its final form the *Humble Petition* was delivered to Parliament on 13 August 1652 this constituted its opening clause.

Memorandum, Leith, 16 January 1652

fo. [9h]^{r}[18]

This day the Lord Saint Johns was not well but kept his chamber at Dalkeith.[19]

Memorandum, Leith, 17 January 1652

fo. 10^{r}

This day I went to Dalkeith where I saw all the commissioners except the Lord St Johns who kept his bed.

[William Clarke], Leith, to unknown recipient, 3 February 1652

fo. 20^{r}

Sir

~~There having [been] nothing considerable <happening here>[20] of late . . .~~Nothing considerable happening of late in these parts, I have

[16] There may, however, be a hint of it in the petition's call for 'speedy consideration . . . of such Quallifications for future and successive Parliaments as tend to the Election only of such as are pious and faithfull to the interest of the Commonwealth, to sit and serve as Members in the said Parliament'; *To the Supreame Authoritie the Parliament of the Common-Wealth of England The humble Petition of the Officers of the Army* (London, 1652).

[17] P. 58.

[18] The foliation throughout Clarke's manuscripts is erratic. Where there are more unfoliated pages than unallocated folio numbers I have added lower case letters in alphabetical order.

[19] Although St John was frequently in poor health (Worden, *Rump*, p. 178), I have found no other evidence that he was unwell at this particular time. He appears to have attended the commissioners' initial discussions on the 16th; *S&C*, pp. 31–32.

[20] Interlined.

forborne to trouble your honour with any account of affairs here nor should I now, had not the inclosed <letter intended to the Lord General>[21] come to my hands which not knowing whether your honour has seen, I have presumed to send you a copy thereof. Your honour will perceive by it the drift of the intentions of those who would be called the godly party here which is to exalt their government etc.[22]

William Clarke, Leith, to [Thomas Pury (?) Senior], 2 March 1652[23]

fo. 38^{r}

Sir

You may justly wonder that I should not send to your honour in so long a time as now I have been absent from you but the not knowing of your being in town and, when you were, that while we had anything considerable you had it from Colonel Downes[24] I forbore to ~~give you any intelligence of those~~ trouble you with any letter. It has now so pleased God that it is our happiness that we have little or no news to write ~~and upon that account I have forborne to give~~ which should bespeak <it>[25] the best of times, in which respect I have also forborne to write lately to Colonel Downes or any of the honourable committee ~~whom I should be <as>~~[26] ~~willing to serve [here/though]~~ ~~[. . .]~~ as also for that since the coming down of the commissioners of Parliament

[21] Interlined.

[22] Similarities between this and a newsletter written on 31 January 1651 (printed in *S&C*, pp. 32–33) suggest that the enclosure in both cases was the letter drawn up by Archibald Johnston of Wariston and others some time around 21 January 1652; *Mercurius Politicus*, 86 (22–29 Jan. 1652), pp. [1378]–[1380].

[23] Clarke's reference to Mistress Pury in the last line of this letter suggests that it was to Thomas Pury, father or son, that Clarke was writing (for Pury Sr, see *DBR*). Both were fellow MPs of Col John Downes. Thomas Pury (? Sr) was a member of the Army Committee (possibly that to which Clarke refers) of which Downes was chairman; Worden, *Rump*, pp. 59, 389–391; C.H. Firth and R.S. Rait (eds), *Acts and Ordinances of the Interregnum 1642–1660*, 3 vols (London, 1911), II, p. 562. Both Clarke and Pury were present during the treaty negotiations at West Wycombe in July 1647; Worc. MS CX, fo. 119^{r}; Pury's name is misread as 'Povey' in the version printed in *CP*, I, p. 148.

[24] A list of those to whom Clarke sent letters during the last months of 1651 shows that he wrote to Downes weekly. Pury's name is not on the list; Worc. MS CLXXXI, fo. 243^{r}.

[25] Interlined.

[26] Interlined.

and their bringing secretaries and clerks with them for ~~all affairs~~ management of all their affairs myself and some others who have forsaken our country and hazarded our lives in the field in the worst of times are now laid aside and those of yesterday know all and we nothing.[27] I speak not this but that I am in an indifferent posture as to [livehood][28] but that it renders me less serviceable to the honourable committee whom I should have been ready to have been supplying with an account of affairs as formerly [~~. . .~~] <and>[29] I shall yet do when I have anything considerable ~~although~~ <and have>[30] since my coming in Scotland. For ~~near these 12 months past I~~ these 20 months I have had only 20*l*. ~~I offer not this unto you as that you should be ingaged to move that from me~~ Yet if I might be useful to them and in them the publike I should not at all neglect any opportunity of writing unto them.

What we have at present is scarce worth your reading. On Saturday last Master Cadwell the messenger who went from the commissioners at Dalkeith to the marquis of Argyle[31] returned ~~from the Highlands. He stayed~~ [him] with only an overture of the marquis wanting to meet any commissioners from us at <or near>[32] Dunbarton which he doubted not but did give all due satisfaction concerning these by post carriage.[33] The messenger stayed there 2 days and was well entertained by the marquis who keeps a plentiful table and has a very great retinue of about 80 servants, many persons of quality in his house besides his son the Lord Lorne and his daughters. Neither has he any soldiers nor guard about him more than his own family [where/when] his chaplain in his prayers doth earnestly pray for the king under the title of a distrest prince which the marquis seemed to excuse.[34] Yet [thereupon/thereby] we may judge his affections and

[27] This sentence supports the view that Clarke's attempts to see Oliver St John were made either in order to secure some position with the commissioners or to obtain information about their well-guarded proceedings.

[28] Although the outline is clear, this word does not appear in the *OED*.

[29] Interlined.

[30] Interlined.

[31] Cadwell's departure from and return to Leith are noted in *Mercurius Politicus*, 91 (26 Feb.–4 Mar. 1652), p. 1446; *Severall Proceedings*, 129 (11–18 Mar. 1652), p. 1998.

[32] Interlined.

[33] Clarke accompanied the commissioners, Maj.-Gen. Deane and Maj. Salwey, on this mission to Dumbarton, which took place on 17–18 March 1652; Worc. MS XXII, fos [51]^{r}–[54]^{r}; Terry, p. 131.

[34] This phrasing is very similar to the report in *Severall Proceedings*, 129 (11–18 Mar. 1652), p. 1998, apparently one of Clarke's weekly letters to the Speaker (and found in longhand in Worc. MS XXII, fos 38^{v}–[39]^{r}).

which way his disposition inclines him rather to a monarchy than a commonwealth ~~yet~~ but a few days will bring the business between him and the commissioners to an issue which I fear will be too good for so ~~vile and wretched~~ perfidious and bloodthirsty man [*sic*] as he is and has always been, true to no interest nor relations but worshipping money and his own security before all [~~. . . .~~] <duty>[35] and services whatsoever either to God or man.[36]

fo. 38v

<The right honourable>[37] commissioners of Parliament are now settling of the affairs of this nation. The 2 things they are now principally about are the sequestrations and judicaturers[38] for both which most of these gentlemen following are named: *Colonel* West, Colonel Syler, Master Saltonstall, Master Desbrowe, Lieutenant-Colonel [Brayne] etc.[39] And for the judicatories amongst others the Laird Craighall, Hopton, Swinton etc. who are men that we have found most integrous and to come nearest to our [principles/particulars] of any of the Scots whatsoever so far as we can discern them. Master [Sweeten] of Newcastle is to farm the customs ~~at Leith~~ of Scotland which unless there be a free trade with Holland and France for all commodities in their own bottoms will come ~~to little or nothing yearly~~ to no considerable yearly revenue and [indeed] you should not look to get much any way from Scotland. Your greatest mandate will be to keep them from hurting you by incursion and [intercessions] but to bring in a revenue or profit to the Commonwealth of England they will never be able to do.

[35] Interlined.

[36] Clarke's optimism was misplaced. Argyle was still spinning out the negotiations some two months later; *Perfect Account*, 70 (28 Apr.–5 May 1652), p. 559.

[37] Interlined.

[38] Perhaps written in error for 'judicatories'; the word is not found in the *OED* but the shorthand outline is clear.

[39] The three commissioners for sequestrations, based at Leith, were Richard Saltonstall, Samuel Desborough, and Col Edmund Syler; *S&C*, p. xxxi. West is presumably Col Francis West, Lieutenant of the Tower of London, whose regiment served in Scotland and who died in August 1652; F&D, I, p. 341; II, pp. 477, 484, 490, 548, 571–572. Lt-Col William Brayne played a prominent role while with the army in Scotland; in 1656 his regiment was sent to Jamaica, where he became governor; *S&C*, pp. 19, 173, 338; *S&P*, *passim*; F&D, II, pp. 704–705.

Sir, I shall not trouble you any further with these particulars of so little weight or concernment but with my most humble service to Mistress Pury ~~in the~~ I rest your [*sic*]

your most humble servant

William Clarke

Major-General Deane intends to visit Dundee and other garrisons northwards the latter of this week upon whom I shall attend that journey.[40]

Memorandum, Leith, 4 March 1652

*fo. 41^r^*

This day Sir Henry Vane and Colonel Fenwick began their journey for London from Dalkeith.[41] ~~They were~~ The occasion of their business was.[42]

Newsletter from R.H., Westminster, 3 July 1652[43]

*fo. [112]^r^*

There have been 2 great meetings of the officers the two last Thursdays.[44] They agreed [to/upon] a committee to peruse their remonstrance etc. It appear[s] when they were ingaged upon report of them the last day the word ingagement[45] would not go down nor be digested,

[40] Clarke was in Dundee on 6–7 March and Perth on 8–9 March. He returned to Leith on the 13th and set out again for Dumbarton and Ayr on 15 March; Worc. MS XXII.

[41] Vane and Fenwick were instructed on 1 March 1652 to return to London on 4 March to convey to Parliament the commissioners' recommendations regarding an act of union. They arrived in Berwick on the same day; Terry, p. 68. As this memorandum shows, *Severall Proceedings*, 128 (4–11 Mar. 1652), p. 1994, is mistaken in dating their arrival there as the 3rd. They reported to Parliament on 16 March 1652; F.D. Dow, *Cromwellian Scotland 1651–1660* (Edinburgh, 1979), p. 45.

[42] Blank. Although Clarke's note breaks off here, he can hardly have been unaware of the reason for their mission, despite his complaint of two days previously (p. 55 above).

[43] 'R.H.' is almost certainly Richard Hatter, one of Clarke's friends and regular informants. His signature, as secretary to the Council of Officers, appears on the officers' petition of 13 August 1652, *To the Supreame Authoritie the Parliament of the Common-Wealth of England*. . . , the product of a series of meetings including those reported here.

[44] i.e. 24 June and 1 July 1652. Previously the earliest known date for the officers' meetings has been early August; Worden, *Rump*, p. 307; Woolrych, *C–P*, p. 40. See my comments above, p. 52.

[45] I have discussed the possible implications of this word above (pp. 52–53).

but that they [must/should] fall upon debate upon some of the [very] things mentioned in the papers and some were very high for a new representative and a shorter time for the period of this then they had set down,[46] but it was laid aside and a petition is to be drawn mentioning the very things we would have done, but indeed we are begun again with the propagating of the gospel when we shall be lost and I fear lose all.[47]

R.H.

[46] In their draft declaration the officers called for an immediate dissolution of Parliament. They were probably persuaded by Cromwell to modify this demand in their final petition at the meeting which they held with him on 10 August 1652; Worc. MS XXIV, fo. 5[r]; Worden, *Rump*, p. 307; Woolrych, *C–P*, pp. 41–42.

[47] See my comments above, p. 53.

4. NOTEBOOK XXIV

25 September 1652–9 March 1653[1]

Introduction

After the return of the English commissioners in April 1652 Dalkeith House became the army's new headquarters and residence of the commander-in-chief, and so the centre of Clarke's working life.[2] Of the eight or nine incoming shorthand newsletters in this notebook,[3] five were from the newsbook editor Henry Walker, a regular informant over the next two years.[4]

In September Clarke's old colleague John Rushworth sent word of the recurring problems caused in Parliament by low attendances of MPs.[5] During April the relatively high attendance figures of the previous winter had begun to fall away.[6] As Rushworth reports, this process had continued to such an extent that there were difficulties in finding the necessary quorum of forty MPs.

Rushworth also makes reference to the parliamentary committee headed by John Carew and appointed in response to army pressure to consider the provisions for the next Parliament. The army, as it made clear in its petition of 13 August 1652, strongly favoured the dissolution of the Rump and fresh elections for its successor.[7] There was however a strong lobby among MPs to perpetuate themselves by means of 'recruiter elections' to fill vacant places. It has now been established beyond reasonable doubt that the bill which came before Parliament on 20 April 1653 did not contain any such proposals.[8]

[1] Worc. MS XXIV.

[2] He appears, however, to have retained his house in Leith.

[3] The letter from Thomas Fulford (p. 70) may or may not be a genuine newsletter.

[4] Pp. 62–69; see also p. 7 above.

[5] P. 62.

[6] Worden, *Rump*, pp. 297, 313, and 392–394, where the difficulties of trying to assess attendances are discussed.

[7] *A Declaration of the Armie To His Excellency the Lord General Cromwel for the dissolving of this present Parliament*; Worden, *Rump*, pp. 306–310; Woolrych, *C–P*, pp. 41–42. The army's stand was reported to the Scottish headquarters by an anonymous correspondent on 10 August; Worc. MS. XXIV, fo. 5^{r}.

[8] The history of the bill for a new representative is most comprehensively traced in Worden, *Rump*.

Although, unfortunately, Rushworth's wording regarding the precise nature of the committee's recommendation is ambiguous, his letter reveals that both options were still on the cards in September 1652.

I have been unable to verify the strange story in a letter written on Christmas Day 1652, apparently to Clarke himself, by one of his colleagues at the Scottish headquarters, Thomas Fulford.[9] If the episode did take place, we are left to guess the reason for the young man's protest.[10] Perhaps it concerned the Rump's unpopular prohibition of the celebration of Christmas,[11] or one of the particularly contentious matters which were due to come before the House on the day of the incident, 23 December.[12] The 23rd was, for example, the deadline for bids for farming the posts, which ties in with Fulford's reference to Edmund Prideaux, jointly Attorney-General and Postmaster-General.[13] From Fulford's final sentence, however, this may simply be a private joke between two colleagues in the austere climate of a Christmas which could not now be celebrated as before.[14]

By mid-March 1653 it was generally known that Major-General John Lambert was to be sent to Scotland to replace Richard Deane as commander-in-chief there.[15] A month earlier, however, Gilbert Mabbott – assiduous as ever in providing his brother-in-law Clarke

[9] In addition to deciphering intercepted letters, Fulford acted as messenger, intelligencer, and advocate; K&C, pp. 168, 180, 181, 185, 193, 195, 201–202; Chequers, MS 782, fo. 25[v]. In October 1651 he was described as clerk to Henry Whalley, the Judge Advocate at Leith; H. Whalley, *At a Court Martiall At Leith* (London, 1651). He had written to Clarke at least once before, in December 1650; *L-P*, p. 79.

[10] P. 70. Unlike a recent attack on the Speaker (p. 69), the dramatic incident of 23 December described by Fulford is not reported in the newsbooks.

[11] *CJ*, VII, p. 235; *Resolved by the Parliament That the Markets be kept to Morrow*... (London, 1652); *The Vindication of Christmas* (London, 1652); *Flying Eagle* 4 (18–25 Dec. 1652), p. 31; 5 (25 Dec. 1652–1 Jan. 1653), pp. 34–37.

[12] One was the petition of the executors of the former Royalist Lord Mayor of London Sir Richard Gurney, the other the long-standing matter of claims against the public faith; *CJ*, VII, p. 230; *Flying Eagle*, 4 (18–25 Dec. 1652), p. 31; Worden, *Rump*, pp. 293–294.

[13] *CSPD 1652–1653*, p. 110; *SS*, p. 272. Prideaux's first attendance at the fifth Council of State was on 22 December (*ibid.*, p. xxviii). The considerable competition for the office among both new contenders and those who felt they had hereditary claims upon it is described by P. Gaunt, in 'Interregnum governments and the reform of the post office, 1649–59', *Historical Research*, 60 (1987), pp. 284–287.

[14] Although I have not discovered Fulford's whereabouts at this precise time, he was sending news from Inverness-shire during August 1652; Worc. MS XXIV, fo. [8][r]. He was killed on active service in September 1653; *Mercurius Politicus*, 172 (22–29 Sept. 1653), pp. 2751–2752; Chequers MS 782, unfol., entry for 26 October 1653.

[15] *CSPD 1652–1653*, p. 242; *LRHO*, p. 52. Deane was recalled from Scotland to act as General of the Fleet along with Generals Blake and Monck for whom Lilburne was acting commander; *S&C*, p. 62; *Perfect Account*, 105 (29 Dec.–5 Jan. 1653), p. 836.

with useful information – had notified him of this impending change; Clarke concealed the news by writing it in shorthand.[16]

Lambert was said to be unwilling to accept the appointment,[17] and in the heightened political tensions of the first few months of 1653, relations between himself, Harrison, and Cromwell had become increasingly strained.[18] It is possible that the move was being considered as a convenient way to remove him from the capital;[19] if so, we do not know who was its instigator.[20] The proposal assumed mounting urgency in the weeks before the dissolution of the Rump until on 14 April Cromwell was instructed in no uncertain terms to send Lambert to Scotland for six months.[21] A week later the Rump was no more, and Lambert remained in London.

Newsletter from John Rushworth, London, 25 September 1652[22]

*fo. 28*r

from another thus

General Blake is come into the Downs and west of the Dutch fleet yet 2 Guinea ships were taken and brought into our harbour of good value but their Eastland fleet of 45 sail are all got home.[23]

[16] P. 71. Although the letter, which is otherwise written in longhand, is unsigned, it is clearly from Mabbott who wrote an identical letter (but without this postscript) to Hull on the same day; Hull CRO, BRL 555. Mabbott obtained information about the proceedings of the Army Committee from its clerk and parliamentary news from the written journal of the House; Hull CRO, BRL 554, 563.

[17] Worc. MS. XXV, fo. 9r.

[18] *Calendar of State Papers, Venetian Series 1653–1654*, pp. 12, 60; C.H. Firth (ed.), *The Memoirs of Edmund Ludlow Lieutenant-General of the Horse in the Army of the Commonwealth of England, 1625–1672*, 2 vols (Oxford, 1903), I, p. 346; *C&P*, II, p. 181. But see also Worden, *Rump*, p. 329; Woolrych, *C–P*, p. 72.

[19] Bodl., MS Clarendon XLIV, fos 223, 270, quoted in C.H. Firth, 'Cromwell and the expulsion of the Long Parliament', *English Historical Review*, 7 (1893), pp. 528–529; however see Gentles, *New Model Army*, p. 428.

[20] 'One can imagine Cromwell himself reacting . . . with strong suspicion [to such a proposal], especially if the Council made its first approaches to Lambert without his knowledge'; Woolrych, *C–P*, p. 73. Cromwell was absent from Council meetings from 14–20 February, but attended all sessions on the 21st and 22nd, the date of Mabbott's letter; *CSPD 1652–1653*, p. xxx.

[21] *Ibid.*, pp. 242, 260, 263, 266, 279.

[22] This letter's informal and at times unguarded tone suggest that it may have been to his old colleague, William Clarke, that Rushworth was writing.

[23] The capture of these rich prizes was widely applauded (see, for example, pp. 63–64 below; Worc. MS XXIV, fo. 28r; [J. Stoaks], *A great Victory obtained by the English Against the*

The Parliament sits about nothing else but money and yesterday ordered the sale of [the 500/1500][24] men's estates to be sold which they intend to pass next week and in regard most part of this summer they could hardly get 40 Members to make a House before 12 a clock they have ordered the House to be called the 3rd of *9bris*.[25]

2 great officers at Drury House are dead, Colonel Manwaring and Colonel Sheffield.[26]

The committee for expediting the new representative [do/did] sit and it is conceived when the House doth meet in *9bris* they will either resolve on a new representative or to recruit vacant places to the ancient number of the House.[27]

John Rushworth

Newsletter from Henry Walker, Westminster, 28 September 1652

*fo. 30*r

Yesterday the Portugal ambassador was received by order from the Council of State and brought to Sir Abraham Williams' house.[28] He has a great attendance and divers gentlemen very rich attending him, amongst whom his son, a young lord, and others. This day Master Speaker reported to the House letters that he had received from the said ambassador which were read, superscribed, *Illustrissimo Domino Gulielmo Lenthall Esquire Prolocutori Parliamenti Reipublii Angliae: A Comite*

Dutch... (London, 1652); and most of the newsbooks). De Ruyter's evasion of the English fleet is described in *C&P*, II, pp. 134–136.

[24] The shorthand is ambiguous but the former figure is probably the correct reading; the confiscation bill, when passed on 18 November 1652, named 678 royalists, the figure having been enlarged in the interim; *A&O*, II, pp. 623–625; Worden, *Rump*, p. 313; Woolrych, *C–P*. p. 44. No figure is given in the *Commons Journal* for 24 September; *CJ*, VII, p. 185.

[25] See above, p. 59.

[26] This refers to the Registrar-Accountant Col Robert Mainwaring, and not Col Randall Mainwaring Sr, Comptroller for the sale of royalists' lands, who died shortly afterwards; *SS*, pp. 108, 363–364. Replacements for both Mainwaring and Sheffield were appointed on 24 September; *CJ*, VII, p. 185.

[27] The scheme to recruit Members to fill vacant places, first mooted in January 1650 and revived in late 1651, was vigorously opposed by the army, most recently in its petition of 13 August 1652; Woolrych, *C–P*, pp. 10–11; Worden, *Rump*, pp. 265–266; p. 58 above.

[28] This house was regularly used as an official residence; see, for example, Abbott, I, p. 733; III, pp. 205, 223 *et seq.*; *CSPD 1651–1652*, *passim*. The ambassador had been at Plymouth since early August, and the Council of State discussed arrangements for his reception on 20 and 24 September; *Perfect Diurnall* 140 [N&S 503. 140A], (9–16 Aug. 1652), p. 2094; *CSPD 1651–1652*, pp. 409, 417.

Cubiliarcho Extraordinario Legato. 1 is dated 28 *September* the other 7 *July* 1652 but they were [redirected][29] to the Council of State.[30]

The House ordered that Captain Willoughby be Commissioner at Portsmouth in room of Captain Moulton deceased.[31] The House voted that the remainder of monies which shall be raised upon the 1st act for sale of several lands and estates forfeited to the Commonwealth for treason and not yet disposed of or assigned by the Parliament to any particular person be imployed for the use of the navy and the House voted that there be 30 new frigots built for the service of the Commonwealth, and referred it to the Council of State to see it done.[32] An act reviving a former act for relieving of persons upon articles was this day read [the] 3rd time, and the House voted that the continuance of the said act be from 28 *September* 1652 to the 28 *September* 1655 and the commissioners for the said act are voted to be Colonel Barkstead and Master Anthony Samuel besides those formerly named and the House/voted

fo. 30[v]

voted that the quorum be made 7. A proviso was made to this act [thus] that this act or anything therein contained shall not extend or be construed[33] to prejudice, alter or make void any resolutions, votes or judgement given in Parliament touching any the articles aforesaid or any persons claiming thereupon. But this proviso was rejected. Several amendments were made to [the] bill and then it was voted that the further debate should be adjourned until to morrow morning.

On the 21th instant Captain Stokes came into Plymouth and brought with him 2 ships which came from Guinea bound homewards towards Hamburgh.[34] In the one is a great quantity of gold to the value of 40 or 50,000*l* sterling as the skipper confesseth, but it is

[29] *CJ*, VII, p. 185 reads 'superscribed' for '[redirected]'.

[30] The details provided here amplify the brief official record (*ibid*, p. 185). The ambassador's retinue and reception are further described by other correspondents in Clarke's notebook (below, pp. 65–66; Worc. MS XXIV, fos 30[r], 31[r-v], in longhand).

[31] Capp, *Cromwell's Navy*, p. 49.

[32] The order for the new frigates, which were to cost around £300,000, was made on the day of Blake's important victory over the Dutch at Kentish Knock; *C&P*, II, pp. 140–141.

[33] *CJ*, VII, p. 186 inserts 'to extend'.

[34] Also reported in longhand on fo. 28[r] of the same notebook (Worc. MS XXIV). *Severall Proceedings*, 157 (23–30 Sept. 1652), p. [2464], which gives a similar account, omits 'bound homewards towards Hamburgh'. Dutch ships frequently transferred goods on to Hamburg ships to protect them from capture; *Perfect Diurnall*, 146 (20–27 Sept. 1652), p. 2169. Several newsbooks reported that these particular vessels were flying the Swedish flag (e.g. *The Dutch Intelligencer*, 4 (22–29 Sept. 1652), p. 28).

bruited[35] to be worth much more; in that ship is also 8,000*l* or 10,000*l* worth of elephants' teeth; in the other ship is about 4,000*l* worth of elephants' teeth. In the ship[36] were found several letters to the Dutch for Amsterdam and Zealand. The gold is fast sealed in chests and [lands][37] and secured in the hands of the collectors for prize goods.[38] There [are/were] also 3 or 4 salt prizes[39] brought in that day, Dutchmen, the loss of which they will feel.

Our fleet then in the Downs had some discovery of a Dutch fleet and prepared to make sail towards them 2 or 3 days since, but a great storm rising they did not think fit to weigh anchor and the next news they heard was that the Dutch were gone again, so that a navy is still in the Downs.

Henry Walker

Newsletter from Henry Walker, Westminster, 2 October 1652[40]

fo. 31ᵛ

On Thursday last[41] an act for stating the accounts of several officers and soldiers was this day read the 3rd time and ordered that the debate thereupon be adjourned until that day fortnight. The Parliament ordered that the Lord Commissioner Lisle did bring in the Great Seal into the House. Ordered that it be referred to the Committee for the Army to take in consideration the business of Lieutenant-Colonel Salmon and the rest of the garrison of Hull and to send for him and confer with him how satisfaction may be made to them for their arrears either by bill or otherwise and to report their opinion therein to the Parliament on that day sennight. A letter from *Amerigo Salvetti* dated 13[42] *September* 52 the great duke of Tuscany's agent was read and the House ordered that a letter be sent to the great duke

35 *Severall Proceedings*, 157, p. [2464] reads 'counted' for 'bruited'.

36 *Ibid.* reads 'ships' for 'ship'.

37 Clearly intended to be 'landed', as in *Severall Proceedings*.

38 The Council of State immediately took measures for the safe transfer of both the booty and the equally valuable captured papers to London; *CSPD 1651–1652*, pp. 417, 420, 433.

39 In shorthand, 'prices'.

40 The wording of this newsletter is closely similar to the parliamentary record for 30 September–1 October 1652; *CJ*, VII, pp. 187–188.

41 i.e. 30 September 1652.

42 *Ibid.*, p. 187 reads '18' for '13'.

of Tuscany taking notice of his civility to the English merchants and that it be referred to the Council of State to prepare the letter, and that Master Speaker did sign the same.[43] Master Speaker reports a like letter from the State of Venice directed *Reipublicae Angliae Parliamento* which is ordered to be taken into consideration on Thursday[44] next. A bill disabling several persons to have any votes in [election] of officers in cities or burghs or to bear offices was this day read the 1st and 2nd times and upon the question committed to a committee.[45] The House voted Mistress Hamilton[46] to have 200*l* for supporting of her and her children and for her sending her away into Ireland. The Council of State to see it paid. A bill for issuing a statute made for the repairing of Sherborne Causey was read the 1st and 2nd time and upon the question committed.[47]

The House being informed by the Sergeant that the ambassador from the king of Portugal was ready and did attend to present himself to the Parliament, the Sergeant with his mace went to attend the lord ambassador to the House. So soon as the lord ambassador was entered he uncovered himself. Master Speaker and all the members stood up bare. When the lord ambassador was come as far as the bar, the Master of the Ceremonies[48] and the Sergeant attended him, the one on the right hand and the other on the left until the lord ambassador came to the chair appointed for that purpose which was placed on the north side of the House upon a Turkey carpet with a cushion in it and a footstool before it. The ambassador's name was John Roderick who is Lord High Chamberlain of Portugal[49] who after a few words addressed to Master Speaker he presented his letters credential which were by the Master of the Ceremonies delivered to Master Speaker and afterwards declared the substance of his embassy delivering a copy in English, of what he delivered by word, to the House. Master Speaker informed the ambassador by the Master of the Ceremonies that he would acquaint the Parliament therewith. And then the lord ambassador with the Master of the Ceremonies and the

[43] Thurloe received orders to draft the letter on 10 November 1652 and it was finally ordered to be sent on 23 November; *CSPD 1652–1653*, pp. 485, 504.

[44] *CJ*, VII, p. 187 reads 'Tuesday' for 'Thursday'.

[45] *Ibid.* adds the names of the committee members.

[46] Wife of Archibald Hamilton, an Irish trader hanged by the Scots as a traitor on 25 April 1651; *CSPD 1651–1652*, p. 414; *Mercurius Politicus* 49 (8–15 May 1651), pp. 795–796; W.C. Douglas, *Cromwell's Scotch Campaigns 1650–1651* (London, 1898), p. 243n.

[47] *CJ*, VII, p. 188 names the members of the committee.

[48] Sir Oliver Fleming; *CSPD 1651–1652*, p. 409.

[49] *CJ*, VII, p. 188 omits 'who is Lord High Chamberlain of Portugal' and substitutes two asterisks.

Sergeant-at-Arms attending him withdrew. Master Speaker reported to the Parliament the letters credential from the king of Portugal and the treaty.[50] He also reported what was delivered by the lord ambassador by word of mouth which was also read, which business was ordered to be taken into consideration on Tuesday next.

Yesterday[51] the Parliament ordered that the committee to whom the act touching the Treasury was referred be revived and that they meet at 2 a clock in the afternoon and bring in the names of fit persons for supervisors of the Treasury and to make their reports on Friday morning next. Ordered that the Commissioners of the Navy do make report on settling the business of the Admiralty on Friday morning next and that they [be] thereby impowered to present the names of fit persons to be intrusted therewith etc.[52]

Henry Walker

Newsletter from Henry Walker, Westminster, 16 October 1652[53]

fo. 36[r]

The Parliament has these 2 days past been about some particular lands and forests and chases and such like, redirecting it to be [reatched] such as are not to be sold for the best advantage and honour and profit of the State.

A petition of trayners about some such lands they should have had is referred and a petition of some in Southwark about a manour there was referred.[54] Letters were read from Master Bradshaw, agent at Hamburgh of the state of affairs thereabouts, but it was transmitted to the Council of State.[55]

The main business is about letters from Copenhagen of the stay of our English ships by the king of Denmark. An imbargo is certainly laid

[50] *Ibid.* omits 'and the treaty'.

[51] i.e. Friday 1 October.

[52] Also reported in a newsletter of 2 October 1652; Worc. MS XXIV, fo. 31[v], longhand.

[53] Most of the items in this newsletter are confirmed by *CJ*, VII, p. 191, but the wording is less similar than is the case with other letters from Walker (e.g. pp. 62–66 above).

[54] The petition from Southwark referred to the manor of the Maze; the petition from the train artillery and others, 'heretofore Members of the Train' referred to the Hare-Warren and also some meadows at Hampton Court; *CJ*, VII, p. 191.

[55] A letter of 5 October 1652 from Richard Bradshaw was read on 14 October (*ibid.*). On 22 October 1652 the Council of State ordered him to proceed to Copenhagen as Resident there; *CSPD 1651–1652*, p. 452. For the outcome of his mission see *CSPD 1652–1653*, pp. 170–171, 194.

upon our merchants there.[56] Some letters say that it was because our men of war being thereabouts gave no account of their intents to that nation. Others suspect worse, that it is upon a design carried on against us upon the Dutch interest with whom they are in league.[57] Some say that one of our captains of the men of war sent to have the merchants' ships released (for it is only the merchants that are stayed) or that they would be fetched out or something to that purpose which did much, say some, exasperate. What the event may be God knows. The men of war [were then in] treaty about it and [some] overtures were with the king of Denmark for their release.[58] There is at this time a resident here at London from the king of Denmark and also an ambassador extraordinary, and they both sent to the Parliament to desire their discharge to take their leave and be gone. Which occasioned the calling for the report on the treaty by representatives from the Parliament between the Council of State and the Danish ambassadour and the House also gave instructions to the Council of State to acquaint the said ambassador with their hearing of the stay of their merchants' ships by the king of Denmark and the particulars thereof, and to desire his answer therein. And the Parliament has ordered that report thereof shall be made to the House on Tuesday morning next, for without all question the Parliament will have account of the ships at Copenhagen before they and the agent or the ambassador are [allowed to] depart out of England.[59]

Master Feake [did] his part extremely in speaking plain English before the Parliament the last fast day which was kept very strictly on Wednesday last,[60] though divers of the Presbyterians would not open their church doors.

[56] As widely reported in the newsbooks, Frederick III had reneged on a previous undertaking to protect the Commonwealth's merchant ships; e.g. *A Perfect Diurnall*, 143 (30 Aug–6 Sept. 1652), pp. 2135–2136; 144 (6–13 Sept. 1652), p. 2147; 150 (18–25 Oct. 1652), p. 2234.

[57] The Danish king's growing support for the Dutch was made much of in the newsbooks; e.g. *Perfect Diurnall*, 146 (20–27 Sept. 1652), p. 2183; 149 (11–18 Oct. 1652), p. 2227; *Dutch Intelligencer*, 4 (22–29 Sept. 1652), pp. 25–26. See p. 71 below.

[58] Here *CJ*, VII, p. 191 merely records that letters of 18/8 October were read; no further details are given.

[59] On 20 October 1652 the Council of State ordered that the Danish ambassadors be informed that Danish ships would continue to be detained in the Thames pending the release of the impounded English vessels; *CSPD 1651–1652*, pp. 447–448.

[60] i.e. 13 October. Another correspondent wrote that 'The pulpet spoke plaine Englisch to the Parliament that day'; Worc. MS XXIV, fo. 35^{v}. For Christopher Feake, a prominent Fifth Monarchy preacher, and his connections with the regicide MP Thomas Harrison see *DBR*, 'Feake', 'Harrison'; for the background to their association and this sermon see Worden, *Rump*, pp. 304, 309, 315.

Divers considerable parties in Ireland have submitted to come in to the lieutenant-general since he got into Ireland.

Henry Walker

Newsletter from Henry Walker, Westminster, 23 October 1652

fo. 40v

Thursday last the Parliament received the report from the Council of State touching the Denmark ambassador and the staying of our merchants' ships by the king of Denmark with the narrative of the whole business[61] and on Friday the Council of State received further directions to proceed therein and a letter is to be sent to the king of Denmark about it and a narrative to be given to the ambassador of the particulars. Friday come sennight[62] is appointed for naming of sheriffs. Several votes passed about appointing of ammunition for the officers of the ordnance.

Some propositions about settling the isle of Jersey were referred to a committee.[63] Master Attorney-General[64] and the rest of the Council for the Commonwealth and Master Hurst are appointed Council of the Commonwealth to the Commissioners for Articles. An act for continuing of several commissions granted by the commissioners in Scotland until May 1653 was read twice and it is thought will pass on Tuesday.[65]

The Scots king is very busy at the French court for a general peace, for the cardinal and court are ingaged to give all assistance to him after that is concluded.[66]

Henry Walker

[61] Discussed by the Council of State on 14 and 21 October. Also on the 21st Bulstrode Whitelocke reported to the House on the outcome of a meeting which took place between English and Danish representatives on 20 October; *CSPD 1651–1652*, pp. 438, 450; *CJ*, VII, p. 192.

[62] i.e. 5 November (*ibid.*, p. 193).

[63] For these propositions see *ibid.*, pp. 193–194.

[64] Edmund Prideaux.

[65] The bill passed on Tuesday 30 October 1652 (*ibid.*, p. 195).

[66] Reported in a newsletter from Paris of 20/30 October 1652; *Severall Proceedings*, 161 (21–28 Oct. 1652), p. 2524. Charles's efforts to secure a Franco-Spanish alliance against the Commonwealth are described in *C&P*, II, p. 132.

Newsletter from Henry Walker, Westminster, 6 November 1652[67]

*fo. 48^v^*

On Thursday last[68] Master Speaker by way of report informed the Parliament that as he was coming to do his duty in Parliament one Samuel Arnold[69] threw a brick which hit the Sergeant's man[70] and narrowly scaped hitting the Sergeant on the head as he waited on the Speaker, and that he threw another stone which hit Master Speaker on the face. The Parliament voted that he should be brought in as a delinquent which was done. He said he was born at Grantham in Lincolnshire. He said that nobody persuaded him to throw these stones, but he did it to try them.[71] So the House committed him to Bridewell there to be kept to hard labour and daily corrected until the Parliament take further order.

The House ordered that Master Emott[72] and 6 more attend Master Speaker according as formerly they have done. Reports were made[73] of the charge of the navy and what is needful for them to come. A letter from General Blake from aboard the Triumph in Stokes Bay *November* 2 1652 and an order from the Council State [*sic*] 30 *October* were all read with a list of such ships as are of this winter's guard at or near ports where they may be soonest set forth, which were read and returned back to the Council of State.[74] Tuesday next was appointed to consider which way to raise monies and how provision may be made for defraying the charges both by sea and land and the House referred it to the Council of State to consider the state of the treasuries and also to state the business of Weavers' Hall bills and present the account thereof to the Parliament.[75] A committee was chosen, to whom it was referred to consider how incouragement may

[67] Again the wording of Walker's newsletter echoes that of *CJ* VII, pp. 209–210, and the official newsbook, *Severall Proceedings*, 163 (4–11 Nov. 1652), pp. 2551–2552.

[68] i.e. 4 November 1652.

[69] Elsewhere this man's name is given as Solomon Arnold; Worc. MS XXIV, fo. 47^r^ (in longhand); Hull CRO, BRL 532; *CJ*, VII, p. 209.

[70] *Ibid.* reads 'mace' for 'man'.

[71] *Ibid.* reads 'he answered that they might try him' for 'he did it to try them'.

[72] Lancelot Emott, Provost-Marshal for Middlesex and Westminster; *ibid.*, p. 209; *CSPD 1653–1654*, p. 452; *CSPD 1654*, p. 170.

[73] By Sir Henry Vane Jr; *CJ*, VII, p. 210.

[74] *Ibid.* reads 'to Sir Henry Vane' [junior] here. The Council dealt with these two matters on 4 November and 10 November respectively; *CSPD 1651–1652*, pp. 473, 484.

[75] Discussed by the Council of State on 26 August 1652 and 9 November 1652 (*ibid.*, pp. 382, 484); the act for ascertaining the time of payment of moneys due upon Weavers Hall bills was passed on 16 December 1652; *A&O*, II, p. 688.

be given to such merchants as at their own charge will set forth any ships for war for the public advantage[76] and the Parliament ordered that the commissioners appointed by act of Parliament on 25 *August* 1652[77] for stating the accounts of such officers and soldiers as have formerly served the Commonwealth in Ireland be injoyned to go forthwith into Ireland to attend their duty and service (according to the act) without further stay and that the said commissioners shall have power by themselves or their deputies to require copies from all committees of accounts, auditors, treasurers and other accountants in Ireland of their payments on the place relating to the soldiery and of all muster rolls there or extracts thereof.[78] This day the Parliament kept the thankgiving.

Henry Walker

Thomas Fulford to [William Clarke], 25 December 1652[79]

*fo. 85^v^*

On Thursday last[80] a young man clad all in armour, an arrow in his hand upon a white horse, cost 16*l* the Friday before, rode up to the further end of the hall and asked if the House were seated or not, answer being given yes. Also some say he asked for Master Prideaux.[81] He returned forth again. The horse guard seized on him took away his horse, [his money] with a watch. I pray [silence] your jollity of this [peradventure].

Thomas Fulford

[76] The names of those appointed to this committee are given in *CJ*, VII, p. 210.

[77] The act was passed in answer to the army's demands of 13 August 1652; *To the Supreame Authority the Parliament*; pp. 57–58 above; *A&O*, II, pp. 603–612.

[78] Although this item does not appear in the official proceedings for this day (4 November), Sir Henry Vane reported to the House on the matter on 27 November 1652; *CJ*, VII, pp. 210, 222.

[79] On Friday 24 December the House had ordered that Christmas Day was not to be marked (*ibid.*, p. 235). Gilbert Mabbott reported to the Hull authorities that this had been 'very strictly' observed (Hull CRO, BRL 544). The writer of the letter, Thomas Fulford, was normally based in Scotland; Chequers, MS 782, unfol., payments for 18 September 1652, 26 October 1653. I have discussed this document above (p. 60).

[80] i.e. 23 December 1652.

[81] Edmund Prideaux, Attorney-General, Postmaster-General and a member of the Council of State.

News from [Gilbert Mabbott], Westminster, 22 February 1653[82]

fo. 119[r]

Major Generall Lambert sent for by the Councell of State, in order to his coming for Scotland.[83]

Newsletter from London, 9 March 1653[84]

fo. 124[r]

There were 1,200 Dutch prisoners brought into Portsmouth and 600 into Dover and other places [that] our ships bring in daily prizes.[85] We have set out 27 men[86] to lie to catch the Dutch merchants and others upon the French coasts that [. . .] where the [centre] <fleet upon the coast of France>[87] has taken 2 rich prizes and brought into Dover.

The king of Denmark has dispossessed the English of all their ships and is setting out 20 men of war the least 30 guns to assist the Hollanders. De Witt is to come forth 45 sayle.[88]

[82] This item of news forms the postscript to a letter otherwise copied in longhand. The anonymous sender was certainly Gilbert Mabbott, who on the same day sent an identical newsletter, but with a different postscript, to the Mayor and aldermen of Hull (Hull CRO BRL 555).

[83] The longhand part of this sentence was noted by Austin Woolrych, who correctly inferred the Council's purpose (*C–P*, p. 73). On 30 March 1653 the Council of State ordered the Irish and Scotch Committee to 'report what has been done concerning sending Major-Gen. Lambert into Scotland'; by 26 April 1653 it was generally known that Lambert would not accept the command, although Cornet John Baynes seems to have been aware of this a month earlier; *CSPD 1652–1653*, p. 242; Worc. MS XXV, fo. 9[r]; *LRHO*, p. 52; pp. 60–61 above.

[84] Mabbott had already sent word of all the items contained in this newsletter to the Scottish headquarters and to Hull on 5 March 1653; Worc. MS XXIV, fo. 122[v]; Hull CRO, BRL 560.

[85] These would have been prisoners taken at the battle of Portland, 18–20 February 1653; *C&P*, II, pp. 157–161; S.R. Gardiner and C.T. Atkinson (eds), *Letters and Papers Relating to the First Dutch War 1652–1654*, 6 vols (London, 1899–1930), IV, pp. 1–22.

[86] i.e. men of war.

[87] Interlined. The intended position for this insertion is not indicated in the text.

[88] The Council of State received slightly lower estimates on 23 February and 27 March 1653; *CSPD 1652–1653*, pp. 183, 237.

30 Members are to be chosen from Scotland and 30 from Ireland.[89] The Parliament have ordered several of their Members to collect from the rest <to be given to the maimed mariners>[90]

The officers of the army at London have agreed a 100*l* to be gathered in the regiment for supply of the widows of [slain men] and for maimed mariners.

The Switzers' letter for accommodation with Holland [was] read[91] and to be answered Friday last.

The officers [are/were] again met to offer something to the Parliament in relation to their late letters.[92]

The Parliament have passed an act for nominating several persons to translate the Bible out of the original.

There are petitions <[of/by] great [....]>[93] in most counties in England <[~~dispatched~~], some for and>[94] against tithes.[95]

89 The decision to include thirty Members from Scotland was recorded as part of the day's business on 9 March (*CJ*, VII, p. 265); Ireland is not mentioned, but the number for both had been set at thirty on the 2nd (*ibid.*, p. 263).

90 Interlined.

91 On 8 March 1653 (*ibid.*, p. 264).

92 Two days earlier the officers had appointed a committee 'to advise his Excellency concerning a New Representative (the subject matter of their then debate)'; Worc. MS XXIV, fo. 122^{v}.

93 Interlined.

94 Interlined.

95 Such petitions were circulating in early December 1652; *Perfect Account*, 101 (1–8 Dec. 1652), pp. 806–807.

5. NOTEBOOK XXV

2 April–December 1653[1]

Introduction

In 1653 the news was largely dominated by the continuing Dutch war. In Clarke's notebook its course is traced in newsletters from both London and Newcastle, in memoranda, and in two sets of captured Dutch orders (translated, apparently, at the Scottish army headquarters). There are early reports of the engagement of the Dutch and English fleets in the decisive battle of the Texel on 31 July,[2] with the first account of the English victory coming from Newcastle in a letter of 5 August,[3] and a later report from George Downing in London with the important news that the Dutch admiral, Martin van Tromp, had been killed in the battle.[4] Another correspondent rightly forecast the profound effect of the pro-Orangist admiral's death,[5] which was followed in both countries by higher expectations of a successful conclusion to the negotiation of a peace treaty.[6]

In the later months of the year the government also had to face the threat of a major royalist-inspired rising in Scotland. In 1652 John Middleton, appointed by the exiled Charles Stuart as putative commander of an uneasy alliance of lowland nobles and highland chieftains, travelled to Holland to gather funds and reinforcements but was delayed there by illness. In his absence the former earl of Glencairn took his place. While at this stage the Scots army lacked both the internal accord and the resources to launch a major offensive, they made increasingly daring incursions into English-held territory, reaching the outskirts of Edinburgh itself. Apart from two occasions when he accompanied the acting commander-in-chief

[1] Worc. MS XXV.

[2] P. 97.

[3] P. 99.

[4] P. 101.

[5] P. 100. The chequered course of the peace negotiations is comprehensively analysed by S.C.A. Pincus in *Protestantism and Patriotism: Ideologies and the Making of English Foreign Policy, 1650–1668* (Cambridge, 1996), pp. 83–191.

[6] For example, see pp. 119, 127.

Robert Lilburne on brief visits to Dumbarton in October and Stirling in November, Clarke continued his duties at Dalkeith.

There are no newsletters which give details of Cromwell's termination of the Rump on 20 April 1653, and little political news from London until Gilbert Mabbott's letter of 2 August, almost a month after the first session of the Nominated Assembly.[7] From this point onwards many details of the Assembly's proceedings feature in letters from Mabbott, Downing, Walker, Thurloe, Hatter, and others.

They culminate with two anonymous descriptions of the way in which the Nominated Assembly came to its dramatic end on 12 December 1653,[8] and, at a time when discussions about the future form of government were a closely-guarded secret, with details of preparations for the inauguration of the new Protectorate.[9] Both letters refer to the new head of state as a 'governour' – a title which, in preference to earlier suggestions of 'king' or 'protector', was under discussion on the day on which they were written, 13 December.[10] The second letter is explicitly addressed to Robert Lilburne.[11] In its last few lines, the writer's astute forecast of three of the main provisions of the Instrument of Government, still in draft form only and not published until 2 January, indicates that he was extremely well informed, perhaps one of the very small group of officers who were privy to the discussions on 13 December, and possibly even Lilburne's old friend and colleague John Lambert, principal framer of the Instrument.[12]

As usual there is a sprinkling of foreign news unconnected with the war, and there are two accounts of the seamen's mutiny in London on 26–27 October 1653.[13] There are, too, reports of the increasingly disruptive behaviour of the Fifth Monarchists based at Blackfriars,

[7] P. 97.

[8] Pp. 126–128.

[9] P. 129. I am most grateful to Blair Worden for allowing me to read his unpublished paper on the framing of the Instrument of Government.

[10] *C&P*, II, pp. 282–283; *TSP*, I, p. 632; Woolrych, *C–P*, pp. 355, 358. By the following day the title of Lord Protector had been agreed, and Cromwell was sworn in as such on the 16th; *CP*, III, p. 10; *Weekly Intelligencer*, 148 (13–20 Dec. 1653), p. 94.

[11] Unfortunately the writer's address, Axeyard, Westminster, gives us no clue as to his identity. Mabbott and Downing both lived there, but so did many others connected with the army.

[12] Only three members of this group have been identified: Lambert, Berry, and Kelsey; P. Gaunt, 'Drafting the Instrument of Government, 1653–54: a reappraisal', *Parliamentary History*, 8 (1989), pp. 28–42, esp. p. 29; *The Protector (so called) In Part Unvailed: By whom the Mystery of Iniquity, is now Working*... (London, 1655), p. 12. The letter also supports the claim of 'T.M.' that the principal provisions of the Instrument had been finally drafted by the evening of 13 December; *TSP*, I, p. 632. Both letters appear to have reached the Scottish headquarters on about 20 December.

[13] Pp. 115, 116.

foremost among them Major-General Thomas Harrison and the minister Christopher Feake.[14]

The volume includes several letters which describe the arrival in London in June 1653 and subsequent trial of the Leveller John Lilburne, brother of Clarke's commander-in-chief. Lilburne had returned from his exile on the Continent in order to challenge the act of banishment passed upon him in January 1652. Immediately rearrested, he was again put on trial, with a series of hearings during July and August 1653.[15] Although on this occasion, unlike his brother's trial of 1649, Robert Lilburne distanced himself from the event, these letters show that he was kept fully informed about its progress.[16]

In September Clarke wrote to three contacts in London asking them to be of assistance to the eccentric poet Payne Fisher, who had travelled to Scotland in September 1652 in order to write a history of the wars in Scotland, and whom Clarke seems to have befriended.[17]

Authorization for impressment of sailors, 2 April 1653[18]

f. 3v

Whereas Captain William Pestell,[19] commander of the *Satisfaction* frigot, has received [powers] <and authority>[20] from the right honourable the Commissioners of the Admiralty of the Commonwealth of England to impress such and so many able seamen and mariners as he can possibly get and procure, you are therefore on sight hereof to be aiding and assisting unto the same Captain Pestell for whom he shall appoint in the due execution of these warrants and for the [conveying] on shipboard such seamen and mariners as he

[14] Pp. 119, 125, 129.

[15] Clarke's shorthand notes include two vivid eye-witness accounts of the trial (pp. 102–103), of which there is a full account in Gregg, *Free-born John*, ch. 28.

[16] *Ibid.*, p. 298; *DBR*, 'Robert Lilburne'.

[17] Pp. 104–105. The project had the blessing of both the current Scottish commander Richard Deane and the Council of State; *CSPD 1651–1652*, pp. 366, 367, 573; *S&C*, pp. 75–77.

[18] One of the first acts to be passed by the new Commonwealth concerned impressment (*A&O*, II, pp. 9–13). This is fully discussed, with especial reference to 1653, in Capp, *Cromwell's Navy*, pp. 262–272. Around this time the Navy Commissioners wrote to Hull, Leith, and Newcastle to stress the urgency of raising as many men as possible; Gardiner and Atkinson, *Letters and Papers Relating to the First Dutch War*, V, pp. 32–33.

[19] For Pestell's career see B.S. Capp, *The Fifth Monarchy Men* (London, 1972), p. 81; Capp, *Cromwell's Navy*, pp. 171n, 234, 307, 381. By 18 June 1653 he was facing a charge of neglect of duty; Worc. MS LXXXVI, fo. 71r–v.

[20] Interlined.

shall so impress for the publike service, and hereon you are not to fayle.[21]

To all officers and soldiers quartering in Fife and
other parts whom these may concern.

Memorandum, 4 April 1653

fo. [4][v]

Colonel Atkins'[22] ship called the Rook or Adventure, <Captain Edwards, commander>,[23] brought in a vessel, [a] fly boat of 200 tun laden with tallow, hides, stockfish, sturgeon and other commodities valued at 6,000*l* but they pretended to be Lubeckers.[24]

William Lenthall, [London], to the commissioners of the army, Leith, 16 April 1653[25]

fo. [5][v]

Gentlemen

The Parliament having been pleased (according to the inclosed) to order lands of inheritance of the yearly value of 80*l* (rendering 20*l* per annum to the use of the Commonwealth) of confiscated lands in Scotland to be settled upon Thomas Poole of Wedsbury in the county of Stafford and his heirs, and having also required me to write a letter unto you to settle the same upon him accordingly, I desire you will be pleased according to the inclosed order of Parliament to take care that the same be speedily set forth unto him.[26] Thus much I can say of the

[21] The *Satisfaction*, making her way from Orkney to London, was ordered by the English commissioners at Leith to call there especially for this purpose, arriving there on 29 March 1653; *CSPD 1652–1653*, pp. 221, 241.

[22] Presumably Col Samuel Atkins, English merchant at Leith at this time (*ibid.*, p. 464). Another vessel belonging to Atkins, the *Hopewell*, captured the letter which appears below, p. 83; *Mercurius Politicus*, 154 (19–26 May 1653), p. 2469. Atkins played a leading part in the events leading up to the Restoration (pp. 352, 355, 359 below).

[23] Interlined.

[24] *Mercurius Politicus*, 149 (14–21 April 1653), p. 2382 gives a fuller but closely similar account.

[25] In Clarke's notebook, this document is entered under 6 April 1653, the date of the enclosed order. See also pp. 79–80.

[26] For a longhand copy of the order, made on 6 April 1653, see Worc. MS XXV, fo. [5][v]; see also fo. 7[r]; *CJ*, VII, p. 276. Poole arrived at Leith soon afterwards, apparently remaining in Scotland for much of the 1650s; pp. 79–80 below; *S&P*, p. 288; *CP*, IV, p. 129. He was,

party whom it concerns, that his sufferings for the publike have been very great and been so made appear unto the Parliament and therefore I shall not need to say anything to invite you to give all furtherance to a person who has merited so well of the Commonwealth. I desire you to return the cornage up unto me according to the usual course in such cases. I remain

your very loving friend

William Lenthall, Speaker

16 April 1653

For the Honourable the Commissioners at Leith in Scotland, these

William Clarke to William Malyn, [Westminster], 7 April 1653[27]

fo. [6]r

<Letter to Master Malyn>[28]

Sir

This is only an acknowledgement of ~~your respects in~~ <the receipt of>[29] the last by which ~~you have~~ I see yours ~~respecting ours to you~~ <written>[30] in larger characters ~~than I am in a capacity to make real I observe [. . . .]~~ and therefore as to that particular I should ~~suppress~~ contract my [profound] expressions ~~and the gratitude [. . . .]~~ and make the more sudden receipt[31] ~~For the 18,000*l* For [. . .] hereat it was looked upon as a stock for to repay what had been disbursed by For the 18,000*l* Colonel Lilburne has written to Master Rowe~~ Master Bilton[32] out of ~~contingencies~~ the monthly assess here, [that] which was intended chiefly for contingencies, the works at Ayr, St Johnstons and

however, writing to Monck from London in September 1658 (p. 272 below). He may be the Thomas Poole who served as cornet in Clobery's regiment in early 1660; Worc. MS LIII, unfol. For other awards of Scottish lands to Englishmen see *S&C*, p. 74.

[27] William Malyn was Cromwell's secretary between 1650 and 1658 (*SS*, pp. 264–265). The many deletions and alterations in Clarke's letter reveal the care with which it was framed.

[28] Marginated.

[29] Interlined.

[30] Interlined.

[31] Blank.

[32] The career and subsequent disgrace of George Bilton, Deputy Treasurer for the forces in Scotland and, from 1653 or 1654, Receiver-General of the assessment in Scotland, are described in *ibid.*, pp. 145, 245, 399.

Innerness with repairs of Leith and other places ~~will take up the Scots~~ will this summer take up the monthly assess [for] Scotland, which is not above 8,000*l*, ~~or otherwise~~ and in case of fault thereof, either the forces should be unpaid or the works cease, and for provisions the forces here are willing to deposit <3 weeks' or>[33] a month's pay provided it may be in such hands where they may [~~. . .~~] command it and not be deducted by the state when they please. And if the state will but allow freight and convoy they will not at all trouble them to take care of provisions for them, and I think that is the least trouble the state can expect to be put unto by any forces they send into an enemy country as we should yet look upon this.[34]

William Clarke to Samuel Desborough, 15 April 1653

fo. 8[r]

<Letter to Master <Samuel>[35] Disbrowe[36] at [Suffolk] House for my being secretary>[37]

Honourable Sir

That I give you this trouble, it is through that liberty you were pleased to [pass] me by the hand of <my trusted friend>[38] Colonel Syler[39] which is only to mind you of the mission he made to you in my behalf though I know your honour's respect to me (~~though undeservedly~~) <without any merit of mine>[40] [is] such that I shall not need to do more than mention that in case <~~Colonel Lilburne be not [confirmed~~]>[41] your Honour's brother or Colonel Fenwick <or any other in whom you have interest>[42] be designed to ~~this~~ the[43] command <in chief of the forces here>[44] you will move them for

[33] Interlined.

[34] Two days later, on 9 April, similar letters were sent, probably by Robert Lilburne, to the Committee of the Army and to the Speaker; Worc. MS LXXXVI, fos 46[r], 47[r].

[35] Interlined.

[36] A short account of the life of Samuel Desborough is included under the entry for his elder brother John in the *Dictionary of National Biography*, 63 vols (London, 1885–1900).

[37] Marginated.

[38] Interlined.

[39] After his regiment was disbanded in October 1651, Col Edmund Syler remained in Scotland in an administrative capacity; F&D, II, pp. 569–570; *S&C*, p. xxxi.

[40] Interlined.

[41] Interlined.

[42] Interlined.

[43] '[T]he' superimposed on 'this'.

[44] Interlined.

~~me~~ my particular attendance ~~upon them~~ in the quality of a secretary ~~since I should not have troubled you~~ wherein ~~I [presuming not but] through divine assistance to serve them I shall~~ <in which imployment>[45] I shall indeavour (through divine assistance) ~~to shew my~~ to demonstrate my fidelity and diligence in theirs and the publike's service.

Oliver Cromwell, Whitehall, to the English Commissioners at Leith, 26 April 1653

fo. 14^{r}

Gentlemen

This bearer, Cornet Poole, has been faithful to the interest of the Commonwealth from the beginning of the wars and has suffered very much for the publike, which the Parliament has lately taken into their consideration and have thought fit to bestow upon him lands in [Scotland] of the yearly value of 80*l*, he paying thereout 20*l* per annum to the use of the State, wherefore I thought fit to accompany him with this my letter, desiring that you would shew him all lawful favours and that he may have a quick despatch in his business whereby you will very much oblige,

gentlemen

your very loving friend

O. Cromwell

Cockpit, April 26 1653

For the Honourable the Commissioners at Leith in Scotland these.

Colonel Thomas Harrison, Whitehall, to the English Commissioners at Leith, 27 April 1653

fo. 14^{r}

Gentlemen

Cornet Poole, this bearer, having from the beginning of the wars faithfully served the Commonwealth and received great losses for the publike, which the Parliament taking in consideration did bestow upon

[45] Interlined.

him lands in Scotland of the yearly value of 80*l*, he paying thereout 20*l* per annum to the use of the State and in regard I have known much of the integrity and suffering he has undergone I now make this request to you that you will afford him your [lawful] favour in his applications to you for a despatch upon this business, which shall ever be acknowledged as a great respect to,

gentlemen,

your very affectionate friend to serve you

T. Harrison

Whitehall, 27 *April* 1653

For the Honourable the Commissioners at Leith in Scotland.

William Clarke to Commissary-General [Edward] Whalley, [London], 9 May 1653[46]

fo. 44v

<Letter to Commissary-General Whalley to recommend me as secretary to the commander-in-chief to come into Scotland>[47]

May it please your Honour

~~Having <lately>~~[48] ~~been [so generously] remembered~~ [*sic*] ~~in your letters to your [. . .] worthy brother the Judge Advocate~~.

Having ~~lately~~ <formerly>[49] received many ~~expressions~~ testimonies of your ~~respect~~ favours towards me (far above my merit) <and more lately>[50] in your letters to your worthy brother, Judge Advocate Whalley, ~~I should be I am I can~~ I [may] conceive it my duty ~~bound~~ to return my humble acknowledgment and more particularly for your Honour's ~~respect freeness~~ freedom[51] to entertain me in the quality of a

[46] The many deletions and alterations in this draft letter to Edward Whalley indicate the care with which Clarke chose his words.

[47] Marginated. Clarke, who was mustered in one of the troops of Whalley's regiment, had recently received word that John Desborough (p. 78 above) had refused the post of commander-in-chief and that Whalley was 'now conceived to bee the man'; *L-P*, pp. 102, 104; *CP*, III, p. 3. Whalley and his brother, the Judge Advocate, were among those who recommended Clarke for a post in Ireland in October 1650; *CP*, II, pp. 224–225.

[48] Interlined.

[49] Interlined.

[50] Interlined.

[51] '[F]reedom' superimposed upon 'freeness'.

secretary in case your honour had ~~this command~~ been appointed to this command in which respect I should have been far better contented with my stay here but since <divine>[52] providence has left and continued me here so long <(and in that capacity to the present commander-in-chief)>[53] I [must/should] now become a suitor to you that in case the commander here be disposed to any other [hand than whose it is] your Honour will please [to] recommend me ~~thereunto~~ <~~to be secretary~~ to that imployment>[54] and as I shall be careful to express my duty to the publike and those upon whom I shall attend according to my conscience and <blind>[55] obediency so I shall study to be the more <[. . .]>[56] and industrious ~~upon the account of your recommendations~~ which ~~must~~ might cause ~~an~~ a[57] ratifying obligation [~~upon~~] (of/on [. . .] recommendation <[. . . .] your Honour>[58] had not [. . .] provided) [to/upon].

your most faithful and most humble servant

William Clarke

Dalkeith 9th May 1653

The Generals of the Fleet, on board the *Triumph*, to Captain Francis Allen, commander of the *Recovery*, 9 May 1653[59]

fo. [62]r

<Commission to Captain Francis Allen, commander of the Recovery>.[60]

You are forthwith upon sight hereof, wind and weather permitting, to set sayle with the ship under your command towards the ports of the east coasts of Scotland and there to remain for protection of the trade

[52] Interlined.
[53] Interlined.
[54] Interlined.
[55] Interlined.
[56] Interlined.
[57] '[A]' superimposed upon 'an'.
[58] Interlined.
[59] Although dated 9 May, this document was entered by Clarke under 2 June, the day on which one of its signatories, Richard Deane, was killed in a sea battle against the Dutch; *CSPD 1652–1653*, p. 389.
[60] Marginated.

of this Commonwealth or any of the people under their obedience and protection. As also for conveying of provisions, ammunition and other things necessary for the service of this State from one port to another, following therein such orders and directions as from time to time you shall receive from the Council of State, Commissioners of the Admiralty and Navy, ourselfs, or the commander-in-chief in Scotland in relation to that service. And further in your said voyage to your station, as also during your stay there and return from thence, you are to give your protection and assistance to any of the vessels (as well merchant men as men of war) belonging to the Commonwealth of England or under their protection whom you shall meet with passing or trading (to and fro[)] on that coast or in your course hither and thence, as also to take and seise and in case of resistance to sink or otherwise destroy any of the ships or vessels, men of war, or others, belonging to the people of the United Provinces, to the French king, or any of his subiects or any other prince or state or any of their subiects in hostility with this Commonwealth/as

fo. [62]^{v}

as also all pirates or vessels of any other person or persons who shall any way disturb the safe and peaceable trading of the good people of this Commonwealth or under their obedience and protection.[61] Hereof you are not to fayle and this shall warrant your so doing. Given under our hands and seal on board the Triumph the 9th May 1652 [*sic*].

R. Deane

George Monck

To Captain Francis Allen Commander of the Recovery[62]

[61] All along the coast, as far north as Leith, the capture of English merchant ships by the Dutch navy had for the past year severely affected lines of supply. Especially serious was the resultant rise in coal prices; Pincus, *Protestantism and Patriotism*, pp. 175–177.

[62] The *Recovery* was regularly employed on such convoy duties at this time. On 4 June Capt. Allen was in Leith Road awaiting orders, and on 9 June he was sent from Leith to deliver powder and shot to Yarmouth for the use of the navy; Worc. MS LXXXVI, fo. 65^{r}; *CSPD 1652–1653*, pp. 593, 595.

Franse Cornelise [Dewick/Dewitt] to Admiral Martin Van Tromp, [17] May 1653[63]

fo. 52r

Right Honourable

My Lord

The bearer hereof is Master *Aryen Cladslen*,[64] who is bound to seek your Lord<ship>[65] at sea with letters from the high and mighties[66] the States General with this express command, if he [met/meet] with any English ships to throw the letter[67] overboard, and if it should happen the said letters should so miscarry these are to acquaint your Lordship that in case need should require, a considerable number of men of war should be forthwith sent to you. In[68] the meanwhile we are in expectation that the Lord will grant us a firm peace between both Commonwealths. And in regard great indeavours are used for the accomplishing of it, and it being of such concernment to my own particular as well as to the publike, I could not omit the acquainting your Lordship therewith. Never the less what I write is my own private conception and thus wishing your Lordship his[69] happiness and prosperity to the service of our native country, I commit you to the protection of the Almighty and remain

your Lordship's most humble and faithful servant

Franse Cornelise [Dewick/Dewitte][70]

[63] The letter is dated 6 May 1653 N.S., but Clarke entered it under 17 May, presumably the date of its translation. A copy of the English version was forwarded to Cromwell and appears, together with an account of its capture by the *Hopewell* ketch with minor variations in *Mercurius Politicus*, 154 (19–26 May 1653), pp. 2469–2470 (Worc. MS LXXXVI, fo. 62v). This gives the sender's name as 'Denick' (in *Perfect Diurnall*, 181 (23–30 May 1653), pp. 2734–2735, 'Denic'). Clarke's handwriting is unclear, but may read 'Dewitt'. *CSPD 1652–1653*, p. 334, simply records that the letter was from 'the States of Holland'. The letter's capture was noted in Bulstrode Whitelock, *Memorials of the English Affairs*, 4 vols (Oxford, 1853), IV, p. 11.

[64] Identified as Aryen, or Arien, Claesen in *Mercurius Politicus* and in Worc. MS XXV, fo. [54]v, where it is reported that he was captured on the 14th, and brought into Leith on 17 May.

[65] Interlined.

[66] *Mercurius Politicus*, 154, p. 1470, reads 'high and mighty Lords' for 'high and mighties'.

[67] *Ibid.* reads 'letters' for 'letter'. It was standard procedure if captured to jettison important correspondence (see, e.g., *CSPD 1654*, p. 190).

[68] *Mercurius Politicus*, 154, p. 1470 omits 'In'.

[69] *Ibid.* reads 'all' for 'his'.

[70] *Ibid.* reads 'Denick'.

In haste at *Maessland Slugh*[71]
the 16th of May 1653 *Novo*[72]

For the right honourable and valiant the Lord Martin Harperen[73] Tromp Lord Admiral of Holland and West Friesland[74] these present at sea.

Journal of Major Dorrill, Commander of the *Adventure*, 21 May 1653[75]

fo. 56r

The diurnall of Major Dorrill, commander of the Adventure frigot, a private man of war.

<The 13th>[76] of May. Coming out of the Sound off the Naes[77] we discovered about 10 in the morning a fleet of some 60 or 70 great ships with 5 great convoyers. They were 2 English miles to the weather of us and they stood southeast for the sound. We stood along the land northwest. The wind was south and by west stormy.

<The 15th>[78] The wind blew very hard. We stood into the sea northwest some 6 or 8 glasses[79] standing again to the shore south. We discovered a great sayle to our windward about 4 in the afternoon. We aimed to be between him and the shore, being close hard by a wind, he steering likewise our same course south. But looking out we discovered about[80] 100 of great ships with many convoyers and after them we discovered 18 more in[81] sight of the said fleet. The wind blew west-northwest. We kept our course for the shore. They came within half a league of us and one of their great convoyers having a galliot

[71] *Ibid.* reads 'Maesland Sluyck'. A correspondent wrote from The Hague that 'Tromp and De Witt do keep with their fleet about the Maese'; *TSP*, I, p. 237.

[72] *Mercurius Politicus*, 154, p. 1470, 'stilo novo'.

[73] *Ibid.* reads 'Harpers'.

[74] *Ibid.* omits 'and West Friesland'.

[75] Printed in *Mercurius Politicus*, [153] (26 May–2 June 1653), pp. 2485–[2486] and reprinted in *Perfect Diurnall*, 182 (30 May–6 June 1653), pp. 2754–2755. Dorrill's daring encounter was also noted by Bulstrode Whitelocke; Whitelock, *Memorials*, IV, p. 13.

[76] Marginated.

[77] i.e. The Naze.

[78] Marginated.

[79] A reference to the time taken by the sand of a sand-glass to run out, at sea usually a half-hour glass (*OED*). Thus the length of time indicated here is probably three to four hours.

[80] *Mercurius Politicus*, [153], p. 2485, reads 'above' for 'about'.

[81] *Ibid.* inserts 'the'.

with him sent him off from the fleet to discover us. We had a Danes' fane[82] up, which when he discovered he came no further.[83]

<The 16th>[84] May at 6 in the morning we tacked to the land, the weather being stormy, under the course of a mainsayle, we steered north-northwest. About 9 of the clock we espied the fleet from Bergen. We kept our course. They came very near us but could not speak us the sea[85] was so high. About 12 of the clock we discovered a great ship in our water athwart our bow and there was in his company above 300 great ships which we afterwards discovered all standing south. We could not possibly miss them but must speak them. We durst not trust to our running but rather by plain dealing or [impudence] either to outface them or deceive them. And so we steered[86] through their whole fleet, kept[87] all our men close except[88] 5 whereof 4 were Danes. The 1st ship that came up to speak us was a ship with 20 guns. He hung out his Dutch colours, we our Danish. He asked us whence we were. We told him from Copenhagen and bound for Bergen in Norway. We asked them from whence their fleet. They answered from Amsterdam, Rotterdam, Flushing, etc. We spake 7 convoyers and 12 merchant men more, who answered[89] as before. It was from 12 to 6 before we were clear of them.

<The 17th>[90] May we took an Hollander who told us that[91] he saw Tromp the 12th May and that he was about 90 in his fleet and 250 merchants' men, whereof 5 bound to the East Indies, the rest to the Straits, Spain and France. He said Tromp was to convoy these out and to meet the fleet coming from France and to convoy them for Holland but said the French fleet was gone by before Tromp came up, and that Tromp and his merchantmen steered from Shetland southwest, that he heard nothing of the English fleet.

So[92] we suppose the fleet we met the 13th could not be Vantromp's but rather the fleet from Spain, Straits etc. The fleet we met the 15 we do (and so doth this Hollander) conceive to be the Russia fleet that should have come home last Michaelmas and was left behind. The fleet we met the 16th was the French fleet.[93]

[82] Meaning flag or pennant (*OED*).

[83] *Mercurius Politicus*, [153], p. 2485 adds, 'This we conceived to be the fleet from Russia'.

[84] Marginated.

[85] *Ibid.* reads 'winde' for 'sea'.

[86] *Ibid.* reads 'stood' for 'steered'.

[87] *Ibid.* reads 'keeping' for 'kept'.

[88] *Ibid.* reads 'but' for 'except'.

[89] *Ibid.* inserts 'us'.

[90] Marginated.

[91] *Ibid.* omits 'that'.

[92] *Ibid.* inserts 'that'.

[93] *Ibid.* adds 'so you see this single man of war hath met with all the Dutch Fleets within three daies'.

News from Westminster, 21 May 1653[94]

fo. [57]^{r}

Colonel Lilburne was named for the bishoprick of Durham, but in regard he was commander-in-chief in Scotland that was laid aside,[95]

and the Lord Grey of Groby who sold his land [. . .] of 800*l* a year to buy the Lord Craven's estate is like to lose his bargain.[96] Also the earl of [Canricard][97] having articles for an estate in Ireland, the Lord President Bradshaw's 1,000*l* which was given him out of the said earl's estate in kind is to be disposed to the said earl.

William Clarke to Clement Oxenbridge, [London], 25 May 1653

fo. [58]^{r}

<A letter to Master Clement Oxenbridge in the behalf of Master Mew>[98]

Honoured Sir

~~Although I have not since my coming in Scotland. Although I have not had any for this long time had the opportunity of correspondence with~~

[94] Most of this newsletter was copied by Clarke *en clair* and is reproduced in *CP*, III, pp. 6–7, where no indication is given that it contains these two passages in shorthand. The first begins immediately after the sentence ending, 'by order from the Kinge of Spaine were recalled'; the second, beginning 'and the Lord Grey of Groby', comes at the end of the document, i.e. after 'to stand in the pillory.' (both *ibid.*, p. 7).

[95] Although I have found no other supporting evidence, I take this to mean that Lilburne was at one stage considered by the Council of Officers for membership of the forthcoming Nominated Assembly. The list of candidates, on which the Council of Officers had been working throughout May was ready to be presented to the Council of State by 23 May 1653; Woolrych, *C–P*, pp. 134–135.

[96] Craven's estate was forfeited to the Commonwealth under the terms of the act of 4 August 1652; *A&O*, II, p. 591. A year later Payne Fisher wrote that Grey would be £42,000 out of pocket (p. 181).

[97] Ulick Burke, marquis of Clanricarde. Excepted from the act for the settling of Ireland (*A&O*, II, p. 599), he later capitulated to Parliament (*OxDNB*, 'Burke').

[98] Marginated. Edmund Prideaux's tenure of the post had effectively come to an end with the dissolution of the Rump and it was not until 30 June that the contract to farm the posts was given to John Manley; *CSPD 1652–1653*, p. 455. In the interim a group known as the New Undertakers, headed by Clement Oxenbridge, which in 1652 had set up in opposition to the official post, appears to have filled the gap; Gaunt, 'Interregnum governments and the reform of the post', p. 289. Mew was still acting as postmaster at Leith in August 1653 (*LRHO*, p. 64). Oxenbridge petitioned on behalf of the Undertakers for the inland posts on [30] January 1654; *CSPD 1653–1654*, pp. 372–373.

~~you yet I hope it has not in the length between time and distance of place The long distance~~ [Presuming] time and distance of place [are] that since ~~I have been deprived of the [. . .]~~ we have had opportunity of converse together has obliterated ~~the remembrance of our former acquaintance~~ the remembrance of me with you, I am the rather ~~willing~~ <inclined>[99] ~~to trouble you with these few lines by these lines a little to [. . .]~~ ~~to trouble you with these lines and~~ to give <you>[100] the trouble of perusing of these lines ~~to you~~ ~~in the beh~~ in the behalf of <~~Master~~>[101] Nathaniel Mew, postmaster at Leith ~~contin~~ and to desire his continuance in ~~his~~ that[102] implyment under yourself and the rest of the Undertakers which he had under Master Prideaux. The man is so well known to Master Malyn[103] ~~and other gentlemen from whom you have may further~~ whom you esteem, that I shall ~~need only to tell you that I~~ <say the least only in general>[104] I have ~~from the beginning~~ <always>[105] observed him to be of a sober and righteous conversation, to which I may add ~~since his 1st time in the late post change change~~ [*sic*] ~~himself without offence or blemish~~ that upon the ~~probability~~ 1st probability of the late change of the post officer which yourself and the rest have now so happily effected for public good, he carried himself without offence ~~to these who then imployed him [or not~~] offence [*sic*] or blemish, and being ~~was~~ so confident of his own integrity that as he followed his duties faithfully ~~so far as~~ while he was ~~so~~ intrusted ~~[. . .] though he wished more and doubted not but if it came into other hands~~ by the other, so he wished and waited for such ~~a~~ an[106] alteration thereof as might render him serviceable in a more [keepable][107] manner, and therefore I doubt not but you will afford him the fruits of his expectance at the instance of

your humble servant

William Clarke

Dalkeith 16 May 1653

[99] Interlined.

[100] Interlined.

[101] Interlined.

[102] '[T]hat' superimposed on 'his'.

[103] In April 1651 Mew was appointed postmaster at Berwick at Cromwell's request, as Malyn, as Cromwell's secretary, would have known; *CJ*, VI, p. 568; *CSPD 1651*, p. 165.

[104] Interlined.

[105] Interlined.

[106] '[A]n' superimposed upon 'a'.

[107] i.e. 'capable'?

William [Badnell] and Edward Rowbotham to George Dawson, Newcastle, 26 May 1653[108]

fo. [58]^{v}

These are to acquaint that there is come in the [Arbour Tree] of Hamburgh, John [Lopkin/Lupkin] master [. . .] who has nothing but ballast. He saith he came through our fleet on Tuesday last off the Dogger Sands. They were 110 sayle. They lie between the Dogger and the Flie.[109] That the Holland fleet can get no way but our fleet must meet with them. He saith that our fleet has taken 6 great ships from Dantzick laden with rye. This is all at present from

your servants

William [Badnell]

Edward Rowbotham

[Skelbo], May 26 1653

To Master George Dawson, collector of the customs these at Newcastle

Newsletter, 1 June 1653

fo. 61^{v}

<From Colonel Atkins letter of secrecies>[110]

Honoured Coz

The great ambition that I have to serve you inflames me with such a zeal thereupon that you cannot command any thing that lies within my honour but all my power presently moves towards the doing thereof, as towards the centre. I have procured the best composal[111] I could to your [desired . . .], and thank you for your good intelligence in the postscript of it. [~~I hope our~~] I shall not much value the success either of the duke of Vendosme's or the Spanish fleet, having things of great

[108] Information from this newsletter was passed to the Council of State on 26 May; *CSPD 1652–1653*, p. 353.

[109] i.e. Vlie.

[110] This marginal comment appears to indicate that the letter was intercepted by Atkins, or one of his vessels, rather than that he wrote it. His contribution of captured intelligence at this time was much valued by Robert Lilburne; Worc. MS LXXXVI, fo. 69^{v}. Most of the news items are confirmed by *Mercurius Politicus*, [153] (26 May–2 June 1653), pp. 2474, [2479]–2480, [2484]; 156 (2–9 June 1653), p. 2488.

[111] i.e. act of composing (*OED*).

concernment in my eye that concern our nearer allies, and should be glad to hear that Deane and Monck had met with the Batavian fleet. The king of the Romans is not yet chosen, but it's thought that the ~~emperour~~ king of Hungaria will be the man, which will indifferently suit with our affairs,[112] and need not [*sic*] tell you of the good success ~~of~~ that[113] the Polonian army have had against the Cossacks, having slain 5,000 of them and taken 2 other towns, [~~. . . .~~] so that I now believe the Turk will have less mind to help them with supplies. If your fleet ~~be ready it~~ (I will not say of the singular number) be ready, it will be good that you get some men from the prince [or emperour] to raise the siege of Bellegarde <in Burgundy>[114] which I hear is in some danger from people of the duke of Espernon[115] being before it, and the earl of Boytville who commands for Condé in some distress, <though he killed above 1,500 of the besiegers in a late sally>.[116] I pray in your next send me what you have from the grand [buccaneer] at Copenhagen[117] that we may know how manage things in relation to him. If you have any [express] to send to the States of affairs you may send it by the cardinal Antonio Barberini[118] ~~that he be not~~.

Memorandum, 21 June 1653[119]

fo. 74^{r}

This day Colonel Atkins'[120] ship called the[121] which was the packet boat formerly taken by him from the Dutch brought in a prize

[112] Ferdinand IV, king of Bohemia and Hungaria was unanimously elected king of the Romans at Augsburg on 22 May 1653; the exiled Charles Stuart wrote immediately to congratulate him; *Mercurius Politicus*, 158 (16–23 June 1653), p. [2527]; *TSP*, I, p. 248; W.D. Macray and H.O. Coxe (eds), *Calendar of the Clarendon State Papers*, 5 vols (Oxford, 1869), II, p. 213.

[113] '[T]hat' superimposed upon 'of'.

[114] Interlined. Though not indicated in the original, the intended position of this insertion is clear.

[115] See *Mercurius Politicus*, 156 (2–9 June 1653), p. 2488.

[116] Interlined. Boutville was the governor of the besieged Bellegarde. The duc d'Espernon had recently made some progress in his attempt to take the town and was confident that he would soon capture it. There were rumours of a private understanding between the two men; *TSP*, I, pp. 261, 285–286.

[117] Presumably a reference to Frederick III, king of Denmark.

[118] Having been forbidden by the Pope to enter papal territory, Barberini was sent as ambassador to the Italian princes in June 1653; *Perfect Diurnall*, 178 (2–9 May 1653), p. 2696; 183 (5–13 June 1653), p. 2776.

[119] For a closely similar account see *Mercurius Politicus*, 160 (30 June–7 July 1653), p. 2549.

[120] Presumably Col Samuel Atkins; the account in *Mercurius Politicus* states that this vessel had been 'set out by a Merchant of Leith for a private man of War'.

[121] Blank.

of[122] loaden[123] with flax and iron valued at near 1,000*l.* The master of it said that 2 or 3 days before he was taken there were 50 sayle of merchant ships loaden going from the Sound for Holland, having 12 Danish men of war to convoy them. That the king of Denmark had 22 sayle of men of war to go besides, [and one] having 100 guns.

Also Captain Rudlee, captain of the Falcon frigot brought in 2 Dutch vessels laden with fish, one of them [~~worth~~] of about 60 tun. They belonged to Emden.[124]

Memorandum, 23 June 1653

fo. 75^r

This day Judge Swinton went towards England as one of the next Parliament, and the day following my Lord Hopetoun followed him post.[125]

Appeal on behalf of victims of a fire at Marlborough, Wilts, 25 June 1653[126]

fo. 76^r

Whereas in the latter end of April last there happened a very sad and lamentable fire in the <~~once flourishing~~>[127] town of Marlborough in Wiltshire wherein was consumed 250 houses ~~and those the chiefest the [. . .]~~ in the town, whereby many families ~~[are/were] ruined~~ who were once able to relieve others [are/were] ruined and stand in need of ~~relief~~ <supply>[128] from others, and the town which was ~~once~~ <lately>[129] ~~famous~~ very [distinguished] for trade being wholly impoverished, I do hereby recommend it unto you seriously to

[122] Blank.

[123] i.e. heavily laden (*OED*).

[124] Bulstrode Whitelocke recorded Rudlee's prizes, and also the fifty merchant ships sailing towards Holland from the previous paragraph; Whitelock, *Memorials*, IV, p. 20.

[125] Both Swinton and Sir James Hope of Hopetoun had been summoned as Scottish members to the Nominated Assembly which was to convene on 4 July 1653.

[126] On 18 May 1653 the Council of State launched throughout England and Wales an appeal on behalf of victims of the fire which had devastated Marlborough on 28 April 1653. Cromwell issued a similar request to the army on 20 November 1654; *CSPD 1652–1653*, pp. 336–337; *CP*, II, p. xxxvii.

[127] Interlined.

[128] Interlined.

[129] Interlined.

consider the woeful calamities and sad afflictions of your Christian brethren and countrymen of that town so as to administer ~~such relief~~ unto ~~the re edifying of~~ their relief and re-edifying of that now [deprived] and desolate place. Given etc.

William Clarke to Major-General Venables, Ireland, 30 June 1653

fo. [78][v]

<Copy of my letter to Major-General Venables commander of the forces in Ulster in Ireland>[130]

Honourable Sir

Understanding lately from my quondam [mentor] Captain William Johnston that you are pleased with much freedom and civility <and why I wrote not to you by him which indeed I intended and promised to do had he not gone away unexpectedly and when he could not conveniently call for his letters>[131] to inquire concerning me and being desirous to [retrace] any opportunity to renew that former acquaintance and correspondence which I had once the honour to have with you, I have taken the [boldness] to send you these lines ~~with the presentation of my humble prayer~~ to which I desire you will please to return an answer. And in case that you have not the intelligence from England so speedily where you are as you may have it [hence] I shall presume ~~now and then when any~~ when anything comes considerable to acquaint you with it. ~~The posts come hither in 4 days~~ The posts come constantly hither in 4 days, and ~~usually are at Aire~~ ~~we make it then returns~~ we dispatch [later] to Aire in 2 days from whence I suppose it may be soon with you.

At present we have not any ~~thing considerable~~ news of much [concernment] either at home or abroad. ~~Since the [. . . .] of MacNaughton's party and~~ The <late>[132] signal success which God gave our fleet against the Dutch has ~~now much~~ <something>[133] distracted ~~Glengarry~~ our highland neighbours from those attempts they intended [~~. . . .~~] resolvedly to prosecute for Charles Stuart's interest. Yet they still continue their meetings about Lochaber, where

[130] Marginated.
[131] The intended position for this insertion is not indicated.
[132] Interlined.
[133] Interlined.

we hear Glengarry, Glencairn, Belcarris and others do still meet [~~and tend off~~] and give out that Middleton with forces for their assistance will ~~land them~~ be with them about the middle of next month. But in case they should have their expectation therein, they would be able to do us little hurt, [as] the forces in most parts here (notwithstanding the wet season of the year) [~~are drawn~~] <lie down>[134] in the field to be in readiness upon any infall of those wild people in the lowlands.

The last [~~news~~] we had from London is that our fleets did still keep etc.

Newsletter from Colonel Thomas Fitch, Westminster, 2 July 1653

fo. [79]^{v}

It is certified by letters out of Holland to some of the foreign agents here that there are 4 eminent towns revolted from the States and stand for the prince of Orange,[135] and the rabble there run up and down crying up the prince of Orange in so much that troops of horse are disposed of in The Hague and other places to keep the people from [headiness], and there is a general zeal amongst them to have a peace with us, crying out they are come undone.

Several merchants here have letters that our fleet has taken 23 sayle of merchants' men from them. They [shewed] a list of it at the Council door, which is 3 Straits men, 3 Canaries men, one Guinay man, one laden with 200 brass pieces of ordinance; some say 2 ships laden with ordinance and some 10 or 12 East India ships.[136]

Thomas Fitch[137]

[134] Interlined.

[135] The towns were Enkhuizen, Goes, Hoorn, and Medemblik; *Mercurius Politicus*, 159 (23–30 June 1653), p. 2545. For these events see Pincus, *Protestantism and Patriotism*, pp. 143–145. The republicans recaptured Enkhuizen only two months later (p. 106 below).

[136] Lists of prizes taken between 19 and 25 June 1653 appeared in, e.g., *Mercurius Politicus*, 160 (30 June–7 July 1653), pp. 2562–2563; *Moderate Publisher of Every Daies Intelligence*, 140 (1–8 July 1653), pp. [1119]–1120.

[137] Although Fitch's regiment was at Inverness, he is known to have been in England at this point; F&D, II, p. 511; Firth, *S&C*, pp. 154, 203.

Newsletter from George Downing, [Westminster], 2 July 1653[138]

fo. [79]v

From another thus

Very great distraction[s] appear in Holland: that in Enchusen is at present quelled, so as that the town magistrates by article are not to come into the councils of war there.[139] The train bands in Harlem marching through the town, one company had great Orange colours which the magistrates sending and taking away they would not march till they were returned.[140] In Amsterdam [in listing] seamen they mention not Vantromp who it's said has declared for Orange and De Witt for the States General.[141] All our Holland letters say we have taken about 20 sayle of theirs lately, *vizt* about 16 of their Eastland in which are said to be about 187 guns bought in Sweden for the frigots building in Holland, 4 from the West Indies, 3 from the Straits, one from Guinea.[142]

It's Exchange news that young Tromp[143] with about 40 sayle from the Straits is upon our coasts. Letters from Yarmouth say near the same, but nothing yet from our fleet.

Monday the officers met to consider what to say to the new authority[144] and how to receive them.

The Spanish ambassador has printed the breach of articles against his master.[145]

George Downing

[138] The similarity between several of these news items and an undated letter of intelligence sent to Thurloe suggests that that was the source of Downing's information; *TSP*, I, p. 253, where, although clearly it was written in late June, it has been placed between two earlier letters.

[139] *CClarSP*, II, p. 223; *TSP*, I, p. 253. Enkhuizen had been the first town to declare for the prince of Orange the preceding month; *The Faithfull Post* [N&S 149], 119 (28 June–5 July 1653), p. [1071]; *The Faithful[l] Post* [N&S 148], 121 (15–22 July 1653), p. 1081.

[140] This took place on St John's Day, 24 June; *TSP*, I, p. 253.

[141] Confirmed by an undated letter of intelligence to John Thurloe (*ibid.*). It was around this time that Cromwell made a secret attempt to have Van Tromp dismissed by the States General; *C&P*, II, p. 341. His death during the following month and the subsequent appointment as his successor of the anti-Orangist Jacob Van Wassenaer had a profound effect on the conduct of the war with England; Pincus, *Protestantism and Patriotism*, pp. 153–155.

[142] This is another version of the list sent by Thomas Fitch on the same day (previous document).

[143] Cornelis van Tromp, son of Admiral Martin van Tromp.

[144] i.e. the Nominated Assembly, which assembled on 4 July. For Cromwell's reception of the Members, at which 'as many of the Army Officers as the room could well contain' were present, see *Mercurius Politicus*, 160 (30 June–7 July 1653), pp. 2563–2564; also *CP*, III, pp. 8–9.

[145] Confirmed by an undated letter of intelligence from Holland (*TSP*, I, p. 254).

The Council has given the Dutch deputies a paper for satisfaction and security before a further treaty.[146]

Memorandum, 27 July 1653

*fo. 105^r^*

The copy of one of the instructions found in one of the Dutch vessels taken by Captain Robert Drew[147] near Bressay Bay in Shetland the 3rd of July 1653.[148]

Translation of captured Dutch orders, 27 July 1653

*fo. 105^v^*

Copy

Instructions for Dirsk Jans Dick[149]

He is charged that he with [1st/best] opportunity shall put to sea according to[150] done by Peter *Niesen*.

And without any delay sayle northwards and remain there [cruising] twixt Shetland and Faroe at least 5 weeks, and 6 weeks at longest.

Keeping a journal and taking notice from day to day of all passages, giving us account of all ships you meet with under the hands of the shipmasters or chief officers' hands.

In your passage to the north as also during the time of your [cruising] there and your return from thence you are to indeavour to speak with all ships you discover and give them notice that the English keep our coasts guarded and therefore that they shall not come for their own coast but put in the 1st and best[151] harbour they can. And that they

[146] For this see *C&P*, II, p. 341.

[147] For Drew see Capp, *Cromwell's Navy*, p. 170n.

[148] There follows in longhand a set of instructions in Dutch (Worc. MS XXV, fo. 105^{r-v}) of which the next document is a translation. Drew's statement is found in longhand in Worc. MS LXXXVI, fo. 81^{v}. On 20 September 1653 Robert Lilburne wrote to Cromwell about the large number of foreign vessels which used Bressay Sound, suggesting that it 'may easily be secured by a very small Fort' (*ibid.*, fo. 111^{v}).

[149] In the original Dutch, 'Dirk Jans Dyck'; Worc. MS XXV, fo. 105^{r}.

[150] Blank.

[151] Or 'best and 1st'; in Clarke's shorthand the two words are indistinguishable.

accordingly regulate themselves and that you shew colour commands to all you weather.

In Amsterdam *Adij 2 July 1653*

by us the deputed[152] by the Lord Burgomaster

of Amsterdam

William Clarke to Gilbert Mabbott, [Westminster], 28 July 1653

*fo. [106]^r^*

<Letter to my brother Mabbott concerning my letter to Master Malyn being read in the Council>[153]

Dear Brother

I received thine of the 23th instant and thank thee for thy advice to me and care expressed of me therein. I [must/should] confess I did not expect that letter of mine to Master Malyn should have come to so publike a scanning which perhaps may give offence to those gentlemen named therein. But for the truth of what I have written concerning the treasury and forces here, Master Bilton will make it clear, so that I believe neither Captain B. nor C.D.[154] will have much to say to the contrary. For my expressions in relation to the design of bringing in free quarter here, if it have not happened before this time, no thank to them, for had not the officers ~~but~~ and[155] the soldiers most of the money they have or can raise, it must necessarily have fallen out. And now what shall [do/not] the poor soldiers [. . .] any man might easily imagine, having received no pay since the muster of 2d of May and the field forces (most of them) lying abroad having nothing but biskit and cheese and the want of money to buy drink and other [conveniencies] too.[156] It makes many of them to fall sick, all which if the enemy in the

[152] Blank.

[153] Marginated. A letter written by Clarke on 14 July 1653 was referred on 21 July by the Council of State to the Irish and Scotch Committee; *CSPD 1653–1654*, p. 40.

[154] Presumably Capts John Blackwell and [Richard] Deane (cousin of the admiral of the same name), joint Treasurers-at-War and Receivers-General of the Assessment, both of whom were to be consulted about Clarke's letter; *ibid.*, p. 40; *SS*, p. 99.

[155] '[A]nd' superimposed upon 'but'.

[156] Robert Lilburne had written to Cromwell in the same vein a month earlier (*S&C*, p. 149). Years later Monck would place a similar emphasis on the importance of maintaining adequate supplies; George Monck, duke of Albemarle, *Observations upon Military & Political Affairs* (London, 1671), ch. 16, esp. p. 77.

Highlands should have made any bustle this summer (which they are designing)[157] might have been of ill consequence. Besides that just upon the late [revolution][158] the treasurers should [forget] the returning of money from hence and have not the least care of sending down supplies any other way to the soldiers [~~to me [without] the ill favourability~~] but answered the desires of supply with disputes [to me . . . the ill favourability] and would not have [occasioned] well with others. And therefore I think my zeal for the publike good herein should not to be construed to my prejudice. You may acquaint what friends you think good, either of yours or mine, with these particulars and if you consult with Master Bilton[159] he will give you fuller satisfaction then I shall need to [. . .] in a letter. However it happen [*liberas omnium meum*].

William Clarke to George Bilton, [London], 28 July 1653[160]

fo. [106]^{r}

<Abstract of the letter to Master Bilton about the same business>[161]

Dear Father

I believe before this you have seen what a dust [. . .] pour upon their [. . .] the while has raised (as to the regiments of some). My earnest writing for a supply of the forces here may peradventure quicken those at the helm for giving order therein though not intended by me to have come to the perusal of so [high] a [council] which has given offence to some. Yet I think there was nothing writ but what you can make good, the necessities of the forces here making me more quick and something too rigid against some persons in my private letter. Yet since it is done I hope the best story will be made of my zeal for the publike therein in which I know I shall have thy [assistance], only please to hint how high B.[162] takes it etc.

[157] Intelligence had recently been received by the Scottish headquarters that the highland chiefs were currently gathering for the royalist-inspired rising which had been in preparation since 1652; *C&P*, II, pp. 389–397; *S&C*, pp. 161–165.

[158] Presumably a reference to the dissolution of the Rump on 20 April 1653.

[159] For George Bilton see also the following document.

[160] Although Bilton (for whom see *SS*, p. 145) was based in Scotland, it appears that at this time he was in London (p. 95). For his spectacular downfall see p. 264 below.

[161] Marginated.

[162] Probably Capt. John Blackwell (as above).

Newsletter from Gilbert Mabbott, Westminster, 2 August 1653

fo. [108]v

Yesterday letters came from the governor of Deal Castle that by 2 ships lately come in he informed that the fleet ingaged on Thursday last.[163] One of them saw both fleets draw up for ingagement. The other saw them actually ingaged.

Upon a report yesterday from the Council of State, the House ordered that 500*l* per annum be settled upon the earl of Derby and his heirs from his late father's estate. They referred the grievance of granting wine licenses to a committee, passed the act for taking away fines upon bills, declarations and original writs and committed the bill for restraint of appeals from courts in Ireland to commissioners in England. A petition was this day presented to the House in the name of many thousands apprentices and young men in London and Westminster on the behalf of Lieutenant-Colonel John Lilburne.[164] The House ordered the petition a breach of privilege, scandalous and seditious and the printers and authors thereof to be secured. Lieutenant-Colonel Lilburne to be committed close prisoner and not receive [benefit] of pen, ink or paper and referred the examination of the design therein to the Council of State. There are [now/new] preparations to proceed against him the next sessions. The rest of the day was spent in passing the bills for taking away fines upon original writs.[165]

Gilbert Mabbott

Newsletter from George Downing, Whitehall, 2 August 1653[166]

fo. [108]v

The Parliament has passed an act against fines on original writs. Also read an act against appeals to the court of justice in Ireland to the

[163] This was the battle of the Texel, during which the pro-Orangist Dutch admiral, Martin van Tromp, was killed; *C&P*, II, pp. 346–347; p. 101 below.

[164] *To the Parliament of the Commonwealth of England. The humble petition of divers wel-affected, and constant adherers* . . . (London, 1653).

[165] For all these items of parliamentary business see *CJ*, VII, pp. 293–294, 1–2 August 1653, which, however, omits the clause depriving Lilburne of writing materials.

[166] While the two letters differ in detail, all the items of news in this newsletter were reported by Mabbott on the same day (previous document).

courts here. This day a high peremptory petition was delivered by 6 apprentices in the name of many apprentices on behalf of John Lilburne.[167] Being asked their names who delivered it they replied they had not his charge from those that sent them to answer to queries and refused. The Parliament ordered them to the Sergeant, the petition to be burnt by the hangman and the business to be examined further by a committee and John Lilburne be to be [*sic*] close prisoner.[168]

Saturday came a ketch from our fleet that saith Friday and Saturday till night our fleet was ingaged with Tromp we being 120 sayle and he 80. That then De Witt was not come in. We also have sent 12 sayle of frigots from Harwich.[169]

From Paris came news that Burdieux is delivered but no news thereof from Burdieux.[170]

George Downing

[William Clarke] to [John] Rushworth, 4 August 1653

fo. 109^{v}

<Letter to Master Rushworth [by] Commissary Eldred>[171]

Honoured Sir

Having so great a favour offered to me as to receive an invitation from your own hand for my meeting of your [*sic*] at Morpeth the 8th instant, I cannot but return my hearty thanks and assure you that I should have esteemed it a very great happiness to have seen ~~your~~ the[172] face of one whom I so much honour, and whom I should esteem it the greatest happiness to be in a capacity to serve, ~~but in regard I am not now my own man~~ though with the [neglect/necessity] of my greatest particular concernment. But being not at my own disposal and many businesses ~~of the commander-in-chief~~, besides my attendance

[167] *To the Parliament of the Commonwealth of England. The humble petition of divers wel-affected and constant adherers.*

[168] For all this, see *CJ*, VII, pp. 293–294 (1–2 August 1653). Lilburne's imprisonment was reported in the newsbooks, e.g., *Mercurius Politicus*, 164 (28 July–4 Aug 1653), p. 2625.

[169] Confirmed by *ibid.*, pp. 2624–2625.

[170] Possibly based on an intercepted letter of 6 August 1653, N.S.; *TSP*, I, p. 380. A report from Bordeaux appeared in *Mercurius Politicus* the following week; 165 (4–11 Aug. 1653), p. 2630.

[171] Marginated. Eldred was commissary of provisions at Leith; Chequers MS, 782, unfol., entries for 20 June 1653, 22 August 1653; *S&P*, pp. 299–300, 398. In December 1653 he was in London; *S&C*, p. 288.

[172] '[T]he' superimposed upon 'your'.

on the commander-in-chief[173] lying upon me, I must humbly crave your excuse pardon [*sic*] that I cannot <now>[174] wait upon you ~~which was and remain~~ but by these lines only [to testify] the desire I have to express <myself>[175] your most obliged [humble] servant.[176]

Newsletter from Newcastle, 5 August 1653[177]

fo. 110^{r}

Right Honourable

The wind having been fair these 5 days to bring ships from the south, and there being already some 300 sayle arrived at this place, and they severally giving us good intelligence from our fleet, I thought it my duty to impart the certain news, which is that on Tuesday last Master Wiseman, with other masters coming by Yarmouth roads about 10 hours in the morning, spied a galliot hoy with her flag [by] her main top and her colours out, making for our shore. They bore up to know what news. They told them that on Thursday the 28th of July, Vantromp with 90 sayle came forth from the Wielings, and that Friday, at 4 in the afternoon, our fleet ingaged them and fought [whilst] 9 at night. Saturday, the seas were so high that they could do nothing. Sunday morning by 5 hours, both fleets were hotly ingaged and so continued very sharply until night parted them, and Monday the 1st instant they fell to it again until 4 in the evening and then the Dutch ran for it. General Monck sent some to pursue and <drew>[178] the rest in a body, but Tromp was [as shortly] in port, for he making for the Texel one squadron for that guard put him by. Only 3 got in to join with De Witt who all this time was locked up with a north-east wind. At night General Monck with this galliot hoy away with an express to

[173] i.e. Robert Lilburne.

[174] Interlined.

[175] Interlined.

[176] Two months previously Robert Lilburne had invited Rushworth to become agent in London for the Scottish officers, an appointment given to Clarke's brother-in-law William Cary on 13 August 1653 (Worc. MS LXXXVI, fo. 90^{v}); it is tempting to speculate that this may explain Rushworth's wish to see Clarke. Rushworth was born near Morpeth, and though based in London from the early 1640s kept up his connection with the North throughout his life. Business commitments in Newcastle around this time may explain his presence in the area; *DNB*, 'Rushworth'; R. Howell, *Newcastle upon Tyne and the Puritan Revolution* (Oxford, 1967), pp. 296, 308.

[177] Though differing in some details, in general this account of the battle of the Texel is confirmed by Monck's report of 31 July to the Commissioners of the Admiralty; *Mercurius Politicus*, 164 (28 July–4 Aug. 1653), p. [2628].

[178] Interlined.

my Lord General, who landed it at Winterton[179] on Tuesday and says that from the Dutch we have taken bounty and sunk 35 sayle.[180]

Newsletter from John Rogers, [5] August 1653[181]

fo. 110r

From London thus

The fleets [were/are] ingaged and that young Tromp has taken the Harry Bonaventure (a merchantman in the State's service) with a prize newly taken by her in the Straights worth 12,000*l*. The French packet informs Burdieux to be delivered up to the king, and with it the life of the Condé-ish interest in France which is imputed to the [dull] production of the Spanish councils who will not alter the pace of their affected gravity upon any emergency [effecting world [...] too late].[182] Their ambassador was by [permission] bargaining with some merchants here to do that in few weeks which themselfs could not effect in many months.

Our treaty with the Dutch agents is concluded *re infecta*.[183] Whether it will be renewed upon the event of this ingagement time will shew. The chief points insisted on are satisfaction, security and co-alliance.[184] They would not understand what was meant by the 1st but were willing to depute 1 or 200,000*l* for quietness' sake. The 2d would not in any case be admitted of because it would open a door to us to overrun the country at pleasure. The last being an hard word and understood by them for 'collation' they sent to know what was meant by collation, which their Highnesses had a better stomach to than an incorporation with us, though [time/that] may tell [them/that] it is a greater privilege then they deserve.

179 Winterton, Norfolk, was used as a landmark by Vice-Admiral William Penn; *Perfect Diurnall*, 176 (18–25 Apr. 1653), p. 2664. After this battle the English fleet made for Southwold Bay, just to its south; *Mercurius Politicus*, 165 (4–11 Aug. 1653), p. 2638.

180 The Dutch losses were in fact calculated at twenty-six ships; *C&P*, II, p. 348.

181 This newsletter from London appears to have been sent from Newcastle, and was perhaps enclosed with the preceding document.

182 The Spanish force retreated from Bordeaux in late July; *TSP*, I, p. 363.

183 On 3 August 1653 two of the Dutch deputies, Jongestall and Nieupoort, had returned to report to the States General. Their meetings were held in strict secrecy; *ibid.*, pp. 414, 419, 420, 439; *C&P*, II, pp. 345–346.

184 The substitution of this word for the more usual 'coalition' detracts somewhat from the sneering pun later in this paragraph. The English demand – that the only acceptable alternative to open war was union between the two nations – caused disbelief and outrage among the Dutch; Pincus, *Protestantism and Patriotism*, pp. 137–142.

This day which was Tuesday some prentices petitioned for John Lilburne's liberty. [I rest thereon]

Newcastle John Rogers[185]

Newsletter from George Downing, Westminster, 11 August 1653

*fo. 112*r

Yesterday another petition was presented in behalf of Lieutenant-Colonel Lilburne.[186] The Parliament upon a report from the Council has ordered that a new High Court of Justice shall be erected.[187] This afternoon Lieutenant-Colonel Lilburne is to be tried.[188]

A little before the [fight][189] the province of Holland did declare against a stadtholder and that no foreign prince did come within their dominions without licence, since there are great hurly-burlies.[190] They have 94 sayle of their 125 arrived at the Texel and Goeree.[191] Tromp is certainly killed with a musket bullet under the left pap.[192] It's written that De Win[193] is stabbed by his own captain after they were within the Texel. All preparations are making there for a new fleet.

George Downing

[185] The well-known Fifth Monarchy preacher John Rogers had by now returned from Dublin to St Thomas Apostle's in London. There is no way of knowing whether it was he who sent this letter. Another man of the same name was a preacher in Barnard Castle; Capp, *Fifth Monarchy Men*, p. 261; Howell, *Newcastle upon Tyne and the Puritan Revolution*, pp. 220n, 372.

[186] *CJ* makes no reference to this petition, R. Willis, *A Voyce from the Heavenly Word of God... in the behalf of Mr John Lilburne* (London, 1653); the document may have been circulated to MPs privately.

[187] *CJ*, VII, p. 297.

[188] On the preceding day Parliament ordered that the order for Lilburne's close imprisonment be rescinded in order that he could come to trial (*ibid.*).

[189] i.e. the battle of the Texel.

[190] It is not clear whether this phrase belongs to the previous or to the following sentence. Holland was one of the states which refused to elect the infant William III stadtholder in succession to his father, William II (d. 1650); J. Israel. *The Dutch Republic: Its Rise, Greatness, and Fall* (Oxford, 1995), pp. 720–721.

[191] The figures are close to those reported from Paris on 22 August 1653 N.S.; *TSP*, I, p. 413.

[192] The entry point of the bullet was deemed by one correspondent to be particularly appropriate as 'that cabinet where the wicked thoughts of beginning this warre were first harboured'; *Mercurius Politicus*, 166 (11–18 Aug. 1653), p. 2655.

[193] A rumour only, as reported from The Hague on 22 August 1653 N.S. (*TSP*, I, p. 412). Witte De With, Dutch Vice-Admiral, lived until 1658.

Newsletter from London, 12 August 1653

fo. 113ʳ

Brief of some passages against John Lilburne gentleman, at the sessions upon Friday and Saturday the 12th and 13th of August 1653.[194]

On Friday about 4 of the clock he was brought into the court where he demanded oyer of the Parliament against him and also of the offences that he had committed for which he was banished but they said they could or would not shew them, and he did earnestly urge and desire them according to law which they absolutely denied him.

Whereupon he absolutely denied that there were any judgement, act of Parliament or offences by him committed for which he was banished, and further said that he was never called legally to answer for himself or to answer to any accusations or to speak or answer to any thing for any offence committed by him against the law or against any man, nor never committed any felony or ever was summoned or called to hear judgement, nor did ever know nor can believe that ever any such act or judgement was or could lawfully be pressed against him; and whereas the day before oath was made by the Clerk of Parliament's clerk that there was no rule or record of that act in Parliament, but only in pieces of paper scratched and interlined. Yet this day there was a pretended act brought in by the Clerk of the Parliament which [he] will or was accorded and the prisoner was [asked] and urged to plead to that act presently and to put himself to the jury of which new found act and a [certiorari] brought with it Lilburne did earnestly desire a copy and time to be advised by his council what to plead unto it. And they answered him that if he would acknowledge that to be an act of Parliament and waive his former exceptions he should have longer time and copies, which he yielded unto, and then they would give him no longer time than until this Saturday at 2 a clock. /And

fo. 113ᵛ

And about 6 a clock this evening he was sent for again and much pressed to come to an issue and [put] himself to the jury and he said he could not hazard himself to a jury as long as the law was firm for

[194] Reports of Lilburne's trial which appeared almost all the principal newsbooks (although not in the official *Severall Proceedings in Parliament*) confirm the details of both this and the following account. *The Tryall of Mr Iohn Lilburne at the Sessions House in the Old Baily. Together with a diurnal of each days proceedings, in order to his tryal, 13 July to 13 Aug. Taken in Short-hand* (London, 1653), purporting to be written by an anonymous eye-witness, is much less detailed than either of the descriptions reproduced here and is unlikely to have come from either of these sources. The Council of State was required to examine the shorthand reports of the trial; *CJ*, VII, pp. 306, 309.

him without a jury and then he pressed hard again for oyer of the said judgement and causes of his crime for which they demanded he was banished and withall he put in a new plea to the said act and desired longer time for him and his counsel to consider of it and they have given him a further time until Tuesday next at 2 a clock.

Those that are his judges and councillors against him did hear and press things so extremely against his life that it was generally held to be far more than men in their place in case of life usually [do/did] or by law ought to do, so that many would honour and pity him for his so standing to maintain his life and the fundamental laws.

Newsletter from London, 13 August 1653

fo. 113^{v}

From another thus

Coming to the Old Bailey I found numbers of people attending the trial of Lieutenant-Colonel Lilburne, generally supposing this would have been his fatal day. I got as near as it was then possible and then clambering up upon the wall could see into the court and catch at some syllables but not considerable to make any conclusion thereon. Yet it was something observable to see how the people's [emotions] fell and rose, for in the middle of the business some soldiers that were in Holborn or Fleet Street near hand discharged 2 or 3 vollies whereby it was supposed that soldiers begirt them round, and that sentence would this night pass upon him. Indeed like Aesop's hares[195] the most part were full of fears and some went away. At last the court caused the officer to call the jury and then [I dare say every man's heart] (near me) thrilled within him for fear they were then to be impanelled. But it proved to be only to summon them to appear again on Monday and that the lieutenant-colonel should come again on Tuesday about 2 of the clock. At which there was a sudden [apparition/operation] of zeal and much [advice] to [stand to] in their acclamations, but that some fully fear it might rather prejudice then do otherwise and appear in contempt of the court. Yet when he appeared without the guard in the Old Bailey they could not so well contain themselfs, but as formerly raised another [shot/shout] and so conducted him to the prison. *Nihil est infelicius eo cuj unquam contigit Adversi.*

But truly I should desire only to have a smack of it but not always to drink it in my cup.

[195] A reference to the fable of the hares and the frogs; B.E. Perry (ed.), *Babrius and Phaedrus*, (London, 1965), p. 37.

William Clarke to Gilbert Mabbott, [Westminster], 8 September 1653

fo. 124^{r}

<To my brother Mabbott>[196]

Dear Brother

This gentleman, Major Fitzpayne Fisher, having been about some 10 months in Scotland about the transmitting of the history of the wars here, which he intends to write in Latin heroick verse[197] ~~and being having some occasion now to repair to the Council of State~~ and in that time having had much knowledge ~~of~~ and[198] experience of him, I cannot but recommend him unto your acquaintance as a gentleman who for his learning and integrity will merit what favour you can shew unto him. I remain

William Clarke to [Richard] Hatter, [Westminster], 8 September 1653

fo. 124^{r}

<To Master Hatter>[199]

My dear Bro

Having had 10 months' knowledge of this gentleman, Major Fitzpayne Fisher, in Scotland, and finding him to be both likeable and honest, I cannot but recommend him to ~~your~~ the[200] ~~acquaintance and that thou wilt show him~~ knowledge of my friends, not doubting but thou wilt find ~~a [. . .] of benefit and~~ him worthy of thy acquaintance, and what civility you shall shew unto him shall be acknowledged as done unto

your affectionate [serv] friend and servant

W.C.

[196] Marginated.

[197] Fisher had travelled to Scotland in September 1652, and in January 1653 wrote asking for assistance for this project (which had the official blessing of the Council of State) from the then commander-in-chief in Scotland, Maj.-Gen. Richard Deane; *CSPD 1651–1652*, pp. 366, 367, 573; *S&C*, pp. 75–77. I am most grateful to Professor David Norbrook for information about Fisher.

[198] '[A]nd' superimposed upon 'of'.

[199] Marginated.

[200] '[T]he' superimposed upon 'your'.

William Clarke to William Malyn, [Westminster], 9 September 1653

fo. 124^{v}

<To Master Malyn in recommendation of Major Fisher>[201]

Honoured Sir

This ~~bearer~~ gentleman, Major Fitzpaine Fisher being <upon his coming down in England [following] 10 months here>[202] recommended to ~~the Commander in Chief in~~ Major-General Deane by some members of the late Council of State[203] ~~upon his coming down in for his [. . .]~~ for what incouragement and information could be given him concerning the proceedings in Scotland from the army's 1st advance hither, he intending to commit to posterity ~~the affairs thereof and the~~ the affairs thereof in Latin heroick verse. And having had experience of his integrity and industry for the completion ~~thereof~~ of that history in which some materials are wanting that have drawn him up to London, where he will stay for some time, I am desirous to recommend him unto you to shew him what favour you may in any of his addresses unto his Excellency, whereby you will very much cherish <and incourage him [in/his]>[204] ~~[. . .] a gentleman [. . .] and oblige [. . .]~~ commendable indeavour, and very much oblige

yours etc.

Newsletter from Westminster, 10 September 1653

fo. 125^{r}

The bill for sale of papists' estates is ordered to be brought in.[205]

The Protestants in Languedoc having declined the nomination have chosen a gentleman to be their general.[206] The court has ordered the *Comte de Rieux* being prosecuted for having disturbed their synod at *Vals* and that their church be [refuge] and that the edict at Nantes be punctually observed. Thoren's[207] army [musters]. It's decreased within a month 6,000 and had been in a mutiny for pay had not the king

201 Marginated.
202 Interlined.
203 *CSPD 1651–1652*, p. 367.
204 Interlined.
205 *CJ*, VII, p. 317.
206 This was the Sieur de Cassagne; *TSP*, I, p. 454.
207 i.e. Marshal Turenne.

come among them. De Win[208] set sayle with 55 men of war and 200 merchantmen from the Texel on Wednesday was sennight towards the Sound. Amsterdam has possessed themselves of Enchusen by men in hired boats.[209]

Memorandum, 14 September 1653

fo. [127]^r

From Aberdeen there came in a little man of war who had taken 2 Dutch vessels; most of the men he has put ashore here to go towards London.[210]

Newsletter from Gilbert Mabbott, Westminster, 20 September 1653[211]

fo. [130]^r

Yesterday the House ordered that a bill should be brought in Tuesday sennight by the committee for the law for settling the business for probate of wills throughout the parts of this Commonwealth. The Committee for the Admiralty was ordered to bring in a bill for sale and disposal of prizes in some better way than that service is yet performed. They have likewise ordered to consider how the inequality of taxes upon the several counties of this Commonwealth may be rectified, and this is referred to a grand committee of the whole House. This day the House ordered that there be an offer of Hampton Court to his Excellency in exchange for New Hall upon a proportionable value. A committee was appointed to consider how forest lands may be sold.[212]

Gilbert Mabbott

[208] i.e. Witte De With (as on p. 101).

[209] All these news items are confirmed by other foreign correspondence; *Mercurius Politicus*, 168 (25 Aug.–1 Sept. 1653), p. 2699; 169 (1–8 Sept. 1653), p. 2717; 170 (8–15 Sept. 1653), pp. 2729, 2731; 171 (15–22 Sept. 1653), p. 2749; *TSP*, I, pp. 446, 447, 454, 459.

[210] For this incident see *Perfect Diurnall*, 199 (26 Sept.–2 Oct. 1653), p. 3035, which confirms that the prisoners were landed at Aberdeen. Bulstrode Whitelocke also noted it; Whitelock, *Memorials*, IV, p. 39.

[211] Mabbott sent a virtually identical letter to the mayor and aldermen of Hull on the same day (Hull CRO, BRL 591).

[212] *CJ*, VII, pp. 320–322, (19–20 September 1642) confirms all these items of parliamentary news.

Newsletter from Gilbert Mabbott, Westminster, 24 September 1653[213]

fo. 132^{v}

Wednesday the House ordered that the committee for inspections should give order to the Commissioners of the Excise to farm the excise of such counties in England and Wales for 3 months as they shall think fit to the best advantage of the State so as they farm them not at less value then formerly. The bill for relief of creditors was read the 2nd time and recommitted. A bill was ordered to be brought in for sequestering the estates of such as are delinquents since the 30th January 1648[214] and for allowing a 6th part to any that shall make such discovery of any such delinquents. The bill for Ireland was ordered to be read tomorrow. Thursday the Irish bill was read. A clause was referred to be inserted therein for erecting a mint in Ireland for certain years, but passed in the negative. This was the business of the whole day. Friday the House considered of several propositions in order to the sale of forest lands, and thereupon ordered a bill to be brought in to that purpose. A committee was appointed for preservation of the customs and to prevent the deceits and abuses therein. The petition of the officers of the army and supernumeraries whose arrears are comprized in the late king's lands and the forest lands left as an additional security is referred to a committee. The House this day spent all night upon the Irish bill and ordered the consideration thereof to be resumed Monday next.[215]

Gilbert Mabbott

Captain Chillenden has lost his commission for getting a wench with bairn,[216] and Lieutenant-Colonel Joyce committed to the marshal-general for saying he wished Lockier had fired when he presented the pistol against his Excellency.[217]

[213] Mabbott sent a virtually identical letter (but omitting the postscript) to the mayor and aldermen of Hull on the same day (Hull CRO, BRL 592).

[214] i.e. 30 January 1649, the date of the execution of Charles I.

[215] *CJ*, VII, pp. 322–324 (21–24 September 1653) confirms all these items of parliamentary business.

[216] *OxDNB*, 'Chillenden'. No doubt the authorities were glad to get rid of Chillenden, a Fifth Monarchist, who was becoming increasingly engaged in subversive activities; F&D, I, pp. 226–227. Both Clarke and Mabbott knew him and were mustered in his troop; p. 18 above; *L-P*, pp. 102, 104–105.

[217] *CClarSP*, II, p. 254 (newsletter of 16 September 1653). The army Leveller Robert Lockyer was executed for his part in the mutiny of April 1649 (*OxDNB*, 'Lockyer'). Joyce describes his own imprisonment and subsequent cashiering in G. Joyce, *A True Narrative of*

Newsletter from George Downing, Westminster, 27 September 1653

*fo. [134]*r

Yesterday the general[218] gave in his answer to the offer of the Parliament touching the exchange of Hampton Court for New Hall, wherein he acknowledgeth the great respects of the Parliament towards him therein and desireth that they would dispose thereof according to their former resolution. The Parliament ordered thereupon that Hampton Court with the outhouses and gardens and little park be stayed from sale.

The act for satisfying the adventurers and soldiers in Ireland is passed. The bill for the High Court of Justice is to be brought in on Wednesday next. The bill for relief of creditors and prisoners is ordered to be ingrossed. The countess dowager of Derby is admitted to her composition.[219]

This day the general went to Wollage to see the Swiftsure launched and to meet General Monck.[220]

George Downing

Newsletter from Gilbert Mabbott, Westminster, 1 October 1653

*fo. [135]*r

Wednesday the House sat in a grand committee touching the equalities of taxes, and ordered the consideration thereof to be committed this day fortnight. The question was put that the bill for erecting a High Court of Justice should be reported tomorrow. It passed in the negative. A petition from Hampshire for continuance of tithes was read.[221] The answer was that their business was under consideration, and that they would do therein as God should direct them. <Judge Mosley's words>.[222] Thursday the bill touching wills and administrations was read the 2nd time and committed. A bill for better [electing/election]

the Occasions & Courses ([London, 1659]), pp. 3–4. Though it appeared in 1659, Clarke chose to bind his copy with pamphlets of 1653, listing it under that year.

[218] i.e. Cromwell (see p. 106 above).

[219] *CJ*, VII, pp. 324–325 (26–27 September 1653) confirms all these items of parliamentary business.

[220] For the launching of the *Swiftsure* from Woolwich, see *CClarSP*, II, p. 264.

[221] *CJ*, VII, pp. 325–326.

[222] Marginated. Edward Moseley was one of seven Commissioners for the Administration of Justice in Scotland appointed in April 1652; *CSPD 1651–1652*, p. 210. He remained there

of jurors was twice read and committed. Friday the House passed the bill for accounts and publike debts which was the business of the day.

The many thousands of weddings that have been in London this week (the new act for marriages taking place yesterday) is incredible. [. . .] reported General Monck is come hither thereupon.[223] We have many considerable squadrons upon the coast of Holland and elsewhere.

This day General Monck took his place in Parliament as a member.[224] The Speaker gave him the thanks of the House. An act was twice read inabling the Committee of the Army to take the account of the soldiers from 1647 to July 1653.[225] The rest of the day was spent upon private business.[226]

Gilbert Mabbott

News from London, 6 October 1653

*fo. [137]*r

Tomorrow my Lord General and the officers of the army entertain the sea officers.

Newsletter from George Downing, Westminster, [8] October 1653

*fo. [138]*r

Friday *October* 7

The act for accounts and clearing of public debts and for discovery of frauds or concealments of any thing due to the Commonwealth this

during the 1650s, and was still in this position in March 1660; Dow, *Cromwellian Scotland*, pp. 55, 59, 176, 221–222, 261. He may have acted as a messenger from Monck to Fairfax in York in November 1659; Worc. MS XLIX, fo. [110]V.

[223] This act, which was to be effective from 30 September, was passed on 24 August 1653; *A&O*, II, pp. 715–718. It decreed that only marriages performed before a Justice of the Peace would be formally recognized. This newsletter suggests that Monck had married Ann Radford (née Clarges) in a civil ceremony some months before their wedding at St George's, Southwark on 23 January 1654. This is supported by a London correspondent who in October 1653 wrote that Cromwell strongly disapproved of Monck's marriage; J.D.G. Davies, *Honest George Monck* (London, 1936), pp. 130–131; *CClarSP*, II, p. 266.

[224] The honours conferred upon Monck and the other admirals after the battle of the Texel are described in *Mercurius Politicus*, 165 (4–11 Aug. 1653), p. 2641.

[225] More precisely, from 5 October 1647–25 July 1653; *CJ*, VII, pp. 327–328.

[226] *Ibid.*, pp. 325–328 (28 September–1 October 1653) confirms all these items of parliamentary business.

day passed. The bill for the union of Scotland to be read on Tuesday next.

Saturday 8

The bill concerning recusants for disposing of 2 parts of their estates ordered to be ingrossed.[227]

George Downing

Newsletter from Gilbert Mabbott, [Westminster], [8] October 1653[228]

fo. 139^{r}

Wednesday the House passed the bill for relief of creditors and poor prisoners which was the business of the whole day. Thursday it was referred to the committee for prisoners to make a general inquiry of all persons that are in prison for criminal causes and the several causes of their commitment. And they have power to send into the counties for the copies of the records and mittimuses upon which any were imprisoned with the copies of the examinations and informations, and report matter of fact to the House. The captain of the Elizabeth frigot bringing 20 Dutch merchants into our ports and beating off 3 men of war that were their convoy, the House referred it to the Council of State to give him a gratuity and provide for the wife and children of his master, slain in that service.[229] Friday the House passed the bill for accounts and public debts.[230] This day an act passed inabling the commissioners of Haberdashers' Hall to compound with recusants at a 4th or else that their estates be exposed to sale. The House confirmed Alderman Viner[231] Lord Maior of London.[232]

Gilbert Mabbott

[227] *Ibid.*, pp. 331–332 (7–8 October 1653) confirms all the items in this newsletter.

[228] Mabbott sent a virtually identical letter (now in a fragile condition and partly missing) to the mayor and aldermen of Hull on the same day (Hull CRO, BRL 595).

[229] *CJ*, VII, p. 331, simply records the payments, omitting the account of the *Elizabeth's* exploits; see also *CSPD 1653–1654*, p. 189. The letter written to the Council of State on 4 October 1653 by the ship's captain, Christopher Myngs, is printed in *Severall Proceedings of Parliament*, 12 (4–11 Oct. 1653), p. 151. See also *OxDNB*, 'Myngs'.

[230] Here Hull CRO, BRL 595 inserts 'The rest of the day was . . . upon pr[ivate] business'.

[231] Thomas Vyner.

[232] *CJ*, VII, pp. 330–331 (5–9 October 1653) confirms all the items of parliamentary news in this letter.

Newsletter from George Downing, Westminster, [11] October 1653

fo. 139^{v}

Monday 8bris 10. An order inserting several persons[233] in the act of naturalization. Ordered that the petition of divers congregated churches be committed to the committee for tithes.[234] Ordered that there shall be a declaration for giving fitting liberty[235] to all that fear God within this Commonwealth. General Blake came to the House and took his place as a member. Ordered that there be an act for the taking away the powers of the former committee of the <former publike>[236] revenue except such augmentations to ministers as the Council of State shall approve of.

Tuesday 11th

The bill for incorporating Scotland into one free state with England read the 2nd time and committed to a grand committee of the whole House.

Instructions for Bulstrode Whitelocke, Lord Commissioner of the Seal, for his embassy to the queen of Sweden agreed.[237]

Almost all our men of war to the westward are come in with prizes,[238] the Assistance 1 or 2, the Warwick 1, the Nightingale 1, the Pearl 2.[239] The Sapphire met with a fleet of French of 9 sayle, fought them from 7 in the morning till 8 at night, took the St John of Grace of St Malo, vice-admiral, 300 tuns, 22 guns, 80 men, of which 14 slain, the captain, lieutenant and 15 others wounded. Most of them [....] of full bulk with linen cloth; the Three Kings, rear-admiral, 260 tun, 10 guns, 50 men, in which 40 tons of wheat, the rest linen cloth; the Sea Flower, 80 tuns, 2 guns a victualler of ours taken by them and now retaken, laden with beef and pork. The Sapphire had only 4 men slain. Our lieutenant, boatswain and 5 were mortally wounded.[240]

George Downing

[233] Listed by name in *ibid.*, p. 332.

[234] This petition, printed in *Mercurius Politicus*, 174 (6–13 Oct. 1653), pp. 2788–[2791], came from the congregational churches in the northern counties; it is discussed in Woolrych, *C–P* (pp. 333–334).

[235] i.e. liberty of conscience.

[236] Interlined.

[237] *CJ*, VII, pp. 332–333 (10–11 October 1653) confirms all this parliamentary news.

[238] In shorthand, 'prices'.

[239] For the prizes taken by the *Warwick*, *Nightingale*, and *Pearl*, see *Perfect Diurnall*, 201 (9–16 Oct. 1653), p. 3059.

[240] A report of the engagement involving the *Sapphire*, written by her commander Capt. Nicholas Heaton, appears in *Mercurius Politicus*, 174 (6–13 Oct. 1653), pp. [2793]–2794. It is also noted in Whitelock, *Memorials*, IV, p. 41.

Newsletter from George Downing, Westminster, [15] October 1653

fo. [142][r]

Friday 14 *October*

Resolved that the next assessment throughout the nation shall be in a fixed sum on each county and shall be levied by a pound rate upon the estates real and personal, and to make it particular referred to the Committee of the Army.

Saturday

Commissioners appointed by the act for accounts etc. shall have use of the Duchy House.[241]

Resolved that the proceedings in Chancery be adjourned for one month longer, original writs to be issued out under the Great Seal notwithstanding.[242]

We shall speedily see whether a peace intended with Holland.[243]

George Downing

Newsletter from George Downing, Westminster, [18] October 1653

fo. 144[r]

Monday 17 *October*

Order that the bill for appointing a way to determine the present causes depending in Chancery be brought in on Wednesday next.

Tuesday 18

The House was in a grand committee to debate on the bill for the uniting and incorporating Scotland into one free state with England and sit again thereupon this day sennight.

[241] It was a quarrel over who should have the use of Worcester House which led to the Commissioners for Accounts and Public Debts being ordered to move to the Duchy (of Lancaster) House (*SS*, pp. 105–106).

[242] *CJ*, VII, pp. 334–335 (14–15 October 1653) confirms all this parliamentary news.

[243] Downing appears here to be referring to the imminent return of the Dutch commissioners Nieuport and Jongestal from their consultations in The Hague; *C&P*, II, pp. 345–346, 363; p. 100 above.

Letter from Ireland with some resolutions of the commissioners there read and referred to the Council of State.[244]

George Downing

Newsletter from Richard Hatter, Westminster, 22 October 1653

fo. 144v

Monday 17 *October* 1653. An act for stay of hearing causes in Chancery according to the 15th of June read and passed in the negative. Ordered that a bill be brought in for determining causes in Chancery. Tuesday a grand committee for uniting England and Scotland. Letters from the commissioners in Ireland with some resolutions inclosed referred to the Council of State. Wednesday an act for taking away the English Court or Court of Equity in Chancery and for appointing commissioners to hear and determine causes depending read in the House and committed. An act for taking away the ingagement read and laid aside, and ordered that an act be brought in for taking away the abuses of it in pleading [upon/to] stop of judgements etc.[245] An act for redemption of captives be brought in and an act for education of papists' children[246] in protestant religion. Thursday an act for discovery of thieves and highwaymen read twice and to be ingrossed. Friday an act for thieves passed and an act for sale of 2 parts of 3 of papists' estates for the benefit of the Commonwealth passed. Saturday a bill for the disforestation, sale and improvement of the forests and [*sic*] read the 1st time and ordered to be read the 2d time on Wednesday next. A bill for constituting commissioners for hearing and determining causes of equity in Chancery this day read and the question was for reading it the 2nd time. It passed in the negative.

Committee of the law to sit this afternoon upon the bill for the Chancery, which was committed, and to bring in the same with amendments on Monday morning.[247] Post business is to be reported on Monday.

[244] *CJ*, VII, pp. 335–336 (17–18 October 1653) confirms all these items of parliamentary news.

[245] The 'Act for Repealing of a Branch of a certain Act . . . for Subscribing the Engagement' (4 November 1653) specifically addressed this problem; *A&O*, II, pp. 774–775.

[246] Specifically, Irish children (*CJ*, VII, p. 336).

[247] *Ibid.*, pp. 335–338 (17–22 October 1653) confirms all these items of parliamentary business.

Joyce hard at it.[248] Many fault finders without just cause as is conceived.

Richard Hatter

Newsletter from Gilbert Mabbott, Westminster, 22 October 1653

fo. 144[v]

From another thus

2nd time no payment should be made out of the receipt of the revenue for 6 days. Thursday an act was read allowing 10*l*[249] to him that shall discover an highwayman. The letters credential and commission for the Lord Whitelocke to go ambassador for Sweden passed. The bill for highwaymen likewise passed.[250]

An imbargo is put upon all English vessels for one month.[251]

Gilbert Mabbott

Newsletter from George Downing, Westminster, 25 October 1653

fo. 145[r]

Report concerning the affairs of Scotland. Ordered that the commissioners nominated in the Commission for Administration of Justice (except Master March and Master Owen) are required to proceed in the execution of the several and respective commissions. Master Edward Hopkins and Master William Lawrence put into the commission instead of Master March and Master Owen. Master Alexander Pearson also to be put into the commission. Tuesday 25th

[248] George Joyce had been imprisoned about a month earlier (p. 107 above). He was now strenuously resisting attempts to force him to resign from the army, from which he was subsequently cashiered; Joyce, *A True Narrative of the Occasions and Causes* . . . , pp. 3–4.

[249] Though not defined in the official parliamentary record for this day, the sum is specified in the act; *CJ*, VII, p. 336; *A&O*, II, p. 773.

[250] *CJ*, VII, pp. 336–338 (19–21 October 1653) confirms all these items of parliamentary business.

[251] This was the general embargo placed on 19 October 1653 by the Council of State upon all vessels lying in the port of London; *CSPD 1653–1654*, p. 207.

the House was in a grand committee on the bill for uniting of Scotland and to sit again on a grand committee on Friday next.[252]

George Downing

Newsletter from George Downing, Westminster, [27] October 1653

fo. [147]v

Wednesday 26th 8bris 1653, bill for redress of delays and mischief arising from writs of error in several cases was this day read. Bill concerning the sale of forest lands twice read and committed. The minister from Sweden took his leave.[253] A bill to be brought in to make persons incapable of places that are suitors for places, and a bill for regulating of fees in courts of justice. Thursday amendments to the bill concerning the Chancery brought in and the bill with the amendments adjusted and other bills to be brought in on Tuesday next by the committee for the law.[254]

Yesterday many seamen gathering together in a mutinous way came to Whitehall. They were [quietly] answered and returned. This day they gathered about 1,000 of them upon Tower Hill where General Monck coming to them and demanding what they desired they gave him a petition in which they desired that for the future they may be pressed only by sea officers, and a course might speedily be taken to pay them their prize money, who told them both would be done, whereon they promised to return to their homes, which most of them did, except about 200 who marched thence to Whitehall, where General Monck meeting them drew upon them and fell to routing them. They presently ran. About 40 or 50 of them were wounded. Some of them will be made examples.[255]

George Downing

[252] *CJ*, VII, pp. 338–339 (24–25 October 1653) confirms all these items of parliamentary business.

[253] The Swedish ambassador, Lagerfeldt, travelled to Sweden around the same time as Cromwell's ambassador, Bulstrode Whitelocke, acting as a translator between Whitelocke and the queen of Sweden; R. Spalding, *The Improbable Puritan* (London, 1975), p. 160.

[254] *CJ*, VII, pp. 339–340 (26–27 October 1653) confirms these items of parliamentary news.

[255] *C&P*, II, pp. 360–361. After hearing Walter Strickland's report on the affair on the day following the riots, Parliament hurriedly amended the articles of war, to make such mutinies punishable by death; *CJ*, VII, pp. 340–341; *An Additional Article to the Laws of War and Ordinances of the Sea* (London, 1653).

Newsletter from Gilbert Mabbott, Westminster, 29 October 1653[256]

fo. [147]^{v}

From another thus

The act for sale of forests [*sic*] lands was read the 2d time and committed. They ordered that all persons who sought for any imployment shall be made incapable of having any [conferred upon/offered to] them. The queen of Sweden's agent had audience of a committee of Parliament and is gone over into Sweden with the Lord Whitelocke, our ambassador. Thursday the bill for hearing causes in Chancery was read and adjusted, and another ordered to be brought in.[257]

Our seamen having received their full pay randezvouzed on Tower Hill, where they concluded upon a petition – 1. that they might not be pressed by a land soldier, 2. that they may have what is due unto them for the prizes taken by them which the State thought fit to detain until they are again on shipboard. This petition was delivered to General Monck who [promised] his indeavours to have it granted, but 300 of many thousands of them being discontented came down to Charing Cross, where giving ill language and not retreating at his Excellency's and General Monck's command, some of the lifeguard fell on them and with little hurt dispersed them. Guards of horse and foot were left in several parts to prevent any mischief. Friday night they beat up their drum for another randevouz but few appeared.

They ordered the money impressed upon compositions for recusants' estates for the use of the navy. They passed the inclosed declaration and *X*[258]

fo. [148]^{r}

X and articles of war against seamen.[259] They voted the widows of the captains slain in the late fight considerable gratuities.[260] This

[256] Several of the news items from the previous document are repeated here. Mabbott's letter confirms the dates of the seamen's disturbances, and supports the conclusion that Downing wrote on 27 October previous document.

[257] *CJ*, VII, p. 340 (26–27 October 1653) reports all these items of parliamentary business.

[258] In Clarke's notebook the letter continues at '*X*' on the following page, after an intervening document.

[259] *An Additional Article to the Laws of War and Ordinances of the Sea.* The Council of State published its own proclamation on the affair; England, Council of State, *By the Council of State appointed by authority of Parliament. Whereas for the encouragement of Sea-men*... (London, 1653); *CSPD 1653–1654*, p. 219. It may be to this that Mabbott referred as a 'declaration'. The two broadsides survive in Clarke's collection of pamphlets, the second bearing a minor correction probably in Mabbott's hand.

[260] As requested by Monck in his letter of 2 August 1653, written from on board the *Resolution*, *A True Relation of the Last Great Fight at Sea* (London, 1653), p. 5.

day a bill for advance of trade was twice read. A report was made for the strengthening of the Isle of Wight. The Lord Commissioner Whitelocke took his leave this day of the House. An act for continuing the power of commissioners for compounding etc for advance of money and for indemnity. They ordered a bill to be brought in for settling powers touching indemnity in the several counties.[261]

Gilbert Mabbott

Newsletter from Danzig, 6 November 1653[262]

fo. 166v

Danzig, *6 November/6 December 1653*

This morning there arrived here a messenger from the king of Poland unto the lords, with mandates requiring them immediately without delay to secure the goods and persons of all English in this place for damages which some nuns received which were coming to the queen of Poland by the State's frigots. He expresseth in the general precious stones, rich goods for their church, linen and woollen [cloths/clothes], besides the abuse of the nuns, which he aggravates highly.[263]

[William Clarke] to Oliver Cromwell, [Whitehall], 15 November 1653

fo. 156v

To his Excellency etc,
the humble petition etc

sheweth

That whereas your petitioner being in England the latter end of March 1651, Master Richard Cadwell[264] then one of the messengers to the army ~~being~~ being in want of money, I desired that in regard the

[261] *CJ*, VII, pp. 340–342 (28–29 October 1653) reports all these items of parliamentary business.

[262] Apart from minor variations, this is a copy of part of the letter of intelligence sent from John Benson to John Thurloe; *TSP*, I, p. 579.

[263] 150 nuns travelling from France to Poland were brought into Dover on 19 August 1653 (*ibid.*, p. 431). In the event, the Senate of the city of Danzig, which owed only a nominal allegiance to the Polish king, John Casimir, was reluctant to accede to this request; *Mercurius Politicus*, 183 (9–16 Dec. 1653), p. 3027.

[264] Richard Cadwell had been a messenger for the army since at least September 1647 and had distinguished himself by being the first to reach London with the news of Cromwell's

[petitioner was] gone back from Scotland and he ~~imployed upon the business about sending of [wages] thither~~ and should not be there suddenly, that I would account with him for those journeys that he had gone from the army <and some time [before]>[265] rid in Scotland till that time, which [according] I did, and knowing that the greatest part if not all his bill would be allowed to him, paid him [then and before] the sum of 230*l* ~~of his bill~~ <~~which account which came in all to 288*l*~~>[266] which as he acknowledged, as by his bill of journeys hereunto annexed ~~may appear and that thereupon your petitioner took his bill of journeys~~ written with his own hand may more particularly appear, and that accordingly each other subscribed a note of the said agreement, wherein I acknowledged that his bill being allowed by your Excellency there would be 58*l* due to him from the State, and accordingly took the bill down with me into Scotland in May following and presented it to your Excellency to sign, but in regard divers of those journeys he set down were for the time he was imployed about buying of hay and had pay and other great advantages from the Council of State,[267] your Excellency thought not fit to sign it at that time, and afterwards the army marching for England, I was appointed to attend Lieutenant-General Monck, and that Master Hatter might disburse the contingencies for that march. After which the army continuing in England and your petitioner in Scotland, your petitioner sent up a copy of the said bill with the agreement to Master Hatter, and desired he would either <thereon>[268] charge the bill of 214.17.6 upon my account, and I would pay him 158*l*, which was the 58*l* remaining and another 100*l* Master Cadwell had paid upon my account <in the interval>[269] or else that he would pay me the 130*l* remaining and charge the whole bill to his account ~~to contingencies but he doing neither did pay me~~ notwithstanding which Master Cadwell received over again ~~the greatest part of the~~ from Master Hatter the greatest part of the same bill, whereby the State should be either defrauded or your petitioner lose everything he paid unto him upon account thereof, ~~being~~ which amounted to 66.15.6 as by the exact accounts will appear.

victory at Dunbar in September 1650; K&C, p. 144; *CSPD 1650*, pp. 333, 335; T. Carte, *A Collection of Original Letters and Papers*, 2 vols (London, 1739), I, pp. 380–384, esp. p. 380.

[265] Interlined.

[266] Interlined.

[267] On two occasions in November 1650 Cadwell was paid £250 and £140 respectively for buying hay for the army at King's Lynn; *CSPD 1650*, pp. 598, 601.

[268] Interlined.

[269] Interlined.

Your petitioner <humbly>[270] prays that <your Excellency shall give order that>[271] the same may be allowed him either out of such monies as are due to the said Master Cadwell or out of his estate.

And your petitioner shall ever pray etc.[272]

News from Westminster, 19 November 1653[273]

fo. [159]r

Major General Harrison and some who exercise at Blackfriars may make some trouble.[274] Major-General Lambert is sent for.[275]

Newsletter from The Hague, 25 November 1653

fo. 166r

Hague, 25 November/5 December 1653

They are here in expectation of the success of the treaty but have received no particulars of it from their deputies, who write that they have given in their propositions to the Council, but have yet received no answer other than by the word of mouth at 2 conferences.[276] The particulars whereof they excuse the sending of because of the secrecy promised on both sides,[277] to the end that the ministers and agents of foreign states and kingdoms may not penetrate into the negotiations and thereby disturb and countermine the peace. But yet the Orange

[270] Interlined.

[271] Interlined.

[272] Apparently Clarke's petition was unsuccessful, as his letter to Cadwell's widow of 12 May 1654 (p. 183 below) demonstrates.

[273] This brief shorthand passage appears at the end of a newsletter otherwise written in longhand.

[274] Attacks on the establishment by those preaching at the weekly spiritual exercises at Blackfriars were at this time becoming more and more extreme; Woolrych, *C–P*, pp. 324–325. Separate copies of an anomymous eye-witness account of the meeting held on the Monday before this letter was written were sent to Cromwell and Thurloe on Wednesday 16 November; *TSP*, I, pp. 591–592.

[275] The Council of State's purpose in sending for Lambert was to discuss the military situation in Scotland; Woolrych, *C–P*, p. 322.

[276] The death of van Tromp and the recapture of Enkhuizen had strengthened the hand of the anti-Orangists and improved the prospects of peace; Pincus, *Protestantism and Patriotism*, pp. 150–155.

[277] Cromwell had recently sworn the Dutch commissioners to complete secrecy over the negotiations; Woolrych, *C–P*, pp. 322–323.

party are very well satisfied that the deputies did not send an account at large of all that passed in the treaty, and have a very great jealousy and opinion that the States of Holland have and do receive copies and *Memoranda* of all that is done and that they know the secrets. Yet some do believe that already a peace is made between England and the Provinces of Holland, and the commissioners [do/did] write that the English are so civil as to release all the prisoners for a small ransom, and the poor fishermen, which is believed here to be a forerunner of a cessation of arms, and that the business of Amboyna,[278] the herring fishing and other things of difficulty will be passed over, and the late accident happened 29/19 May 1652[279] was paid off by way of provision that so all hostility may cease and then the rest might be cleared at leisure.[280]

However the letters from Brussels do inform that there was sent to the archduke the propositions and *memorandums* which their Lordships' commissioners in England had made and delivered in to the Council, and that there was no likelihood of any agreement between both states.[281]

In the meantime Chan[u]t, the ambassador of France, having performed his visits of honour to the queen and the princess lies still and continues in the condition of an ordinary ambassador giving out he is come only in general to maintain the good intelligence and [correspondences/correspondency] without desiring to ingage himself in any particular negotiation.[282] And yet I know it for certain that his chief aim and design is to ally this state again to France and by this means to [. . .] deliver in sensibly and indirectly this house of Orange and the interest thereof, a business which will be very agreeable and pleasing to the people, and much talking with the great ones, and there is no question but this embassy was promoted upon that interest.[283] And I know that the Orange party as well in Zealand

[278] There were renewed English demands for Dutch compensation for the massacre at Amboyna in 1623; *C&P*, II, pp. 81, 366, 371; *A Memento for Holland: or A True and Exact History of those Villainous and Barbarous Cruelties* . . . (London, 1653).

[279] The date of the opening battle in the Anglo-Dutch war.

[280] Another correspondent writing from The Hague on the same day reported that 'the Amboyna business, and the herring fishing &c. . . . is made of an end of and finished'; *TSP*, I, p. 611.

[281] The recent arrival of the archduke Leopold in Brussels was reported in *Mercurius Politicus*, 182 (2–9 Dec. 1653), p. 3015.

[282] The French ambassador to The Hague, who had arrived there on 17 November 1653, had private instructions to do all he secretly could to hinder the treaty with England; *Perfect Diurnall*, 208 (28 Nov.–5 Dec. 1653), p. 3015; *TSP*, I, p. 595.

[283] Chanut's visits to the princess of Orange, eldest daughter of Charles I, and his efforts in the Royalist cause are confirmed by another correspondent writing from The Hague on the following day; *Mercurius Politicus*, 182 (2–9 Dec. 1653), p. [2819].

as elsewhere will be very suddenly to speak again of a captain and lieutenant-general and they only stay for the news of the success of the peace in England, which the Orange party believe will come to nothing and in the meantime the parties and factions here on both sides do very much embroyle with great violence one against another, the party of Orange having the favour of the people of France, of Denmark and all the monarchies. How can the otherside subsist without a peace with England?

The States here have paid off most of their hired ships and some few of the rest are re-victualling to cruze in the sea and to fetch home the single East India ship at Norway and other ships in the Baltique Sea, and the Commissioners of the Admiralty have advised their lordships that they intend to send 4 or 5 ships of war for the purpose aforesaid, there being but 2 convoyers with the aforesaid ships, and that they had desired the admiralty of the north quarters and that of Friezland to add each one man of war. In the meantime they labour very much to have a very considerable fleet out the next spring, and that very early, and the resident, *Devers*, in his letter of the 22th writes from Copenhagen that having been with his majesty the king of Denmark to give him thanks for the favour done to the fleet and their lordships, and for the care he had of the East India ships, his majesty assured him of all good amity on his part and wished them good success in their war against the English, and that there had been a contribution made towards the maintaining a fleet at sea which was so [spiritual] that he intends to set forth a fleet of 50 ships to sea the next spring. Some captains and officers of soldiers imployed at sea pretending to have their share of their prizes, their lordships referred the business to the commissioners for sea affairs, who thereupon having advised have made report that they have nothing to pretend to.

[284]The 28th of the last month the Rhinegrave writes of some regiments of the duke of Lorraine and prince of Orange were come into the country of Luxembourg and that they gave out that they are to march towards the country of Overmaze.[285] And that 4 of the regiments that the earl of Ligneville had with him were passed the Maze near Ruremont, marching towards their quarters which they intend to take up in these parts, and the other 2 regiments remain yet in the same quarters, near Thoor and Kissemich.[286] The same day

[284] From here this newsletter contains selected quotations from letters of intelligence sent from the continent; *TSP*, I, pp. 611, 612, 616.

[285] A letter of 7 December 1653 (N.S.) reported from Brussels that Lorraine and his army were quartered between Marville and Stenay, very close to the Luxembourg border, and that he planned to make for Overmaze; *Mercurius Politicus*, 182 (2–9 Dec.1653), p. 3015.

[286] 'Hessenich' in *TSP*, I, p. 616.

their lordships received a letter from the lord ambassador, *de Brune*, wherein he signifies that before the receipt of their letter he had spoken with the archduke and other chief ministers to prevent and hinder the passage and quartering of the Lorrainers, not only upon their borders, but also in the country of Overmaze.[287] The earl of Ligneville[288] writes also to their lordships that he hoped that the governor of Maastricht had signified unto them in what good order he had lived with his troops during their abode upon their lordships' territories without suffering the least hurt or damage to be done to any one inhabitant, and that the duke his master did desire to live/in

fo. 166v

in good correspondence and amity with the State and did likewise hope that their lordships would quietly permit 2 or 3 regiments to quarter in the country of Gemert and Megen which did absolutely depend upon the Empire, which the governor of the Bosh did oppose. Their lordships returned the like compliment to the said earl, but for the countries of Gemert and Megen, they said they did not depend upon the empire but did absolutely and immediately belong unto their lordships. Order [was] given to our country men not to carry any provision to the Lorrainers, *ut Jejunio eijciatur hoc demonioque Genus.*

The commissioners of the elector of Colin[289] upon an order presented from him have desired recredentials to [gone],[290] which being debated in the Generality, the most part of the provinces were sorry that this defensive alliance is not concluded. But the considerations taken by Holland thereupon (who had rather defend their own limits and the borders favoured by the [rivers] than to engage so far in the country of [. . .]) are so weighty that the rest will do nothing against them so that they have agreed to give unto them letters recredentiall and therewith a dismission wherein is to be inserted the consideration of Holland, *vizt* that they are ready to permit[291] the alliance as soon as any other members of the Westphalian council or[292] others shall be willing to joyn in the said alliance. The judges appointed for the chambre mipartie (except the Lords *Doublet & Sallick*[)] are agreed to go from hence on Monday next. They take along with them for advocates *Paets, Andel, Stryen, Pandelaer and Cauw*, and the Lord Huygens

[287] For other references to opposition to the Lorrainers' attempts to quarter, see *ibid.*, pp. 560, 570, 574, 592.

[288] Commander of the duke of Lorraine's army; *ibid.*, p. 592.

[289] i.e. Cologne.

[290] Possibly 'be' is omitted before this word.

[291] *Ibid.*, p. 611 reads 'perfect' for 'permit'.

[292] *Ibid.* reads 'as' for 'or'.

is to go to take the oath of those of the king, but his voyage is only to [lay] the platform for them to proceed on hereafter.

The states of Groningen and Ommeland have removed their great cause which depended here before the judges' delegates, having constituted 12 judges[293] in their own province[294] and Count William[295] for president to decide their differences. This doth highly please Count William for his party who were lower here doth prevail there and is master now.

Schellekens has writ it to their lordships[296] from Frankfort that he has advice from Regensberg that the marriage of a Roman king with the infanta of Spain doth proceed, and that there is for this purpose a stately embassy sending thither and that the king will stay this winter at Regensburgh to decide the differences between the princes.

Newsletter from Amsterdam, 25 November 1653

fo. 166v

Amsterdam *25 November/5 December 1653*

You shall do very well to examine specially those herringers that your fleet will meet with for most of the Dutch trade is [driven in] those meetings and now there rides in the Texel 12 or 13 ships which are going westwards under the colours of Hamburgers and Swedes and so most of their trade is now driven.[297]

Newsletter from Richard Hatter, Westminster, 3 December 1653

fo. 166r

Monday 28th *November* 1653, order concerning inclosures that have been or shall be made, and to prevent depopulations and decay of tillage, referred to the committee for the poor. Order concerning paying the salary of the Clerk of the Parliament and other officers.

[293] *Ibid.*, p. 612 inserts 'of and'.

[294] *Ibid.* reads 'provinces' for 'province'.

[295] Willem Frederik, count of Nassau and Stadholder of Friesland and Groningen. The Stadtholder's role in the appointment of magistrates is discussed in Israel, *Dutch Republic*, pp. 703–704.

[296] Presumably it was to the States General that the Dutch spy Schellekens was writing.

[297] A month earlier two Dutch pinks masquerading as Hamburgers had been brought into Leith; *Perfect Diurnall*, 203 (24–31 Oct. 1653), p. 3092.

Order concerning paying servants to committees. Tuesday, bill for excise upon English tobacco twice read. Debate upon the rates of excise proceeded in. Wednesday, the [House] proceeded further in the debate on the rates for excise. Thursday, bill for taking away right of patrons to present to be read on Tuesday morning next. Bill to be brought in for continuing the duty of excise according to the rates already voted. Friday, report from committee for tithes made and that the present possessors have propriety in tithes.[298]

Richard Hatter

Newsletter from John Thurloe, Westminster, 6 December 1653

fo. 166[v]

I have received yours of the 25th of 9bris from Stirling, and am sorry things have so ill an aspect in Scotland at such a time as this is. I hope the Lord will answer for you as heretofore, and scatter those clouds that now hang over us.

The treaty with the Dutch is still on foot, and many particulars are under consideration but no agreement yet made nor any such step made towards it as will worthy conclude the thing.[299] A few days will discover more.

I have herewith sent you [the] foreign intelligence.[300] Here at home there is not much consistency in our Council, and I fear things which are good in themselves are too much and too unsensibly insisted upon. But I trust God will guide them in things for His glory and the peace of the nation.[301] The fleet goes to sea tomorrow with Monck and Penn. The Parliament have added Major-General Disbrowe and Penn to Monck and Blake, to be Generals of the Fleet for the next 6 months.[302]

John Thurloe

[298] *CJ*, VII, pp. 358–361, (28 November–2 December) confirms all these items of parliamentary business.

[299] On 2 December 1653 Thurloe had informed the English ambassador in Sweden, Bulstrode Whitelocke, that 'The treaty with the Dutch still proceeds, butt lento pede'; S. G. von Bischoffshausen, *Die Politik des Protectors Oliver Cromwell . . . seines staatssecretars John Thurloe* (Innsbruck, 1899), p. 146.

[300] This refers to documents on pp. 117 and 119–123 above.

[301] Blank.

[302] *CJ*, VII, pp. 361–362 (3 December 1653).

Newsletter from Westminster, 6 December 1653

fo. 167[r]

We hear that there are 18,000 arms going privately from Holland to the Highlanders in Scotland.[303]

This day the Parliament was again upon church work which makes a great division amongst us.[304] Master Feake the rest [*sic*] which meet at Blackfriars are very high and much against the Parliament meddling with church work. Many of the Parliament men meet at Blackfriars and privately in other places.[305]

Newsletter from Henry Walker, Westminster, 8 December 1653

fo. 167[v]

Though the Dutch brake up the last time they met in the treaty, as if they would come no more but take leave and be gone, yet some eminent persons are of opinion they will meet again, and that there are yet hopes they will agree. But of that there can only be a guess.[306]

The Parliament have been these 3 or 4 days last past upon the business of religion reported by the committee for the tithes etc. The committee reports are that tithes are due by law, before reformation of what is amiss in the farming thereof, which it is thought the House will concur in, but in all probability it will not be by tenths of all over and over again, but the pound's rate. The committee have also named 8 ministers and 8 gentlemen to be sent commissioners to go in all parts (as judges go the circuits) to purge out and eject scandalous and ignorant ministers and place able and godly in their stead, Master Sidrach Simpson,[307] Dean Owen,[308] Master Goodwin[309] and other

303 The large supply of arms which Lt-Gen. John (later Earl) Middleton had successfully secured in Holland for the royalist cause was listed in a letter of intelligence from The Hague, on 18/28 November 1653; *TSP*, I, p. 594.

304 *CJ*, VII, p. 363.

305 For instance at the house of the Fifth Monarchist Arthur Squibb. By this time Feake was making personal attacks against Cromwell; Woolrych, *C–P*, p. 326.

306 Although the Dutch commissioners demanded their passports on 5 December 1653, they did not leave, possibly as a result of inside information that the government was about to change; *ibid.*, p. 324.

307 Independent minister and Master of Pembroke Hall, Cambridge since 1650.

308 John Owen, Dean of Christ Church, and Vice-Chancellor of Oxford University.

309 Thomas Goodwin, Independent minister and chaplain to the Council of State, at this time closely associated with John Owen; *DBR*, 'Goodwin'.

ministers, and Major-General Skippon[310] and other gentlemen. What the House will do it in it [*sic*] is not yet known for it is only in debate and the 3 or 4 last days have been wholly taken up in debate of it.[311]

Henry Walker

Newsletter from Gilbert Mabbott, Westminster, 10 December 1653

fo. 169[r]

Wednesday, Thursday and Friday[312] were wholly spent in debate of the report from the committee for tithes. The House likewise this day proceeded in their debate of the same touching ejecting ignorant, profane and scandalous ministers. The 1st clause brought in by the committee was read, and the question being put to agree it passed in the negative.[313]

Gilbert Mabbott

Newsletter from Westminster, 13 December 1653[314]

fo. 170[r]

Upon Saturday last[315] I came late to London where I found things were [long] and ready for a change.[316]

No peace betwixt Holland and us because they could not find a people as the state of affairs then stood of either faith or constancy to make peace with all but hurt to the next relations or else [the former] might easily if not quite violated yet be sufficiently evaded.

310 Philip Skippon, alleged by Clement Walker to have been responsible for listing dissentients in Goodwin's congregation, was shortly to become a member of the Protector's first Council, but was not on the list of proposed commissioners presented to Parliament on 2 December, who numbered twenty-one, not sixteen as Walker reports; *CJ*, VII, p. 361.

311 *Ibid.*, p. 363 (6–10 December 1653) confirms these items of parliamentary business.

312 i.e. 7–9 December 1653.

313 *Ibid.*, p. 363 (7–10 December 1653) confirms all these items of parliamentary business.

314 Both this and the following newsletter were written on the day after the termination of the Nominated Assembly. Both add details not contained in the official parliamentary record (*ibid.*). The event and its consequences are comprehensively described in Woolrych, *C-P*, chs 10 and 11.

315 i.e. 10 December 1653.

316 Presumably referring to the imminent dissolution of Parliament.

On Monday morning[317] the House met as formerly. The question put whether they should sit any longer carried in the negative whereon the Speaker with the mace before him went out, accompanied with the most of the House, leaving about 27 persons sitting, whom Colonel Goffe[318] and Lieutenant-Colonel White[319] now persuaded that they were not a House to rise, which they accordingly did, and divers of them, as well as those went out 1st, met after at Whitehall and then thus under their hand in writing was conveyed to my Lord General the power of him formerly conveyed to them, and with all making him Lord Governour of England, Ireland and Scotland.

A peace with Holland is not much doubted.[320]

Westminster 10bris 13 1653

Newsletter from London to Colonel Robert Lilburne, 13 December 1653[321]

fo. 170^{v}

<For the Honourable Colonel Lilburne Commander-in-Chief these are>[322]

Sir

This last Parliament consisting of men abounding with zeal but wanting a due balance of Christian prudence had thereon run them [selfs] upon strange inconveniencies and [incapacities] of doing the public work and thereby the majesty of authority lost and all manner of interest of [enemies] gaining daily besides the inconsistency of principles among them and the strangeness of [many] [. . .] of them to the amending of all manner of rules of law, preaching or propriety, and declaring an universal war with the whole world. This a party among them being [wholly] sensible of did yesterday morning in the Parliament house declare that they saw no way to save the nation but by resigning their power to the general[323] from whence they had it, and

[317] i.e. 12 December 1653.

[318] The regicide, William Goffe; *DBR*, 'Goffe'.

[319] The Army radical, Francis White; *ibid.*, 'White'.

[320] Millenarians both inside and outside Parliament had been deeply opposed to any form of treaty with the Dutch; Woolrych, *C–P*, p. 322. The end of the Nominated Assembly greatly lessened their influence and improved the prospects for peace.

[321] As the original volume has been rebound, shorthand outlines on the inner margin of this page are sometimes obscured. Like the preceding document, this letter describes the dissolution of the Nominated Assembly.

[322] Marginated.

[323] i.e. Cromwell.

thereupon immediately [. . .] and came to Whitehall together with the Speaker,[324] and there in the chamber where their commission was delivered to them did [resign] up their power by their subscription to a parchment to that effect. About some 15[325] of them stayed in the [Parliament] whereon the rest being all gone Colonel Goffe went in to them, civilly desired them to depart the Parliament having [. . .] themselfs. Care is taken for a settled government that we may not be every day at this work, which is both trouble[some] and hazardous. What think you of a chief Governour with a Council and triennial Parliament chosen by the people?

Axeyard, Westminster, Decembris 13 1653

Newsletter from Henry Walker, Westminster, [17] December 1653

fo. 167ʳ

Westminster, December [17][326]

The Dutch deputies are now gone home in good earnest and are under sayle, yet we [are/were] persuaded that they will suddenly come again, and therefore a vessel of ours that is gone with them is ordered to stay 6 days for an answer.[327] But there is a report that there is an answer ready by the States, and indeed the letters from [thence] speak of God's wonderfully handling them by his own immediate hand upon them going more [vigorously/rigorously] then yet he has done. For about a fortnight since there fell such a storm as scarce ever was known the like, the effect whereof has been [sad] to them. Between 50 and 60 of their ships that were then in the Texel are so shattered that

[324] Francis Rous.

[325] The number is at variance with that given in the previous account, twenty-seven. Another newsletter (printed in *CP*, III, p. 10) reported that the figure twenty-seven included several who had left the House and then returned. If the number of fifteen reported here is to be believed, then some twelve MPs did so.

[326] The date is not clearly written and could be 7 or 17 December. In Clarke's letter-book, which is usually arranged by date of document, the letter is found on a page headed '6 Dec. 1653' and between letters of 6 and 8 December. However, its reference to Cromwell as 'the Lord Protector' and 'his Highness' indicate that it must have been written sometime after the proclamation of the Instrument of Government on 16 December; *CSPD 1653–1654*, pp. 297–298. Clarke had reached the end of his notebook with the previous letter. It was not unusual for him to backtrack to an empty page in order to complete the year in the same notebook.

[327] The Dutch commissioners, who had asked for their passports on 5 December, did not return home until 4 January 1654; *C&P*, II, pp. 365, 367.

not half of them are fit for any present service, and at least 20 of them sunk, besides some that are ran on ground and broken and spoyled, and 2 of their East India ships that was going out also. Besides in several other places where they had ships, much loss, the particulars so many that letters from all parts of Holland speak of it. A cross-stone and great vane and round ball that was on the top of one of their steeples in Amsterdam was blown down and of mighty weight brake into the church, brake pews and the very grave stones, and graves and vaults broke into. Many mills burnt by the mighty violence of the storm being not able to stay them took fire and in north Holland some hundreds of houses burnt with the church, town-house and some ships at a key and in several parts a very great harm done. They have an Eastland fleet to come home of about 150 sayle, and are in a very great perplexity. There is a report that some of the States' best friends to England have been under question and some deserve to have taken away their lives. What the issue will be the Lord knows.

They are very busy at Whitehall about preparations for the Lord Protector to come, and the next week I think the old council chamber will be finished for the Council to meet in.[328] There is great seeking for places and everyone making their friends, but I think in the conclusion it will be done by his Highness. They do still at Blackfriars kick at the present way of government, but divers of their own followers and of the church of that association fall off from them in that particular, but the rest of the churches about [thereupon], especially such who have ministers for their pastors, are very well satisfied.

Henry Walker

[328] The first meeting of the new Council was on 16 December; *CSPD 1653–1654*, p. xxxv.

6. NOTEBOOK XXVI

30 December 1653–2 December 1654[1]

Introduction

While this volume is considerably slimmer than most of the others in the series, it holds a much higher number of items in shorthand than any other, and the highest proportion of shorthand to longhand.[2] Many date to between 10 May and 25 August 1654, when Clarke was with Monck on his gruelling march round the Scottish Highlands in pursuit of the Royalist army during Glencairn's Rising.[3] At least some of the incoming newsletters may have been delivered by Cromwell's special messenger from London, George Downing.[4]

Early in the year, the success of Scottish royalists in preventing the army's collection of the Scottish sess resulted in the deployment of three more English regiments,[5] and in late January, on orders from Charles Stuart, Lieutenant-General John Middleton returned to Scotland from Holland with a small number of men.[6] Thurloe immediately notified the Scottish headquarters, and the Protector himself urged Lilburne to be on his guard. Despite all possible precautions, Middleton's arrival on the Moray Firth in early March[7] enabled the Scots to embark on a full-scale offensive.[8] The royalist

[1] Worc. MS XXVI.

[2] In the present category there are 140 documents in shorthand and 30 in longhand, most of the latter coming after 16 November 1654. Hence there are very few excerpts from this volume in *CP* III. Much of the shorthand in the volume is particularly cramped and difficult to decipher (e.g. documents on pp. 146–147).

[3] Clarke recorded his whereabouts daily, often noting the distance travelled from one location to another; Worc. MS XXVI, *passim*. The route is conveniently summarized in *C&P*, II, pp. 415–419, and with more detail in *S&P*, pp. 104–156.

[4] *Ibid.*, p. 154.

[5] P. 140. Also Dow, *Cromwellian Scotland*, pp. 110–111.

[6] *C&P*, II, pp. 389, 407. Middleton had been appointed by Charles as lieutenant-general in command of his forces in Scotland in June 1652.

[7] Pp. 152, 160, 163. See *C&P*, II, p. 407, which gives the date of Middleton's landing as February.

[8] Pp. 155, 163. The rising is fully described in *C&P*, II, pp. 389–419 and in Dow, *Cromwellian Scotland*, pp. 115–135. It is known as 'Glencairn's Rising', although the earl of Glencairn, as interim commander, surrendered without hesitation the position of commander-in-chief upon Middleton's return to Scotland. He was less happy with the

threat was not confined to Scotland, and newsletters from late May onwards are full of the developments in a major royalist plot uncovered in London.[9]

The protracted peace negotiations with the Dutch, which received a new impetus with the inauguration of the Protectorate,[10] dominated most of the London newsletters during the earlier part of the year, before the ratification of the treaty in April.[11] The change of government in England was viewed differently by pro- and anti-Orangist factions in Holland, each with its own aspirations.[12] Royalists hoped for a continuation of the war, which would place a further strain upon English resources,[13] and both supporters and opponents of the house of Orange awaited the outcome of the current royalist rising in Scotland before committing themselves to a peace with the Protectorate.[14] In France, Charles Stuart was hopeful that the change would be to his advantage. By contrast, the altogether more pragmatic reaction of Cardinal Mazarin would soon mean that Charles had outstayed his welcome at the French court.[15]

In London, the outspoken opposition of Fifth Monarchists to the proposed treaty was swiftly suppressed.[16] One of their leaders, Major-General Thomas Harrison, who in December 1653 was stripped of his commission after refusing to recognize the Protectorate, had a long conference with the Protector some time in early to mid-January, before being banished to Staffordshire.[17] By early March, when a treaty with the Dutch seemed inevitable, the Fifth Monarchists were said to have 'fallen off from their principles' and to be 'very quiet'.[18] By the end of July, their leading preachers Christopher Feake and John

appointment of Sir George Munro as Middleton's second-in-command; *C&P*, II, pp. 407–408.

[9] See pp. 186, 187, and 195 for details of the plot, mentioned in almost all the following newsletters until after the execution of the plotters on 10 July and subsequent arrest of others involved (pp. 196, 200).

[10] Pincus, *Protestantism and Patriotism*, is essential reading for an understanding of the war, particularly pp. 161–191.

[11] Pp. 179, 182. Up to Mabbott's description of the peace celebrations in London on 26 April 1654 (p. 179), only nine out of a total of sixty-two incoming newsletters make no mention of the negotiations; pp. 137, 148, 164, 167–168, 170, 171, 176.

[12] Pp. 135–136.

[13] Royalist opposition to the resumption of the dialogue with the anti-Orangist Dutch emissary Beverning was, for example, noted by Thurloe in his newsletter of 26 January (p. 146).

[14] Pp. 155–156. A correspondent earlier in the month believed that the chances for peace or war were about even (p. 150).

[15] P. 137.

[16] Pp. 146, 147, 149, 150.

[17] Capp, *Fifth Monarchy Men*, p. 99; pp. 141, 150 below.

[18] Pp. 159, 168–169.

Simpson had bowed to the status quo, and even the most vociferous, John Rogers, had been silenced.[19]

As the prospects for a successful outcome to the negotiations waxed and waned in an atmosphere of mutual suspicion,[20] both countries braced themselves for a formal renewal of the war.[21] The diplomatic deadlock in Sweden, where Queen Christina waited for news of the treaty before committing herself to an alliance with England, added to the tension surrounding the exchanges with the Dutch.[22]

When a fragile peace was finally reached in late April, the formal ratification of the treaty was greeted with celebrations in both countries. There were, however, some hostile reactions in Holland, particularly among pro-Orangists after a secret article excluding the infant Prince William from any active part in Dutch politics became general knowledge.[23]

Between the abrupt termination of the Nominated Assembly in December 1653 and the opening of the first Protectorate Parliament in September 1654, Cromwell governed the country without a Parliament. Although one correspondent as early as 4 March 1654 believed that a new Parliament would soon be called,[24] election writs were not sent out for another two months.[25]

The new Council held its first meeting on the day on which Cromwell was installed as Lord Protector, 16 December 1653, and there are many glimpses of the way in which Council business during this critical interval was conducted, and of Cromwell's part in it.[26] Much of it consisted of ratifying the numerous ordinances which took the place of parliamentary acts, and which often resulted from direct petitioning.[27] Two letters written by Gilbert Mabbott, on 29 August and 2 September 1654 respectively, highlight the urgency with which the Council passed as many ordinances as possible before the inauguration of the Protectorate's first Parliament on 3 September.[28]

[19] Pp. 198, 201.

[20] Pp. 166–167, 173.

[21] Pp. 137, 139, 151, 156, 159, 161–163.

[22] P. 165.

[23] Pp. 182, 185, 189, 200, 204.

[24] P. 159.

[25] Pp. 188.

[26] Pp. 151, 165, 167–168, 179–180, 182, 198, 201–202.

[27] I. Roots, 'Cromwell's ordinances: the early legislation of the Protectorate', in G. E. Aylmer (ed.), *The Interregnum: The Quest for Settlement* (London and Basingstoke, 1974 edn), pp. 143–164. To contemporaries the difference between the two terms was blurred. Walker, Downing, and Mabbott all referred to ordinances as 'acts' (see, for example, pp. 139, 179, 190, 193).

[28] P. 205.

There are descriptions of the elaborate preparations and ceremonial which accompanied the opening of the Parliament,[29] which was marred by the exclusion of several of the elected MPs under the terms of the twenty-first clause of the Instrument of Government. After scrutiny of the election results the Council had instructed the Clerk of the Commonwealth in Chancery to refuse them certificates of election or 'tickets'.[30] Among them, wrote Gilbert Mabbott on 5 September, was Major John Wildman, whose exclusion before the opening of the Parliament is now conclusively demonstrated.[31]

Cromwell laid the Instrument of Government before the new MPs for their approval, about which he did not foresee any difficulty.[32] There were objections, however, and on 12 September he excluded all the sitting Members, who were readmitted only if prepared to take an oath, or recognition, of loyalty to the Protectorate. The incident, and the gradual compliance of a majority of MPs, are reported in some detail by both Downing and Mabbott over the next three weeks.[33]

Almost all the newsletters reflect the premier concern of the Parliament during the rest of its life (that is until January 1655) – the dissection and minute examination, clause by clause, of the Instrument of Government. During the surrounding debates, the House frequently dissolved itself into a grand committee, the proceedings of which were not minuted in the journal of the House but were frequently communicated by Clarke's London correspondents.[34]

At some time around 18 October the 'petition of the three colonels', heavily critical of the Protectorate, was published.[35] While there are

[29] Pp. 205–207.

[30] *SS*, p. 87.

[31] P. 207 below. In answer to Dr Ashley's assertion in his biography of Wildman that '[Wildman] was not in his seat . . . when Parliament was opened on 3rd September', Dr Taft, writing in 1978, correctly pointed out that at that time there was 'no evidence to support a conclusion that Wildman was excluded before the House met'; M. Ashley, *John Wildman, Plotter and Postmaster* (London, 1947), p. 85; B. Taft, '*The Humble Petition of Several Colonels of the Army* . . . ', *Huntington Library Quarterly*, 42 (1978), p. 20n. Mabbott used the outdated title of 'Clerk of the Crown', as did an unattributed account of the same procedure before the first meeting of the second Protectorate Parliament in 1656; *CP*, III, pp. 73–74.

[32] Roots, 'Cromwell's ordinances', p. 158.

[33] Pp. 209–210, 211–214, 216.

[34] Pp. 212–216, 220–222. The parliamentary diary of Guibon Goddard is another useful source for the proceedings of grand committees in later parliaments; J.T. Rutt (ed.), *The Diary of Thomas Burton Esq. Member in the Parliaments of Oliver and Richard Cromwell from 1656 to 1659*, 4 vols (London, 1828), pp. i–cxcii.

[35] Entitled *The Humble Petition of Several Colonels of the Army* . . . but signed by only three of them (Alured, Okey, and Saunders), the petition was framed by Maj. John Wildman. It is extensively discussed by Dr. Taft in '*The Humble Petition of Several Colonels of the Army* . . . ', pp. 15–41.

no direct references to the petition in Clarke's shorthand, the meeting of 'some officers' five days later is likely to have been among the first of a series held in response to it by officers loyal to Cromwell.[36]

In a letter of 29 August, otherwise largely concerned with the 'western design', Gilbert Mabbott made casual mention of a rumour that 'an emperour will be chosen before the end of the next month'.[37] In December the regicide MP Augustine Garland would propose to the first Protectorate Parliament that Cromwell again be offered the crown.[38] Although the matter was dropped, it was revived in the summer of 1655 when apparently there was uncertainty over whether the Protector would take the title of king or emperor.[39] Without supporting evidence, unfortunately, it is impossible to be certain whether Mabbott meant that the title was being discussed as early as August 1654, or whether he was making a light-hearted reference to the Protector's territorial ambitions in the West Indies.

In the second half of 1654 there were several guarded allusions to the western design, Cromwell's ill-advised scheme to attack Spain in the West Indies.[40] Gilbert Mabbott reported at the end of June 1654 that it had been shelved upon its 'discovery'[41] and the culprit 'severely punished'.[42] Even in late August, reliable information regarding the plan was hard to come by, both Rushworth and Mabbott believing that the expedition was intended to consist of 8,000 troops, rather than the more accurate figure of 3,000.[43]

The launch of the expedition was jeopardized by a threatened mutiny of the seamen of Vice-Admiral Penn's fleet, who were awaiting their departure for the West Indies at Portsmouth. They had been encouraged by Vice-Admiral John Lawson (who had contacts with John Wildman and others associated with the 'three colonels petition') to submit to Parliament a strongly-worded petition listing their grievances.[44] The authorities took the matter seriously enough to despatch Penn and Desborough immediately to Portsmouth where

[36] Pp. 220–221, 226–229.

[37] P. 205.

[38] C.H. Firth, 'Cromwell and the crown', *English Historical Review*, 17 (1902), p. 429.

[39] Michael Roberts (ed.), *Swedish Diplomats at Cromwell's Court, 1655–1656*, (London, 1988), pp. 78–79. Previously Whitelocke assured Coyet that Cromwell had 'greater power than any king of England before him: yea, that he was *re vera Anglorum Imperator*'; (*ibid*, p. 63).

[40] Several correspondents corroborate S.R. Gardiner's statement that until August 1654 plans surrounding it were kept secret; *C&P*, II, p. 475. T. Venning, however, has written that 'the plan was not a secret' at this point; *Cromwellian Foreign Policy* (Basingstoke, 1995), p. 56.

[41] In the sense of 'disclosure' rather than 'detection'.

[42] P. 193. Other veiled references to the design will be found on pp. 196, 200, and 202.

[43] Pp. 204, 205. In the event not more than 2,500 appear to have embarked; C.H. Firth (ed.), *The Narrative of General Venables* (Camden Society, N.S. LXI, 1900), p. xviii.

[44] Capp, *Cromwell's Navy*, pp. 135–136.

most of the demands were settled with substantial amounts of cash. George Downing, writing on 4 November, described the petition in quite different terms, as swearing loyalty to the regime, but it was not until two days later that Penn could safely write that the revolt had been quelled.[45]

In October Mabbott made reference to a scheme to rename Ireland as 'West England' which had been discussed in committee[46] – probably that appointed on 29 September 1654 to meet on 2 October in order to consider the affairs of Ireland.[47] The proposal was intended to go before Parliament, but perhaps never did so, or was dismissed by MPs, as there is no mention of it in the official journals of the House. In 1682 the designation was also used by Richard Lawrence, who had been closely involved in Irish affairs during the 1650s and was a member of the committee appointed during the month of Mabbott's letter to survey forfeited Irish lands.[48]

Newsletter from The Hague, 30 December 1653

fo. [5]v

Hague 9 January/30 December 1653/4

All our expectations here are about a peace with England concerning which our deputies with you wrote by their letter of the 2nd of January 1654 that they were almost come to an issue either to conclude the peace or quite to break it off, and had been hitherto hindered by the late change of government which had lost them a day or 2 which they say was excused to them by the master of the ceremonies; and that since they had been formated under one consent with commissioners appointed by his Highness when they had propounded that which they thought necessary and especially the including of [allies] according to the resolution of the States General and that they had since sent in writing what they had debated by word of mouth and hoped that now the power of concluding did rest in one person they should have better success.

However, this news of the alteration of the government and the placing in the Lord Protector is diversely understood here, some

[45] P. 223; *TSP*, II, p. 709; *C&P*, III, p. 56.

[46] P. 216.

[47] *CJ*, VII, p. 371.

[48] 'Ireland is become West England'; Richard Lawrence, *The Interest of Ireland in its Trade and Wealth Stated in Two Parts* (Dublin, 1682), II, p. 51 (I am most grateful to Dr Toby Barnard for providing me with this reference); *DBR*, 'Lawrence'.

judging it to be the greatest blow to the house of Orange and the Stewarts which they ever received and that it will make much for the peace; others are of another opinion and especially those of the party of the [prince] who although they judge the peace necessary as seeing no way to continue the war with [. . . .] do wish a rupture of this negotiation, judging that something will fall out for the prince of Orange from the war but nothing from the peace, and this party do so much fear the domination of the States of Holland that they would not be [angry] although Holland should lose their trade and commerce which must of necessity follow from the war.[49]

In the meantime the king of Denmark is very jealous concerning his own condition lest the States General should leave him out of their present treaty with England and therefore notwithstanding the former promises this state has made unto him on this behalf, he has writ a letter to the States General desiring that their commissioners in England would procure a pass for an agent of his to be sent into England to treat with that state.[50]

They write from Sweden that although the ambassador from England is well received that yet the queen has declared that she will not treat in any wise to the prejudice of this state with England so that we do not care much what Sweden will do.

The French ambassador Chan[u]t here is very busy upon the articles of the treaty with France against England and all the provinces but Holland comply fully with him.[51]

Newsletter from Amsterdam, 30 December 1653

*fo. [5]^v^*

Amsterdam 9 *January 1653*[52]

There was upon the last Tuesday such a storm that incredible loss has happened in Holland and we fear the like in Zealand and other parts. Also there were at the time riding at anchor in the Texel [between] 50 ships, merchant men, 33 whereof were cast away and the rest cast

[49] A letter of intelligence from The Hague, written some time in January 1654, is full of the Orangists' opposition to the treaty; *TSP*, II, pp. 20–21.

[50] Compensation for the English ships held by Frederick III was covered by articles XXVIII–XXIX of the treaty; Abbott, III, pp. 903–904.

[51] French hopes of this were dashed in early February 1654 (p. 149 below). By late February Chanut was making attempts to be included in the Anglo-Dutch treaty (pp. 157, 160 below).

[52] New Style.

away upon the sands and lee shore which they hope to get off again. Also one East India ship called the Lily cast away and another named the Marigold shattered exceedingly.[53] We fear the same of our ships coming home from the Sound being in all 150 ships whereof we hear no news yet. Much hurt has also been done here in the town by the same storm. A malt mill in the storm fell on fire and with 4 houses more was burnt down and divers such harms we hear of in other places, especially in a place called Rype. In the north Holland a mill fell on fire and was burnt down with 5 or 600 houses more, 2 churches and the town house and divers small ships and boats that lay in the haven were burnt and consumed with fire.[54]

This doth somewhat discourage them yet they do truly intend the equipping of their summer navy. 30 new ships are taken on to be built, the least of 40 guns and some more, 2 whereof shall be as big as the new ship of the admiral of 70 pieces of cannon.[55] Amsterdam is to build 10, the rest at several towns and if no agreement be made there is no doubt but they will bring to sea a very good fleet.

Newsletter from Paris, 31 December 1653

fo. [5]ᵛ

Paris *10 January 1653* new style

This winter season the armies lie still and both sides preparing for the next [field],[56] but that which most of all takes up the mind of the court is your new government which Charles Stuart seems to glory at as thinking his game to be the fairer. But Mazarin easily sees the contrary and that now affairs are in hand of a person who has done so great things, his neighbours notwithstanding, to [consider] him. Besides he sees the consequence thereof will be peace with the Dutch and therefore his State, but considering Charles Stuart's interest he contrives ways of holding correspondence with your Protector.[57] He has already restored some merchandizes to the English which the Protector long since wrote to him about but nothing could be done in

[53] The loss of these ships is reported in several newsbooks, e.g., *Faithfull Scout*, [127] [N&S 150.160B] (6–13 Jan. 1654), p. 1268.

[54] Accounts of the storm which include many of these details were carried in most of the newsbooks, e.g., *Perfect Diurnall*, 214 (9–15 Jan. 1654), pp. 3261–3262.

[55] The English were at the same time building up their fleet against the eventuality of a renewal of the war; *CSPV 1653–1654*, p. 180.

[56] i.e. campaign.

[57] Mazarin was well informed about the treaty negotiations with the Dutch in London; *ibid.*, p. 173.

it until now. He also speaks of sending an ambassador hither to congratulate his Highness.[58]

The reformed churches here do also greatly [rejoice] in this alteration and their ministers and deputies came to me and to express [all/their] gladness, and told me that they had no [belief] in the court here but did expect that England would take consideration of the sending of their [condition].

Newsletter from Westminster, 3 January 1654

fo. [2]r

The Dutch deputies sent to the Council for a pass for all to go back to Holland,[59] it seems supposing the Lord Protector would fawn upon them to yield more then formerly to what was before done, seeing the people here affected so much [with] peace, but a pass was granted and no notice taken of anything, since which they have returned themselfs and treated all day yesterday, and it is again brought into a way of [probability] of agreement, but all is very private.[60] 5 prizes were brought in of merchants' ships signified by letters from the generals-at-sea.

An ordinance is passed for commissioners for the excise and an ordinance for probate of wills.[61] The Lord Protector and his Council with the officers of the army kept a fast on Friday last. Master Sterry, Master Thomas Goodwin and Master Lockyer prayed and preached and dealt plainly and faithfully with his Highness. His Highness also was so far from preaching in his stead that whereas a cloth of state was put up and a cushion of state, he sat at the end of the pew all the while and leant against the wall [quite] beside him.[62] Both the inclosed were read in [New . . . Chambers].[63]

Westminster *January 3 1653*

[58] Mazarin's special envoy the Baron de Baas had, in all, three audiences with Cromwell, the first on 13 January 1654. He reported favourably on them on his return to France; *ibid*, pp. 175, 183.

[59] Their request is printed in *TSP*, I, p. 650.

[60] A correspondent from The Hague (5 January 1654) noted the secrecy observed by the Dutch deputies in their reports; *TSP*, II, p. 7. The Venetian resident in London claimed that 'although the negotiations have been conducted with great secrecy, they have not been quite hidden from me'; *CSPV 1653–1654*, p. 171.

[61] These ordinances passed on 29 and 24 December 1653 respectively; *ibid.*, pp. 316, 310.

[62] The fast was held in the chapel at Whitehall; *Severall Proceedings*, 223 (29 Dec. 1653–5 Jan. 1654), p. [3533].

[63] There is no indication what these enclosures might have been.

Newsletter from Henry Walker, Westminster, 5 January 1654

fo. [3]ʳ

Letters are come of the safe arrival of the Lord Ambassador Whitelocke in Sweden.[64] The Dutch deputies had their last meeting on Monday last from 9 in the morning till 4 at night.[65] All is very secret. They took their [goods] and since were gone to Gravesend. A letter came from them to his Highness last night and an officer sent down to them or to the fleet, but things are very private.[66] Denmark should [see/seek] to indeavour as much as may be for something which I believe is under difference in debate about them.[67] [Men's/many] opinions are [various], but there is this night a whispering among some great ones of something that makes them confident of an agreement, but we have besides the fleet with the generals about Spithead out at sea which are about 50, some say 60. There is a squadron out and some scouts in several places, so that we have at this present about 70 men of war out at sea.

The act for continuance of the act for propagation of the gospel in the northern counties is by the Council almost finished and shortly to pass. My Lord Protector has been very busy at home with his officers and in private about business of some great concernment so that his Highness could not for 2 days past come to the Council.[68]

Mistress Lilburne solicits for her husband in person to whom it is said will be allowed 40*s* a week.[69]

Henry Walker

[64] Whitelocke reported his arrival to Cromwell on 18 November 1653; *TSP*, I, pp. 601–602.

[65] This was 2 January. The date is confirmed by most newsbooks, e.g. *The True Informer*, unnumb. (30 Dec. 1653–6 Jan. 1654), p. 4. *The True and Perfect Dutch-diurnall*, unnumb. (3–10 Jan. 1654), p. 18 reports the meeting in detail but assigns its date to 3 January.

[66] See also p. 138.

[67] Walker was right. It was the question of the king of Denmark's part in the treaty which was presented to the deputies at Gravesend; Pincus, *Protestantism and Patriotism*, p. 180.

[68] Around this time the Venetian ambassador noted that many of the officers had refused to take an oath of allegiance and that Cromwell was 'trying to gain them with art and flattery'; *CSPV 1653–1654*, p. 172. Cromwell attended the Council only five times during January 1654, all of them after the 15th; *CSPD 1653–1654*, p. xxxviii.

[69] The order was made on 6 January 1654; *ibid.*, p. 457.

Newsletter from Westminster, 7 January 1654

fo. [4][r]

The Dutch commissioners treated with ours Monday last from 9 in the morning till 6 at night. Wednesday night at 9 of the clock they took barge to Gravesend in order to their voyage to Holland. Wednesday a letter of expedition of one word insisted much on in the treaty was sent to them and their answer returned the same day. Hereupon General Blake and General Desbrowe were sent to the fleet with instructions for a preparation and as some say a [. . .].[70] The Dutch commissioners since their going to Gravesend have made application to his Highness and his Council for a further treaty for an accommodation whereby their return is speedily expected. This makes several discontented persons give out that these commissioners went not further then they had commission.

The Dutch, we hear for certain, have lately received a great loss by [burning] and tempest, there being 500 houses burnt thereby near Amsterdam and about 50 merchants' ships sunk in the Texel besides many other prejudices by this storm.[71]

The highlanders of Scotland begin to plunder the lowlanders so that they are not able to pay their assessments, for preventing whereof Major-General Lambert's, Commissary-General Whalley's and Colonel Barkstead['s] regiments are ordered to march thither speedily.

Letters came yesterday from Swethland that our ambassador is safely arrived there and that his lordship and his retinue are very honourably entertained.[72]

The Council has this week allowed Lieutenant-Colonel Lilburne 40*s* per week and such persons to speak with him as the Lieutenant of the Tower shall approve of.[73]

Westminster

[70] Blake and Desborough acted as intermediaries and also facilitated the commissioners' return home on board the *Amity*; *ibid.*, p. 554; *TSP*, II, p. 9; p. next document.

[71] Varying accounts of the disastrous effects of this storm appeared both in the printed newsbooks and in written newsletters, e.g., *Perfect Diurnall*, 213 (2–9 Jan. 1654), p. 3256, which reports that forty ships were sunk; *TSP*, II, p. 7.

[72] *TSP*, I, pp. 601, 645–646.

[73] *CSPD 1653–1654*, pp. 344, 457, 458.

Newsletter from George Downing, Westminster, 7 January 1654

fo. [4]r

In the letters mentioned in my last were the Dutch deputies'. There was not only a declaration of their being fully satisfied with what was granted by his Highness as to the whole treaty, but that they intended speedily to depart and that they doubted not but their superiours would ratify the same, and instead of the frigot which was [allotted unto] them to carry them over they desired the Amity frigot which accordingly is granted and she is to stay after her arrival in Holland 6 days in expectation of some answer from them.[74]

There has been lately a very great storm upon the coast of Holland by which 33 sayle were [drowned/downed] in the Texel [Holland bound] or cast away among one which one East India ship was cast away and another very much shattered into divers parts. Also from Holland there have been divers houses burnt down by the firing of oil mills and in one town of north Holland, Rype, 600 houses burnt down.[75]

George Downing

Newsletter from John Spencer, London, 14 January 1654

fo. [7]v

I cannot yet hear that General Monck is appointed for Scotland but it is universally believed he will be sent down if we have peace with Holland.[76] My Lord Protector saith if we have not it will lie wholly upon them and make our war the clearer with them. Major-General Harrison was this week 4 or 5 hours with my Lord Protector but he cannot be satisfied for those that meet at Blackfriars are as unsatisfied as ever.[77]

[74] As requested by Blake and Desborough in their letter of 5 January 1654 from Gravesend; *TSP*, II, p. 9.

[75] Similar accounts appear in many of the newsbooks, e.g., *Mercurius Politicus*, 188 (12–19 Jan. 1654), p. 3201; 189 (19–26 Jan. 1654), p. 3207; *True Informer*, 2 (6–13 Jan. 1654), p. 12. Estimates of the damage varied considerably. For example, *Faithful[l] Scout*, [127] [N&S 150.160B] (6–13 Jan. 1654), p. [1238] reported that 500 houses were destroyed.

[76] Monck left London to assume command in Scotland on 10 April 1654 (p. 176 below).

[77] The dissolution of the Nominated Assembly on 12 December 1653 and Cromwell's installation as Lord Protector had caused an immediate and irreconcilable breach between Harrison and Cromwell; *DBR*, 'Harrison'. On 21 December 1653 Harrison had declared that he would not serve under the new regime and was stripped of his commission; Capp, *Fifth Monarchy Men*, p. 99.

Master Powell is gone down to Wales and desired all of them to be much within his [prayer] and not to meddle any more with the government having as he said [laid] their witness against it.[78] I find but very few officers dissatisfied.

John Spencer

Newsletter from George Downing, Westminster, 17 January 1654

fo. 10[r]

His Highness is very busy inacting things in a good mould and frame. All the commissions for Justices of Peace are daily [altering] that so that great trust may be put into the best and steadiest hands. What concerns the acts that are passing for Scotland are near ending this day.[79] The Venetian and Hamburgh agents congratulated the late change of government.[80] There has been a strong report upon the Exchange that the treaty with Holland is confirmed, but we have nothing thereon as yet at Whitehall.

George Downing

Draft Order, 19 January 1654

fo. 10[v]

<[. . .] proposed for my Lord Protector to sign for taking mine and Master Hatter's accounts but another form signed>[81]

Whereas there have been several ~~large~~ sums of money paid by warrant from myself unto Master William Clarke treasurer for

[78] Despite difficulties with the authorities since speaking publicly against Cromwell on 18 December 1653, the Fifth Monarchist Vavasor Powell continued preaching against the regime. After a warrant was issued for his arrest on 10 January 1654, he preached again at Blackfriars and Christ Church before escaping to Wales; *CSPD 1653–1654*, p. 353; R.T. Jones, 'The life, work, and thought of Vavasor Powell', Oxford D.Phil. thesis, 1947, 2 vols, I, pp. 113–114, 117–119. According to Thurloe, Cromwell chose 'patient [*sic*] towards him rather than severity'; von Bischoffshausen, *Des Politik des Protectors Oliver Cromwell*, p. 154.

[79] The ordinance for uniting the people of Scotland into one commonwealth with England was read for the first and second times and referred to a committee on 20 January 1654; *CSPD 1653–1654*, p. 364.

[80] Paulucci's description of this audience with Cromwell is found in *CSPV 1653–1654*, p. 177.

[81] Marginated. Clarke's submission concerning these accounts may be connected with the forthcoming ordinance for appointing a Committee for the Army and Treasurers-at-War (28 January 1654), which made provision for satisfying the arrears of the army in Scotland prior to 20 October 1651; *A&O*, II, pp. 835–839.

contingencies in Scotland from the first advance of the army under my command towards Scotland of which no account has yet been given ~~for the [matter]~~ ~~now~~ for that end therefore that the State may not be damaged and that the said Master Clarke may be discharged ~~for so much of the [bearer's]~~ of what monies he has so disbursed by my order for the publike service in Scotland these are therefore to authorize you on sight hereof to take the account of the said Master Clarke for all such monies as he has received for contingencies from the 4th of July 1650 to the 1st of January 1651[82] from which time ~~he has~~ (as I am informed) he has cleared accounts with you ~~and to give him such discharge and~~ to take in such warrants as shall be produced by him for the payment of the same which you are to allow and give him ~~a~~ discharge ~~thereupon the same~~ thereupon.

And whereas upon the army's march into Scotland there was 6,000*l* paid to Master Richard Hatter <secretary to the Council of War>[83] upon warrants in the name and with the subscription of the said Master William Clarke (while he was in Scotland) ~~and to the end both the said Master Clarke~~ you are ~~therefore on sight hereof~~ also hereby authorized to take and examine the account of the ~~same Master~~ Hatter for the said 6,000*l* and to give such discharge or discharges for the same or so much thereof as he has discharged by warrant ~~from myself~~ as may clear both the <said>[84] Master Hatter and Master Clarke from any further question for the same[85] and the Treasurers-at-War or their deputies in Scotland are ~~to give you~~ hereby required to give you a charge of what monies have been received of them in name of the said Master Clarke aforesaid and for the presents this shall be your warrant.

Newsletter from George Downing, Westminster, 19 January 1654

fo. [11][r]

The Amity frigot is returned from Holland.[86] The sum of what news we have from here and the post hints to this much, that the Dutch

[82] In his account books Clarke began each new year on 25 March. Thus this date probably refers to 1 January 1651/2; Thoresby, MS SD IX; Chequers, MS 782. In the former entries cease on 26 June 1650; in the latter there are none between the end of June 1650 and January 1651/2, coinciding with the period specified here.

[83] Interlined.

[84] Interlined.

[85] Blank.

[86] The *Amity*, on her return after carrying home the Dutch commissioners, set out from Holland on 10 January; *TSP*, II, p. 18.

deputies having escaped much danger from a violent storm [arrived] upon Tuesday was sennight[87] at Goree. Wednesday they came to The Hague and gave an account of what they had done here,[88] whereupon the States General have ordered meetings of the States Provincial to advise thereupon and the States of Holland were to assemble the Tuesday following.[89] They have taken away all freedom from excise and other impositions from the prince of Orange a thing heretofore unheard of among them.

George Downing

William Clarke to George Monck, 19 January 1654

fo. [11]^{v}

<Letter to General Monck in my brother Cary's and my own behalf>[90]
Right Honourable

Understanding that your [. . .] Honour is appointed to ~~come hither~~ to [*sic*] command our forces [~~in~~] <in this nation>[91] I have presumed to [~~---~~] acquaint this bearer, Master William Cary (who is imployed by Colonel Lilburne as agent to the forces here),[92] that ~~you will please to continue him in his imployment and that if there be any~~ for his continuance in ~~his imployment~~ <his agency>[93] and that you will please to lay your commands upon him wherein he may be serviceable <serve your coming away from London>[94] in which I doubt not but you will find him faithful and diligent.

I shall not ~~trouble~~ need to trouble your Honour with any long narrative of the state of affairs here since you have it from better hands.

[87] i.e. 10 January.

[88] The commissioners' point-by-point observations on the proposed treaty are listed in *ibid.*, pp. 16–18.

[89] 17 January. Several extracts of the resolutions taken at this meeting are printed in *ibid.*, pp. 28–30.

[90] Marginated. Two days later Robert Lilburne wrote to Monck recommending Clarke as 'an old Gentleman of the State's' and commending his 'abilitie and honestie'; *S&P*, p. 21. Shortly before coming to Scotland in April 1654 Monck was allocated an allowance of 10s a day for a secretary and 5s a day for a clerk; *CSPD 1654*, p. 77. Clarke must have written this as soon as he received John Spencer's letter of 14 January (p. 141 above).

[91] Interlined. Rumours to this effect had been circulating for some time. See, e.g., an intercepted letter from Paris of 22 December 1653; *TSP*, I, p. 641; p. 141 above.

[92] Clarke's brother-in-law, the London goldsmith William Cary, was appointed on 13 August 1653; Worc. MS LXXXVI, fo. 90^{v}.

[93] Interlined.

[94] Interlined.

The enemy ~~while conceiving themself~~ (now looking upon themselves as considerable) are fallen in to Morayland with their greatest strength <[....]>[95]. ~~The particulars which they could Major~~ Colonel Morgan is drawing all the [~~strength~~] <[....]>[96] he can make in these parts to remove them[97] ~~if he can~~ having only Colonel Rich's and Colonel [Harrison's] of horse and Colonel Ashfield and Colonel Salmon's of foot, ~~some of which will be ingaged to keep some small garrisons to~~ Captain Farmer's and Major Bramwell [*sic*] troops of dragoons to make his field <force>[98] out of and ~~divers of them are [with]~~ some part of these regiments. Both horse, foot and dragoons are ~~in small garrison~~ distributed in small garrisons ~~upon the whole~~ ~~my~~ near the regiments of horse [intire]. What with sick, absent men or servants, I cannot think those two regiments will <be drawn>[99] from above 400 horse in the field. It is therefore very necessary since a troop of 50 men is so small that those in Scotland at least in this time of service might be recruited 20 in a troop which would be less charge upon the public than to raise any new forces. Another ~~particular you will want will be a considerable supply of money and your ingagement being expedited will~~ it will be of absolute necessity that your Honour get ~~supply of a~~ a considerably supply of money <and ingagement from the treasury that necessaries may not be sufficient for the future>[100] the foot soldiers here having before above these six months past not received above 3*s* 6*d* a week and now both horse and foot are the <26 weeks>[101] musters of 9bris 28 and of the 9th of January behind. ~~which~~ ~~but I shall too much trouble your Honour~~ But I fear I have already transgressed too much upon your Honour's [patience]. I shall therefore humbly crave pardon for giving you this trouble and with the tender of myself to serve you (to my greatest ability) in my present situation, subscribe myself

your honour's most humble servant

Dalkeith 19th *January 1653*

I suppose I need not hint your Honour you have Leith as well as Scotland in your commission for the time was when ~~commands of~~

95 Interlined.

96 Interlined.

97 News of these troop movements appeared in the newsbooks, e.g., *True Informer*, unnumb. (6–13 Jan. 1654), p. 15; *Several Proceedings*, 228 (2–9 Feb. 1654), p. [3600]. A letter from Dalkeith of 31 January 1654, reported that Morgan had chased the enemy from 'Murrayland' to Ross; *Mercurius Politicus* 191 (2–9 Feb. 1654), p. [3261].

98 Interlined.

99 Interlined.

100 Interlined.

101 Interlined.

~~that [. . .] were disputed~~ if I mistake not that was disputed whether in your commission or not.

News from [London], 26 January 1654[102]

fo. 15^{r}

Master Beverning was at the 1st news of him with his Highness the Lord Protector though so late. Master Feake and 2 more[103] since the [draughting] of the ordinance for treason were apprehended for what they have since spoken.[104] Here is great hopes of sweet [composure] and peace and the hearts of people are much [revived] in expectation of a settlement that trade may again be revived.

Newsletter from John Thurloe, Westminster, 26 January 1654

fo. 15^{v}

Westminster January 26

Yesternight arrived here the Lord Beverning one of the Dutch deputies that departed hence about a fortnight since.[105] He has brought with him the agreement of the province of Holland to the peace and assures that the States General will send their confirmation of it in a few weeks, deputies being sent into all the provinces to get a despatch [thereof/thereon] so that there is very little doubt of a peace which every body rejoiceth in. But a few of the Blackfriars men who throw doubt upon every person and thing which suits not with their [oppressions], they grow so unreasonable and extravagant that

[102] It is unclear whether or not this is a postscript to an immediately preceding newsletter in longhand.

[103] The Fifth Monarchist John Simpson was arrested with Feake and both imprisoned in Windsor Castle; *CSPD 1653–1654*, p. 371; p. 147 below.

[104] The Council of State ordered the drafting of this bill on 21 December 1653, the day on which Feake and Vavasor Powell were brought before the Council. It was presented to the Protector on 17 January 1654 and proclaimed on the 23rd; *ibid.*, pp. 308, 362–364, 365. Feake was rearrested three days later; *Perfect Diurnall*, 216 (23–30 Jan. 1654), p. [3298]. *A Perfect Account*, 160 (25 Jan.–1 Feb. 1654), p. 1279 explicitly connects Feake's arrest with the ordinance.

[105] Beverning landed at Harwich on 24 January, arriving in London on the 25th; *TSP*, II, p. 54. He returned alone, sent by the anti-Orangist Grand Pensionary of Holland, John de Witt, and ahead of the other deputies; this caused ill feeling in London; Venning, *Cromwellian Foreign Policy*, p. 165.

the Council are necessitated to restrain Master Feake and Master John Simpson. Upon Monday last they spoke against the government in express terms and affirmed it should not stand the year about reproaching all persons in government. In the meantime the other congregational churches and all other sober Christians send in their suffrages and express their joy for the alteration.

Jo. Thurloe

Newsletter from George Downing, Westminster, 26 January 1654

fo. 15[v]

Axeyard, Jan. 26

Yesternight came to this town the Lord Beverning who landed at Harwidge and was one of the 3 that went last away.[106] He saith his arrend[107] is to let us know that the States of Holland have agreed to the articles of peace and that they have sent to the rest of the provinces and doubts not of their very speedy concurrence and that thereupon there shall come a grand embassy to confirm the treaty.

The lord ambassador Whitelocke is entered Upsal (where the Swedish court intends to winter by reason of the plague at Stockholm)[108] the [20]th of 10bris being honourably received with 18 coaches of 6 horses in [every] coach and as many senators and courtiers as were there. The next day he presented a copy of his credentials to the master of the ceremonies to her Majesty which was wanting somewhat in her [exact] title *vizt potentissima Domina*[109] of which [defect] the Dutch agents at [London had] certified <long>[110] before, thereupon hoping at least a confirmation of the business, but it was interpreted an [. . .] and no voluntary act [. . .]. As soon as the credentials were accepted [wherefore on considering] my lord

[106] Capt. Henry Pack's account of the comings and goings of the Dutch deputies is found in *CSPD 1653–1654*, pp. 366–367.

[107] An early form of 'errand' (*OED*).

[108] *Perfect Diurnall*, 214 (9–15 Jan. 1654), p. 3249. Whitelocke wrote to Thurloe on 22 December 1653 that he had arrived safely at Uppsala; von Bischoffshausen, *Die Politik des Protectors Oliver Cromwell*, p. 155.

[109] H. Reeve (ed.), *A Journal of the Swedish Embassy . . . written by the Ambassador Bulstrode Whitelocke*, 2 vols (London, 1855), I, p. 226. The Swedish commissioner Bonnel committed a similar gaffe when he arrived in London to present a congratulatory letter from Christina to Cromwell some two months later; *ibid.*, II, p. 143.

[110] Interlined.

ambassador had audience. Her Majesty heard the speech interpreted by parts in French, at the end of the whole replied ex tempore pertinently and in order to every head,/concluding.

fo. [16]ʳ

concluding that she was very ready to enter into a stricter confirmation of the Commonwealth of England then had formerly been between the 2 nations. The 26th *December* the lord ambassador had private conversation with her Majesty betwixt 2 or 3 hours with mutual satisfaction on both sides. *December* 29th my lord ambassador exhibited in the articles of the treaty which were well relished so that there are hopes of a convenient despatch according to our desire.[111]

George Downing

Master Feake having been before a committee of the Council and being charged with seditious and treasonable words replied that as an Englishman he was subject to such government as it pleased God to set over him, but as a preacher that he had a liberty to expound histories and prophecies. Master John Simpson being called and charged in like manner replied that the [words] as charged upon him were none of his but that it was indeavoured so to place expressions as might make against him. They are both committed to the sergeant's men.[112]

Newsletter from [London], 2 February 1654

fo. 18ᵛ

This week's letters from Holland produce little. No other of the provinces has as yet declared. The Orange faction doth stickle very high against the peace. [France] carry themselfs so as if they cannot hinder the peace they may be included in it. Condé is like to be generalissimo of the Spanish army in France. Fuensaldagna to be returned.[113]

[111] Most newsbooks carried extensive reports of Whitelocke's negotiations in Sweden, e.g., *Mercurius Politicus*, 190 (26 Jan.–1 Feb. 1654), *passim*.

[112] As noted above (p. 146n), both were imprisoned in Windsor Castle.

[113] Count Fuensaldaña was overall commander of the Spanish army and therefore superior in rank to the more able Condé; *C&P*, II, p. 474.

Newsletter from Westminster, 2 February 1654

*fo. 18^v^*

Axeyard, Westminster

The French ambassador offered the State from the French king to bear half the charges of the war with England in case they break off the treaty and continue the wars,[114] but the Hollanders considering their loss of trade and maintaining war would be greater prejudice than that [act] did them [help], they voted for a peace which it is believed will be done when the Zealand lords come to meet with the States General.[115]

Master Feake and Master John Simpson are in Windsor Castle where is also Judge Jenkins, a new companion to them.[116] The Lord Protector has been so [urged] and solicited[117] by the aldermen of the city to come into London that after many addresses about it his Highness has now at the last consented to go and is to dine on Saturday next at Grocers' Hall where they intend a great solemnity.

Newsletter from [London], 2 February 1654

*fo. 18^v^*

Master Feake and Master Simpson contriving to preach their invective [misery/missives] against the present government, they were thereupon apprehended and sent prisoners to Windsor Castle.

The 2 full tides that we had this day at London Bridge in 3 hours' time causes [some discourse] and much admiration, the wind being northerly.[118]

Master Walwyn lately committed to the Tower of London is by his Highness's special order discharged.[119]

[114] Chanut's offer was reported in *A Perfect Diurnall*, 218 (6–13 Feb. 1654), p. 3328.

[115] The meeting had already taken place, on 27 January; *Severall Proceedings*, 228 (2–9 Feb. 1654), p. 3618.

[116] The following month the Welsh judge David Jenkins was said to be 'declin[ing] exceedingly'; *Moderate Intelligencer*, 167 (28 Feb.–8 Mar. 1654), p. 1333. He was not released until January 1657; *CSPD 1656–1657*, p. 239.

[117] *A Perfect Diurnall*, [215] (30 Jan.–6 Feb. 1654), p. [3100], paints a somewhat different picture, merely recording that the aldermen 'invited' Cromwell.

[118] The same phenomenon had occurred just before the execution of Charles I, and, in conjunction with the collapse of part of St Paul's, was now the cause of much foreboding; *CSPV 1653–1654*, p. 185; *Politique Informer*, 2 (30 Jan.–6 Feb. 1654), p. 16; *Certain Passages*, 3 (27 Jan.–3 Feb. 1654), p. 18; pp. 150, 162 below.

[119] The Leveller William Walwyn was ordered to be imprisoned in the Tower on 29 August 1653; *CSPD 1653–1654*, p. 111. His release is reported in *Certain Passages*, 3 (27 Jan.–3 Feb. 1654), p. 18.

Newsletter from London, 4 February 1654

fo. 19v

London February 4

On Tuesday last another messenger came from the Dutch with further assurances by word of mouth that all the haste is made that possibly can be acted in the rest of the provinces to subscribe as Holland and West Friezland have done,[120] and great assurances did come from other letters from merchants and others of good repute to that purpose so that now there is great probability of peace or war.

On Thursday last here was 2 tides in the forenoon an hour and half difference betwixt each tide. Wednesday next is the great feast at Grocers' Hall in London whither the Lord Protector is to be conducted by his soldiers from Whitehall to Temple Bar and there (and from thence) the Lord Maior, aldermen and Common Council in their gowns and liveries do receive him and conduce[121] him from Grocers' Hall towards the feast. Every alderman has subscribed 24*s* and every Common Council man 10*s*.

General Monck is preparing provisions for Scotland.[122] In Ireland there is some dissatisfaction.[123]

Newsletter from John Thurloe, Whitehall, 7 February 1654

fo. 21v

Whitehall February 7

The Dutch business stands as it did. Beverning remains here for further orders without doing anything. The 2 ministers[124] remain in prison in Windsor. The 2 ministers remain in prison at Windsor. [*sic*] Harrison is confined to Stanfordshire[125] that [fire] being to go out and so will everyone that is not of the Lord's [kindness].

[120] The resolutions were passed on 19 January 1654. Extracts are printed in *TSP*, II, pp. 34–36.

[121] Meaning 'conduct' (*OED*).

[122] Orders for shipping both Monck's personal goods and cloth for regimental uniforms were issued some two months later; *CSPD 1654*, p. 434.

[123] This contrasts with the 'much satisfaction and great solemnity' marking the proclamation of the Protectorate in Ireland which was reported in the official *Severall Proceedings*, 229 (9–16 Feb. 1654), p. 3633. Shortly afterwards the Venetian resident described widespread Irish opposition to such proclamations; *CSPV 1653–1654*, p. 187.

[124] Christopher Feake and John Simpson (p. 148 above).

[125] i.e. Staffordshire; *Certain Passages*, 5 (10–17 Feb. 1654), p. 38.

Tomorrow the Protector dines in the city and was invited by the Lord Maior, aldermen and Common Council upon which occasion the city has declared itself even as one man for the government. The last letters from Ireland bring that Murtogh O'Brien with his party is come in which was all the strength the enemy had in that country.[126]

John Thurloe

Newsletter from London, 10 February 1654

fo. 24r

London February 10

We have heard nothing from the Dutch of late only that Zealand have agreed with Holland to the treaty[127] and that their preparation of [150/the 50] sayle of men of war goes on [effectually].

Tuesday last Colonel Mackworth, governor of Shrewsbury was added to the Council,[128] who do little of business but what is referred to them by his Highness. The 2 Masters of Requests make report of petitions every Tuesday and Thursday to his Highness, who gives a speedy and satisfactory answer to them.[129] Yesterday his Highness was entered into the city.[130] The lifeguard marched before him and the heralds followed. The foot captains went bare on each side of his rich coach, wherein his Highness, Major-General Lambert and the Lord President of the Council[131] rode to Temple Bar. Commissary-General Whalley led up all the field officers and Commissary-General Reynolds brought up the rear. The Lord Maior and aldermen received him at Temple Bar and delivered up his sword, which was speedily redelivered to his Lordship, who rid bare before his Highness (then mounted) to Grocers' Hall where the Recorder made a congratulatory speech,[132] as likewise at his entrance into the city, which was railed from the Temple to Grocers' Hall, where all the livery men of the

[126] The surrender of Murrough O'Brien, Lord Inchiquin, was greeted with disbelief on the Continent; *TSP*, II, pp. 108, 119. The articles of surrender were printed in several newsbooks, e.g., *Mercurius Politicus*, 193 (16–23 Feb. 1654), p. 3281–3286.

[127] *Ibid.*, 192 (9–16 Feb. 1654), p. 3277.

[128] *Ibid.*, p. 3273.

[129] For these officials, see *SS*, pp. 32, 46, 71.

[130] This was Cromwell's first state visit as Protector. It was apparently greeted with some popular disfavour; *C&P*, II, pp. 308–309; *CSPV, 1653–1654*, pp. 184–185.

[131] Henry Lawrence.

[132] Recorder William Steele's speech was printed by several newsbooks, e.g. *A Perfect Diurnall*, 218 (6–13 Feb. 1654), pp. [3329]–[3332].

city stood all along to receive him. His Highness and officers were royally entertained, the Lord Maior sitting on his right and the Lord General Cromwell[133] on his left hand. The rest that sat at his table were all of his Council. After dinner they were entertained with a sumptuous banquet[134] and then his Highness knighted the Lord Maior and intended the like to the Recorder if he could have been found.[135] Upon his Highness's return, the great guns at the Tower were twice discharged and the bells of the city commanded to be rung.[136]

This day Master Recorder, Master Nudigate, Master Twisden, Master Maynard and Master Hugh Windhum were sworn serjeants of the court.[137] It's conceived they will be made judges this term and ride the next circuit.

Newsletter from John Thurloe, [Whitehall], 11 February 1654

fo. 23^v

February 11

I have intelligence from Holland that Middleton is gone or going from thence with 300 men, whereof there is 30 officers, into Scotland.[138] Zealand and [Utrecht] have agreed with the province of Holland in the ratification of what their deputies have done here[139] so that the greatest part by much have consented to the articles and ambassadors [----] named though delay to conclude the peace. Charles Stewart is going from France, some say for Scotland, others for Germany.[140]

[133] Henry Cromwell.

[134] i.e. dessert. A closely similar account up to this point is found in *Perfect Diurnall*, 218 (6–13 Feb. 1654), p. [3332].

[135] *Severall Proceedings*, 229 (9–16 Feb. 1654), p. 3628 noted that 'Mr Recorder was called for, but had been sent away upon speciall businesse before'.

[136] Cromwell's reception in the city was widely reported by the newsbooks, e.g., *Perfect Account*, 162 (8–15 Feb. 1654), p. 1291.

[137] *Mercurius Politicus*, 192 (9–16 Feb. 1654), p. 3273 confirms these appointments.

[138] A report from The Hague of 2 February put Middleton's force at 200 men; *Severall Proceedings*, 229 (9–16 Feb. 1654), p. 3633. For Middleton's landing in Scotland see p. 163 below.

[139] News of the ratification was sent to Thurloe on 31 January 1654; *TSP*, II, pp. 60–61.

[140] Rumours that Charles was about to leave France appeared in several newsbooks, e.g., *Perfect Diurnall*, [203] (13–20 Mar. 1654), p. 3399. It was not until July that he finally arrived at the German town of Spa; *TSP*, II, p. 448.

I think it doth not concern anybody much whither he goes. He has neither friends nor money.[141]

John Thurloe

William Clarke to George Bilton, [London], 13 February 1654

fo. 24v

<Letter to Master Bilton with thanks for his [reposals]>[142]

Honoured Sir

~~I received yours~~ I cannot but return you many thanks for those friendly overtures you propose in my behalf by your last ~~I shall not~~ which however they succeed ~~I cannot but express a~~ I cannot but look upon myself as ~~exceed~~ deeply obliged unto you, and [~~----~~] shall only trust Providence with the issue being resolved to be content with ~~its disposal~~ my lot in what place so ever it shall be and knowing that what the Almighty has appointed shall be best for me, and I praise God I am not so ambitious of preferment or amorous of imployment as to indeavour to put any by who have a fairer turn or [opener] way made for them. But I keep you too long from the [good] news which is.[143]

Newsletter from London, 14 February 1654

fo. 25r

London *February 14*

Friday last about noon the States General despatched an express hither to the Lord Beveringen[144] stating that the 5 provinces having assented to the peace they had sent to the other 2, Gelderland and Groningen, to let them know that unless they sent very speedily they would lose their votes.[145] About 12 the last Friday night the States General despatched

[141] Charles had outstayed his welcome in France, where his presence at the French court compromised any projected negotiations with England; p. 137 above; *Perfect Diurnall*, [203] (13–20 Mar. 1654), p. 3399.

[142] Marginated. 'Reposals' from 'the act of reposing (trust, confidence, etc.)' (*OED*).

[143] Blank.

[144] i.e. Beverning.

[145] It was planned to go ahead with the treaty despite the objections of both provinces; *TSP*, II, pp. 26, 47–48, 80–81, 98; *Severall Proceedings*, 229 (9–16 Feb. 1654), p. 3635.

another express hither to Beveringen with a new commission making him lord ambassador[146] and signifying that Gelderland and Groningen had also sent in their assents, and that their ambassadors would be here very speedily. Within 10 days we expect that we also expect speedily the great French marquis.[147]

Richard Beke, Uppsala, to [Robert Lilburne], 17 February 1654[148]

fo. 26v

This negotiation of necessity does make a stand until the ultimate resolution of the treaty between England and Holland be certainly known for according to the success of that [affair] so there will be a variation of their counsels here and [suitable], therefore, their answer will be to our proposals.[149] The queen has assured my lord that she will not make [hostage] in the least for an answer after she has received true information and satisfaction touching the treaty.

Richard Beke

Newsletter from George Downing, London, 18 February 1654

fo. 27r

London February 18

It is not certain that General Monck comes down for Scotland though the peace with Holland (whereof there is much [probability])

[146] The commission is printed in *TSP*, II, p. 76. Beverning had arrived as an unofficial emissary from Grand Pensionary John de Witt; p. 146.

[147] Mazarin's second envoy, Bordeaux, had a cool reception in London when he arrived in early March 1654; *C&P*, II, p. 433. He was not granted an audience with Cromwell until 28 March; pp. 168, 172 below.

[148] Richard Beke was in Sweden at this time, as captain of Whitelocke's guard. This letter was probably addressed to Robert Lilburne, who had married Beke's sister some time around 1649. On 23 March 1654 Lilburne wrote to Cromwell asking that despite Beke's absence he should be remembered in any forthcoming changes in the lifeguard, of which Beke became captain in 1656; *S&P*, p. 59 and n.

[149] The way for the treaty with Sweden, which concerned only matters relating to trade and free passage through the Sound, was cleared by the inclusion of Denmark in the Anglo-Dutch agreement. This removed the need for Whitelocke to press for military support from Sweden against the Danes; *C&P*, II, pp. 377, 380.

is concluded. I hear there is a design (upon which he is to go) for the Straights with part of the fleet to seek reparations for some injuries done by the grand duke of Florence that will engender the truth.[150]

Divers persons of disparate fortunes with some of indifferent estates associated with several apprentices of London made an oath of secrecy have been for divers months indeavouring to carry on a design for Charles Stuart and had drawn in and are indeavouring to draw in others in divers parts of the nation, as the Lord Loughborough, the Lord Byron etc.[151] One of their number did from time to time give notice of their actions and upon Tuesday night being come to some resolutions among themselves 12 of them were apprehended on Tuesday night, one person whereof they will not discover his name as yet.[152] They say that Massey[153] is in this town and that Charles Stuart was to have been here in the spring etc.

Beverning had audience by virtue of his plenipotentiary's commission. He spake very high on behalf of my Lord Protector and the present government declaring the speedy coming over other ambassadors and that in case they should not be here some time the next week he alone could sign the articles of peace in hopes whereof there is extraordinary rejoicing in Holland.[154]

George Downing

Newsletter from John Thurloe, Westminster, 21 February 1654

fo. 28^{v}

I received yours which brings the good news of the defeat of Glencairn which is a very seasonable mersy and will tend very much to the settlement of affairs.[155]

The Dutch do look to that party as very considerable and without question are very willing to see the issue thereof before they would

[150] Monck received his instructions to take over as commander-in-chief in Scotland on 6 April 1654 (p. 175 below).

[151] Both Byron and Loughborough were implicated in the plot, which was being discussed at meetings in London taverns from at least November 1653; *TSP*, II, p. 96.

[152] The newsbooks were full of the plot. A list of the twelve who were sent to the Tower on 13 February 1654 appears in *The Moderate Intelligencer*, 165 (16–23 Feb. 1654), p. 1315.

[153] Edward Massey, appointed by Charles as major-general to the duke of Buckingham in May 1651.

[154] Beverning reported the meeting to the States General on the same day; *TSP*, II, pp. 92–93.

[155] Lilburne reported on the encounter, which took place on 8 February 1654, to both Cromwell and Lambert; *S&P*, pp. 43–44, 46–48; *TSP*, II, p. 95.

come to a conclusion. Yet lay upon the same [guard] before the fight at Worcester and fell in the pit they digged for others and if they remain yet in the same temper God will find them out. Beverning and one of their deputies have been here some weeks without doing anything and now he acts to desire a proceeding, but I can assure you in very ambiguous terms. However I hope this side have done their duty and will have comfort in all events. I do not write this out of despair. It is more probable we shall have peace then otherwise, but I think every [man] ought to look to their charge as if there were to be a war. Our fleet of 100 sayle is at sea. The Dutch have none yet as I know.

Jo. Thurloe

<Westminster 21 *February*>[156]

Newsletter from George Downing, Westminster, 23 February 1654

fo. 29v

Axeyard, Westminster *February 23 1654*

The Dutch ambassadors imbarked from Holland last Lord's day in the morning.[157] In regard of fowl weather they steered for Zealand.[158] The stories of the discontents and risings amongst them were but stories. This news we have from one that came from thence the same day in the afternoon and keeping out to sea then got hither before them.

I am sorry you should desire anything from me that is not [. . . .] which [. . .] [the/thee more use] then Major-General Lambert's letters by the last post. The truth is I am desirous for your sake *omnem movere lapidem* but I find it will not do, the Lord Cranston being so obnoxious a person.[159]

George Downing

[156] Marginated.

[157] Nieupoort and Jongestal were formally authorized to act on behalf of the States General; Venning, *Cromwellian Foreign Policy*, p. 165.

[158] These details are confirmed by a letter of 21 February from The Hague; *TSP*, II, p. 107.

[159] 'Obnoxious' is used in its seventeenth-century sense of being open to censure or punishment (*OED*). Cranston had been placed on parole at Edinburgh following his capture at the battle of Worcester. His bearing impressed Robert Lilburne sufficiently for Lilburne to write to both Lambert and Cromwell on his behalf; *S&P*, pp. 44, 80. On 26 June 1654 Cromwell signed a pass for Cranston to travel overseas; Bodl., MS Rawlinson A. 328, p. 81. In June 1656, at the request of the king of Sweden, Cranston's estates were discharged from confiscation; *TSP*, V, p. 129.

Newsletter from George [Felsherd], London, 25 February 1654

fo. 31^{r}

Further advertisements are come from Holland which confirm the signing of the treaty by all the provinces, and four ambassadors were shipped at Flushing when the messengers came away. Lodgings are provided for them at Sir Abraham Williams' house.[160] It is said they [are/were] landed at Harwich [——]. The French <agent>[161] has now produced letters of credence whereby he is commissioned as an ambassador, and accordingly has had his audience and labours very much to be included with the Dutch.[162]

Colonel Henry Cromwell is sent into Ireland by the Lord Protector, there being some of the army there of the Anabaptist judgement who do oppose the proclaiming of the Lord Protector in Ireland,[163] Colonel Ludlow, Captain Vernon and Adjutant-General Allen[164] being the chief that seem unsatisfied, but if the peace with the Dutch be concluded, of which there is little doubt, this humour will quickly vanish.

George [Felsherd]

Newsletter from Gilbert Mabbott, Westminster, 28 February 1654[165]

fo. 32^{r}

There were two ambassadors landed at Dover the last Lord's Day.[166] They are expected to be about Thursday in town. Nothing is yet

[160] *Severall Proceedings*, 231 (23 Feb.–2 Mar. 1654), pp. [3664], 3673–[3674] confirms this, giving some details of the house's refurbishments and the ambassadors' intended move to York House in the Strand after their audience.

[161] Interlined.

[162] *TSP*, II, p. 130. At The Hague the French agent, Chanut, was 'labouring very hard' towards the same end; *Perfect Diurnall*, [203] (13–20 Mar. 1654), p. 3396.

[163] Cromwell left Chester on 22 February 1654, the reason given being to update Fleetwood with affairs in England; *Mercurius Politicus*, 194 (23 Feb.–2 Mar. 1654), p. 3304; *TSP*, II, p. 130. He reported to Thurloe on 8 March that the Anabaptists were quiet but that Ludlow and Col John Jones were against the government (*ibid.*, p. 149). He was back in London by 29 March; *Severall Proceedings*, 235 (23–30 Mar. 1654), p. 3738.

[164] Incriminating letters from Allen were intercepted by Thurloe in the following April; *TSP*, II, pp. 214–215.

[165] On the same day Mabbott wrote an identical letter to the mayor and aldermen of Hull; Hull CRO, BRL 596.

[166] i.e. 26 February, as confirmed in letters from Beverning and Thurloe. From Dover they went to Gravesend to await their formal arrival in London on 3 March; *TSP*, II, p. 124; below, p. 158–159.

known of their business but common fame gives it out they come to sign articles upon the late treaty. Great state will be used upon their occasion and barges are gone down this tide to attend them.

Gilbert Mabbott

Newsletter from Gilbert Mabbott, London, 4 March 1654

fo. 34r

Yesterday the Lord Newport and Youngstal[167] ambassadors from Holland, were honourably attended with near 50 coaches through the city to Sir Abraham Williams his house in the Palace Yard, Westminster, and were with as much state brought this day from thence to Whitehall where they had audience of his Highness and Council.[168] All the Dutch prisoners were discharged lately which makes the people conclude a peace. The Portugal and French ambassadors attended these from the Tower in their coaches. Next week they begin to buckle to their business.

Gilbert Mabbott

Newsletter from George Downing, [Westminster], 4 March 1654

fo. 34r

From another hand

Yesterday the Dutch ambassadors came to town. The French and Portugal ambassadors sent their coaches [to] the Tower to wait upon them, from whence they were brought to Westminster by Sir Gilbert Pickering and Master Strickland in a very handsome manner with a great number of coaches. This afternoon my Lord Protector gave them audience in [the] Banqueting House at Whitehall, and the beginning of next week they will fall [to/upon] their business.[169]

George Downing

[167] i.e. Jongestal.

[168] Sir Gilbert Pickering and Walter Strickland were ordered to meet the ambassadors on 3 March and attend them to Westminster; *CSPD 1654*, p. 3. Their arrival was reported in detail in the newsbooks, e.g. *Severall Proceedings*, 232 (9–16 Mar. 1654), pp. 3682–3684.

[169] For a more detailed account of the ambassadors' reception in London see the following document.

Newsletter from John Spencer, [London], 4 March, 1654

fo. 34r

From another of the same date

The Holland ambassadors came through London this Thursday last. There went for them some of the Council and many of the officers. There were 26 coaches with 6 horses in a coach, many with 4 and with 2. My Lord's own coach brought them through London. This day at 4 a clock they have audience in the Banqueting House of Whitehall. It is most richly hung and at the upper end only to stand on a step or 2 there the chair of state is to be, where my Lord Protector is to sit. There are great hopes thereon of peace.

<Yet there is now a-marching with all speed a thousand foot to Portsmouth to be shipped for some design. We make all haste out with our fleet as if there were no peace like to be. General Monck has no order yet to come to relieve you.[170] My Lord will not yet dispose of his regiment. Major-General Harrison is very quiet and most [of the] people of God begin to be satisfied.[171] It's thought my Lord will suddenly call a Parliament.

John Spencer>[172]

Oliver Cromwell, Whitehall, to Robert Lilburne, [Dalkeith], 7 March 1654[173]

fo. 35v

<Letter from his Highness for the sending up for the 3 ministers>[174]

Sir,

Having some occasion to speak with some godly ministers and Christians to accommodate the interest and to beget a good understanding between the people of God of different judgements in this nation, and remembering well you did once hint to me some

[170] It was not until 5 April that Monck's orders were 'read, amended, agreed and passed by his Highness and Council'; *CSPD 1654*, p. 76.

[171] *The Moderate Intelligencer*, 168 (8–14 Mar. 1654), pp. 1333–1334, reported that Harrison had 'declared to live peacably'.

[172] Marginated.

[173] A copy of this letter, taken from BL, MS Egerton 2620, fo. 11, is printed in Abbott, III, p. 211. Cromwell's purpose in sending for the three Scottish ministers is discussed in Dow, *Cromwellian Scotland*, pp. 196–198.

[174] Marginated.

purpose of Master Patrick Gillespie's thoughts to come up hither in order (as I suppose) to somewhat relating[175] to the people of God in Scotland, I have thought fit to require the coming up of Master John Levingstone, Master Patrick Gillespie and Master John Menzies to which purpose I have here inclosed sent to each of them a letter appointing them the time of their appearance herein. I desire you to speed their letters to them especially to Master John Menzies who is so far remote as Aberdeen.[176] I desire you to let them have 20*l* apiece to defray the charges of their journey. Let it be out of the treasury in Scotland. Not doubting of your care and diligence herein, I rest

your loving friend

Oliver P.

Cockpit 7th of March 1653

I desire you to contrive your care to look out after Middleton upon the coast for I hear he was driven back by foul weather.

I desire you not to make too publike the end of sending for these gentlemen.

Oliver P.

For the honourable Colonel Lilburne, commander-in-chief of the forces in Scotland these.

Haste, haste, post haste
for the service of the State.

Newsletter from Henry Walker, Westminster, 9 March 1654

fo. 36^v

The French agent (who has now clothed his footmen) has already credentials and will soon desire audience and that though he be not included in the treaty with the Dutch in those articles, yet that he has been so far treated with and it is so ready that he will [sign/soon present] after the Dutch, which it is thought they will do before this day sennight. Sir Gervase [Lucas] and other cavaliers beyond the seas are making suit to his Highness to have passes to come over into England if it might be. Major-General Brown is inlarged and

[175] Superimposed on an illegible outline.

[176] Lilburne replied on 16 March that Gillespie and Livingstone had already received their letters, and that he had despatched that to Menzies; Worc. MS, L, fo. 22^r.

come home to his house in London.[177] There is a committee of the Council appointed to draw up such grievances for the business of religion and settling of ministers as shall be by them thought fit upon consultation with Master Lockier and the other ministers that have been with his Highness. It is thought it will begin the [regulation] when the Committee for Plundered Ministers find it [. . .] that have been settled since to pass the test of commissioners that shall be established and so for all such as shall be placed in any livings to receive publike maintenance in any parish or from the State's pay for [time] to come.

There are 3 Dutch vessels taken in the narrow off which are come letters. This day there are justices come [newly] from Ireland to the Council.[178] This day is the very great settling and [in effect turn] and general conference of the officers and soldiers and also of the inhabitants in our quarters and that the enemy is not at all considerable.

There is one to have a patent here for the making of brass farthings. It is thought they should be of intrinsick value.[179]

Henry Walker

Newsletter from Gilbert Mabbott, Westminster, 11 March 1654

fo. [37]ᵛ

Since my last the Dutch ambassadors have treated several times with the English commissioners which are the Lord Lisle, Major-General Lambert, Master Lawrence, Sir Gilbert Pickering, Colonel Montague and Master Strickland, and their [result/resolution] upon the whole tends to a speedy union to which purpose the articles of agreement are ordered to be drawn into form and fairly ingrossed that so they may be speedily signed. Yet the drawing this week 1,000 men out of regiments to march towards the sea coasts occasions some to be stayed in their hopes of this so much desired peace. But both this and the command which was also this week given for all officers to repair to their charges in Scotland [signifies] at present rather an act of policy

[177] Brown's release after long-term imprisonment in Ludlow Castle was reported in several newsbooks, e.g., *Certain Passages*, 6 (17–24 Mar. 1654), p. 47.

[178] There were at this time ongoing problems with finding judges to act in Irish courts; *TSP*, II, pp. 89, 94, 224.

[179] On 16 March 1654 the Council laid aside several petitions and proposals concerning the widespread abuse in making farthings; *CSPD 1654*, p. 32. Various aspects of the problem are illustrated by *Faithful[l] Scout*, 169 [N&S 150. 169B] (10–17 Mar. 1654), p. 1341; *Perfect Account*, 159 (18–25 Jan. 1654), p. 1265; *Severall Proceedings*, 234 (16–23 Mar. 1654), p. 3718.

then fear, Charles Stuart and his mother having lately withdrawn themselfs into the duke of Orleans his country to sojourn there for some time; and the people here giving out they are banished thence gives an [advantage] to the French ambassador to be [earnest] for a union with the nation, but nothing is yet done therein.[180]

A great part of Paul's fell this week and has done much hurt, which puts the Council upon thoughts of taking it down.[181] His Highness has been in a course of fisick this week more to prevent then remedy distempers. An ordinance is passed for the trial and approbation of such ministers as have been preferred within 6 months last past.

Gilbert Mabbott

Newsletter from George Downing, [Westminster], [11 March 1654]

fo. [37][v]

Another thus

The Dutch treaty is yet in the dark. They do desire some [explanations] of some articles and indeed do a little balk among themselfs. We, on the other hand, use all possible care to make ready our fleet and they are now more active therein than they were.

George Downing

Newsletter from George Bilton, [London], [11 March 1654]

fo. [37][v]

Another thus

Things are kept private still which are or shall be done. The report is that all is agreed upon. The articles are ingrossed fit to be signed. Some horses were yesterday landed sent from the States of Holland as

[180] It was only in the following month that Charles was reported to have escorted the queen from Paris, either to Orleans or to the house of the duc d'Orleans at Blois; *Perfect Account*, 172 (19–26 Apr. 1654), p. 1373.

[181] This was the latest of several similar incidents; *Moderate Publisher*, 3 (27 Jan.–3 Feb. 1654), p. 18. The Council was now said to be considering dismantling the building, although according to the official record its main concern appears to have been to prevent looting of the fallen stones; *Moderate Intelligencer*, 168 (8–14 Mar. 1654), p. 1336; *CSPD 1654*, p. 19.

a present to the Lord Protector. Yesterday [from] a dry dock at [Horse Head Down] was lifted a gallant frigot which will carry 70 guns but will not be fit to go to sea this month or 6 weeks. The most part of the navy, near to an 100 sayle, are at Portsmouth ready for to [attempt] 300 soldiers out of each regiment being sent thither to them.

George Bilton

Newsletter from Gilbert Mabbott, London, 14 March 1654

fo. [39]r

Since my last nothing considerable has intervened. This evening the Dutch ambassadors had audience of commissioners of the Council in order to a consultation on this great business which will be permitted in few days. In the interim preparations go on very fast for the removal of his Highness to Whitehall which is expected on Friday next, against which time cloth coats will be made ready for his guard.[182]

Gilbert Mabbott

Newsletter from John Thurloe, Westminster, 14 March 1654

fo. [39]r

I thank you for your last which although I had the certain news of Middleton's landing[183] yet it proves so very inconsiderable that certainly his coming will be a discouragement to his party[184] especially when they shall hear that he has brought all with him that he is to expect and that the low countries will not only refuse to give him assistance but to suffer any of his party to abide in their dominions. Whereupon they will be obliged by the treaty if it take effect as I doubt not but it will. This week has been spent upon one point which was of the most difficult consideration and that being overcome the rest will

[182] The Protector was suffering from a cold, and spent only one night at Whitehall before returning to the Cockpit (p. 168 below).

[183] Middleton's landing in Sutherland was widely reported, e.g., *Severall Proceedings*, 233 (9–16 Mar. 1654), p. 3699; 234 (16–23 Mar. 1654), p. 3708. News of it came in a letter written to Thurloe on 3 March from The Hague, and in Robert Lilburne's letter to Cromwell of 4 March; *TSP*, II, p. 131; *S&P*, p. 52.

[184] Middleton was said to have landed with only 200 men and comparatively few arms; *TSP*, II, p. 131; *S&P*, pp. 56–57.

go down [more] smoothly, and very probably this week may end this business. Besides the 9 <Dutch>[185] ships I hear you have taken upon the northern coasts, we have taken [7] more. We have also taken the great pirate Beaches in a ship of 39 guns; the old Warwick took him after a hot and sharp dispute.[186]

Jo. Thurloe

Newsletter from George Downing, Westminster, 16 March 1654

fo. [40]ʳ

Yesterday an ordinance passed the Council for appointing commissioners for approbation of publike ministers.[187] This day the Council ordered Hampton Court and the Mews should be forthwith cleared for the use of his Highness.[188] An ordinance for the disposing of the confiscated lands in Scotland this day also passed the Council, so that now the whole acts that concern the settlement of Scotland are before his Highness.[189]

The Constant Warwick frigot has taken Beaches the arch English pirate. He had a new frigot built at Brest with 42 guns and 200 men.[190] He has done very much spoyle and had 60 prisoners then aboard him. The fight continued for about 5 hours, not many men killed but it pleased God that the Warwick frigot's [1st/best] shot down his fore top [. . .] his main yard and so dangerously hit him in the hull that he had 5 foot water [*sic*] in the hold,[191] that he had no other choice left than a certainty of drowning or a probability of hanging.

George Downing

[185] Interlined.

[186] The *Constant Warwick* had almost taken Beaches, or Beach, only a month before; *Severall Proceedings*, 231 (23 Feb.–2 Mar. 1654), p. 3650. Operating out of Brest, he had been carrying out attacks on both English and French shipping for some time; *Politique Informer*, 2 (30 Jan.–6 Feb. 1654), p. 13. News of his capture was carried by most of the newsbooks, and occasioned a celebratory verse in one; *Grand Politique Post*, 170 (21–28 Mar. 1654), p. 1353.

[187] *CSPD 1654*, p. 30.

[188] *Ibid.*, p. 32.

[189] This was incorporated in the 'ordinance of pardon and grace to the people of Scotland', 12 April 1654; *A&O*, II, pp. 875–883.

[190] *Mercurius Politicus*, 197 (16–23 Mar. 1654), p. 3346, like John Thurloe in the previous document, put the number of guns at thirty-nine.

[191] These details are confirmed by the account in *Perfect Diurnall*, [203] (13–20 Mar. 1654), p. 3309.

A Dutch ship of 400 tons laden with masts and iron was brought into Harwich yesterday.[192] There was a conference with the Dutch ambassadors upon the [old] articles and matters are brought already near a closure.

George Downing, Westminster, to [Robert Lilburne], 18 March 1654[193]

fo. [41]r

Yesterday the petition for the officers of the Chester brigade was read and committed.[194] An ordinance was read and committed to make voyd all patents and writs in the old style.[195] The ordinance for the excise is passed.[196] Upon a letter from yourself to his Highness it is referred to Major-General Lambert and some others to provide money for the services therein mentioned and further to attend his Highness about the affairs of Scotland.[197]

The queen of Sweden did lately solemnly in her Council desire to resign her government, the States of Sweden allowing her competent maintenance.[198] This is thought to be done to make trial who are her own friends and [. . .] not for the confining of her in point of her marriage. Our negotiation there stands still till the certainty of the conclusion of the Dutch business.

George Downing

Newsletter from J.R. [Westminster], [18 March 1654][199]

fo. [41]r

From another thus

The business is not yet settled concerning the Dutch though last night a commission did pass under the great seal in order to the complete

[192] The ship also carried pitch and tar; *Mercurius Politicus*, 197 (16–23 Mar. 1654), p. 3347.

[193] That Downing is writing to Lilburne is made clear by his reference to Lilburne's letter to Cromwell.

[194] *CSPD 1654*, p. 35.

[195] *Ibid.*, p. 36.

[196] *A&O*, II, pp. 845–854; *CSPD 1654*, p. 35.

[197] Lilburne's letter to Cromwell, which was written on 11 March 1654, is printed in *S&P*, pp. 57–58.

[198] Beuningen, Dutch ambassador in Sweden, wrote on 18 February to the States General informing them of Christina's decision. Daniel Whistler sent the news to Cromwell on the same day; *TSP*, II, pp. 103, 104. Unknown to Whitelocke when he set out on his embassy, the queen had decided on this course of action some time before; *C&P*, II, p. 379.

[199] Possibly from John Rushworth.

settlement thereof. The fault is ours not theirs it is not done and there is some reason of state why it is deferred. You must not ask me what it is.[200] I hope by the next post to send you a more particular account of this great business. In the meantime I remain

yours, *J.R.*

Newsletter from Gilbert Mabbott, [Westminster], [18 March 1654]

*fo. [41]*ʳ

From another thus

The Council has this week passed the ordinance to appoint commissioners for approving of ministers and also that for disposing estates in Scotland forfeited to this nation, and ordered upon Thursday last that the Mews and Hampton Court should be cleared for the use of his Highness.

The Constant Warwick has taken Beaches the arch pirate at Brest who had a frigot of 42 guns and 100 men.[201] A Dutch ship of 400 ton was brought into Harwich laden with masts and iron.[202]

Upon Wednesday's consent with the Dutch ambassadors there are great hopes of speedy conclusion.

His Highness lodged in Whitehall Thursday and the rest of his family and retinue are likewise removing.

Gilbert Mabbott

Newsletter from W.W., [20 March 1654]

*fo. [42]*ʳ

I have it in a letter from The Hague of a witty description of the present state of things by an emblem pictured there where his Highness the Lord Protector is pictured treading with one foot on an Englishman another upon an Irish and a Scotsman between his legs raising up a Dutchman before, with cap in hand bowing for peace, besides his breeches down and [skirt/shirt advanced] which the king of Spain is

[200] The delay, which was resolved by 1 April, was over the compensation for English ships detained by the king of Denmark; pp. 168, 170, 172 below.

[201] These figures can be compared with those on p. 164.

[202] On the same day all the foregoing news was also communicated by George Downing (p. 165 above).

hastening to kiss but thrust back by the king of France to be there before him. This is a way much used by that beastly people the Dutch to express things, and truly though it be a beastly emblem yet I thought good to let you know it that you may not only smile at the conceit but see how much the state of things are at present thereby too freely [deregulated].[203]

W. W.

Newsletter from George Downing, Westminster, 21 March 1654

fo. [42]v

An ordinance for making the highways, an ordinance for approbation of ministers passed his Highness and the Council.[204] Order is given to prepare Sir Abraham Williams his house for the reception of Monsieur Burdieux.[205]

Lord Bradshaw[206] has accepted of and continued his place of Chief Justice of Chester.

George Downing

Newsletter from Gilbert Mabbott, [Westminster], [21 March 1654]

fo. [42]v

Another thus

Friday the Council read and committed the petition of the officers of the Chester brigade. They likewise passed the ordinance for the excise and read and committed another ordinance to make voyd all patents

[203] I have been unable to identify this print. It is not listed in the British Museum *Catalogue of Prints and Drawings, I: Political and Personal Satires* (London, 1870). It shares some motifs with a print in the Sutherland Collection, Ashmolean Museum, Oxford, but differs from it in other respects. On stylistic evidence, the Sutherland example is probably later, dating perhaps from the last quarter of the seventeenth century. For guidance on this last point I am most grateful to Richard Sharp.

[204] For both of these see *CSPD 1654*, p. 40 (20 March 1654).

[205] The house had been vacated by the Dutch ambassadors after their audience on 4 March 1654; *Severall Proceedings*, 231 (23 Feb.–2 Mar. 1654), pp. 3673–[3674]; p. 159 above; *Mercurius Politicus*, 198 (23–30 Mar. 1654), p. 3370.

[206] i. e. John Bradshaw.

and writs in the old style. They referred Colonel Lilburne's letters for monies to Major-General Lambert and others who are likewise to attend his Highness about the affairs of Scotland.

By letters from Sweden we understand the queen has solemnly of late desired in her council to resign her government [from] the States, they allowing her convenient maintenance on purpose to try who are for her [. . .] in point of marriage.[207]

Gilbert Mabbott

Newsletter from Henry Walker, Westminster, 23 March 1654

fo. [43]^v

It is believed a few meetings more will finish the treaty with the Dutch to be sealed. Monsieur Bordeaux has from the king of France sent to the Lord Protector that he has letters of credence to be ambassador[s] extraordinary and desires to be received and have speedy audience.[208] It was thought he should have had audience on Monday but it will be [1st] seen whether there can be a conclusion with the Dutch which the Dutch ambassadors press.[209] A despatch of the [greatest halt] is about the Eastland merchants and other losses sustained [from] the king of Denmark as to the sum of money to be allowed.

The Lord Protector lay only one night in Whitehall, being not well, and his old rooms liking him best whilst he is ill, which is only a cold, but it's hoped he mends of it.[210] He goeth abroad and is now about choosing his footguard for the guard of his person at court. It is thought they will be all or most of them members of the army.[211]

Those that are the great followers of Master Feake and Master Simpson are many of them much fallen off from their principles, and Master Rogers of Thomas Apostle's is under admonishment of the church that [walks] with Master Squibb, whereof he is a member and has been several times sent for, but refuseth to come among them.

[207] All the items of news in this letter were also reported by Downing on 18 March (p. 165 above).

[208] Bordeaux had first sought an audience with Cromwell four weeks previously; *TSP*, II, p. 113.

[209] The most recent meeting between Cromwell and the ambassadors had taken place on 21 March; *Mercurius Politicus*, 197 (16–23 Mar. 1654), p. 3358.

[210] *Moderate Intelligencer*, 170 (22–29 Mar. 1654), p. 1353.

[211] The life guard of foot belonged to, and was maintained by, the Protector's household, as distinct from the life guard of horse, which was part of the army establishment; R. Sherwood, *The Court of Oliver Cromwell* (London, 1977), pp. 80–81.

The greatest part of them comply with the present government, but Master Rogers doth much [rayle] against it.[212]

The Lord Maior of London and justices of Westminster have sent strong precepts to the inhabitants to shut up their shops and to keep tomorrow a very strict fast so that what with the episcopal party on the one side that so wholly honour that day as to receive the [. . .] thereon, the presbyterian party with my Lord Maior's [protection], and the moderate independent satisfied in the Lord Protector's sincerity in the [design] it is like to be very strictly kept.[213]

Henry Walker

Newsletter from Gilbert Mabbott, Westminster, 25 March 1654

fo. [44]^v

To tell you the peace between us and the Dutch is concluded is not safe nor convenient, because his Highness and the Council have not, or will not, yet declare it for some reasons of state, especially in respect of negotiations with foreign princes who lie upon the catch[214] in this juncture of time. Both [. . .] our selfs and Holland, and upon this score our ships and theirs must not forbear acts of hostility, and conferences should likewise be continued between our commissioners and theirs twice or thrice a week which induces most men that know nothing of this mystery to question the union. The French ambassador is expected on Tuesday next, some preparations of boats being making ready to bring him up.[215]

The Council has this week passed the ordinance for the approbation of preachers, with others for [renewing] the act for [impressing] of seamen and disposing the estates of lunatiques and idiots, and for continuing the former excise on coals.[216] Yesterday was strictly observed a fast for rain and the crying sins of the nation.

Gilbert Mabbott

[212] Both John Rogers and Arthur Squibb were prominent Fifth Monarchists. Rogers's house was searched in April 1654 and he was imprisoned in the following July. Squibb, a member of the Nominated Assembly, held several official positions until 1654. A gathered congregation, probably Baptist, was meeting at his home from 1649; *DBR*, 'Rogers', 'Squibb'; Capp, *Fifth Monarchy Men*, pp. 261, 263.

[213] The Protector's declaration for the fast, issued on 20 March, is printed in *Perfect Diurnall*, 224 (20–27 Mar. 1654), pp. 3417–3422.

[214] To lie in wait, be on the lookout (*OED*).

[215] Bordeaux travelled the short distance to Gravesend in order to make his ceremonial entrance into London by river on 28 March (p. 170 below).

[216] For all these see *A&O*, II, pp. 854–858.

George Downing, Westminster, to [Robert Lilburne], 28 March 1654

fo. [46]ʳ

I acquainted my Lord Protector with what you have done as to Knox[217] who very well approves thereof and if I mistake not the commissioners for [. . .] have power to put out ministers. As for Colonel Overton's chaplain, he also thanks you for what you have done as to him, and in case he be any way clamourous you shall have an order for his acting for my Lord Argyle. My Lord saith he shall be glad to see him now and thinks it may not be amiss if he come hither this spring.

As for a foot regiment, I suppose you are not [. . .] that there are thoughts of turning Colonel Clobery's regiment of foot out of Ireland into Scotland, but in that nothing yet is concluded, and as to money it is debated. But the Dutch business keeps all things at uncertainty. It's wholly agreed except as to the 140,000*l* for the ships stopped in the Sound, and I believe the Dutch officers have sent into Holland an express about that.[218] Our fleet is in a [guard without pay]. We have now above 230 sayle at sea, and shall within 3 weeks have 30 sayle more abroad, and such ships as well fitted as [yet] before and [---] points the course. Yet were the admiralty business well ordered it could be much better then it is.

Your brother Lilburne is shipped for Jersey.[219]

George Downing

Newsletter from Gilbert Mabbott, Westminster, 30 March 1654

fo. [47]ʳ

The French agent having received power from his master to act as an ambassador went Monday last from London to Gravesend to be brought up hence and received here in state which [accordingly] was done and as he was coming through the city he indeavoured to have a French coach immediately to follow that which he was in but the Portugal ambassador's court interposed, the next place being

[217] Lilburne had recently arrested 'Mr Knox of Kelsey' (Kelso) for publicly preaching his royalist sympathies; *Perfect Diurnall*, 225 (27 Mar.–3 Apr. 1654), p. 3438.

[218] A letter of intelligence from The Hague written almost at the same time confirms this, giving a more precise figure of £140,650; *TSP*, II, p. 198.

[219] On 22 March 1654 the Protector and Council ordered John Lilburne's transfer from the Tower of London to Jersey; *CSPD 1654*, p. 46.

his right.[220] This occasioned the laquies of both ambassadors to draw but the soldiers coming in prevented the mischief.[221] Yesterday the French had audience, desiring treaty and union with us. A committee of the Council is appointed to treat with him. Monday last Colonel Rich delivered up his commission to his Highness. Tuesday last Sir Gilbert Pickering gave in his answer and accepted of the place of Lord Steward to his Highness' family. A cofferer from [Bristol] is likewise named[222] with other chief officers and his Highness intends a speedy removal to Whitehall. Yesterday General Monck received his commission and instructions to go commander-in-chief for Scotland.[223] Tomorrow sennight he intends his journey. Lieutenant-Colonel John Lilburne is tomorrow upon removal but [where] is not yet known.

Gilbert Mabbott

50,000*l* was yesterday ordered for the forces in Scotland and the laying and setting the assessment there was referred to the Committee of the Army.[224]

Newsletter from George Downing, [Westminster], 30 March 1654

fo. [47]^r

From another thus

Yesterday the amendments to the ordinance for the relief of creditors passed the Council.[225] The ordinance for continuing the Judges of the Admiralty passed both his Highness and the Council[226] and it

[220] According to the newsbooks, the French ambassador managed to get his way. His own coach came immediately behind the Protector's coach, in which the ambassador was riding; *Perfect Diurnall*, 225 (27 Mar.–3 Apr. 1654), pp. 3433–3434.

[221] The fracas is described in *Severall Proceedings*, 234 (16–23 Mar. 1654), pp. 3731–[3732].

[222] This was John Maidstone; *CSPD 1654*, pp. 92–93; Sherwood, *The Court of Oliver Cromwell*, p. 42.

[223] Monck's instructions were read, amended and passed by the Protector on 5 April 1654, and signed at Whitehall on the 8th; *CSPD 1654*, p. 76; *TSP*, II, p. 222.

[224] *CSPD 1654*, pp. 57–58.

[225] The ordinance suspending the proceedings of the judges named in the act for the relief of creditors and poor prisoners was itself suspended on 31 March 1654, and in its revised form passed on 18 April 1654; *A&O*, II, pp. 860–861, 888–889; *CSPD 1654*, p. 57.

[226] *Ibid.*, p. 58.

was ordered from the Council that the sum of 50,000*l* be forthwith provided and sent to Scotland for supply of the forces there, *vizt* out of the treasuries of Goldsmiths' Hall and Drury House 1,200*l*, out of the monies in the Tower 20,000*l*,[227] out of such other treasuries as the Commissioners for Inspecting the Treasury shall think fit 8,000*l* and out of the rest monies that shall come in from treasurers of Drury House after the said 8,000*l* shall be reimbursed 10,000*l*.[228] The setting of the [assessment] in Scotland is referred to the Committee for the Army and you shall speedily have it done. Yesterday also the French plenipotentiary had audience in the Banqueting House. This day an ordinance was reported from the Council for [better] provision for widows and maimed soldiers in Ireland.[229]

George Downing

Newsletter from George [Felsherd], London, 1 April 1654

fo. [48]ʳ

Last night about 9 of the clock the Dutch business was in effect fully concluded, so that either on Monday or Tuesday at the furthest it will be so finished that 2 of the Council will be sent over into Holland to see the States General, the States of the several principal provinces, to sign and seal as their ambassadors here are waiting to see the Lord Protector and Council of State to sign and seal here. Master Strickland is one who is to sign it to go over upon that account. I write this upon very good grounds so that you may depend upon it for the ruts that were in the way about the Dane are all removed to contentment and there is no other obstruction in the way.[230]

George [Felsherd]

[227] A warrant was immediately issued to the Treasurers-at-War to release this money (*ibid.*, p. 444).

[228] *Ibid.*, pp. 57–58, confirms all these sums. The money was ordered on 7 April 1654 to be sent to Leith by sea, but because of concerns about its safe passage did not arrive there until 23 May; *ibid.*, pp. 86, 135; *LRHO*, p. 70.

[229] *CSPD 1654*, p. 59.

[230] The successful conclusion of negotiations following agreement over the compensation to be paid for English merchant ships detained by the king of Denmark is fully reported in the official newsbook *Severall Proceedings*, 236 (30 Mar.–6 Apr. 1654), p. 3749.

Newsletter from George Downing, [Westminster], 1 April 1654

fo. [48]r

From another thus

The Dutch treaty will be signed upon Monday next if there be any faith in a Dutch man.[231] I believe you heard by the last post how it stands with Colonel Rich.[232]

George Downing

Newsletter from Gilbert Mabbott, Westminster, 4 April 1654

fo. [50]v

On Sunday last the Lord Protector sent a warrant to bring the Great Seal of England to his Highness which accordingly was done. The reason thereof was [that] R. Keble was laid aside and Sir Thomas Widdrington is ordered to succeed him in that place.[233]

Yesterday the English merchants delivered in an estimate of the losses received from the king of Denmark for which satisfaction is to be made by the treaty. Lieutenant-Colonel Lilburne was removed Sunday last from the Tower to the isle of Jersey. 600 of Sir William Constable's regiment are ordered forthwith to march into Scotland.[234] The bill for probate of wills is revived.[235] The Portugal quarrel in the Exchange[236] and the business of improving forest lands is this day referred. The Dutch treaty had been signed before this but that it could not be ingrossed. 1,800*l* was yesterday ordered Colonel Hewson for

[231] English mistrust of Dutch motives was summed up earlier in the year by the *Politique Informer* – 'He that takes an Eele by the Tail hath but slippery hold, and however the Dutch pretend Peace, their actions shew the Contrary'; 1 (23–30 Jan. 1654), p. 3.

[232] In mid-March 1654, Col Nathaniel Rich was implicated in irregularities connected with the farming of the post; *CSPD 1654*, pp. 23, 24. It may be to this that Downing refers.

[233] Widdrington was appointed to succeed Richard Keble (for whom see *OxDNB*) as a commissioner of the Great Seal on 4 April 1654; *CSPD 1654*, p. 73.

[234] They formed part of the reinforcements sent to Scotland to suppress the mounting highland rising; F&D, II, p. 401.

[235] The ordinance was passed on 3 April 1654; *A&O*, II, p. 869.

[236] The trial and subsequent execution of Don Pantaleon de Saa, brother of the Portuguese ambassador, for a murder committed in London in November 1653 was widely reported; e.g., pp. 184, 190, 194, 195 below.

his arrears.[237] Master Bilton this day received 30,000*l* for Scotland,[238] whither General Monck sets not forward till the next week.

Gilbert Mabbott

Newsletter from John Thurloe, [Westminster], 4 April 1654

fo. [50]v

This will bring you the certain news of the conclusion of the peace with the Dutch in every particular, and I think the articles will be signed tomorrow. What the terms of this peace are you will see ere long. They are too large to repeat here.[239] I hope they are honourable and profitable to the nation and the [best/1st] that ever were made with that people.

John Thurloe

Newsletter from Westminster, 6 April 1654

fo. [51]v

The articles upon the treaty with the Dutch were yesterday signed and sealed by commissioners on both sides and within 14 days they are to be signed and sealed by the Lord Protector and the States of Holland, and then to be [dressed].[240] The loss of the English merchants by the Dane amounting to 140,000*l* referred to Master Winslow and Master [Bernard][241] and 2 Dutch merchants who are to sit in Guildhall 20 days thereupon and in case they agree not by that time they are all 4 to be locked up in one room and to have no benefit of fire, candle or provision till they are agreed.[242] The business of Amboyna is referred

[237] The commissioners for prize goods ordered payment of £1,832 9s 3d to Col John Hewson on 3 April 1654; *CSPD 1654*, p. 445.

[238] The amount to be paid out was £28,000; *ibid.*, p. 86.

[239] The articles are printed in Abbott, III, pp. 897–905 (Appendix I).

[240] Following the signature of the completed articles they were despatched to the States General for ratification; von Bischoffshausen, *Die Politik des Protectors Oliver Cromwell*, p. 178; *Severall Proceedings*, 236 (30 Mar.–6 Apr. 1654), p. 3754; *Perfect Account*, 170 (5–12 Apr. 1654), p. 1356.

[241] The two English representatives were Edward Winslow and James Russell; Abbott, III, p. 903.

[242] This was made explicit in the secret article of the treaty, where, however, it was specified that they were to meet at Goldsmiths' Hall, not Guildhall, which was where

to 8 commissioners who are to sit 6 months thereupon, and in case they agree not then the chief magistrates of Switzerland are to be umpire between us.[243] The Lord Protector has passed an ordinance for [adjourning] part of Easter term that [else] many abuses and [corruptions] are crept into the ordinary course and administration of justice both in law and equity, the reformation whereof has not yet been attained, out of a tender care and desire that so necessary and good a work may at length be brought to effect. It is ordered that part of this Easter term from the 1st return called *Quindena Paschae* be forwarded unto the 1st of trinity term called *Crastino Trinitatis*.[244]

Newsletter from George Downing, Westminster, 6 April 1654

fo. [51]v

An ordinance is ordered to be brought in for ejecting scandalous ministers.[245] It is referred to a committee to consider how to take away tithes and otherwise to provide for ministers' maintenance. It is referred to his Highness from the Council as their opinion that the Lord Whitelocke have leave to return from his embassy when he shall think fit. Part of Easter term is put off that in the interim something may be effected as to the regulating of law proceedings. His Highness has passed ordinance for uniting of Scotland to England, as also the bill of grace for Scotland.[246] Last night the Dutch treaty was signed by the commissioners of the council appointed by his Highness, and by the Dutch ambassadors, and they have this day sent an express into Holland to have it ratified, and in the interim there is no cessation of arms.

George Downing

This afternoon his Highness has signed General Monck's instructions as commander-in-chief of the forces in Scotland.[247]

the commissioners considering the 30th article of the treaty were to convene; Abbott, III, pp. 903, 908; *Perfect Diurnall*, 234 (29 May–5 June 1654), pp. 3581–[3582].

243 Followed by a blank. The arrangement had been made public in February; *Severall Proceedings*, 229 (9–16 Feb. 1654), p. 3632.

244 The ordinance, which is found in *A&O*, II, pp. 869–870, was widely published, e.g., *Mercurius Politicus*, 200 (6–13 Apr. 1654), p. 3407.

245 The ordinance was passed on 28 August 1654; *A&O*, II, pp. 968–990.

246 These ordinances were passed on 12 April 1654; *ibid.*, pp. 871–883.

247 The instructions had passed Council on the preceding day; *CSPD 1654*, p. 76; they are printed on pp. 83–85. On 5 April Monck was authorized to employ a secretary and clerk; *ibid.*, p. 77.

Newsletter from Gilbert Mabbott, Westminster, 11 April 1654

fo. 53ʳ

General Monck began his journey yesterday for Scotland,[248] where he is to command in chief, and Commissary-General [. . .][249] has commission to command in chief under him all the horse in that nation. We have heard nothing yet from the Dutch since their commissioners sent the express.

Gilbert Mabbott

Newsletter from George Downing, Westminster, 13 April 1654

fo. 54ᵛ

I have been lately with the fleet indeed I never saw any fleet like this [either] for goodness of ships, well-fittedness and good government. My Lord tells me Colonel Pride's regiment is ordered to Scotland and that it is resolved to forward the work on the hills or behind the hills and my brother Howard[250] is ordered for the borders and to command 6 troops of horse for [quieting] the borders.[251]

George Downing

Newsletter from Henry Walker, Westminster, 13 April 1654

fo. 54ᵛ

From another thus

There is an ordinance coming out for suppressing the planting of tobacco in England where it seems divers acres of ground have

[248] Monck's departure is confirmed by *Mercurius Politicus*, 200 (6–13 Apr. 1654), p. 3414. His arrival in Edinburgh on 4 May was greeted with considerable ceremony; *ibid.*, 205 (11–18 May 1654), p. 3477.

[249] The name is illegible, but presumably this was Commissary-General Edward Whalley, whose regiment of horse was sent to Scotland two months earlier; F&D, I, p. 228. In 1655 Whalley was appointed one of Cromwell's major-generals.

[250] Capt. Charles Howard whose sister, Frances, Downing married in 1654; *OxDNB*, 'Downing'.

[251] These troop movements were ordered on the following day; *CSPD 1654*, p. 100.

been already planted.[252] An ordinance besides the act of grace for Scotland is passed for union with Scotland.[253] An ordinance is likewise coming out for court barons[254] for Scotland. There are no extraordinary preparations against the Lord Protector's coming to Whitehall tomorrow.[255] He is making himself a guard of foot.

Henry Walker

Newsletter from Westminster, 15 April 1654

fo. 55v

The Swede and Hamburgh agents press to be included with the Dutch which is assented unto.[256] An ordinance is passed the Council for continuation of the former act for the customs passed *Anno* 1653 and the last act to be laid aside.[257] An ordinance is also passed the Council for [contracting][258] the imposition upon coals for building of ships. Some amendments also are reported to the act for the excise *viz*: for nulling that clause taking away half customs on goods exported. The business of improving the forests is again referred.[259]

Newsletter from Gilbert Mabbott, Westminster, 18 April 1654

fo. 57r

The Lord Protector removed Friday last to Whitehall with all his family and on Saturday last dined at Hampton Court where he intends to reside for some part of this next summer. The Council has this week

[252] The ordinance was passed on 11 April 1654; *A&O*, II, pp. 870–871.

[253] This information had been supplied by Downing a week earlier; p. 175 above.

[254] i.e. 'courts baron'. The ordinance was passed on 12 April 1654; *A&O*, II, p. 883. Courts baron sat at three-weekly intervals and could exercise jurisdiction of up to 40s on claims from contract, debt, or trespass; A.R.G. McMillan, 'The judicial system of the Commonwealth in Scotland', *Juridical Review*, 1 (1937), p. 251.

[255] The Protector's return to Whitehall was predicted in *Severall Proceedings*, 238 (13–20 Apr. 1654), p. 3771.

[256] After initial difficulties over the superscription of Christina's letter of congratulation to Cromwell, the Swedish agent Bonnel was granted an audience on 4 April 1654; *Severall Proceedings*, 236 (30 Mar.–6 Apr. 1654), p. 3750; Reeve, *A Journal of the Swedish Embassy* . . . , II, p. 143.

[257] The ordinance was passed on 20 March 1654; *A&O*, II, p. 854.

[258] This ordinance, also passed on 20 March 1654, was for 'continuation' of the imposition; *ibid.*, p. 854.

[259] This was referred on 14 April 1654; *CSPD 1654*, pp. 98–99.

revived the business of improving of forests by giving it a 2nd order of [consent]. The Dane and Hamburgh agents have of late been very importunate to be included with the Dutch, which was on Thursday last assented unto. An ordinance is passed the Council for continuing the imposition upon coals for building of ships. An ordinance is passed for continuing a former act for settling of the customs. Yesterday the Dutch ambassadors received a confirmation of the treaty from their superiours the States, who have signed and sealed the same as was desired.[260] The like is speedily to be done by his Highness and then the peace will soon after be proclaimed. Thursday next is given out to be the day for that purpose. The Portsmouth, Middleburgh and Falmouth frigots met on Tuesday last with 48 sayle of French, and after 5 hours fight, took 4, sunk 3 of them.[261] They had only provisions and some salt in them and bound for the Newfoundland.

Gilbert Mabbott

Newsletter from Gilbert Mabbott, Westminster, 22 April 1654

fo. 59[r]

The treaty with the Hollanders was signed on Wednesday last[262] by his Highness and a proclamation of the peace is hourly expected here.

His Highness lives as politely at Whitehall as he did at the Cockpit without the addition of any more attendants.

3 of our frigots fell upon 48 of the French fleet bound for the Newfoundland and elsewhere, sunk 3 of their best ships and took 4 more of them. We have also 400 prisoners taken out of French ships.

Gilbert Mabbott

Wednesday next proclamation is to be made here and in Holland of the treaty.[263]

[260] The date is confirmed in the ambassadors' reply to the States General; *TSP*, II, p. 245.

[261] Richard Bradshaw, English resident at Hamburg, had heard a greatly exaggerated report that sixty French ships had been captured. The encounter took place off St Malo (*ibid.* p. 259).

[262] i.e. on 19 April.

[263] i.e. 26 April.

Newsletter from George Downing, [Westminster], 22 April 1654

fo. 59[r]

From another

This night the Dutch treaty was ratified. Wednesday next proclamation <thereof>[264] is to be made both here and at The Hague and within 12 days after, all ships taken within these seas are to be restored and all taken from thence to the Cape of Saint Vincent's within 6 weeks, and all from thence to the line[265] within 10 weeks, and all on the other side of the line within 8 months.[266] This will a little relieve the Hollanders who by this war besides other losses has lost to the Portugal all those fighting in Brazil and the isle in the East Indies in which grew all the cinnamom.

George Downing

The Scots acts are passed and this night will be sent you.[267]

Newsletter from Gilbert Mabbott, Westminster, 27 April 1654

fo. 61[v]

Yesterday the peace was proclaimed at Whitehall before his Highness and Council (who stood in the council chamber window), at Temple Bar and the Exchange with 4 heralds and 6 trumpets.[268] Some bells rung and some bonfires were made [hereupon] and towards the evening the great guns went off at the Tower. The Dutch ambassadors consummating the whole kept [. . .] upon the river Thames from 9 till 12 at night. This day 400 dishes of meat were raised at Whitehall to entertain the Dutch ambassadors and their retinue, the Council being in their best habits and his Highness' guard having all their new grey coats (with black velvet and lace in every set) to attend

[264] Interlined.

[265] i.e. the equator, or, in *Mercurius Politicus*, 202 (20–27 Apr. 1654), p. 3439, the 'Aequinoctial line'.

[266] *Ibid.* prints the proclamation (pp. 3444–3445).

[267] The acts were to be published in all the Scottish shires by the commander-in-chief, although not, it seems, in England; Roots, 'Cromwell's ordinances', p. 157.

[268] These details are confirmed by *Severall Proceedings*, 239 (20–27 Apr. 1654), p. [3801]. The proclamation was printed in many of the newsbooks, e.g. *A Perfect Diurnall*, 230 (1–8 May 1654), pp. 3517–3519.

them.[269] Master Nathaniel Fiennes was yesterday chosen sit [*sic*] as a member of the Council.

Gilbert Mabbott

Newsletter from [London], 1 May 1654

fo. [63]ᵛ

The Lord Protector's daughters being in [. . . .] in Hyde Park with Colonel Ingoldsby and others, the people set up a shout which made them go out at a back door.[270]

Newsletter from George Downing, Westminster, 2 May 1654

fo. [64]ʳ

The Committee of the Army are ordered to bring in an act for continuing the act of the monthly assessment.[271] The merchant ships imployed in the service of the States are ordered to be discharged and also some others to the number of about 40 sayle.[272] An act is drawing up to continue the powers of the commissioners for inspecting the treasuries for 7[273] months.

George Downing

Newsletter from Payne Fisher, Whitehall, 8 May 1654

fo. 67ᵛ

My Lord's great officers, most colonels, dined with him this day and I heard Colonel Hacker say my Lord desires their company every

[269] The new uniforms of the life guard were noticed in several newsbooks, e.g. *Severall Proceedings*, 240 (27 Apr.–4 May 1654), pp. 3803–3804; *Faithful[l] Scout*, 178 (5–12 May 1654), p. 1406.

[270] Hyde Park was the focus for the May Day celebrations in 1654, one eyewitness estimating that there were some 1,500 coaches there. The Protector's three daughters were 'all in green-a', galloping round the Park in their coach 'and all that great multitude hunted them, and caught them still at the turn, like a hare, and so after them again, that I never saw the like in my life'; quoted from the correspondence of Lord Scudamore in J. Ashton, *Hyde Park from Domesday-Book to Date* (London, 1896), p. 16.

[271] The order was made on the same day as this newsletter; *CSPD 1654*, p. 144.

[272] *Ibid.* does not give the size of the proposed reduction.

[273] This should read '3' months as in *ibid.*, p. 145.

Monday. Colonel Hacker believes he shall go down for Scotland. Okey was on his way and was sent for by one of his Highness' messengers, but is again dismissed and takes his journey tomorrow. Rich's regiment is conferred upon Colonel Ingoldsby for which some horse officers grumble but [toss] in their gizzards. Major Husbands is discontented and has laid down.[274] Great preparations by sea, divers of our ships being sheathed, the hopes and expectation of the merchant being matched with great designs in hand. Lord Whitelocke is ready to open the articles being agreed, and amiable interchanges fly. The Dutch ambassadors have some private offers in behalf of their friends and, 'tis thought, that of settling the Lord Craven again in his estate by a [great/grand] request which will annoy Grey of Groby who is out 42 thousand pounds, and other petty adventures.

Payne Fisher

Whitehall, Master Peters'

Newsletter from Gilbert Mabbott, [London], 8 May 1654

fo. 67[v]

From another thus

The Lord Whitelocke has concluded a peace with Sweden and himself is coming over for England.[275] Colonel Okey, having lately [spake] some despising language against the present authority is come up on his Highness' special order to answer the same.[276]

The Lord Broghill and Sir Charles Coote's brother are come over lately from Ireland with a congratulatory message from a general council of officers in Ireland.[277] The resolution as to civil affairs there will be speedily known.

Gilbert Mabbott

[274] See F&D, I, p. 149.

[275] The news was announced in *Perfect Diurnall*, 230 (1–8 May 1654), p. 3528.

[276] I have not found any other reference to this incident, although in October of the same year Okey was court-martialled for his part in signing the 'petition of the three colonels'.

[277] The mission was reported in *ibid.*, 231 (8–15 May 1654), p. 3541.

Newsletter from Henry Walker, Westminster, 11 May 1654

fo. 69r

There is some [muttering] this night of some letters from Holland that there are some soldiers discontented in Holland at the peace that have plundered some houses, set on by the Orange party. There are 14 more of his Highness' guard listed, and I believe will be received in tomorrow, which some think will be all, besides the 20 put in before, that he will have of 40.[278] His Highness' Council have under consideration the sending of some body to Holland to appoint as deputy and the sending ambassadors to Turkey and other places.[279]

Henry Walker

Newsletter from George Downing, [Westminster], 11 May 1654

fo. 69r

The peace is proclaimed in Holland with very great joy and very great preparations there for all merchants' voyages as well here as there.[280]

The queen of Sweden is gone to Nicoping[281] to visit her mother. The articles of alliance are in the meanwhile ingrossing so as there will be nothing to do at her return but to sign, and she is expected within about 8 days after her departing.[282]

George Downing

[278] Presumably the life guard of horse, of which the strength was forty; Sherwood, *The Court of Oliver Cromwell*, p. 83.

[279] Richard Lawrence, the Levant Company's agent at Constantinople had complained on several occasions that he had been prevented from taking up office by the self-appointed ambassador there, Sir Thomas Bendish. In 1652 Maj. Richard Salwey was appointed to succeed him at such time as the company's flagging trade recovered. This was confirmed on 14 August 1654, but Salwey never went, asking to be released from the appointment in 1655; *CSPD 1654*, pp. 215, 340; Abbott, III, p. 399.

[280] The merchants of both nations had suffered greatly as a result of the hostilities; Pincus, *Protestantism and Patriotism*, p. 179.

[281] i.e. Nyköping Castle, frequently used as a royal residence during the sixteenth and seventeenth centuries, although less so after Christina's abdication. (I am grateful to Dr Svante Norrhem for this information.)

[282] One of the aims of Christina's visit was to show the articles of the treaty (which Whitelocke had scrutinized with Count Axel Oxensternia) to her intended successor, the future Charles X; *TSP*, II, pp. 232, 243. The queen returned to Uppsala on 23 April 1654; Reeve, *A Journal of the Swedish Embassy*, II, p. 153.

William Clarke, Stirling, to Mrs Cadwell, 12 May 1654

fo. 69ᵛ

<Letter to Mistress Cadwell to pay her husband's debts>[283]

Good Mistress Cadwell

~~Having written I am sorry that I should have this occasion to trouble you with any remembrance of the~~ [. . .]

~~Your hus~~

Having written several times to my brother Cary concerning ~~some monies~~ <60 [odd] pounds>[284] which [were/are] due to me from your late husband, and hearing that you seem unsatisfied to pay it, I thought good by [these] to put you in mind of it, and to assure you that ~~if you appoint any friend~~ upon <the exact>[285] perusal of what you have to offer for your husband and my brother for me, it will clearly appear that the said monies are due unto me, and if you will seriously <consider>[286] ~~peruse~~ of that one paper written with your husband's own hand wherein he acknowledges to have received 230*l* of me for that very bill of journey for which Master Hatter afterwards paid him you will find that the account is clear enough. For I can safely take my oath that I never had more to discount with your husband than <before the [death]>[287] [the] 100*l* which was paid by him upon a bill of trade between [~~. . .~~] Colonel Atkins[288] and me myself, and for his bill in my Lord Fairfax's time, all which I have clearly stated. ~~I desire you will~~ Refer it to any friend to be chosen by my brother Cary for me and another for yourself to peruse it and give their opinion. I [must/should] further profess that as my life has hitherto been unblamable as to the ~~deceiving of any man~~ <rendering any man his due>,[289] so I desire it but my duty in this, and that what money is justly mine may not lie in your hands as part of that left by your husband ~~and so consume and~~ and bring a curse instead of a blessing upon the rest, which I leave to your serious consideration and remain

Your very assured friend and servant

[283] Marginated. On 15 November 1653 Clarke had petitioned Cromwell (unsuccessfully, as this letter shows) asking him to intercede in the recovery of this debt (p. 117 above).

[284] Interlined.

[285] Interlined.

[286] Interlined.

[287] Interlined.

[288] Col Samuel Atkins.

[289] Interlined.

Newsletter from Gilbert Mabbott, Westminster, 13 May 1654

fo. 70[r]

A commission of oyer and terminer is ordered to be drawn [upon] Lord Chief Justice Rolles, Justice Atkins, Sergeant Steele, Dr Zouch, Dr Turner, Dr Clarke, Sir Henry Bunt, Richard Lucy Esq., Alderman Tichborne, for trial of Don Pantaleon *de Sa* the Portugal ambassador's brother.[290] An ordinance is ordered to be brought in for the settling of Jersey.[291] An ordinance is passed for doubling 20,000*l* more upon dean and chapter lands.[292] A declaration is passed for observing the 27th[293] instant a day of thanksgiving for the peace with Holland and the late seasonable rain which the nation has received.[294]

Gilbert Mabbott

Newsletter from George Downing, Westminster, 16 May 1654

fo. 71[v]

12 sayle of the state's ships are this day ordered by his Highness and the Council to be laid up.[295] There is also an ordinance passed for relief of debtors in Scotland in cases of extremity.[296] For the proclamation it pleases his Highness well, only they say [if ~~a~~ the[297] generals' heads be worth a great [. . .] but 200*l*] then surely you think the head of a colonel of high worth.[298]

George Downing

[290] These details are confirmed by *CSPD 1654*, p. 159. The trial arose from the shooting in the London Exchange of Thomas Howard on 22 November 1653. There is an eye-witness account in *TSP*, II, pp. 222–223.

[291] *CSPD 1654*, p. 156.

[292] *A&O*, II, pp. 890–897.

[293] Clearly an error. The thanksgiving was ordered for 23 May; *CSPD 1654*, pp. 162, 167.

[294] The declaration was printed in several newsbooks, e.g. *Mercurius Politicus*, 205 (11–18 May 1654), pp. 3480–3483.

[295] Presumably this was one of seven unspecified orders approved on this day; *CSPD 1654*, p. 177.

[296] The ordinance was approved on 16 May and passed on 26 May 1654; *ibid.*, p. 165; *A&O*, II, pp. 898–899.

[297] '[T]he' superimposed upon 'a'.

[298] This refers to Monck's proclamation issued from Dalkeith on 4 May 1654 and printed in, for example, *Mercurius Politicus*, 205 (11–18 May 1654), pp. 3490–3492.

Newsletter from Gilbert Mabbott Westminster, 20 May 1654

*fo. 73^v^*

We had [17] sayle of ships that made some attempt to secure Saint Malo's (as the governour thereof says) but say we it was only to get some fresh victuals, which appears by the landing of some of our men in the country who indeavoured to drive away their cattle, but prevented by the [insurrection] of the people. However 2 of our ships [. . . .] were left ashore by the going out of the tide which they indeavoured to seize, but could not, only brought down some ordnance to batter them and upon a high wave our frigots got off. This occasioned the governour thereof to plunder, devour and abuse the English merchants in that town and this week the French ambassador had audience about his business, but nothing yet resolved.[299]

The 8th instant the deputy of Friesland protested against the peace.[300] The deputy of Gelderland deferred going back pretending their ambassadors have exceeded their power. The deputies of Zealand and [Utrecht] deferred their assent. The Lords the States General have [published] their declaration upon the treaty. The deputy of Groningen protested against the excluding the prince of Orange and his successors by this treaty. Amalia princess of Orange has likewise in her own name and in behalf of the grandmother and guardians of the young prince[301] desired their lordships' interposition concerning his Highness in these articles of peace and that nothing before may come to an actual end in dissatisfactions but the strange reports here, but you will find them of very little damage to the articles.[302]

The writs for calling the next Parliament are almost finished and will be speedily sealed.[303] The Council has ordered to hear no private business till 1 *June* next. His Highness and several of his Council dined this day at Wimbledon, the Lord Lambert's house.[304]

Gilbert Mabbott

[299] See also previous document.

[300] i.e. 18 May N.S.; Israel, *The Dutch Republic*, p. 723.

[301] William III, posthumous son of William II who had died in November 1650.

[302] The bitter wrangling which took place over the exclusion clause in the treaty, and its outcome, are fully described in *ibid.*, pp. 722–726.

[303] On 18 May 1654 the warrant and writs for the election were approved by the Council; *CSPD 1654*, p. 182.

[304] The Council did not meet formally on this day, a Saturday; *ibid.*, p. xxxviii.

Newsletter from George Downing, Westminster, 23 May 1654

fo. 75r

Commissary-General Whalley, Colonel Goffe and myself thought we should have been for some time out of town, but upon a discovery made [from/by/of] a great cavalier privy to the conspiracy but detesting so [heinous] an act, we are returned hither.[305] There are about 10 of them who had [intended] to murther my Lord Protector taken. Sir Gilbert Gerard, a cavalier, and one John Gerard, a brother of his, were of them, and Commissary-General Whalley's apothecary and 2 doctors of fisick and one that had [obeyed] a promise to be a [fencer] under the master of the horse. Most of them were lately in France where the design was hatched. They did resolve to have acted their villainy Saturday was a sennight as his Highness was upon his way to Hampton Court but, some of their company not coming, durst not attempt it. One Captain Fitzjames, who was the person [designed] in France to act it, coming from thence, the vessel he was in a fight with a Dutch [. . .], / sunk

fo. 75v

sunk and although he was an excellent swimmer yet he was the [. . .] person that was [drowned]. The generalty of those who were taken will confess nothing but one of them seems ingenuous and gives in the names of divers conspirators.[306]

George Downing

Newsletter from Henry Walker, Westminster, 25 May 1654

fo. 76r

The great business here is about the plot mentioned in the inclosed which the Lord Protector and the Council are very close every day

[305] A Royalist informer had first revealed details of the plot on 18 May; *A True Account of the Late Bloody and Inhumane Conspiracy Against His Highness the Lord Protector and this Commonwealth* (London, 1654), p. 6.

[306] While the plot was widely reported in newsbooks and newsletters, the most detailed contemporary account, published five months later, reproduced the statements under examination of all those involved in the plot. It confirms all these details (*ibid.*, *passim*).

upon.[307] It is supposed that Charles Stewart is about London and that was the cause of the inclosed proclamation,[308] but it doth not yet appear so, but there are divers apprehended the last night *vizt* the Lord Willoughby, the Lord Montague, a knight whose name I know not, one [Bell] and about 10 or 12 more.[309]

Henry Walker

Newsletter from George Downing, Westminster, 1 June 1654

fo. 79ᵛ

Tudor the chirurgeon upon examination looking upon himself as in a desperate condition did yesterday morning discover divers persons and that the Saturday night before Whitsunday there were 3 parties of them out to have met with his Highness, and that having despatched him they doubted not to have surprized the Mews and James's and to have made a [. . .] in the City and [. . . .] at dinner. Being committed to 2 warders of the Tower, they gave him leave to go in the house of office in Whitehall garden through which he leapt into the Thames and so escaped, a very great loss. Colonel Alridge and a [tewter] in London, both officers under the earl of Essex, and Alexander the horse [rider] are by his information yesterday apprehended, as also one Wiseman.

Tomorrow the ordinance for the assessment will be read again. The old commissioners of the Admiralty are issued an ordinance by committee to give liberty to transport corn, butter and cheese.[310]

The Lord Digby's brother is taken in a shallop going for France.[311]

George Downing

307 The Council immediately issued orders to all ports to prevent all departures and detain any new arrivals; *CSPD 1654*, p. 184. Stringent measures were also taken to identify possible suspects in London.

308 Probably the proclamation issued on 23 May requiring a census of all lodgers within London, Southwark, and Westminster and controlling their movements for the next ten days; O. Cromwell, *By the Lord Protector, A Proclamation ordering a return from the house-keepers of London, Westminster and Southwark*. . . (London, 1654); *CSPD 1654*, pp. 184–185. Clarke's copy survives in Worcester College library.

309 As neither Willoughby nor Mountague seems to have been implicated in this plot, this appears to be an unfounded rumour; *A True Account of the Late Bloody and Inhumane Conspiracy*; D. Underdown, *Royalist Conspiracy in England* (New Haven, 1960), pp. 100–102.

310 *CSPD 1654*, p. 195.

311 The capture of John, brother of the second earl of Digby, was reported to the Council on this day; *ibid.*, pp. 195–196.

Newsletter from Gilbert Mabbott, Westminster, 1 June 1654

fo. 79^{v}

His Highness sent a warrant on Tuesday last to the Lords Commissioners of the Great Seal to issue out writs for electing members for the next Parliament.[312] The same day Sergeant Pepys was sworn one of the barons of the Exchequer, Sergeant Newdigate one of the judges of the Upper Bench and Sergeant Wyndham one of the judges of the Common Pleas.[313] Several are apprehended daily for having an hand in the grand plot.[314] One Master Tudor, chief man therein, going with his keeper yesterday to the house of office in Whitehall orchard to ease himself made his escape down the walls, it being the low water.[315] An ambassador that speaks French and one or 2 of his Highness' family were likewise said to be guilty thereof.

Gilbert Mabbott

Newsletter from George Downing, Westminster, 3 June 1654

fo. 80^{v}

Ann Trapnell, the great prophetess, is committed to Bridewell.[316]

The Council has agreed upon the [distribution] of parliament men for Scotland and the writs are issued out for England. The act of assessments for England is passed the Council and to be 12,000*l* [*sic*] per mensem for the 1st 3 months and 90,000*l* per mensem for the last 3 months,[317] and it's committed to consider of the assessments of Scotland that both may issue out together. General Desborow will go

[312] Both this and the date of the elections, 12 July 1654, were published in the newsbooks, e.g. *Faithful[l] Scout*, 182 (2–9 June 1654), pp. 1438–[1439], 1444. The Parliament opened on 3 September 1654.

[313] *Perfect Diurnall*, 234 (29 May–5 June 1654), p. 3588.

[314] This sentence exactly replicates the wording of Daniel Border's *A Perfect Account*, 178 (31 May–7 June 1654), p. 1420, perhaps revealing something about Mabbott's – or Border's – sources. See also p. 192n.

[315] Tudor's escape was made much of in the newsbooks, e.g. *Mercurius Politicus*, 207 (25 May–1 June 1654), p. 3524; *Perfect Diurnall*, 234 (29 May–5 June 1654), p. 3583. He was recaptured at Norwich on 31 July; *Mercurius Politicus*, 216 (27 July–3 Aug. 1654), p. [3668].

[316] Anna Trapnell was arrested in Cornwall before being brought to Bridewell, where later in the month her religious trances attracted large crowds, especially followers of the Fifth Monarchists; *CSPD 1654*, pp. 197, 436; *Faithful[l] Scout*, 184 (16–23 June 1654), p. [1458].

[317] *CSPD 1654*, p. 196.

for Ireland with 3 others who are to be the Council there. One of them now there, 2 more to go.

George Downing

Newsletter from John Thurloe, Westminster, 6 June 1654

fo. 82r

Sir

It has pleased God to bring to light a bloody and barbarous design hatched against the Protector by the old cavalier party and I hope to defeat it. Several of the contrivers are taken and their crime will be fully proved against them. Some disabled, several are escaped as Colonel Charles Finch, Major Thomas Henshaw, Colonel Deane and others of good quality.[318] They intended to have murthered the Protector and at the same time to have seized upon the guards about Whitehall and Saint James's and then to have proclaimed Charles Stewart king.

The peace between this and the commonwealth of the United Provinces is like to make a war between the provinces themselfs. 6 of the provinces protest against Holland for something done in this treaty against the prince of Orange and if persuaded would proceed from paper protestations to arms if they feared not the Protector's [. . .] which side he would declare for in such a contest.[319]

My Lord Whitelocke is expected home daily, he having dispatched his business in Sweden in April last.[320] That queen holds her resolution of resigning the crown for what reason no man yet comprehends unless it be to retire to a life of contemplation.[321]

Jo. Thurloe

[318] For their parts in the plot, see *TSP*, II, p. 416.

[319] A few days earlier Thurloe sent word to John Pell in Zurich that the secret article in the treaty (whereby the States of Holland and West Friesland agreed to exclude the prince of Orange from being either Stadtholder or Captain General) was causing grave difficulties between Holland and the other provinces; R. Vaughan (ed.), *The Protectorate of Oliver Cromwell*, 2 vols (London 1839), I, p. 8; the secret article is printed in Abbott, III, pp. 906–909.

[320] The treaty with Sweden was signed on 29 April and Whitelocke had his last audience with Queen Christina on 12 May 1654; *Mercurius Politicus*, 207 (25 May–1 June 1654), p. 3511; 209 (8–15 June 1654), p. 3551. He left Stockholm on on 1 June; *Perfect Diurnall*, 239 (3–10 July 1654), p. 3656.

[321] The scene of the queen's abdication is described in Whitelock, *Memorials*, IV, pp. 121–122.

Newsletter from George Downing, Westminster, 15 June 1654

fo. 87v

There is a commission in hand for ordering matters ecclesiastical in Scotland and the commission for causes civil in Scotland is under commitment, there being no alteration therein save only the leaving out the Lord Hopetoun. [The] same names are to be for causes criminal.[322]

The trial of the Portugal is now hastened on and all the judges are detained in town till further order.[323] A letter is sent to Colonel Saunders to [suppress] the great meeting in Derbyshire under the notion of quaking.[324]

George Downing

The petition of persons fined in Scotland is referred to the Council.

Monsieur *de Baas* who was in commission with *Bond* must forthwith depart being in the last plot.[325]

Newsletter from Gilbert Mabbott, Westminster, 17 June 1654

fo. 88v

The act for 120,000*l* per mensem for the next 3 months assessment and 90,000*l* per mensem for the next 3 months after is likewise ordered.[326] Great preparations are made for the design by sea by pressing of men.[327] [And otherwise] there were yesterday 2 men executed at Charing Cross for conniving at the escape of some persons apprehended upon this plot.

Gilbert Mabbott

[322] These matters were dealt with by the Council on 14 June 1654; *CSPD 1654*, p. 211.

[323] The order was made on the day on which this letter was written; *ibid.*, p. 212.

[324] *Ibid.*, p. 211.

[325] Cardinal Mazarin's envoy, the baron de Baas was questioned several times in early June on his part in the plot; *TSP*, II, pp. 364–365. Authority was given for him to return to France on 17 June; Bodl., MS Rawlinson A.328, pp. 76–77. Cromwell's letters to Louis XIV and Mazarin are reproduced in Abbott, III, pp. 347–349.

[326] *A&O*, II, pp. 902–907. The amounts are listed by county in *Faithful[l] Scout*, 183 (9–16 June 1654), pp. 1450–1452.

[327] Another newsletter had recently reported that a number of frigates were being boarded up to prevent tropical worm damage; Worc. MS XXVI, fo. 83r. The subject of an undefined 'western design' apparently first came before the Council on 5 June 1654; *CSPD 1654*, p. 201. The discussions were cloaked in secrecy, and were temporarily laid aside when security was breached; *C&P*, II, p. 475; below, p. 193.

Newsletter from George Downing, Westminster, 22 June 1654

fo. 90ʳ

The 13th instant the Lord Whitelocke was at Hamburgh.[328] We now expect him daily. The queen of Sweden has publikely affronted the agent of Portugal.[329] This day Colonel Ingoldsby was sent to the Tower for striking a countryman upon a private quarrel in Whitehall. He will be speedily out again.[330] This [plot] takes up all the time. 17 of the High Court of Justice are sworn.

George Downing

Newsletter from Gilbert Mabbott, Westminster, 27 June 1654

fo. 92ᵛ

Colonel Ingoldsby is committed to the Tower for striking another gentleman in Whitehall that stood against him for an election in the county of Bucks, and the [. . .] was this impudent severe act of justice in the case because the soldiers should not appear obstructors in the elections.[331] Master Scot, a member of the late Parliament, was chosen the last week for a [corporation] in the said county of Bucks.[332] Justice Atkins and Judge Aske and some others of the long robe are not free to take the oath or act as members of the High Court of Justice.[333] The rest met this day in the Painted Chamber and adjourned to the Chancery Court till Thursday next, which place is making ready for them.[334]

Gilbert Mabbott

[328] Whitelocke was entertained with much ceremony during his stay at Hamburg between 10 and 17 June; *Mercurius Politicus*, 212 (29 June–6 July 1654), pp. 3602–[3603]; *Perfect Diurnall*, 239 (3–10 July 1654), p. 3656.

[329] *TSP*, II, p. 374. Christina was reported to have said that 'she did not know him as the King's embassadour at all, but rather an envoy from duke de Braganza'; *ibid.*, pp. 386–387.

[330] *Faithful[l] Scout*, 185 (23–30 June 1654), p. 1454. Ingoldsby was released on 24 June (p. 192 below).

[331] Ingoldsby was imprisoned on 22 June (see preceding document).

[332] There was controversy over Scot's nomination; *Weekly Post*, 185 (20–27 June 1654), p. 1454.

[333] Both men were among those appointed on 14 June. Atkins's reasons for being unable to act are given in the official record. Aske did in the event take the oath; *Perfect Account*, 180 (14–21 June 1654), p. 1435; *CSPD 1654*, pp. 233–234.

[334] According to *Mercurius Politicus*, 211 (21–29 June 1654), p. 3588, they were expected to adjourn to the Chancery Court on Friday 30 June.

Newsletter from George Downing, Axeyard, Westminster, 27 June 1654

fo. 92ᵛ

Saturday night Colonel Ingoldsby returned home from the Tower. The High Court of Justice are sitting to order their business. The Chancery Court is preparing for them to sit in. John Gerard and one Vowell, schoolmaster of Islington, and one Somerset Fox of [London] are like to be 1st tried. Yesterday one Mistress Barbara Slingsby and this day Sir Thomas Ingram's lady was committed to the Tower as accessories to the plot.[335] As I writ in my last on Saturday last the ordinance for the Scotch assessments passed.

George Downing

Newsletter from Gilbert Mabbott, Westminster, [30 June] 1654

fo. 94ʳ

Westminster 30 July[336] *1654*

Yesterday the High Court of Justice sat in the Chancery at Westminster when John Gerrard, Somerset Fox and Peter Vowell were upon their trial.[337] It was proved against each of them that they were knowing of and had a hand in a design to take away the life of the Lord Protector and his Council and at the same time to seize the guards, secure the Lord Maior and afterwards proclaim Charles Stewart king. The court gave no judgement but have adjourned till [Thursday][338] next.

[335] Although Lady Ingram's imprisonment is confirmed in *CSPD 1654*, p. 274, I have not been able to trace the arrest of Barbara Slingsby, wife of Sir Henry Slingsby and daughter of the 1st Viscount Fauconberg (*OxDNB*, 'Slingsby').

[336] Evidently 'June' is intended. The same slip occurs in Daniel Border's *A Perfect Account*, 182 (28 June–5 July 1654), p. 1453. However, the trial began, not as implied here on 29 but on 30 June; *Mercurius Politicus*, 212 (29 June–6 July 1654), p. 3599; Vaughan, *Protectorate of Oliver Cromwell*, I, p. 15. The letter appears therefore to have been written on 1 July. This is confirmed by its reference to Whitelocke's arrival which took place on 1 July; *Perfect Diurnall*, 239 (3–10 July 1654), p. 3655; *Faithful[l] Scout*, 182 (30 June–7 July 1654), p. 1472.

[337] There is a very full account of the trial by the court's president, John Lisle, in *CSPD 1654*, pp. 233–240.

[338] The outline is unclear, but appears to read 'Thursday'. The court reconvened on Tuesday 4 July and was adjourned once more until Thursday 6 July, when the judgement and sentence were passed; *CSPD 1654*, pp. 235, 236; Vaughan, *Protectorate of Oliver Cromwell*, I, p. 22. *Mercurius Politicus*, 212 (29 June–6 July 1654), p. [3604] agrees with these dates, although

Sir Thomas Ingram's lady was Wednesday last committed to the Tower upon this design.

An act is [draughted] for electing members in Ireland and Scotland[339] [whereby sits our cause] and [. . .], another against fighting of duels.[340]

The western design is at present laid aside the party that discovered it being severely punished.[341] The ordinance concerning preaching and regulating the Chancery have taken up much time this week.

The Lord Whitelocke safely arrived here this morning with all his retinue. He [came] in privately without any ceremony.[342]

Gilbert Mabbott

Newsletter from George Downing, Westminster, 4 July 1654

fo. 96r

Right Honourable,

I am sorry to hear (as we have done by the way of Ireland) of the loss under Lieutenant-Colonel Brayne.[343] This day an order is issued out to the Lieutenant of the Tower to deliver the body of the Portugal's brother to the sheriff of Middlesex in order to his trial.[344] This day also the High Court met in private to gather the evidence in order to a sentence which probably will be given by Thursday next.

Many old Parliament men are chosen, as Sir Henry Vane junior in 2 places, Lieutenant-General Fleetwood in 2 places, Lord Whitelocke at [Marlow].[345]

George Downing

another account in the same issue (pp. 3599–3602) states that the court met on Monday 3 July.

339 The ordinance was passed on 27 June; Roots, 'Cromwell's ordinances', p. 157.

340 *CSPD 1654*, pp. 228, 227.

341 Cromwell's instructions for the undertaking of the western design were not issued until 18 August 1654 (printed in Abbott, III, pp. 413–415).

342 Whitelocke reported officially to the Protector and Council on 6 July; Whitelock, *Memorials*, IV, p. 115.

343 A party of reinforcements which Brayne had brought from Ireland to Scotland was ambushed with severe losses sometime in late June; *Severall Proceedings of State Affaires*, 250 (6–13 July 1654), p. [3967].

344 See p. 190 above.

345 Whitelocke was elected for the county of Buckinghamshire; *Perfect Diurnall: or, Occurrences*, [11] (17–24 July 1654), p. 89.

Newsletter from Axeyard, Westminster, 6 July 1654

fo. 97r

Charles Stewart is gone from France towards Flanders.[346]

This day Don Punteleon with 3 other Portuguezes with an Englishman were condemned to be hanged on Monday next for the murther committed by them at the New Exchange.[347] The High Court of Justice has also condemned Gerard, Vowell and [Lex].[348]

Newsletter from Gilbert Mabbott, Westminster, 8 July 1654

fo. 98r

This week the Portugal ambassador's brother and 4 of the rest that joyned with him in committing the late murther in the New Exchange were brought to trial before Judge Rolle and others upon a commission of oyer and terminer. The prisoners answered by an interpreter of their own, another interpreter on the behalf of the State being present. They were all found guilty of murther and condemned to be hanged. The execution is deferred for some certain time and in the interim all possible means are used by the ladies and others to beg their pardon or reprieve. The ambassador's brother came to and returned from his trial in a coach with 6 horses and has yet all his meat served up in plate at Newgate, denied at 1st to be uncovered to the court or plead, but upon 2d thoughts became bare and put himself to a jury which were half English and half foreigners.[349]

An ordinance is passed prohibiting horse races for 6 months.[350] His Highness and his Council sat this day and gave audience to the French ambassador who came to mediate for the life of the Portugal ambassador's brother.[351] The Portugal ambassador had likewise audience. He pretends a desire to return home and the

[346] Charles set out from Paris for the town of Spa on 30 June, 'giving out that he is going to Spain'; *Perfect Diurnall*, 239 (3–10 July 1654), p. 3668; Vaughan, *Protectorate of Oliver Cromwell*, I, p. 22.

[347] *Mercurius Politicus*, 213 (6–13 July 1654), pp. [3612]–3613.

[348] Presumably meaning 'Fox'. Somerset Fox was then reprieved (*ibid.*, p. 3615).

[349] Some but not all of these details were carried by the newsbooks, e.g., *Perfect Account*, 183 (5–12 July 1654), pp. 1458–1461.

[350] The ordinance was passed on 4 July 1654; *CSPD 1654*, p. 242.

[351] Bordeaux's intercession is reported in *TSP*, II, p. 447, but not in official Council records; *CSPD 1654*, pp. 246–247, 8 July.

Council is as free to give him a safe conduct. Monday next Fox, Gerard and Vowell are to be hanged before the Mews gate.

Gilbert Mabbott

The Scottish nobility and gentry are ordered to pay in a 3d part of their fines by the 1st day of payment in the ordinance mentioned, and all their cases referred to commissioners in Scotland.[352]

Newsletter from Richard Hatter, Westminster, 11 July 1654

fo. 99v

Yesterday was executed upon a gallows near to the Mews Master Vowell, late schoolmaster at Islington, who died resolutely and with the word king in his mouth. Another of them, Master Gerard, upon the petition of some ladies on his behalf lost his head on a scaffold [toward hill][353] he being condemned before to be hanged.[354] The 3d conspirator, Somerset Fox, through submission and penitences, was reprieved the same day.[355] The Portugal ambassador's brother lost his head in the same place and upon the same scaffold with [. . . .] as Gerard. He came to execution with coach and 6 horses in mourning, made confession to his priest, and died resolutely.[356] The English boy, one of the 5 condemned with the Portugal, was hanged at Tyburn but to make the act [respectable] his Highness and Council pardoned all the rest of them yesterday at 6 in the morning.[357] The Portugal ambassador signed the treaty of peace, took leave of his Highness, and intended speedily after to be begone,[358] his barge being ready and being indebted above 30,000*l*, and his creditors having notice thereof, arrested and secured all his goods.[359]

Richard Hatter

[352] *Ibid.*, p. 246.

[353] Presumably 'Tower Hill' is intended here, the site of the execution; *Perfect Account*, 183 (5–12 July 1654), p. 1463; Vaughan, *Protectorate of Oliver Cromwell*, I, p. 25.

[354] *Perfect Account*, 183 (5–12 July 1654), p. 1463.

[355] *Ibid.*, p. 1464. Fox was imprisoned and subsequently deported to Barbados in May 1655; *TSP*, III, pp. 453–454.

[356] A last-minute bid to help him escape was foiled; *Mercurius Politicus*, 213 (6–13 July 1654), pp. 3619–[3620].

[357] *Perfect Account*, 183 (5–12 July 1654), p. 1464.

[358] This use of 'begone' is not given in the *OED* where the word is given as an imperative only. However, the shorthand outline is clear.

[359] The Portuguese ambassador left London for Gravesend on the morning of his brother's execution, but was not allowed to leave England until money had arrived from Lisbon to pay off his debts; *TSP*, II, pp. 439, 517; *Perfect Account*, 185 (19–26 July 1654), p. 1473; 186 (26 July–2 Aug. 1654), p. [1485]; Bodl., MS Rawlinson A. 328, pp. 97–98, 101–102.

Newsletter from George Downing, Westminster, 13 July 1654

fo. 100v

William Ashburnham, the French doctor[360] and the blind doctor[361] are like to come before the High Court.

George Downing

Newsletter from George Downing, Westminster, 18 July 1654

fo. 103r

Our fleet that are to go abroad and what concerns it is now close in debate and the [. . .] etc. to go with it. So also for the sending persons to govern Ireland, that country suffering much for want of fit persons settled there.[362]

The French are making strong preparations to relieve Arras and some private letters speak as if it were already relieved.[363] The Spaniard has seized on the Genoa goods in Naples and divers other [. . .] of his dominions and there appears much probability of quarrel between them about the customs of Final (the only port of Milan) which were granted by Charles the 5th to the Genoese.[364]

George Downing

You will see from the list inclosed that some parties have been much [. . .] in their strong indeavours.[365]

360 Dr Theodore Naudin petitioned the Protector for his release on 7 August 1654, but appears still to have been imprisoned in September 1654; *CSPD 1654*, p. 289; *TSP*, II, p. 384.

361 This was Dr Hudson, whose alleged part in the plot is described in *ibid*.

362 See also p. 199 below. Commissioners were appointed and instructions issued on 17 August 1654; R. Dunlop (ed.), *Ireland under the Commonwealth*, 2 vols (Manchester, 1913), II, pp. 437–443.

363 *Severall Proceedings*, 252 (20–27 July 1654), p. 3986. It was to be more than a month before word was received that the siege had been raised (p. 205 below).

364 A Genoese news-sheet claimed that Cromwell had promised to help the Genoese against the Spanish; Vaughan, *The Protectorate of Oliver Cromwell*, I, p. 33. A Genoese ambassador was sent to England and had audience with Cromwell in January 1655; *CP*, III, p. 18.

365 There is no indication of what the enclosure might have been; it was possibly the list of MPs elected in England and Wales, published on this day; *A List of Knights & Burgesses for several counties elected . . . 12 July, to serve in the next Parliament . . .* (London, 1654), not found among Clarke's papers. The list subsequently appeared in *Perfect Diurnall*, 241 (17–24 July 1654), pp. 3688–3695.

Marston the great Leveller that being sent for by the Council killed 2 of the messengers is apprehended by a party of horse sent for him and dangerously wounded in the taking.[366]

Newsletter from Gilbert Mabbott, Westminster, 22 July 1654

fo. 106v

Right Honourable

His Highness and Council have sat very seldom these 6 weeks in public council but rather choose to meet in private. His Highness (yesterday) gave audience to the Venetian ambassador[367] and the duke of Oldenburgh his agent who presented his Highness with 6 noble coach horses.[368] The consideration of several persons elected members has taken up some time this week.[369] The western design begins to be revived and expedition, it's thought, will be used therein. The queen of Sweden's removal to a Jew's house in Hamburgh (some say in man's apparel) is the subject of much discourse here.[370]

We had a sad accident on Thursday last. A ship was fired which indangered the blowing up of London Bridge, and yesterday another ship fired and was blown up. Divers persons lost their lives. It was a great mercy that the bridge, their ships, and the houses on both sides were not burnt.[371]

Gilbert Mabbott

[366] Marston, an associate of John Lilburne, was hanged for these murders, committed four years previously, on 21 August 1654; *Mercurius Politicus*, 219 (17–24 Aug. 1654), p. 3716; *Severall Proceedings*, 256 (17–24 Aug. 1654), pp. 4056, 4057–4061. His funeral is described in *Certain Passages*, [37] (18–24 Aug. 1654), p. [300].

[367] Paulucci, Venetian secretary in England, sent a lengthy account of his audience to the Venetian ambassador in France; *CSPV 1653–1654*, pp. 243–244. The address which he presented to the Protector is printed in *TSP*, II, p. 470.

[368] These appear to be in addition to the '8 magnificent horses' presented to Cromwell in June; *CSPV 1653–1654*, p. 226. Authorization was given on 8 July 1654 for a further six horses from Oldenburg to be landed; it may be these to which the present letter refers; Bodl., MS Rawlinson A. 328, p. 91. Oldenburg's gift almost cost the Protector his life; Vaughan, *Protectorate of Oliver Cromwell*, I, p. 74.

[369] Paulucci describes Cromwell vetting the list and ordering some of the MPs elect to be struck off; *CSPV 1653–1654*, pp. 246, 251–252.

[370] Confirmed by S. Åkerman, *Queen Christina and Her Circle*, (Leiden, 1991), p. 184. Christina arrived in Hamburg on 3 July 1654; *TSP*, II, p. 423. Her mannish behaviour and dress caused comment wherever she went; *ibid.*, pp. 404, 499, 536, 546.

[371] *A Perfect Diurnall; or Occurrences*, no. [11] (17–24 July 1654), pp. 95–96.

Newsletter from Henry Walker, Westminster, 27 July 1654

fo. 110r

An ordinance is passed for the compositions of Henry Hennings an infant. Also an ordinance touching the ministry of [Gould] and the school called Peter's School,[372] and an ordinance for George Raleigh and Henry Clark to have the benefit of the articles given upon rendition of Oxford.[373] Master Rogers was this day apprehended and brought before the Lord Protector and Council for preaching and writing a book against the present powers.[374] Master John Simpson preached at Ware and prayed for the present government.[375] Master Feake sent a letter to his people that though he was a loser in his estate and was in prison yet he didst very much rejoice in these conditions.[376] The godly are more and more satisfied in the present power.

Lord Protector and Council sat this day in private very early and long.[377] A committee of the Council sat for despatch of petitions.[378] Master Hughurst[379] has given in his answer to his charge which is very unsatisfactory. He is committed to Lambeth prisoner and presseth for a [despatch]. The names of the commissioners for the several counties for ejecting of scandalous ministers are brought in, and that ordinance, it is believed, will shortly be passed. Some think we shall agree with France.

Henry Walker

372 This was passed on 14 July; *CSPD 1654*, p. 253.

373 Passed on 25 July; *ibid.*, p. 257.

374 John Rogers's arrest on 27 July and the background to it, are discussed in Capp, *Fifth Monarchy Men*, pp. 103–104.

375 It was said that Simpson (recently freed from imprisonment at Windsor on compassionate grounds with Cromwell's pardon and liberty to preach within ten miles of London) 'now owns and prays for the present Powers'; *Perfect Diurnall; or Occurrences*, 13 (31 July–7 Aug. 1654), p. 100; *Severall Proceedings*, 252 (20–27 July 1654), p. 4000; 255 (10–17 Aug. 1654), p. 4044.

376 *Certain Passages*, 28 (21–28 July 1654), p. 220, noted that Simpson's release had ended 'the great Disputes between Mr Feake and Mr Sympson at Windsor, (the one for Baptisme, and the other against it)'.

377 Cromwell's attendance is not recorded on this day, when a considerable amount of Council business was conducted; *CSPD 1654*, pp. xl, 264–270. He was, however, present on the previous day, when Whitelocke wrote that 'the lord protector sat very close with his council'; *ibid.*, p. xl; Whitelock, *Memorials*, IV, p. 125.

378 Many of the ordinances were generated by individual petitions; Roots, 'Cromwell's ordinances', p. 148.

379 In *Certain Passages*, 31 (11–18 Aug. 1654), p. 239, 'Haghurst', and in *Faithful[l] Scout*, 191 (4–11 Aug. 1654), p. 1516, 'John Hurst'. He was charged with blasphemy.

Newsletter from George Downing, Axeyard, Westminster, 27 July 1654

fo. 110r

The coming over of Colonel Jones, one of the commissioners in Ireland,[380] and thereby there being not a quorum left upon the place to act in regard that Lieutenant-General Ludlow doth not act, this puts his Highness [to/upon] an immediate settlement of that affair. Master Recorder Steele, Colonel Robert Hammond and Master Robert Goodwin will, I suppose, be speedily despatched thither as commissioners and whether my Lord Henry and General Disbrowe shall go is yet uncertain.[381] The business of regulating the Chancery is very far proceeded in by the Council.

George Downing

Newsletter from Richard [Saltold], Newcastle, 28 July 1654

fo. 110v

There is a great trial at Durham this assizes concerning a murther which was some 14 years since committed. There is one Ricketts which committed the murther and this Ricketts was servant to one Master Hall, a great and rich man in Durham. It's thought it will go hard both with the master and the man and will be [just with God] to bring such a hideous murther to light and the offenders to certain punishment.[382]

Richard [Saltold]

[380] Col John Jones's instructions for his meeting with the Protector are printed in Dunlop, *Ireland under the Commonwealth*, II, p. 436.

[381] Henry Cromwell was not among those appointed; *ibid.*, pp. 437–443. Following a petition from the city of London, Steele successfully avoided being sent to Ireland; Hammond was to die there in October 1654; *Certain Passages*, 30 (4–11 Aug. 1654), p. 237; p. 200 below; *Severall Proceedings*, 265 (19–26 Oct. 1654), p. 4169.

[382] Clarke must have had a particular interest in this case for him to copy it down in shorthand. It may be relevant that Clarke's father-in-law took the name of Hall when he moved to Hebburn, near Jarrow, in the 1630s; *L-P*, pp. xiii, 269. Another possible connection is the pamphleteer John Hall of Durham, whom Clarke would have known during Cromwell's Scottish campaign of 1650–1651; *CSPD 1654*, p. 163.

Newsletter from Gilbert Mabbott, Westminster, 29 July 1654

fo. 111ʳ

The treaty with France goes on [effectually] so that a speedy union is expected with that nation,[383] the consideration whereof has brought down the price of French wines here (within these 14 days) a penny and in some places 2*d* per pint. 2 ships laden with French wines sailed out of the river Thames the last week to [Calis] to be sold there, our city merchants not coming up to their [shop/ship] prices. Here are great preparations for sea but none know certainly the design. The press for mariners has continued for several days together. Some land men are shipped with them. The 2 Ashburnhams and several of the chief prisoners in the Tower which were secured upon this last plot are lately made close prisoners, which makes us conceive they will be speedily brought to trial.

The contents of Sir Kenelm Digby's letters of raising the siege at Arras by the French army and killing 6,000 Spaniards hold not truth, for our French letters this week that that [*sic*] leagure is yet continued.[384]

Gilbert Mabbott

Newsletter from George Downing, Westminster, 29 July 1654

fo. 111ʳ

The Common Council of London have petitioned his Highness that Master Recorder Steele may not be taken from them and sent for Ireland.[385] However, I think he will be sent, and my Lord Broghill, Commissary-General Reynolds and the rest of the Irish officers here are going back. The last letters say that the Spaniards are yet like to carry Arras and the French Stenay. The Hollanders are preparing a manifesto against the prince of Orange his being Stadtholder.[386]

[383] The recent royalist conspiracy had interrupted negotiations for the treaty; Vaughan, *The Protectorate of Oliver Cromwell*, I, p. 8.

[384] On 21 July Paulucci wrote to the Venetian ambassador in France that this rumour had not pleased Cromwell; *CSPV 1653–1654*, p. 242.

[385] The petition was successful; although Steele was appointed to the Irish Council he never acted in this capacity; *Certain Passages*, 30 (4–11 Aug. 1654), p. 237; Dunlop, *Ireland under the Commonwealth*, II, p. 437n. See also p. 199 above.

[386] The following month Holland was reported to be pursuing this resolution despite the opposition of the other provinces; *Certain Passages*, [37] (18–24 Aug. 1654), pp. 295, [300].

Master Rogers a principal of the All Hallows[387] way is yet under restraint, but nothing yet done about him.[388]

George Downing

Newsletter from George Downing, Westminster, 5 August 1654

fo. 114v

Ordinance for the universities in Scotland is passed, as also an ordinance for the approbation of ministers in [. . .] Scotland.[389] The ordinance for removing scandalous ministers in England will I suppose be this day quite finished. General Blake departs hence on Monday for the fleet he is to command to the [southward], indeed a gallant fleet.[390] My lord Henry is now again hot for Ireland,[391] as Colonel Howard,[392] Steele, Goodwin and I think Colonel Thomlinson. The Spanish news by the last letters is very much diminished [by the rowting] only a part and in probability not above 4 or 500 which had taken a Spanish convoy with 100 wagons.

George Downing

An extraordinary ambassador is coming from Genoa to his Highness.

Newsletter from Gilbert Mabbott, Westminster, 8 August 1654

fo. 116r

They have proceeded to an electing of members for some parts of Ireland and have chosen Sir Robert King and Sir John Temple for

387 Another leading Fifth Monarchist, Christopher Feake, was a weekday lecturer at All Hallows; *DBR*, 'Feake'.

388 'Mr Rogers . . . prayes and preacheth to all that come to the prison at Lambath-House to visit him, but having not yet received the new light of conformity to the present Government, he perseveres in his Invectives against it'; *Certain Passages*, 31 (11–18 Aug. 1654), p. [242].

389 *CSPD 1654*, p. 290.

390 *Severall Proceedings*, 254 (3–10 Aug. 1654), p. 4021. Blake's instructions to sail to Algiers, dated 22 July 1654, are printed in Abbott, III, p. 379.

391 Henry Cromwell's departure for Ireland was reported in *Certain Passages*, 30 (4–11 Aug. 1654), p. 240.

392 Probably intended to be Col 'Hammond', who is among those named by *The Weekly Post*, 193 (22–29 Aug. 1654), p. 1546. See also Dunlop, *Ireland under the Commonwealth*, II, p. 437n.

the counties of Roscommon, Sligo and Leitrim, Colonel Williamson and Alderman Hutchinson for the city and county of Dublin, Major Morgan and Major Meredith for Wicklow and Kildare.[393] The Council has settled a [. . .] exchequer (as to the receipts) and have appointed the 2 Lords Chief Justice,[394] the 3 Lords Commissioners of the Great Seal, Colonel Montague [. . .], Master Massam and Colonel Sydenham Lords Commissioners of the Treasury for the revenue,[395] Captain Falconbridge[396] and Sir William Roberts Auditors. All the 4 Tellers are not yet known, only Captain Stone and Captain Lister.[397] They intend speedily to settle the Court of Exchequer, Sergeant Glynn being already given out to be the Lord Chief Baron.[398]

Colonel Heane is now come from Jersey, which makes many believe the design for sea is near putting in execution, in order wherefore General Blake went yesterday to the fleet, which lies yet in the Downs. There is no talk now of the West Indies, but several whisper the design to lie very near us.[399]

Yesterday his Highness ordered that the pay of his Highness' lifeguard should be made up 7*s* 6*d* a man per diem.[400] They have likewise passed an ordinance for giving indemnity to the English Protestants of the province of Munster in Ireland.[401]

Gilbert Mabbott

Newsletter from Gilbert Mabbott, Westminster, 15 August 1654

fo. 119ᵛ

The last Lord's day here arose a great westerly wind which continued till 12 at night and kept not only the tide out the next day but forced so

[393] These names are included in lists of MPs elected for Ireland published in several newsbooks, e.g., *Faithfull Scout*, 192 (11–18 Aug. 1654), p. 1540.

[394] These were Henry Rolle and Oliver St John; *CSPD 1654*, p. 284.

[395] *Ibid.*, p. 284.

[396] Capt. Thomas Falconbridge or Fauconberg.

[397] In addition to John Stone and Christopher Lister, Edward Horseman had been chosen by 18 September 1654; *ibid.*, p. 367.

[398] For Sir John Glynne see *OxDNB*.

[399] So successful was the secrecy surrounding the plans for the western design, that the Venetian secretary believed that rumours about sending part of the English fleet to the West Indies were simply a ruse to disguise its real destination, the Mediterranean; *CSPV 1653–1654*. pp. 247, 258.

[400] The Council considered the lifeguard's increase of pay on 8 August. When it was approved on the 14th, the soldiers' pay was to be 5s. a day; *CSPD 1654*, p. 290.

[401] For this ordinance see *A&O*, II, p. 933.

much water out of the river of Thames that children of 8 or 10 years of age frequently over the river [*sic*]. The like has not been known for many years past.[402]

Here are so great preparations for so many foot companies falling down near the seaside in order to their going abroad.[403] An ordinance is passed for renewing the last ordinance and former act for relief of creditors and poor prisoners till the 1st of December next.[404] Another ordinance is passed for appointing a committee of citizens and to determine all differences amongst the adventurers of Ireland[405]

Gilbert Mabbott

Newsletter from John Milton, Westminster, 17 August 1654

fo. 120^r

Colonel Venables has accepted to go as commander in chief in the voyage to the West Indies (as is conceived).[406] They are very busy in mustering the forces for that service. There are 6 regiments of foot which will [consist] of 1,200 in a regiment, and an 100 horses. The regiments will not ever be filled up here, but they will be left vacant to receive their [commission] from the English plantations which they shall touch upon in their voyage.

There has been some time spent this week about the elections as to the government, but nothing as yet is concluded upon as to persons. Master Highland, Master Warcup and Master [. . .] have been [first dealt with all].[407]

John Milton[408]

402 The phenomenon is described in *Severall Proceedings*, 255 (10–17 Aug. 1654), p. 4043.

403 That is, in preparation for the 'western design'.

404 *CSPD 1654*, p. 295; *A&O*, II, p. 943.

405 *CSPD 1654*, p. 281; *A&O*, II, p. 942.

406 The appointment of Robert Venables is discussed by Sir Charles Firth in the preface to his edition of *The Narrative of General Venables*, pp. viii–ix. Venables was one of those appointed by Parliament on 29 September 1654 to the committee to 'consider of the Affairs of Scotland'; *CJ*, VII, p. 371.

407 The Protector was reviewing the list of elected MPs and ordering some of them to be struck off; *CSPV 1653–1654*, p. 246. The case involving the election of Highland and Warcup at Southwark is detailed in *CSPD 1654*, pp. 305–306.

408 I have discussed the possible identity of this particular John Milton above, p. 7n.

Newsletter from Gilbert Mabbott, Westminster, 22 August 1654

*fo. 122^r^*

The queen of Sweden has been at Brussels to view the city, but is returned again to Antwerp, where it is thought she will winter.[409] General Disbrowe has been very ill of a fever, but is now upon recovery.

In the United Provinces the divisions grow so high[410] that in all probability there will be [deliberation] on the 6 or the 7th which is Holland and this province continues as resolved for the casting out the Orange family as the other are for restoring it.[411] If they break off the consequence will be that Holland [must/should] admit of a lord protector.[412]

Gilbert Mabbott

Newsletter from John Rushworth, Lincoln's Inn, 26 August 1654

*fo. 123^v^*

Lincoln's Inn 26 *August*

There is great resort of [reduced] officers to Whitehall. Colonel Fortescue, Colonel Buller[413] etc. are [. . .] for this expedition by sea. I understand there are so many officers listed as will head 8,000 men.[414] There goes [2 fleets], one as is reported to the Straits to visit the [port of Gibraltar] the other to the West Indias, but perhaps they may take

[409] The queen arrived in man's clothing, but wore woman's dress on the following day; *Perfect Diurnall: or, Occurrences*, 15 (7–14 Aug. 1654), p. 115. After returning to Antwerp, she went back to Brussels on 5 October 1654; *Perfect Account*, 198 (18–25 Oct. 1654), p. 1575.

[410] 'Every man's head is hot here', began a long diatribe from The Hague on 19 August 1654; *Mercurius Politicus*, 220 (24–31 Aug. 1654), pp. 3727–3728.

[411] In mid-July Holland had asserted its right to negotiate a treaty separately from the other provinces; *TSP*, II, p. 451.

[412] Earlier in the month a correspondent from The Hague wrote that 'it must be the protector, that must by authority, or otherwise, maintain the present government of Holland'; *ibid.*, p. 521.

[413] On Fortescue and Buller, both reformadoes, see Firth, *Narrative of General Venables*, pp. xviii–xx.

[414] The actual number proposed was more in the region of 3,000; *ibid.*, p. xviii, where Fortescue and Buller are included in the list of officers commanding regiments. In the following document Gilbert Mabbott, writing on 29 August, also believed that 8,000 foot soldiers were to be sent on the expedition.

another course. The French have given overthrow to the Spaniards before Arras which makes them very high.[415]

John Rushworth

Newsletter from Gilbert Mabbott, Westminster, 29 August 1654

fo. 125[r]

The Council sits this afternoon to pass ordinances only before the Parliament sit.[416] Colonel Overton is dispatched away for Scotland, where he is to command as major-general of the foot.[417]

It will be yet 3 weeks or a month before the fleet sayles upon their intended design. The number of our forces are said to be about 8,000 foot and one troop of horse which will consist of 100, many of them reformadoes. Whether the approbation or concurrence of Parliament will be desired in this great undertaking is a question much disputed among the people who already report, and some wagers are laid, that an emperour will be chosen before the end of the next month.[418]

Gilbert Mabbott

Newsletter from Gilbert Mabbott, Westminster, 2 September 1654

fo. 127[v]

The Council have this week despatched the many ordinances because of the speedy session of parliament which convenes tomorrow and then, or the next day after, his Highness makes a speech to them in the Painted Chamber where a seat of majesty is erecting much like

[415] The raising of the lengthy Spanish siege of Arras lessened the need for France to sign the projected treaty with England. The news was not welcomed by Cromwell; Vaughan, *Protectorate of Oliver Cromwell*, I, p. 43; *CSPV 1653–1654*, p. 256.

[416] An unusually large number of ordinances was rushed through before the opening of Parliament on 3 September; *CSPD 1654*, pp. 338–339, 342–343, 346–347, 354–355, 361–362.

[417] Overton was governor of Hull. He was soon on his way back to England in disgrace for his part in the so-called 'Overton plot' (pp. 230, 241 below).

[418] There had been a heated discussion of the projected 'western design' at the Council meeting on 20 July 1654 (the main points of which are to be found in *CP*, III, pp. 207–208). Cromwell's orders to the commanders of the expedition were issued on 18 August 1654, well before the opening of the new Parliament on 3 September; Abbott, III, pp. 413–415.

that formerly in the House of Peers and about 100 new large forms ([covered] with mats) are this day set there for the members' repose. The House of Peers is likewise making ready with the same hanging and furniture as formerly.[419]

Colonel Gibbons is made governour of Jersey,[420] and Major-General Harrison's regiment is given to Major Winthrop[421] the ladies' man, and stood this week twice in the pillory for indeavouring the escape of the Portugal ambassador's brother

Gilbert Mabbott

Newsletter from Gilbert Mabbott, Westminster, 5 September 1654

fo. 130r

Sir

The last Lord's day his Highness came after [prayer] by water to the Painted Chamber and desired the members (which were above 300) to meet him the next day at the Abbey where Master Thomas Goodwin preached before them.[422] He went in state by coach to church and from thence by foot to the Painted Chamber[423] where he made a large speech to the members, relating the principal providences of God concerning the changes and turnings of the affairs about the common interest of the 3 nations, the many and great dangers they are in by the divisions at home, and wars with foreign parts had there not been a remedy applied which was instrumentally [~~applied~~] by the present government, it having produced many good things for the healing up of the breaches and the hopefulness of a future lasting peace concluded. He had not said anything to them upon the assumption of any dominion over them, but to joyn with them as a fellow servant to carry on the interest of these great affairs.[424] After this the members

[419] The work was begun on 1 September 1654; *Severall Proceedings*, 258 (31 Aug.–7 Sept. 1654), p. 4085.

[420] Col Robert Gibbon, or Gibbons, was certainly acting in this capacity by November 1654; *CSPD 1654*, p. 577.

[421] Stephen, fourth son of the first governor of Massachusetts Bay, John Winthrop; *DBR*, 'Stephen Winthrop'; F&D, I, p. 191.

[422] The text was Hosea, XII. 3–4; *Mercurius Politicus*, 221 (31 Aug.–7 Sept. 1654), p. 3743, which puts the number at 'above 200', although other sources agree with the figure given here.

[423] The elaborate ceremonial is described in Whitelock, *Memorials*, IV, p. 133.

[424] O. Cromwell, *His Highnesse's the Lord Protector's Speeches to the Parliament in the Painted Chamber, The one on Munday the 4th of September, the Other on Tuesday the 12 of September 1654.*

returned to the House and chose Master Lenthall their Speaker, Master Scobell their Clerk and Master Birkhead their Sergeant.[425] Several members that had not tickets from the Clerk of the Crown[426] were not admitted, *vizt* the Lord Grey,[427] earl of Stamford,[428] Major Wildman,[429] Master Warcup[430] and about 10 more. They ordered likewise that the morning lecture at the Abbey be continued and that a divine did pray in the House every morning of their session before them. They voted a fast day to be observed by the Parliament and those within the late lines of communications and another by England and Wales and another by England and Wales [*sic*] and a 3d by Ireland and Scotland and the future act be brought in <upon Wednesday come sennight>.[431] For that purpose they ordered Master Stephen Marshall and Master Thomas Goodwin do preach before the House on their fast day.[432] This day the House was called in and a committee appointed to consider of elections and double returns.[433] Tomorrow the House considers of the matter of this government. Great are the people's expectations of the results thereupon.

Gilbert Mabbott

Westminster 5th 7bris 1654

Taken by one who stood very near him and published to prevent mistakes (London, 1654). The speech is printed in Abbott, III, pp. 434–443.

425 *CJ*, VII, p. 365

426 The title 'Clerk of the Crown' had now been supplanted by 'Clerk of the Commonwealth in Chancery'. This was Nathaniel Tayler, who in accordance with clause XXI of the Instrument of Government issued Guibon Goddard with his ticket, or certificate of election, on 2 September; *SS*, p. 87; Burton, *Diary*, I, p. xvii; Whitelock, *Memorials*, IV, p. 274. The same procedure for the second Protectorate Parliament two years later is described by a correspondent who also uses the phrase, 'clerk of the crowne'; *CP*, III, pp. 73–74.

427 Lord Grey of Groby; Ludlow, *Memoirs*, I, p. 390.

428 Both the earl of Stamford and his elder son, Lord Grey of Groby, were issued with tickets by the Council on 6 September; *C&P*, III, p. 20.

429 I have discussed the question of Wildman's exclusion *before* the opening of Parliament above, p. 133.

430 Warcup's case, along with Samuel Highland's, had been considered by the Council on 16 August 1654 (see above p. 203). Highland was also prevented from taking his seat; Ludlow, *Memoirs*, I, p. 390.

431 Marginated. The intended position of this phrase is not indicated in the original. The dates proposed for the fasts were (London) 13 September, (England, Wales, and Scotland) 4 October, (Ireland) 1 November 1654; *CJ*, VII, p. 366.

432 *Ibid.*

433 The committee is named in *ibid.*

Newsletter from George Downing, London, 6 September 1654

*fo. 130*ʳ

The Parliament has spent these 2 days in debate whether they should approve of the government by a single person and a Parliament, and have put off the debate [thereof/thereon] till tomorrow morning.[434]

George Downing

Newsletter from Richard Hatter, Westminster, 12 September 1654

*fo. 132*ᵛ

The last week was wholly taken up in debate about the government which grew to a very great heighth,[435] insomuch that his Highness was necessitated to set a guard upon the Parliament door and appointed the Members to go into the Painted Chamber whither he came himself this day about 9 of the clock and there made a very excellent speech to them on the rise of the government,[436] that he[437] called himself to it nor did he bear witness to himself concerning it.[438] I am confident if the things declared by him be [...] all ingenuous and peacable spirits in the nation will receive full satisfaction. He desired that they would but consent to 4 things fundamental, *vizt*, the government to be in one person and the parliament, liberty of conscience, successive parliaments, and the militia to be as the model of the government[439] doth express. For other things, being as circumstantials, they might alter as they should see according and for that end an instrument was prepared under which so many were willing to subscribe might then with freedom fall upon the affairs of the nation. The Speaker and

[434] *Ibid.*, pp. 366–367; Burton, *Diary*, I, pp. xxi–xxiv.

[435] The House had dissolved itself into a grand committee in order to consider the Instrument of Government. It was clause 1 (on government by 'one person and the people assembled in Parliament') which caused these stormy debates; *ibid.*, pp. xxiv–xxxii.

[436] Goddard, who hurried to Westminster on hearing that Parliament had been dissolved by a joint decision of the Council and a council of war, recorded that the Protector's speech began at 10 am and lasted for about one and a half hours; *ibid.*, pp. xxxii–xxxiii.

[437] The word 'neither' is evidently omitted here.

[438] This phrase is a direct quotation from the Protector's speech; O. Cromwell, *His Highnesse the Lord Protector's Speech To the Parliament in London, the Painted Chamber On Tuesday the 12th of September* (London, 1654), p. 3.

[439] i. e. the Instrument of Government.

about 140 more of the members have subscribed the Instrument.[440] It's thought things will go happily on.[441]

Richard Hatter

Newsletter from George Downing, London, 12 September 1654

fo. 132v

Yesterday being also spent in debate in the Parliament, this day his Highness caused the Parliament doors to be shut and the Members desired to go to the Painted Chamber, where his Highness came to them, told them that he did not think they would have spent their time in [reading his foundations] and not considering how thereby they gave occasion to all discontented humours, and that to prevent all as it had been formerly, the custom of all Members of Parliament to take an oath so that he had to prevent such future disputes ordered an ingagement not to alter the present government as on one person and a Parliament to be signed by all before they enter in the House. 140 have this day signed. Tomorrow it is to be kept a fast.[442] It's generally talked that the French have again defeated the Spaniards.[443]

George Downing

Newsletter from George Downing, Westminster, 14 September 1654

fo. 133v

This day the Parliament met and passed the insuing vote that the recognition signed by divers Members of Parliament be declared by the Parliament to concern only so much of the government as relates to it as it consists of one person and a Parliament according

[440] There are differing estimates of the number of MPs who signed the new engagement, the wording of which can be found in *C&P*, III, pp. 32–33 and in Abbott, III, p. 463. *Mercurius Politicus*, 222 (7–14 Sept. 1654), p. 3764, agrees with the figure of 140, as does George Downing (next document) but other sources vary between 130 (*Perfect Diurnall*, 249 (11–18 Sept. 1654), p. 3814), and 180 (*CSPV 1653–1654*, p. 262).

[441] 'The Lord Protector of Heaven and Earth put a period to these Distractions', implored *The Faithful[l] Scout*, 196 (8–15 Sept. 1654), p. 1559.

[442] The fast was held in St Margaret's, Westminster; *Weekly Post*, 196 (12–19 Sept. 1654), p. 1565.

[443] *Mercurius Politicus*, 223 (14–21 Sept. 1654), pp. 3767–3768.

to the indenture,[444] and that the matters contained in the books of government consisting in 32[445] articles be not included therein but reserved for the debate of Parliament for which day they have ordered the [record] of the same book to be brought in the House.[446]

George Downing

George Monck to Oliver Cromwell, 16 September 1654[447]

fo. 134r

May it please your Highness

~~Though I have nothing~~

Affairs here being at present[448] in a quiet posture and parties of the enemy coming in daily I will not <need to>[449] trouble [~~—~~] your Highness with more then [~~—~~ own] that which the necessity of the soldiers does daily earnestly[450] call for, a speedy [re-]supply[451] of money,[452] [~~—~~] their arrears and wants daily increasing, but no [~~—~~] answerable [appointment] of money designed[453] for their satisfaction. ~~This want makes the I shall not~~This want makes[454] my command not altogether[455] so acceptable[456] to me and[457] the pressing occasions for the settling of my affairs and family in England do[458] [reissue][459] my suit unto your Lordship[460] for ~~some other commission than the present~~

[444] On this day the House appointed a committee 'in reference to the Subscription to prepare something to be offered to the House for their further Consideration'; *CJ*, VII, p. 367 names the committee members.

[445] This should read '42'. The articles were read out in Parliament on 15 September; *Severall Proceedings*, 260 (14–21 Sept. 1654), p. 4120, which also prints Parliament's declaration on the engagement, or recognition (pp. 4113–[4114]).

[446] *CJ*, VII, p. 368; *C&P*, III, p. 35.

[447] The number of deletions and alterations in this letter reveal the care with which it was framed. It appears to be a first draft of Monck's letter of the same date found in longhand in Worc MS L, fo. 70v (printed in *S&P*, pp. 184–185).

[448] Worc. MS L, fo. 70v places 'being' after 'at present'.

[449] Interlined. *Ibid.* omits 'need to'.

[450] *Ibid.* reads 'inevitably' for 'earnestly'.

[451] *Ibid.* reads 'supply'.

[452] In *ibid.*, 'moneyes'.

[453] *Ibid.* reads 'allotted' for 'designed'.

[454] *Ibid.* reads 'here renders' for 'makes'.

[455] *Ibid.* omits 'altogether'.

[456] *Ibid.* reads 'desireable' for 'acceptable'.

[457] *Ibid.* reads 'for' for 'to me and'.

[458] Blank.

[459] *Ibid.* reads 'induce me to renew' for '[reissue]'.

[460] *Ibid.* reads 'Highness' for 'Lordship'.

the appointing of[461] some other to take the charge of these forces, and having once settled ~~and [. . .] that little I am~~ that little I have in England I shall ~~observe your Highness' commands~~ attend your Highness' commands if it be to the West Indias.[462] [~~. . .~~] Hoping your Highness will pardon this presumption and grant my earnest request herein I remain.

Newsletter from Gilbert Mabbott, Westminster, 16 September 1654

fo. 134[r]

Wednesday last Doctor Goodwin and Master Marshall preached before the Members.[463] Thursday the House ordered that the sending for ministers from every county to sit here and debate matters of religion should be referred to the committee for privileges. They likewise ordered that the last ordinance concerning marriages should be referred to a committee.[464] They likewise passed the inclosed declaration which made near 80 more Members the next day come in and subscribe the ingagement.[465] Yesterday the House only read the Instrument of Government and deferred the debate thereon till Monday next, and to that day adjourned.[466] His Highness that night made a large speech to the Lord Mayor, aldermen and Common Council men of London at Whitehall on the reasons of his late actings and the necessity thereof, which gave them much satisfaction as was demonstrated by their lowd hemming him up after his speech.[467]

Gilbert Mabbott

[461] *Ibid.* omits 'of'.

[462] *Ibid.* places this phrase in parentheses.

[463] Dr Francis Cheynell was also one of the preachers; *CJ*, VII, p. 367.

[464] Both these matters arose on Friday 15th, not as reported here on Thursday 14th; *ibid.*, p. 368; Burton, *Diary*, I, p. xxxix. The proposal for this 'Assembly of Divines' was soon dropped; *C&P*, III, pp. 22, 43.

[465] The enclosure was presumably the printed broadsheet, *The Parliament doth Declare, That the Recognition of the Government by the Members of this Parliament in the Words Following* . . . (London, 1654), and perhaps the copy which survives in Clarke's collection at Worcester College.

[466] This is confirmed in *CJ*, VII, p. 368.

[467] The Protector's speech lasted for almost two hours, and only representatives of the City were permitted to be present. The speech was well received and 'he was applauded with very great hums at the end, and at every pause'; Stainer, *Speeches of Oliver Cromwell, 1644–58*, pp. 172–173.

Newsletter from George Downing, Westminster, 16 September 1654

fo. 134r

200 [want 13] of the Parliament men have subscribed the ingagement yesterday.[468] The Parliament ordered the act for satisfying creditors on which the commissioners sat at Haberdashers' Hall, and the act for marriages to be considered by a committee and with amendments is to be reported to the Parliament.

George Downing

Newsletter from Gilbert Mabbott, Westminster, 21 September 1654

fo. 136v

Monday the House passed an act for setting the 11th of 8bris next [appearing] for a day of humiliation and ordered a committee to attend his Highness for his assent therein.[469] They ordered that the Judge Advocate should be excused of any longer attendance in receiving the subscription of the Members to the ingagement or recognition, and that any 2 Members may receive the like subscriptions for the future.[470] Tuesday they ordered that Master Griffith should preach before the House the next fast day instead of Master Vennings.[471] The Lord of Salisbury then reported his Highness' assent to the act for a day of humiliation.[472] The rest of the day was spent in debate on the Instrument for Government. Yesterday and this day they sat in a grand committee and resolved that the supreme legislative authority should reside in a Lord Protector and the people assembled in a Parliament, and that the present Lord Protector shall continue during life. They likewise voted that no laws should be repealed nor made and any tax charge or imposition laid upon the people but by

[468] According to *Mercurius Politicus*, around 240 MPs had subscribed the recognition by 19 September; 223 (14–21 Sept. 1654), p. 3780. The *Perfect Diurnall* put the figure at 193 on 15 September; 249 (11–18 Sept. 1654), p. [3822]. See S.R. Gardiner's comments in *C&P*, III, pp. 35, 43n.

[469] The declaration for the fast is printed in *Mercurius Politicus*, 223 (14–21 Sept. 1654), pp. 3777–3779.

[470] *CJ*, VII, p. 368.

[471] The other preachers were Sidrach Simpson and 'Mr Turner'; *Severall Proceedings*, 260 (21–28 Sept. 1654), p. 4126.

[472] *CJ*, VII, p. 368.

common consent in Parliament.[473] There are now about 230 Members that have subscribed. This day likewise the House ordered that an act should be drawn for this Parliament not to be dissolved in 6 months unless by their own consent, and likewise to inable them to sit 3 months after if they see emergent occasion for it.[474] Wednesday next the House is ordered to be called.

Gilbert Mabbott

Westminster 7bris 21 1654

Newsletter from Gilbert Mabbott, Westminster, 26 September 1654[475]

fo. 138r

Since my last the House has been for the most part in a grand committee[476] debating the Instrument of Government and have passed several votes thereupon, *vizt* that the power of the militia shall be in his Highness's Council in the interval of Parliaments only.[477] That this and all other Councils of his Highness shall pass the approbation of Parliament, his Highness being to be present[478] and the Parliament to approve. That the Council now to be approved of shall not continue longer than 40 days after the session of the next Parliament.[479] That the number of his Council shall be 21 and any 7 of them to be of the quorum.[480] That the ordinance appointing commissioners to approve of the settlement[481] the ministers and the several powers thereupon given to[482] them be referred to the examination of a committee who

473 As Guibon Goddard was out of London between 16 and 20 September and returned to the House only on the 21st, we do not have his record of the grand committee's proceedings; Burton, *Diary*, I, p. xl. However, these resolutions are reported in the newsbooks, e.g., *Weekly Post* 197 (19–26 Sept. 1654), p. 1575.

474 Burton, *Diary*, I, p. xl.

475 Mabbott sent the same letter to the mayor and aldermen of Hull on the same day. That document is in a damaged condition, but where I have been able to compare the wording I have added variations as footnotes; Hull CRO, BRL 599.

476 The House formed itself into a grand committee on 22, 23, 25 and 26 September; *CJ*, VII, pp. 369–370.

477 The question was laid aside on the 23rd and resolved on the day of this letter; Burton, *Diary*, I, pp. xli–xlii.

478 Hull CRO, BRL 599 reads 'represent' for 'be present'.

479 This was resolved on 26 September; Burton, *Diary*, I, p. xlii.

480 This was resolved on 25 September; *ibid.*

481 Hull CRO, BRL 599 reads '& settle' for 'the settlement'.

482 *Ibid.* (where the preceding word is missing) reads 'upon' for 'to'.

are to report same with their opinion[483] thereupon to the House.[484] They likewise appointed a committee to regulate the press and to suppress such pamphlets as they shall think fit. A report was likewise made to the House from his Highness of an intended design by[485] sea which was left to their consideration. The House thereupon ordered that it should be referred to his Highness and Council to do therein as they should think fit for the good and safety of the nation.[486] This occasions much expedition in the fleet, which will be ready within 3 weeks at sea.[487]

Several Members come in daily, the bystanders being well pleased in a[488] Parliament taking the Instrument of Government in pieces and his Highness not being offended at the same so that a full House and a right understanding is expected in a[489] short time.

Gilbert Mabbott

Newsletter from George Downing, Westminster, 28 September 1654

*fo. 139^r^*

Sir

Yesterday the grand committee of the House voted that the exercise of the chief magistracy over [these] nations shall be by the Protector assisted as[490] a Council and that this Protector and Council shall govern according to the laws.[491] This day they are about 2 or 3 things relating to the 3d article of the government but came to no resolution.[492]

George Downing

483 *Ibid.* reads 'opinions'.

484 The present commissioners were thought to be 'very incompetent'; Burton, *Diary*, I, p. xli.

485 Hull CRO, BRL 599 reads 'at' for 'by'.

486 Cromwell informed the Speaker of the proposed 'design' in a letter of 22 September 1654 (printed in Abbott, III, p. 468). The House resolved to leave the matter entirely in the hands of the Protector; *CJ*, VII, p. 369; Burton, *Diary*, I, pp. xl–xli.

487 On 28 September the Council ordered that all remaining gunpowder in the Tower was to be sent to Plymouth and other garrisons; *CSPD 1654*, p. 372.

488 Hull CRO, BRL 599 reads 'the' for 'a'.

489 *Ibid.* omits 'a'.

490 This word should read 'with', as in Goddard's account; Burton, *Diary*, I, p. xliii.

491 Here Goddard adds, 'and such limitations as should be agreed upon in Parliament'; *ibid.*

492 This is also confirmed by Goddard, who adds the resolutions of the grand committee; *ibid.*

Axeyard, 7bris 28

Arundel Harry Howard last night killed one Holland, solicitor for the Lord Standford in the rooms without the Starchamber.[493]

Newsletter from Gilbert Mabbott, Westminster, 3 October 1654

*fo. 140*ʳ

The House Wednesday and Thursday last sat in a grand committee debating the Instrument of Government and voted that the supreme magistracy of these 3 nations be invested in the Lord Protector with such limitations as shall be hereafter agreed upon by Parliament that all honours shall be conferred by his Highness, but not to be hereditary without consent of Parliament. That his Highness shall not have power to pardon wilful murther.[494]

The earl of Arundel's brother on Wednesday last stabbed a solicitor in the Starchamber who appeared against him in the probate of the old countess of Arundel her will and cannot yet be apprehended.

Thursday last his Highness took the air in Hyde Park attended with Master Secretary Thurloe and being in some pain with a fit of the stone, got up in the coach box hoping ease thereon, but the horses finding an unusual rein from a new driver got head and ran away upon a full speed with the coach. His Highness sat the box for a mile, the postillion and part of the lifeguard that attended him being not able at that time to give them check. At last his feet being most unhappily [intangled] in the reins his person was thereupon dragged a short way till his shoe was forced off and then received a very mersiful deliverance.[495] The Secretary seeing his Highness exposed to this danger leapt out of the coach to preserve his Highness and himself, but thereon the coach wheels running over his leg whereby it was out of joint and much bruised, was disabled [~~from~~] for[496] some time to rise from the ground.[497]

493 The incident is reported in *Mercurius Politicus*, 225 (28 Sept.–5 Oct. 1654), p. 3796.

494 These points are confirmed by Goddard; Burton, *Diary*, I, p. xliii.

495 A briefer account of the accident appeared in several of the newsbooks, e.g., *Faithful[l] Scout*, 199 (29 Sept.–6 Oct. 1654), p. 1574. The Venetian, French, and Dutch ambassadors all reported it in their official correspondence; *CSPV 1653–1654*, p. 269; *TSP*, II, pp. 652–653.

496 '[F]or' superimposed on '[from]'.

497 Thurloe, describing the affair to John Pell in a letter of 24 October, wrote that it had prevented him from sending his usual letters as 'I have kept to my chamber, and been under so much disposition of body'; Vaughan, *Protectorate of Oliver Cromwell*, I, pp. 69–70.

The same day the House appointed a committee to attend his Highness about raising the force by sea and land whereby the nation might be eased.[498] Friday and Saturday they appointed a committee for the affairs of Ireland and for the affairs of Scotland.[499] Yesterday and this day the House was debating about making war and peace and passed only this act; that no war should be made during the session of Parliament but by advice and consent of Parliament. In whose power it shall be in the intervals of Parliament is the question in debate.[500] The House is now full, 300 Members.[501] The expedition by seas goes on [effectually].

The committee for Ireland yesterday voted that Ireland should be hereafter called West England; whether the House will concur therein we know not.[502]

Gilbert Mabbott

Newsletter from London, 7 October 1654

fo. 142ʳ

The House has all this week been in a grand committee debating the Instrument of Government and for the most part that concerning the number of the members to be chosen in the several countries for successive parliaments, having yet made no alteration therein, but only Scarburgh (for which Major Wildman was returned) and all Surrey, which are made uncapable to choose any more for the future.[503] They have likewise appointed a committee to consider of the ordinance of his Highness and Council for regulation of the Chancery.[504] They ordered that every Wednesday and Friday in the afternoon the House should meet in a grand committee to consider of religion and in prosecution thereof they yesterday voted that there shall be an [asserting/assertion] held forth of the faith of England.[505] A committee is appointed to consider of the transportation of corn, butter and

[498] This was not recorded by either Bulstrode Whitelocke or Guibon Goddard.

[499] Those named for the committees are listed in *CJ*, VII, p. 371.

[500] The outcome of the debate was that this power should rest in the hands of the Protector and Council, 'with such limitations and restrictions as the Parliament shall think fit'; Burton, *Diary*, I, p. xlvi.

[501] This figure is confirmed in *CSPV 1653–1654*, p. 270, and in the newsbooks, e.g., *Certain Passages*, [39] (29 Sept.–5 Oct. 1654), p. 298.

[502] I have discussed this item of news above, p. 135.

[503] This is not reported by Guibon Goddard.

[504] The committee, appointed on 5 October, is listed in *CJ*, VII, pp. 373–374.

[505] *Ibid.*, p. 373.

cheese and that the customs thereon may be raised.[506] His Highness sent a letter to the House with the names of the Chancellour and Commissioners for the Exchequer for the approbation of Parliament according to the Instrument, but they have not yet passed any vote thereupon.[507]

London 8bris 7 1654

Newsletter from George Downing, Westminster, 10 October 1654

fo. 143[v]

Axeyard 8bris 10

Yesterday a committee was appointed for the distribution of the 30 Members appointed for Scotland, and the 30 appointed for Ireland. A committee also was appointed for the considering and [issuing] of the writs of summons for future Parliaments together with the qualifications and manner of elections.[508] This day the committee passed over the remaining articles most whereof are already under particular consideration, until they came to the 30th article, and thereupon ordered the Committee of the Chancery to consider of the ordinances made by his Highness and his Council not already referred.[509] They also appointed a committee to consider of the land not already sold and disposed and how it may be fit to have them disposed.[510]

George Downing

Newsletter from Gilbert Mabbott, Westminster, 14 October 1654

fo. 144[r]

Monday last was spent in debate of elections and appointing a committee to consider of the form of a written indenture with the

[506] *Ibid.*, p. 374. There had been what was viewed as a God-given surfeit of these products in this year; Whitelock, *Memorials*, IV, p. 152; *Faithful[l] Scout*, 200 (6–13 Oct. 1654), p. [1601].

[507] The official record for 6 October does not give any indication of the contents of Cromwell's letter to the Speaker; *CJ*, VII, p. 374.

[508] This is reported in brief by Goddard; Burton, *Diary*, I, p. xlviii.

[509] *CJ*, VII, p. 375.

[510] This was also noted by Goddard; Burton, *Diary*, I, p. xlix.

qualifications of the persons elected and to be elected.[511] Tuesday was spent in debate of the ordinances made by his Highness and Council before the session of Parliament and referred consideration thereof to a committee.[512] Wednesday was <kept>[513] a fast which the House observed within their own walls.[514] Thursday was spent in debate of the business of trades which at last was referred to a grand committee who are to sit every Tuesday in the afternoon thereupon.[515] Friday was spent in debate of the ordinance for regulation of the Chancery (formerly referred) and ordered to suspend the execution thereof till 28th *November* next.[516] This day the House sat not.

His Highness has lost his ague and is well recovering from the lameness of his leg by his late fall from the coach.[517]

Gilbert Mabbott

Westminster 8bris 14

Newsletter from George Downing, Westminster, 19 October 1654

fo. 146[r]

Yesterday the committee of the Parliament voted that the Protector shall be elective and not hereditary. This day was spent in debate whether the Protector shall be chosen by the Parliament or the Council, but nothing therein concluded.[518]

His Highness is in reasonable good health. He takes the ayr every afternoon in Saint James's Park.[519]

George Downing

Axeyard 8bris 19 1654

[511] *CJ*, VII, p. 375 confirms, but does not mention the question of a written indenture.

[512] *Ibid.*

[513] Interlined.

[514] The fast, ordered on 14 September, had been postponed from 4 October; *ibid.*, p. 367. In reporting it *Mercurius Politicus* uses the same phrase, 'within their own walls'; 226 (5–12 Oct. 1654), p. 3832.

[515] *CJ*, VII, pp. 375–376.

[516] *Ibid.*, p. 376.

[517] For which see p. 215 above.

[518] After three days' debate, from 19–21 October, the question of how future Protectors should be elected was decided on 21 October; Burton, *Diary*, I, pp. lii–liii. See following document.

[519] Cromwell was reported on this day to be taking the air in St James's Park in a sedan; *TSP*, II, p. 684.

Newsletter from Gilbert Mabbott, London, 21 October 1654

fo. 147ʳ

Monday, Tuesday and Wednesday last were spent in debating whether future Lord Protectors should be elective or successive. At last it was resolved in the former.[520] Thursday and Friday were spent in debating who should have the power to elect them, but they are not yet come to any result therein. The House sits not this day, having adjourned from Friday to Monday.

His Highness is so well recovered that he has been twice abroad this week.[521]

Gilbert Mabbott

Newsletter from William Rowe, Whitehall, 24 October 1654

fo. 148ᵛ

The House has assigned the electing of the Lord Protector by the Parliament sitting, the Parliament and the Council in the interval limited therein as the House shall hereafter direct, and that chief officers of state and justice be nominated and constituted by the Lord Protector and Council in the interval, but be approved by Parliament. And in conformity thereupon the grand committee turned themselfs into an House and passed votes of [approbation] on the present Lord Deputy of Ireland, Lords Commissioners [of the Seal], 2 Lords Chief Justices and the Commissioners for the Treasuries who are the same 3 Lords Commissioners, 2 Lords Justices and Colonel Montague and Colonel Sydenham.[522]

William Rowe

Whitehall 24 8bris 1654

[520] It is likely that the massive majority of 200 to 65 in favour of the office being elective rather than hereditary reflected Cromwell's own wishes; *C&P*, III, p. 40.

[521] The Protector had been 'abroad in his coach'; *Perfect Account*, 198 (18–25 Oct. 1654), p. 1579.

[522] Guibon Goddard was absent from the House during the debates on Monday 23 October, but gives a lengthy summary of the arguments. He confirms the elections on the following day; Burton, *Diary*, I, pp. liii–lviii.

Newsletter from George Downing, Westminster, 26 October 1654

fo. 149[v]

Axeyard 26th 8bris 1654

Right Honourable

Yesterday the Parliament suspended the ordinance of his Highness and the Council for the relief of poor debtors and creditors.[523] This day the grand committee voted that the true Christian religion contained in the Holy Scriptures of the Old and New Testament be held forth and recommended as the publike profession of these nations, and that the present maintenance for godly, able and painful ministers and tenders for instructing the people and for discovery and confutation of error, heresies and everything contrary to sound doctrine be continued until other provision be made for them.[524] Monday last some of the officers of the army met together. They meet together again tomorrow at Saint James's.

George Downing

Newsletter from Gilbert Mabbott, Westminster, 28 October 1654

fo. 150[r]

Right Honourable

Monday last the House voted that the constitution of his Highness' Council shall be in the Parliament. They likewise voted that the Lords Protectors of this nation shall for the future be chosen by the Parliament (if any Protector die during the session thereof) and in the intervals of Parliament to be chosen by the Council who are to be directed, limited and qualified therein by Parliament. The next day they approved of (upon his Highness 1st nominating of them) the present Commissioners of Ireland, the 2 Lords Chief Justices, the Lords Commissioners of the Great Seal and the Lords Treasurers for the Exchequer.[525] Wednesday was spent (as a House, the Speaker

[523] *CJ*, VII, p. 378.

[524] The wording follows closely that of the thirty-fifth article of the Instrument of Government. Goddard confirms that it was debated on this day; Burton, *Diary*, I, p. lix.

[525] For all this, see also p. 219 above.

being in the chair) in debate of the ordinance and act for relief of creditors and poor prisoners (against all which all the long robe were very bitter) and the question was put for the suspending the execution thereof by the commissioners at Salters' Hall, and it was resolved in the affirmative.[526] Thursday and Friday the House sat in debate on the articles of the faith of the Church of England (ordered by the late assembly of ministers) and agree [*sic*] thereunto with very little alterations.[527]

Friday many officers of the army met to seek God. This day was spent in debate of tender consciences.[528]

The reason of the report of the expedition not [going] on or the [convoy] of any ships I know not, and I believe will [prove] but a bare report.

Gilbert Mabbott

Westminster 28 8bris 1654

Newsletter from George Downing, Westminster, 28 October 1654

fo. 150r

Axeyard 28 *October* 1654

Sir,

Yesterday and this day have been spent in debate of the 36th article of the[529] government, whether any shall be compelled by penalties to the publike profession that shall be held forth, and the further debate thereupon is adjourned till Monday next.

Yesterday the officers of the army met at James's to seek God. There were some glances at civil matters. They meet again on Wednesday next.

George Downing

[526] *CJ*, VII, p. 378.

[527] Apparently referring to article XXXVII of the Instrument of Government, this is at variance with Goddard's account that article XXXV was considered on Thursday 26 October and XXXVI on 27–28 October when '[t]he House being much divided, nothing was, either day, resolved'; Burton, *Diary*, I, p. lix. Goddard's account agrees with Downing's information (next document).

[528] The meeting was reported by *Mercurius Politicus*, 229 (26 Oct.–2 Nov. 1654), p. 3879, and also by George Downing in the next document.

[529] 'Instrument of' omitted here.

Newsletter from George Downing, Westminster, 31 October 1654

fo. 151r

Right Honourable

Yesterday was also spent in debate concerning the 36 and 37 articles of the government, and the debate adjourned till tomorrow.[530] This day the Speaker taking the chair passed the act brought in by the committee for transportation of corn and butter.[531] They also appointed a committee to consider of the whole matter concerning Linsey Level.[532]

George Downing

Axeyard, 31 8bris 1654

Newsletter from George Downing, Westminster, 4 November 1654

fo. 153r

Axeyard 4th 9bris

Right Honourable

Yesterday the Parliament appointed a committee to consider the petitions of the Lord Craven, Sir John Stowell and the tenants of the Dean and Chapter of Durham.[533] They also voted to Colonel Birch, 1,000*l* to be paid him out of the excise for which instead of lands had voted him for [it] out of Sir John Stowell's estate.[534] This day the grand committee took into consideration an oath for the

530 *Severall Proceedings*, 266 (26 Oct.–2 Nov. 1654), p. [4219], reported simply that the grand committee sat 'on the Government, and made further progresse therein'.

531 *CJ*, VII, p. 379.

532 The Council had considered the matter of the drainage of Lindsey level several times during the year, and had passed an ordinance relating to it on 25 August 1654; *CSPD 1654*, pp. 152, 322, 335.

533 *CJ*, VII, p. 381. All three cases concerned confiscated lands; *The Lord Craven's Case briefly stated* (London, 1654); *Reasons humbly offered why the Sale of the Lands and Estates belonging to the late Bishop of Durham should not be confirmed* ([London], 1654); *To Parliament. The Petition of severall well affected persons, purchasers of the estate of William Lord Craven* ([London], 1654); *Reasons for Establishment of Publike Sale. Humbly tendered, as well as in behalf of the Commonwealth, as likewise of the Purchasers of the Estate of Sir John Stowel* ([London], 1654).

534 The sum of £2,500 owed to Birch since an ordinance of 24 December 1647 was voted on 3 November to be repaid to him out of the excise; *CJ*, VII, pp. 381–382.

Protector and Council and a committee is appointed for the framing of them. They also voted a committee to consider how the study of the civil law may be incouraged and ordered a report to be brought in from the committee of 10 appointed to word the articles for liberty of conscience.[535]

The fleet under General Penn sent up a representation to his Highness of their hearty resolution to stand by the present government and yield obedience to it in pursuance of the present design on foot.[536]

George Downing

Newsletter from George Downing, Westminster, 11 November 1654

fo. 156ʳ

Axeyard 11 9bris

Yesterday the Parliament voted that the supreme legislative power of the Commonwealth is and shall reside in one single person and Parliament and that all [proceedings] agreed unto by Parliament shall be presented unto the Lord Protector and in case he shall not give his consent thereunto then they shall pass into and become laws although he shall not consent thereto, provided that the said bill contain nothing contrary to such negatives as the Parliament shall think fit to give unto the Protector. Upon reading the question exceptions were taken to the words thereof and it was ordered that in regard the style of the single person is not yet voted in Parliament that the word single person shall be inserted instead of the word Protector and the debate upon the last clause of the said question was adjourned unto this day and upon the question it was this day resolved that instead of the said words provided that the said bills contain in them nothing contrary to such negatives as the Parliament shall think fit to give the single person be inserted provided that the said bills contain in them nothing contrary

[535] Goddard confirms the items about the oaths and the consideration of civil law, but not that about the committee for the articles for liberty of conscience; Burton, *Diary*, I, pp. lxi–lxii.

[536] On the contrary, the seamen's petition, *To his Highness the Lord Protector, The Humble Petition of the Sea-men, belonging to the ships of the Commonwealth of England* (dated by George Thomason 4 November 1654) was a list of grievances. Cromwell settled the unrest by immediately paying their arrears. By the middle of the month the trouble was over; Taft, '*The Humble Petition of Several Colonels of the Army*...', p. 35; Worc. MS XXVI, fo. 157ʳ. Downing's version is of interest as there seems to have been some attempt to keep the unrest quiet; *TSP*, II, p. 709.

to such matters wherein the single person and Parliament shall declare a negative to be in the single person.[537]

George Downing

Monday last the committee to whom the drawing up of an act for appointing commissioners in several counties to eject scandalous ministers was referred made report thereon and being very long.[538]

Newsletter from George Downing, Westminster, 18 November 1654

fo. 160^r

Axeyard, 9bris 18 1654

<Received 23th>[539]

Right Honourable

Yesterday morning his Highness his mother departed this life, having languished a long time.[540]

Yesterday also the Parliament voted that Oliver Cromwell the present Lord Protector shall dispose such of the standing forces as shall be agreed to be continued upon the charge of the Commonwealth in the intervals of Parliament by the advice of the Council and not otherwise. This day the Parliament debated how the militia shall be disposed of after the death of this Protector and adjourned the further debate thereupon till Monday morning.[541]

George Downing

537 All these details are confirmed and amplified by Goddard's much lengthier account of the two days' proceedings; Burton, *Diary*, I, pp. lxiii–lxxi.

538 Blank. *CJ*, VII, p. 384 confirms this item of business.

539 Marginated. A rare example of Clarke noting the date of receipt of a communication from London.

540 Other accounts record that Elizabeth Cromwell died on the night of 16 November, so perhaps her death came early in the hours of the morning of the 17th; *CSPV 1653–1654*, p. 284; Vaughan, *Protectorate of Oliver Cromwell*, I, p. 81; *Severall Proceedings*, 269 (16–23 Nov. 1654), p. [4267]. On his copy of J. Longe's *An Epitaph On the late deceased, that truely-Noble and Renowned Lady* (London, 1655), George Thomason wrote, 'A very Sad Copie of verses'.

541 Again these details are confirmed by Goddard's fuller notes; Burton, *Diary*, I, pp. lxviii–lxxxiv.

Newsletter from Richard Hatter, Westminster, 18 November 1654

fo. 160^{r}

Since the Parliament is yet upon the government and as to the 24th article being subjoyned to the 1st, the question is resolved with this proviso that such laws contain in them nothing contrary to such negatives as the single person or the Parliament shall declare to be in the single person.[542] The reports of the committee concerning the Lord Protector and the Council's oaths, as likewise of the articles concerning elections and qualifications for members from the 13th article to the 22th read but nothing was resolved, but by the writ for summons sheriffs shall not be returned for their counties, but for any burgh or other county they may be chosen to serve in Parliament. Tuesday the House agreed more [unanimously] than has been observed heretofore.[543] Of late they took care that neither the Protector nor Parliaments shall be able to alter the government from a single person and a Parliament, which is intended to be done by adding a provision to that purpose in the Lord Protector's oaths, and by injoyning that the members of every successive Parliament shall subscribe not to [consent to efface] the same government.

Richard Hatter

Westminster 18 9bris 1654

Newsletter from George Downing, [Westminster], 21 November 1654

fo. 161^{v}

Right Honourable

Yesterday the Parliament voted that after the death of the present Protector the forces should be disposed by the Council until the meeting of the Parliament, and then to be disposed as the Parliament shall think fit.[544] This day the Parliament voted that an assessment be laid upon England of 60,000*l* per mensem for 3 months next ensuing.[545]

[542] Here Hatter is commenting upon the business of 10 November; *CJ*, VII, p. 384.

[543] Guibon Goddard also noted that 'the House seemed very unanimous that Parliament should not be perpetual'; Burton, *Diary*, I, p. lxxiv.

[544] No vote was necessary and the resolution passed without a division; *CJ*, VII, p. 387. Its background and implications are discussed in *C&P*, III, pp. 47–49.

[545] *CJ*, VII, p. 387.

Saturday the council of war met about Colonel Okey. The charge was exhibited against him by the judicature. The court ordered him to be taken into custody and to proceed [further] upon Thursday next, but he hides himself.[546]

George Downing

Newsletter from George Downing, [Westminster], 23 November 1654

fo. 162v

Right Honourable

Yesterday the bill for scandalous ministers was read the 2d time and was committed.[547] A committee was also appointed to consider a way for turning such treasurers and such as have received the publike money to account and to consider how such may be punished as have forged debentures or publike bills.[548] This day the Parliament voted that all ordinances made by his Highness and his Council for raising money for defraying the publike charges [did] stand good and in force until the last day of this Parliament unless they expire before that time or the Parliament take another order to the contrary.[549] They also voted that no law be abrogated, suspended or repealed nor any new made or any tax laid upon the people without common consent of the people assembled in Parliament.[550]

The meeting of officers at Saint James's yesterday dissolved themselfs without [concluding][551] anything concerning their petition.[552]

George Downing

546 With Colonels Matthew Alured and Thomas Saunders, Okey had signed and had been instrumental in producing the so-called 'petition of the three colonels', (see above p. 133n). Okey was acquitted of the charge of treason and after resigning his commission was allowed to go free.

547 *CJ*, VII, p. 387.

548 *Ibid.*

549 *Ibid.*, p. 388.

550 *Ibid.*

551 In the sense of 'dealing with' (*OED*).

552 It was reported in *Certain Passages*, unnumb., (17–24 Nov. 1654), p. [120], that the officers had met on 23 November, '(as they have done divers dayes before)', to consider 'certain propositions' to the Protector and Parliament. John Thurloe wrote to John Pell on 17 November that the officers' meetings to consider their petition to Cromwell had not 'produced much'; Vaughan, *Protectorate of Oliver Cromwell*, I, p. 80.

Newsletter from John Thurloe, Westminster, 23 November 1654

fo. 162v

Westminster 9bris 23

The Parliament has now sat almost 3 months and have not passed any one act or done any one thing of the peace and settlement of the nation. Their whole time has been taken up in debate about the government which the nation expected had been settled before their meeting, and when they will come to the end of their debate is very uncertain. Of the 42 articles they have gone over in the House not above 4 or 5, that is the 1st, 24, 4 and 6 wherein they have made several great alterations. They have put the militia after the death of the Protector wholly in the Parliament. This day they have declared that the ordinance of his Highness and the Council for raising of money for the pay of the army etc. shall be of force during the sitting this Parliament and no longer time, that if they rise without settlement of that business the army is without any provision. The monthly assessment they have reduced to 60,000*l* per mensem which is 30,000*l* less than now is raised,[553] and yet they have not advised his Highness to disband any of our forces in the 3 nations unless it be some inconsiderable garrisons, and yet 'tis evident that as the assessment is now the state [runs in debt]. Where the rest shall be had I know not unless it be by free quarter. We must expect and wait upon God for the issue of these things. I need not mind you of having an eye to busy and discontented persons.

This day Colonel Okey appeared before the council of war having absented himself for some days before. He pleads not guilty to his charge and has put himself upon his trial. He being committed to the marshall desired he might be bayled, but the charge being of a very high nature that was denied him.[554] Colonel Alured stands yet committed and is suddenly to be brought to his trial.[555]

John Thurloe

553 *CJ*, VII, p. 388.

554 This is confirmed by Thurloe's letter to John Pell of 24 November; Vaughan, *Protectorate of Oliver Cromwell*, I, p. 85.

555 Alured first appeared before a court martial on 7 December 1654, but the trial was delayed until the following January (p. 244 below).

Newsletter from Henry Walker, Westminster, 23 November 1654

fo. 162v

Westminster 23 9bris

Yesterday 800 men were drawn out of Colonel Barkstead's regiment, 400 out of the General's, 400 out of Colonel Ingoldsby's and 400 out of Colonel Goffe's, and General Venables with his officers and lifeguard were at the muster. General Penn is returned to the fleet and they are suddenly to go upon the expedition.[556]

Henry Walker

John Spencer, Westminster, to [George Monck], 2 December 1654

fo. 169v

<Captain Spencer's letter to the General concerning the meeting of the officers>[557]

May it please your Honour,

We met last Wednesday at Saint James's.[558] We had a great many officers. We had a good agreement in all those our things we were to propound to my Lord Protector. There was chose out of them about 10 officers to go to my Lord Protector with them, which accordingly we did. My Lord did declare to us his heart was in those good things and did promise to do his best for the [accomplishment] of them. We did also declare that we and all the officers would with our lives stand by him in the doing of those good things.[559] We have met several times this week with my Lord, Major Packer, Major Creed, Captain Empson, Captain Malyn, Colonel Pryde, Colonel Axtel, and myself.[560] We have declared how far we can stand by my Lord. As for the Instrument

[556] Penn's commission and orders for the expedition are reprinted in Abbott, III, pp. 528–552, 530–532. Penn was reported to be putting out to sea on 25 November 1654; *Perfect Account*, 203 (22–29 Nov. 1654), pp. 1622–1623.

[557] Marginated.

[558] *Severall Proceedings*, 270 (23–30 Nov. 1654), p. [4288], reports that the officers met for prayer 'and were long together' at this meeting on 29 November 1654.

[559] At this meeting the officers declared that they would 'live and die' with Cronwell; *CP*, III, p. 10; Vaughan, *Protectorate of Oliver Cromwell*, I, pp. 87–88.

[560] Malyn, Pryde, and Axtel are not included in the group which according to another newsletter presented the officers' proposals to the Protector; *CP*, III, p. 11.

of the Government we desired my Lord not to insist on that for we did believe he would see cause to alter something in it. We did assure him that we could with our souls own him in the doing of all the good things. We are well satisfied in my Lord Protector and my Lord Protector is fully satisfied in us. So all the officers and my Lord are more strongly united than ever.

Colonel Okey and my Lord are very well united.[561] All things [passed over] by my lord. Union amongst us at this time will prove a great blessing to us. Lieutenant-Colonel Lilburne is like to come forth of prison.[562] I desire of God to bless you and yours and shall remain

your faithful servant

John Spencer

[561] Despite the council of war's recent refusal of Okey's application for bail, Cromwell had now ordered him to be set at liberty; *ibid.*, p. 11; p. 227 above.

[562] John Lilburne was transferred from imprisonment in Jersey to Dover Castle in October 1655; Gregg, *Free-born John*, p. 339.

7. NOTEBOOK XXVII

1 January–13 November 1655[1]

Introduction

Several documents in this volume relate to the discovery, sometime towards the end of December 1654, of the so-called 'Overton plot'.[2] On 18 December a group of officers who were dissatisfied with the Protectorate met at Aberdeen to plan a meeting of other disaffected members of the army in Scotland; this was to take place in Edinburgh on 1 January 1655.[3] Colonel Robert Overton, if not the ringleader, was clearly involved, as were Major John Bramston and the chaplain of Colonel Thomas Pride's regiment, Samuel Oates. The plan was discovered before the meeting could take place and the leaders were immediately arrested.[4] Incriminating papers found on Bramston and copied by Clarke in shorthand include the text of a letter addressed to the congregation at the Glass House in London of which until now only the title has been known.[5] Clarke sent a typically discreet account of developments in the affair to his recently departed commander, Robert Lilburne.[6] Two shorthand passages in another intercepted letter otherwise written in longhand from the imprisoned Samuel Oates conceal his poor state of health and a potentially embarrassing message for his colonel, Thomas Pride.[7]

[1] Worc. MS XXVII.

[2] Pp. 231–241, 242–243, 244–245. While Sir Charles Firth chose to place documents relating to the plot with other Scottish material in his *Scotland and the Protectorate*, pp. 234, 238–242, 250–253, I have included them in the present edition in view of their wider implications and the plot's connection with the 'petition of the three colonels', Taft, '*The Humble Petition of Several Colonels of the Army . . .*', p. 37. The Overton plot is also discussed by Barbara Taft, '"They that pursew perfaction on earth . . .", the political progress of Robert Overton', in I. Gentles, J. Morrill, and B. Worden (eds), *Soldiers, Writers and Statesmen of the English Revolution* (Cambridge, 1998), pp. 291–293.

[3] J. Nickolls (ed.), *Letters and Papers of State Addressed to Cromwell* (London, 1743), p. 133.

[4] The design and Overton's part in it are described by in *C&P*, III, pp. 70–76.

[5] *S&P*, p. 238; below, p. 234. Monck forwarded the confiscated papers to Cromwell in mid-January; *ibid.*, pp. 238–239.

[6] P. 240. Lilburne left his command in Scotland in April 1654; F&D, I, p. 270.

[7] P. 244. The longhand is printed in *S&P*, p. 241. Oates is said to have been sickly from childhood; J. Lane, *Titus Oates* (London, 1949), p. 17.

Discoveries of Royalist plots, real or imagined, abounded in early 1655.[8] The Protectorate relied heavily on its informants, and the role played by Major James Borthwick in providing incriminating evidence against his brother, the royalist Colonel William Borthwick, is for the first time substantiated by Clarke's shorthand notes.[9]

On 27 February 1655 a correspondent who was almost certainly George Downing provided Monck with advance information concerning a proposal to establish a separate Council for Scotland.[10] The new body, which was to be headed by the young Lord Broghill, was to play a significant part in establishing a far greater stability than Scotland had known for some considerable time.[11]

Document confiscated from Major John Bramston, 1 January [1655][12]

fo. [1]^r

Reasons why those who did sign the late address to the Lord Protector are not to be communicated within the ordinances of God:

1. Because that they have in so doing made themselves guilty of all the blood which had been shed in all the 3 nations in these late wars against the king and so come under the condemnation of that scripture in Esay[13] 1.15.[14]21.
2. Because they have made themselves under a curse, for it is written, cursed is he that puts forth his hand to build Jericho. The reason was because the Lord had given command that it should be destroyed, Joshua 6, and the apostle saith, Gals 2, if I build again that which I have destroyed I make myself a transgressor.
3. They have highly transgressed a command of God which saith they ought to fear the Lord and the King, but not to meddle with

[8] Pp. 241–242.

[9] P. 245. In a longhand copy of this statement (Worc. MS CLXXXI, fo. 328^r) James Borthwick's name is concealed by being written in shorthand. The identification allows us to connect the document with the incident described in *TSP*, IV, p. 187.

[10] P. 245.

[11] Dow, *Cromwellian Scotland*, pp. 165–194.

[12] There is a longhand version of this document at Worc. MS L, fos 91^v–92^r. Both this and the following document were seized from Major John Bramston when he was arrested in connection with the 'Overton plot' and forwarded to Cromwell by Monck in mid-January; p. 240 below; *S&P*, pp. 238–239. For an account of the plot, see *C&P*, III, pp 70–76.

[13] i.e. Isaiah.

[14] Worc. MS L, fo. 91^v reads, correctly, '14' for '15'.

those that are given to change and he that breaketh the least of God's commands and teacheth men so, the same shall be least in the kingdom.[15]

4. They have made all the blood and treasures[16] spent in the wars fruitless and brought the inhabitants[17] of the nations into a fourfold worse slavery than they were under in[18] the days of the late king.
5. They have ingaged for a power that was purposed to prosecute the Lord's people, it being that spoken of in Revelations 13. A beast whose deadly wound was healed which beast should[19] make war with the saints.
6. They have evidenced it to the world that it has been their own and not the people's good which they have sought[20] contrary to the command of our Lord by the Apostle in the 1 Corinthians and the 10 and 24.
7. They have adhered to a lie and so are guilty of trusting in lying vanities. A righteous man hateth lying, [Proverbs] 13.5, Psalms 119.163, Revelations 22.15.
8. They have caused religion to be everywhere spoken of and so the name of God to be blasphemed amongst[21] the heathen, Romans 2.24, Psalms, 50.18.

*fo. [1]*v

9. They have made themselves guilty of resisting of lawful power contrary to the command of God, Romans 13.1.2.3.4.5.6.7. For sure I am it had been more lawful for Charles Stuart to have been king than O.C. to be protector.
10. They have verified that to be in them which was reported to be in the Anabaptists in Germany so as that for their cause men professing religion shall never be trusted in any publike imployment in after ages.
11. They have denied their 1st principles which were that they would have no king but Jesus, and have set up that which they themselfs have both prayed against, preached against, and[22] fought against.

[15] *Ibid.* adds 'of heaven'.
[16] *Ibid.* reads 'treasure' for 'treasures'.
[17] *Ibid.* repeats 'brought the inhabitants'– evidently a copyist's error.
[18] *Ibid.* omits 'in'.
[19] *Ibid.* reads 'was to' for 'should'.
[20] *Ibid.* reads 'fought' for 'sought'.
[21] *Ibid.* reads 'among'.
[22] *Ibid.*, fo. 92r omits 'and'.

12. They have, contrary to the will of God, willingly walked after the commandments of men mixing themselves among the people *Ephraim* like Hos[ea] 5.11.12 and 11 8th and 9th.
13. They have made a covenant with the workers of iniquity and so consequently with death and Hell, and also said a confederacy with those who have said[23] a confederacy, whereby they came under the condemnation of the sayings of the Lord in Isay[24] 8.11.22.13 and 28 and the 15th verse.
14. They have made it appear to all the world that they are truce and covenant breakers such as all the histories in[25] the world cannot make mention of. Witness their ingagement at[26] Newmarket, their remonstrance at St Albans[27] together with their ingagement to the Parliament upon the taking off the king's head[28] so that they lie under the condemnation of the Lord in Romans 1.31[29] compared with 2nd Timothy the 3rd and the 3rd.
15. They have betrayed that trust which they were intrusted withall by the people together with that cause[30] the Lord has so eminently owned from the 1st undertaking thereof and so are become as those spoken of by our Lord in Jeremiah 9.2 and 2 Timothy 3.4.
16. They have sold themselves to work iniquity as Ahab did, 1 Kings 16. 31. 32. 33. 34.
17. They have not only sold their own and their posterities but all the freeborn people of England, and so are become fornicators and profane as Esau was. Hebrews 12. 15. 16. 17.
18. They have turned all the grace of our God into wantonness in that they have made no better use of all the great and glorious victories the Lord has given them then to turn them into court pride and vanity.[31]

[23] *Ibid.* omits 'said'.

[24] *Ibid.* reads 'Esay'.

[25] *Ibid.* reads 'of' for 'in'.

[26] *Ibid.* reads 'of' for 'at'. The reference is to *A Solemne Ingagement of the Armie under the Command of his Excellency Sir Thomas Fairfax; With a Declaration of their Resolutions*... of June 1647.

[27] i.e. T. Fairfax, *A Remonstrance Of His Excellency Thomas Lord Fairfax... And of the Generall Councell of Officers*... (London, 1648), a key document in the 'petition of the three colonels'; Taft, *The Humble Petition of Several Colonels of the Army*..., p. 21.

[28] The Engagement, to be 'true and faithful to the Commonwealth of England, as it is now established, without a King or House of Lords', was imposed upon army officers, among others, on 12 October 1649; *CJ*, VI, p. 306.

[29] Worc. MS L, fo. 92[r] reads 'Rom.31'.

[30] *Ibid.* inserts 'of'.

[31] Here the writer is identified by an illegible scrawl which in *ibid.* reads 'J.B.' (i.e. John Bramston).

[Major John Bramston] to the congregation at the Glass House, London, 25 December 1654[32]

fo. 2r

For the church of Christ assembled at the Glass House, Broad Street, London, these

Brethren

The fear and dread of the great Jehovah being upon my heart, together with the assured knowledge of the sudden appearing of our Lord when he shall come the 2d time without sin unto salvation, as also the clear apprehension of the present state of most of the churches at this day and time of the bridegroom's tarrying, which is not only a condition of slumbering and sleeping but of eating and drinking with the drunken and beating of their fellow servants, Matth[ew] 24.49.50.51 and the 25th and the 5th. Indeed I have waited long with silence as also with as much love as the Lord would [. . .] me, thinking to have seen something from you tending to the resurrecting of Sion, Esay 52.1. But perceiving your [continuing] with silence, I am now constrained to speak. Otherwise, I should think the stones would cry out against me,[33] though I could rather wish that mine eyes were a fountain of tears that I might weep day and night for the transgressions of the Lord's people or that I had as Jeremiah, 9.1.2.3, in the wilderness a lodging place that I might go from them for they bend their tongues like their bow for lies but are not valiant for the truth upon the earth. This is the condition of the Lord's people of old and it is well if we are not guilty of the same things, but it is too apparent that we are, and therefore it is high time to repent. The harvest seems to be wheat[34] and the summer ended, and we are not saved, <Jeremiah 8.20.21.22>.[35] Is there no balm in Gilead, is there no physician to heal that great backsliding and apostasy which is now amongst men. Will not the Lord come and sit as a refiner's fire and be like fuller's soap to purify the sons of Levi that these may offer unto the Lord an offering in righteousness <Malachi 3.2.[9]>.[36] Surely these things he will do to those that fear him <Malachi 4.2>,[37] but for 3 transgressions of Israel[38] and for 4, saith the Lord, I will not turn away the punishment thereof and therefore 3 transgressions of Judah and for 4 will I turn away

[32] Like the preceding document, this was seized from Maj. John Bramston (p. 240 below).

[33] Luke, XIX.40.

[34] Jeremiah, VIII.20 reads 'past' for 'wheat'.

[35] Marginated.

[36] Marginated. A reference to Malachi III.2–3.

[37] Marginated.

[38] Amos, II.4 reads 'Judah' for 'Israel'.

the punishment thereof because they have dishonoured the law of the Lord and have not kept his commandments. And now, friends, I shall come to shew you wherein you have not kept the commandments of the Lord, <Amos, 2.4.5.6>.[39]

1. The Lord has positively commanded his people, Esay 8.11.12, say not a confederacy to those who say a confederacy; but sanctify the Lord in your hearts and let him be your fear, and let him be your dread. Your [. . .] only seem a confederacy with the [world], but you have made covenants with them and so [. . .] like have mixed yourselfs among them, Esay 28.15. <Hosea 4.8.9>[40]. But consider [. . .] who saith he will lay judgment to the line and righteousness to the plummet and will sweep away the refuge of lies and the waters shall overflow your hiding places.[41]

fo. 2*v*

2. The Lord hath commanded [----], Isaiah 52.11, 2 Corinthians 6.17.18 and Revelation 18.4, an absolute sequestration from the world not only in doctrine and worship but in all things else that may defile. Nay the saints were not so much as to touch the Lord [. . . .] that are unclean but to make covenants with the world and to break them as many of you have done is certainly a defiling of your [sanctuaries] or to bear with those that have so done [. . . 5th].18 as if your selfs had done it.
3. To justify the earth and to stem the scripture are both an obligation to the Lord. 1st have you not justified all that murthering and treason, truce and covenant breaking which has of late been acted by many of us who are your brethren and 2ly have you not, nay do you not still shame those just men as busy bodies and such as suffer as evil doers who are now in bonds for the testimony of a good conscience. Have you forgot since you yourselfs are turned factious and such as are the disturbers and troublers of Israel know you not that he that departeth from iniquity maketh himself a prey. Woe to you that are at ease in Sion, that trust in the mountains of Samaria and go to fend off nations[42] as the house of Israel did, that stretch yourselfs upon your beds of ivory and drink wine in bowls, but remember not the afflictions of Joseph.[43] Think you that there may not arise a king which knew not Joseph? Have you so soon forgotten your strong resolutions which were that you would have no king but Jesus?

[39] Marginated.
[40] Marginated.
[41] Isaiah, XXVIII.17.
[42] Amos, VI.1.
[43] Amos, VI.4,6.

4. Should you now needs be like unto the nations. <1.Sam[uel] 8.7, Hosea 13.10>.[44] Take heed that it be not said of you as it was also of the Lord's people of old that they would not have him to rule over them and as our Lord shall [say true] in answering those mine enemies that would not that I should rule over them, bring them and slay them before me. Is it not a sad thing that you who have so much [abjured] the [court] pride and vanity should now become [humourers] and flatterers there as some of you are, to the great reproach of the truth and the wounding of the hearts of the saints?
5. Has not the Lord commanded that his people should not be conformable to this world, Romans 12.2, and what a conformity is in many of you is high manifest to the world:[45] take heed of having a love to live and be dead. Remember the words of the Lord and think thereon. Whatsoever things are true, whatsoever things are just, whatsoever things are honest, whatsoever things are lovely, whatsoever things are of good report, if there be any virtue, if there be any praise, think on these things <Philippians 4.8>.[46] [Was it of good report] for those who have prayed and preached and fought against the vanity and iniquity of the court now to become courtiers as some of you are?
6. Are you not commanded to look diligently lest there should be root of bitterness sprung up amongst you and thereby many be defiled, Hebrews 12.15?[47] And lest there should be any fornicator or profane person amongst you as Esau was who for one morsel of pottage sold his birthright,[48] how many are there amongst you who have not only sold their own but the whole nation's with which they were [intrusted]/which

fo. 3r

which should be a far higher crime in them than that was in Esau, and yet that was [~~—~~] to [reproach] him for a profane person [upon all eternity].

7. Has not the Lord commanded that prayer and supplication should be made for all men, and that you should remember those that are in bonds as being bound with them? And have you not wholly served this command and [should] neglect nothing to this end? Have not I heard and seen you deny to pray for saints that are in prison because they did contend with this ~~church~~ Christian[49]

[44] Marginated.
[45] The colon is indicated by Clarke.
[46] Marginated.
[47] This text is also cited in the previous document.
[48] Hebrews, XII. 16.
[49] 'Christian' superimposed upon '~~church~~'

power on the earth:[50] take heed for it will be a dangerous thing not to remember the afflictions of Joseph. It will not serve thee much to say Lord, when saw we the sick and in prison and visited them not.

8. Has not the Lord commanded that you should withdraw from every brother that walketh disorderly and from such turn away,[51] and if any man be a fornicator or covetous with such a man not to eat?[52] Sure I am if treason and truce-breaking be a sin, you ought to take notice thereof, and to deal with new [. . .]. But instead of dealing with the persons offending in that case, you hug them to your bosom notwithstanding [you did think you] to take an account of your brethren, however many promises and vows they have made to the people since Newmarket Hall and how many of them they have broken, none of them being kept by them, and also what account they can give to their country, who has trusted them with their army and strengths to defend them against tyranny and oppression, for which they have [. . .] them well. But that trust is most early betrayed. Will not the Lord [himself] be avenged on such a representation as this when they have committed all these abominations? Were they ashamed? No, they were not ashamed, saith the Lord.[53] Say not the temple of the Lord, the temple of the Lord.[54] But if you throughly amend your ways and your doings; if you oppress not the fatherless, the stranger and the widow and shed not innocent blood, but if you trust in lying words that will not profit, as it is [. . .] apparent many of you have done, and yet come to stand before the Lord in his house <Jer[emiah] 7.5.6>.[55] Therefore take heed who gave Jacob to the spoyle, and Israel to the robbers. Did not the Lord, against whom they sinned? <Isaiah 42.24>.[56]

Now friends, the consideration of our Lord's being revealed taking vengeance on all those that know not God and obey not his gospel, 2 Thess[alonians] 1.8, as also that the sinners in Sion shall be afraid, fearfulness shall surprize the heretics.[57] I therefore thought it my duty to awaken myself and indeavour the awaking of you that you might act on your strength and beautiful garments for from henceforth shall no other come in to thee, the uncircumcised or unclean. Therefore

[50] The colon is indicated by Clarke.

[51] 2 Thessalonians, III. 6.

[52] 1 Corinthians, V.11.

[53] Jeremiah, VI.15.

[54] Jeremiah, VII.4.

[55] Marginated. The passage also draws on the following four verses of the same chapter from Jeremiah.

[56] Marginated.

[57] Isaiah, XXXIII.14.

shake your selfs from the dust[58] from all that earthly pride and vanity, and know that no unclean thing shall enter into the Kingdom and that [your] religion [long] undefiled is to keep your selfs [. . .] from the world and if any

fo. 3v

but love the world the [word/work] of the Father [enter] in him. Be not deceived. The Lord will not be mocked.[59] It will be an easier thing to be [. . .] joyned to idols of God than bear your miseries in that case will be to be there alone. *Ephraim* was oppressed and broken in judgment because he willingly walked after the commandments,[60] and grey hairs were here and there upon him before he knew it.[61] But when he saw his sickness and his blood, his going to the Assyrians and in sickness unto the king of Jareb was the aggravation of his sin. Therefore will the Lord be unto him as a lion and as a young lion to the house of Judah.[62] When *Ephraim* spake [. . .] he exalted himself in Israel, but when he offended he died:[63] better it is to be of an humble spirit with the lowly than to divide the spoyle with the proud,[64] for he that exalteth himself shall be brought low and he that humbleth himself shall be exalted.[65] But woe to him that spoyleth for he shall be spoyled,[66] and to him that leadeth into captivity, for he shall go into captivity. Take heed, my friends, of blessing yourselfs in a thing of naught and of trusting in lying words that will not profit.[67] Say not peace, peace when there is no peace.[68] For what peace can you expect? Truly the whoredoms of Jezebel and her witchcrafts are so many.[69] If all be well what needeth then the bleating of the sheep and the lowing of the oxen.[70] What meaneth all the [sighs] and groans and prayers and tears of the saints in this [. . . .]? What meaneth all the reproaches and scorn with which the Lord's people are reproached? What meaneth the cries of the prisoners in the prison houses? Are not the statutes of Omri yet kept up? What meaneth the cries of almost all the people in England, Scotland and Ireland against the army truce and covenant breakers and say these have betrayed their trust with which they were

58 Isaiah, LII.1.
59 Jeremiah, XX.7.
60 Hosea, V.11, also cited in the previous document.
61 Hosea, VII. 9.
62 Hosea, V.13–14.
63 Hosea, XIII.1.
64 Proverbs, XVI.19.
65 Luke, XIV.18.
66 Isaiah, XXXIII.1.
67 Jeremiah, VII.8.
68 Jeremiah, VI.14; VIII.11.
69 2 Kings, IX.22.
70 1 Samuel, XV.14.

intrusted by the people? If all things be so well as you speak of, are you able to justify your brethren as to all the things aforesaid? Then why do you not [end/do] it that we may have something thereby to stop the mirth of gainsayers and to answer the [speakers] and reproaches of our adversaries? Is not the house of the Lord an house of prayer, and will you make it a den of robbers?[71] Shall we commit murthers, fornication, treason and what not and come [naked] before the Lord in his house, and say we are delivered to commit those abominations?[72] If there be no bonds upon us then let us do what seemeth good in his cause [. . .]. But if there be no time from the Lord as who dares dares, then do not hate your brethren in your hearts so as to suffer these upon them. I observed that through all the churches that the great controversy which the Lord has with his people is about their doing violence [to ourself]. Could not Israel the Lord's peculiar ones [eschew] the wrath of God in such cases/and

fo. 4^r

and did you think to be better [dealt] withall than they when you committed the same abominations and that under the profession of a [. . . .] might not they so much as speak even of the rulers of the people and maybe do violence to our rulers as many of us have done to the great dishonour of the Lord and scorn and reproof of the truth, there being as great an ingagement upon us to obey our superiours as ever there was upon the Jews, Romans 13.1.2.3.4,[73] [Titous] 3.1.2.3? These positive commands of the Lord to the [. . .] saints have been wholly violated by many of us, and yet not to do this [. . .] charged a sin by any of our leaders. [What] shall we then say [has] not the leaders of this people [caused] them to [err] and to fear those that were led by them into danger of being destroyed? Is there not a [blow] pronounced against those which [. . . .] ever after [turn] and [turn] ever after as also against those that justify the earth and take away the faithfulness of the faithful from them? Therefore as the fire devoureth the stubble and the flame consumeth the chaff, so their root shall be rottenness and their blossoms shall go up as dust, because they have cast away the laws of the Lord of Hosts and despised the word of the Holy One of Israel.[74] Thus desiring that you may be awaked and put on your strength[75] and that your loyns may be girded and your light[s] burning.[76] For the day of the Lord is coming. It is long at hand and

[71] Jeremiah, VII.11.
[72] Jeremiah, VII.10.
[73] This text is also cited in the previous document.
[74] Isaiah, V.24.
[75] I Samuel, LI.9; LII.1.
[76] Luke, XII.35.

if judgment begin at the house of God when shall the ungodly and sinners appear? I remain

your poor unworthy brother in the kingdom
love and faith of Jesus

J.B.

From my lodging in Aberdeen

25th of the 10th month

William Clarke, Dalkeith, to Colonel [Robert] Lilburne, 2 January 1655[77]

fo. [7]v

<Copy of my letter to Colonel Lilburne concerning the design in Scotland>[78]

Sir

I have not written to you of late, having nothing material to acquaint you with. The common enemy being subdued, we had some danger of more home-bred discords. Some officers who were dissatisfied with the present government had appointed a meeting at *Edinburgh* the 1st of this month to consider of what was fit to be done, of which the general having (accidentally) notice, and the meeting designed without acquainting him, divers of Colonel Rich's late regiment's officers who were coming from Aberdeen (where the business was 1st agitated) were secured at Dundee and since that on Saturday night last Major Bramston and Master Oates were apprehended at Leith. In Major Bramston's pocket there were found some papers of dangerous importance, one paper intituled, 'Reasons why those who did sign the late address to the Lord Protector are not to be communicated within the ordinances of God'. They were in number 18 and did deliver forth many desperate positions against his Highness.[79] There was also a large letter all written by Major Bramston's own hand (as the former was) and signed by himself directed, for the churches of Christ assembled at the Glass House in Broad Street, London,[80] which did also much intreat them against the present government. Some queries were also

[77] It would have been to Robert Lilburne, acting commander-in-chief of the army in Scotland until the end of April 1654, rather than his brother John, that Clarke was writing. Lilburne's regiment was now based in the north of England; F&D, I, p. 270.

[78] Marginated.

[79] P. 231 above.

[80] P. 234 above.

found with Master Oates [. . .] whether they should resist [to blood] etc., and a *Memorandum* in his almanack to this effect, *vizt* Brother *Danvers*[81] said that if it were not that the fear of man would take hold of him it would not be against his conscience to kill every man that was not of his mind. It is hinted that Major-General Overton had some hand in these actings and thereupon he is ordered to be secured. All things are otherwise very quiet in this nation.

W.C.

Memorandum, Dalkeith, 4 January 1655[82]

fo. 9^v

This day Major-General Overton, who was brought the night before to Leith, was sent on board the Basing frigot to be sent to London according to order from his Highness to the general.[83]

Memorandum, Dalkeith, 6 January 1655[84]

fo. 14^v

This day one Master Sumner came with an express to the general from Master Thurloe concerning a new discovery of a design at London (as was conjectured).[85]

Memorandum, Dalkeith, 7 January 1655

fo. 15^r

This day John Dempster[86] wrote a letter to me that he had something of concernment to relate to the general whereupon he was sent for and told many strange relations of [. . . .] that Major-General [Lambert]

[81] Perhaps Col Henry Danvers, for whom see *DBR*, 'Danvers'.

[82] There is a longhand copy of this memorandum at Worc. MS CLXXXI, fo. 308^v.

[83] All this is confirmed in Monck's letter of 4 January 1655 to the Protector; *TSP*, III, p. 76. Worc. MS CLXXXI fo. 308^v adds, 'There was found amongst other papers in his pockets The Character of a Protector &c'.

[84] There is a longhand copy of this memorandum at Worc. MS CLXXXI, fo. 309^v.

[85] *Ibid.* reads 'against his Highnesse' for '(as was conjectured)'. I have been unable to trace the letter from John Thurloe but the 'design' was reported in greater detail by Gilbert Mabbott in a letter of 6 January 1655; *CP*, III, pp. 17–18.

[86] Presumably the same John Dempster who, having been disgraced during the previous summer, was now apparently keen to reingratiate himself; Dow, *Cromwellian Scotland*, p. 144.

was in Wales with Major-General Harrison raising forces, and Colonel Lilburne in the north with 10,000*l* men [*sic*] against his Highness, and other fictitious stories.

Marginal annotation, Dalkeith, 9 January 1655[87]

fo. 16r

<Copy of a letter sent [or taken] going from Hull to Major-General Overton. This copy was inclosed in one supposed from Master Canne.>[88]

[Ann Overton?] to [Robert Overton], [c.9 January 1655][89]

fo. 18r

For your master

Dear Heart

Yours of the 10th, 18 and 21 came all to me this 2d of January[90] which administers great cause of joy and thankfulness on your behalf that our good Father doth still uphold you in your integrity. Truly there is a great stock of faith, love and prayer going on in this and other places for you that the Lord would make you faithful unto death. My dear, fear not but I shall freely give you up into the hand of our dear and loving Father to be [acted] by his spirit. I hope I shall dare to trust you under the shadow of divine protection as I have hitherto done, and had a good account of you. I had rather beg my bread than be any occasion of tempting you to dishonour God, blind your own conscience and desert the most glorious interest of our Lord and King, Jesus. Turn all ways so he return with honour to those [watching

[87] This note is attached to the first of a group of four letters, two dated 19 December 1654 and two undated. Three of them are copied in longhand and one in shorthand (next document).

[88] Marginated. John Canne was chaplain to Overton during his governorship of Hull; A. Laurence, *Parliamentary Army Chaplains, 1642–1651*. (Woodbridge etc., 1990) p. 108.

[89] The letter is signed 'A.O.', and may be from Overton's wife, born Ann Gardiner, whom he married in 1632; *OxDNB*, 'Robert Overton'. See also B. Taft, '"They that pursew perfaction on earth" . . . ', p. 287. Its intended recipient is identified from a marginal inscription (see below).

[90] An anonymous intercepted letter written to Overton by an English correspondent on 30 December 1654 indicates that Overton's wife was in England at this time and that she had not heard from him for some time; *TSP*, III, p. 65.

praying spirits] who now sits in the dust, but God will shortly set the witnesses on their feet. The men of the earth will not be able to bear their testimony but they should for the witnesses most stirred up, and they will not fear the faces of men. The Lord fit us for changes. Profaneness and iniquity doth abound. The inevitable forerunner of ruin, self-love, pleasure, pride, [hypocrisy], was never more in this land. You have [undoubtedly] a controversy with us of this nation for your houses and lands know not yet what to determine, but think we shall have enough cast into our hands for ourselfs, and a [tyrant] also. It is no place for your children in winter, their bodies having been tenderly bred nearer [Lands End . . .]. I shall determine something herein. I shall keep your house etc. Here came a letter lately from you to *cap.* your cozen *O.* I had a great desire to see what was in it, but durst not for I/think

fo. 18v

think it was occasioned from you by some falsities of his to you. As little time and paper would be spent as may be to such persons if you knew what others and I did in this place of their carriages and conditions. The Lord turn their hearts. I have done with the business of [Simson/Wilson/Merson]. I wish you had some of that money in your purse which has been laid out in debentures already but 'tis no great matter who has much or who has little. The Lord gives us His grace and it shall suffice us. His loving kindness is better than life. I shall only add that all yours are well and that Master will I think be not hasty to change our condition. Dear heart I am

yours

A.O.

There is [. . .] up of letters this week which came from London.

What is feared I know not.

Marginal annotation, [Dalkeith], undated

fo. 18v

<A letter to Colonel Overton from Hull in which the former letters were inclosed.>[91]

[91] Marginated. The letter to which this note is attached is unsigned and undated, but begins, 'By my last I acquainted you That your sons Wife was deliver'd of a sonne, & that

Memorandum, Dalkeith, 14 January 1655

*fo. [23]*r

This day the letters from London give an account that Colonel Alured was the last week at a court martial tried and dismissed the army.[92]

Memorandum, Dalkeith, 31 January 1655

*fo. [39]*v

This day a letter came from Lieutenant-Colonel Wilkes wherein the following papers were inclosed.[93]

Samuel Oates, [Edinburgh], to Jack [Jeffries], London, [January 1655][94]

*fo. [40]*r

. . . . *I am very* ill. I have got a flux and a fevour, yet eat my meat, but the trouble lies in my head and joynts. I pray send me word what I had best to do and, if my wife had best to come down to look to me, pray advise her. *Sir pray send mee a Copy of that speciall order which the Lord Protector sent downe for the discharging mee of my place in the Regiment.* Present my service to my colonel[95] and all his family, and my love to all my friends and be you a counsellor to my good wife and present my love

they call him Robert'; this was the second son of Overton's son John; G. Poulson, *The History and Antiquities of the Seigniory of Holderness* (Hull and London, 1841), II, p. 377.

[92] Alured's impending court martial, resulting from his involvement in the 'petition of the three colonels', was reported by Thurloe on 23 November 1654 (p. 227 above). It began on 7 December 1654 but was repeatedly adjourned to allow him opportunity to consider the charge against him. It was finally appointed for 8 January 1655, after which he was cashiered and imprisoned; *CP*, III, pp. 11, 15, 17; *C&P*, III, p. 58; M. Alured, *The Case of Colonel Matthew Alured; or, A short Account of his Sufferings by long imprisonment* . . . (London, 1659); Taft, '*The Humble Petition of Several Colonels of the Army*: . . . ', pp. 15–41; F&D, II, p. 464 states that he was cashiered on 5 December 1654.

[93] The enclosures were: (1) A letter from the Marshals at Leith enclosing a copy letter from Samuel Oates (next document); (2) a covering letter from Col Timothy Wilkes dated at Leith 20 January 1655 (Worc. MS XXVII, fo. [40]r; (3) the examination of John Bramston, dated 22 January 1655 (printed in *S&P*, pp. 241–242).

[94] These two extracts from a letter from Edinburgh written by the imprisoned Oates are copied in shorthand. The remainder, in longhand, is printed in *ibid.*, p. 241.

[95] i.e. Col Thomas Pride.

to yours and be assured I am

your loving friend

Samuel Oates

For his loving friend Master Jack [Jeffries] apothecary in Tower Street right against the Sugar Loaf a little from the great house in Westminster London this.[96]

News from G.D., 27 February 1655[97]

fo. [54][v]

A Council also for yourself in Scotland is thinking of.[98] I doubt not but you will have that person much to your contentment and [the/that] country's good. I dare say no more at present. The business of the [fines] of the [scouts/Scots] will I hope be speedily at an end.

G.D.

Memorandum, Edinburgh, 13 November 1655[99]

fo. [141][r]

Intelligence inclosed in a letter to his Highness of that date being had from one that witnessed it by Colonel Borthwick.[100]

The king, he tells, is just now to receive from the emperour and princes of Germany 2 hundred thousand rix dollars, and he is to expect some from France and some from England, which sum he intends to make a new war with.[101] He is in great hopes of the king of

[96] The document ends with a signed statement by Col Timothy Wilkes of the reasons for seizing the letter, with reports on Oates's examination which precedes it in the printed edition; Worc. MS XXVII, fo. [40][r]; *S&P*, p. 240.

[97] Most probably from George Downing. This passage comes at the end of the newsletter printed in *CP*, III, p. 24 which begins, 'Bagnell uppon his ingenuous Confession', where it is replaced by a row of dots.

[98] The proposal to establish such a council was first raised at a meeting of the Protector's Council on the following day, 28 February; Dow, *Cromwellian Scotland*, p. 165. Downing's father, Emanuel, would be appointed its clerk in the following May; *CSPD 1655*, p. 152.

[99] Another copy of this document, with mainly insignificant variations, is found in Worc. MS CLXXXI, fo. 328[r].

[100] On this same day Lord Broghill reported to Thurloe the receipt of important intelligence from his informant Maj. James Borthwick. On the preceeding night Borthwick with an accomplice had made his brother, Col William Borthwick (a trusted messenger of Charles Stuart), 'merry in his owne chamber to make him speake the more freely'; *TSP*, IV, p. 187. Several references to 'my brother' indicate that the information recorded here came from James Borthwick, and is therefore probably that which Broghill communicated to Thurloe.

[101] At the Diet of Ratisbon, 1653, Charles had been voted supply of 200,000 rix dollars; *CClarSP*, II, pp. 274, 295. Little of it ever reached him; Edward Hyde, earl of Clarendon,

Spain and your falling out, which will contribute much for the present expedition.[102]

It was thought fit that he should <be>[103] presently sent here both for confirming my Lord Glencairn and for the total reconciling him and Middleton, who is now resolved to stand and fall with Glencairn, for Chancellour Hyde told my brother that he was very feared that Glencairn hearing how Middleton was so graciously entertained here might turn my lord desperate. As also he told he would give his left hand that my brother was with Glencairn, for fear that Belcarris should strike in with him having totally fallen out with Middleton, which indeed is fallen out, for Belcarris' friends here are doing all they can to reconcile my lord and him, but my brother thinks to crush that in the bud.

The parties opposite at court are my lord Ormonde, Hyde, Middleton, Newburgh, and Napier for Glencairn. The other party are Prince Rupert, Gerard, Belcarris, and Doctor Fraser,[104] the king's doctor, but he tells me the king carries himself so indifferent as both parties are pleased, only his own judgement inclines to the 1st party and secretly gives them all assurances that he can of his love to them. He tells me likewise that he is imployed to [. . .] see who will ingage for the king in Scotland. There is certainly agents sent to England but as yet I cannot learn that he knows who they are, for he tells me except the king, Ormonde, Hyde and Middleton, there is none knows that he is here but thinks he be gone for Sweden. So you may be assured those that are imployed for the other kingdom are very private.

He tells me the king was hugely offended at the levies he hears are to be in Scotland. He says he counts all that goes out in the country at this time as so many dead men to him. It was resolved if they must bear that they are openly [. . .] that 1st the king of Sweden should be dealt with to desist, and if that could not be effected of those imployed to levy to see if they will joyne the king and withall that the king should disperse abroad his opinion of them all that ingages to be holden by him as rebels and destroyers of their native country.[105]

The History of the Rebellion and Civil Wars in England, 3 vols (Oxford, 1702–1704), III, pp. 393–394.

[102] The royalists actively sought an alliance with Spain and a secret treaty between Charles and Philip IV was signed in April 1656; *CClarSP*, III, pp. 55, 57, 109–110.

[103] Interlined.

[104] Worc. MS CLXXXI, fo. 328^{r} reads 'Forbes' for 'Fraser'.

[105] Acting on information from Maj. James Borthwick the authorities imprisoned Glencairn a month later; Dow, *Cromwellian Scotland*, p. 190. In order to protect his cover Borthwick was arrested at the same time but was later released; *TSP*, IV, p. 770. Col William Borthwick was given a permit to remain in Scotland and was allowed to remain free in order to make his royalist masters believe that it was he who had betrayed Glencairn; *ibid*, pp. 444, 741; Worc. MS XLVII, unfol., 23 November 1655.

8. NOTEBOOK XXVIII

1 March–[October/November] 1656[1]

Introduction

In 1656 a serious shortage of money forced the government to call the second Protectorate Parliament a year earlier than was required by the Instrument of Government. Thurloe sent advance warning of the impending elections to Monck who reacted swiftly, and by the time the official writs arrived on 16 July he had already taken steps to ensure that in Scotland only candidates who were sympathetic to the regime would be elected.[2]

The proposed union between England and Scotland, which began with the deliberations of the commissioners at Dalkeith in early 1652,[3] had still not been formalized. It had been delayed principally by the summary terminations of the Rump Parliament and the Nominated Assembly in April and December 1653 respectively.[4] When the Cromwellian ordinance for union of April 1654 finally came before Parliament for ratification on 4 November 1656[5] there were said to be difficulties about 'some clawses about the lawes' which entailed seeking the advice of senior lawyers,[6] and disagreement about whether Scotland could be, as specified by the ordinance, 'incorporated' into one Commonwealth with England unless the two countries were bound by the same legal system.[7] Specifically, the clause in the ordinance which decreed that 'all Laws, Usages, and Customs' were to be completely abolished and declared null and void did not distinguish between constitutional and common law,[8] and as we learn from an unattributed list of 'Queries upon the Proposed Act of Union'

[1] Worc. MS XXVIII.

[2] P. 254 below.

[3] Pp. 51–52 above.

[4] Progress of the Bill for Union introduced in April 1652 is summarized in Dow, *Cromwellian Scotland*, pp. 120–121, and in Terry, pp. xlviii, xlix, lviii, lxvi, lxxiv.

[5] It received its first reading on 25 October 1656; Worc. MS XXVIII, fo. 96^{v}. The ordinance and its associated measures are printed in *A&O*, II, pp. 871–888.

[6] *CP*, III, p. 80.

[7] *Ibid.*, p. 81; *A&O*, II, pp. 871–872.

[8] *Ibid.*, p. 872. The creation of courts baron dealt with the problem of the administration of the law at local level but did not address the differences between Scots and English law.

in Clarke's notes, the necessity to differentiate the two constituted at least one important issue.[9]

Several measures which affected the process of the law in Scotland had already been introduced. For example, the unpopular Court of Session was replaced in May 1652 by a pancl of four English and three Scots commissioners for the administration of justice and a system of courts baron was set up in April 1654. The procedures of the Supreme Court were radically altered and the use of Latin in the courts was discontinued.[10] However, these new provisions did not address fundamental differences between the legal codes of the two countries.[11] From the 'Queries' it seems clear that at some time during the bill's later stages it was intended to insert an additional clause into the ordinance in order to address the problem. Ultimately no such provision was made and the ordinance was finally pushed through as it stood on 28 April 1657.[12] Clarke's list of 'Queries' ends with the proposition that the Instrument of Government might in itself provide sufficient grounds for a solution.[13]

As several of the documents in this volume show, one of the government's main concerns in the early part of the year was the heavy losses sustained by English merchant ships at the hands of the many privateers sent out from Ostend and Dunkirk – encouraged, it was suspected, by the Dutch.[14] The effects of these, which included a steep rise in the price of coal, were sufficiently serious to cause the English to mount a blockade of both ports.[15]

[9] P. 258 below. Although undated, its position in Clarke's notebook indicates that it was written some time between 25 October and 4 November 1656, the days of the first and second readings of the bill. It precedes a speech made by an unidentified MP on 4 November; Worc. MS XXVIII, fos 104^{v}–106^{v}, printed in *S&P*, pp. 333–336. The importance of the integration of the two legal systems in any proposed union is discussed by B.P. Levack in 'The proposed union of English law and Scots law in the seventeenth century', *Juridical Review*, (1975), p. 112.

[10] These measures are conveniently summarized in A.J.G. Mackay (ed.), *Memoir of Sir James Dalrymple First Viscount Stair* (Edinburgh, 1873), pp. 58–62.

[11] Proposals submitted by Scots commissioners to the English Council on 10 August 1653 merely proposed that courts of justice might be set up 'to judge according to the Law and Practices of the Nation' but which nation that was to be was not made clear; Terry, pp. xlvi–xlvii.

[12] *Ibid.*, p. lxxiv. Under renewed negotiations for parliamentary union during 1670, it was proposed that this should incorporate 'The preserving to either Kingdome their Laws, Civil and Ecclesiasticall entire'; *ibid.*, pp. 197, 203, 211, 215–216.

[13] I have not been able to identify the source of the 'Queries'. Thomas Burton's account of the debate in committee relating to the question of Scots law on 4 December 1656, for example, offers no clues; Burton, *Diary*, I, pp. 12–18.

[14] Some of them were said to be flying the flag 'of the king of Scotland'; *CSPV 1655–1656*, p. 222.

[15] Pp. 249–250 below; *C&P*, III, pp. 477–478, 483–485. Among those called into service was Capt. Jeremiah Smith, a regular news provider not only to Monck but to the Council;

William Clarke, memorandum, 1 March 1656

fo. 1ʳ

Letters from London[16] this day inform that Major-General Harrison, Colonel Rich, Master [Carew][17] and Master Courtney are by order from his Highness set at liberty from the several places where they are prisoners,[18] that the fleet had a randevouz in Stokes Bay.[19]

Newsletter from London, 4 March 1656

fo. 3ʳ

There [are/were] 2 frigots sent to the northward, but not so far as Scotland, to range upon the coast where it seems the Dunkirkers have lately [dominated], so as to alarm some places or houses upon the shore with a fear lest they should fetch people out of their beds.[20] And because it's said the Dutch suffer the Dunkirkers and enemies of this Commonwealth to bring in and make sale of our ships and goods within their ports or waters it's fancied that there is some unhandsomeness suspected from the Dutch.

Newsletter from London, 6 March 1656

fo. 3ᵛ

London 6 March

His Highness has proposed something to the merchants for them to consider of for securing their trade in the narrow seas[21] in case the

pp. 256, 257, 367, 368 and his many letters which are listed in the indices of *CSPD 1655–1656* and *CSPD 1656–1657*.

[16] I have not been able to trace these letters among Clarke's surviving papers.

[17] In shorthand, 'Caro'.

[18] The order, which first came before the Council on 19 February 1656, was rescinded on 7 March; *CSPD 1655–1656*, pp. 190, 202, 215. Harrison was released around 20 March, and John Carew and Hugh Courtney in October 1656. Rich, who also appears to have been released in March, was rearrested in August 1656 and released in October; *C&P*, III, p. 469; *CSPD 1656–1657*, pp. 71, 130.

[19] The fleet was ordered to rendezvous off Portsmouth immediately prior to its voyage towards Spain, which began on on 4 March; *CSPV 1655–1656*, pp. 184, 191. Blake and Mountagu had hurried there from the Downs on the resignation in February of John Lawson; Capp, *Cromwell's Navy*, p. 145.

[20] Only one example of the many reports of daring raids carried out by privateers from Dunkirk and Ostend upon the English coast.

[21] Collectively the English Channel and Irish Sea (*OED*).

war abroad should necessitate the sending the state's fleet into foreign parts.[22]

William Clarke, memorandum, 9 March 1656

fo. [4]ʳ

A report of the Yarmouth frigot that took a Dunkirk man near Newcastle with 12 guns and of the Speaker that had 7 Dunkirkers fell upon her, whereof she sunk 3, took 3 and the other escaped. They did not know her to be a man of war.[23]

Letter from Jeremiah Smith, Birkin, Yorkshire, 18 April 1656

fo. 10ᵛ

<*Berkin* in Yorkshire>[24]

I perceive his Highness is resolute to send me for the coast of Spain and to command on the 2d rate ships that are making ready.[25] There is the James, George, Vanguard, and a new ship that was built at Wollage.[26] I understand that his Highness intends to send those to the fleet that [were/are] gone before Calais and the Straits mouth. His Highness sent for Captain Hall[27] and would have given him command and for Captain Thomas but they both refused to serve.

Jeremiah Smith

[22] The matter was discussed by the Council on 27 February 1656; *CSPD 1655–1656*, p. 200.

[23] Both were relatively new ships. The *Speaker*, under a recently appointed commander, Capt. Richard Stayner, would soon score a notable success against the homeward-bound Spanish silver fleet; Capp, *Cromwell's Navy*, pp. 52, 99, 142; below, p. 258n.

[24] Marginated. Smith's home was at Birkin, where his wife died later in the same year; *OxDNB*, 'Smith'.

[25] Smith, who was now on standby (*CSPD 1655–1656*, p. 531), was shortly to command for a brief period on the *Essex* and thereafter in the Downs on board the *Dunbar*, where he proved an energetic and useful informant, e.g., *ibid.*, pp. 555, 561, 569, 571; below pp. 256, 257.

[26] Woolwich.

[27] One of the navy's most outspoken officers, Edward Hall has been linked with Edward Sexby around this time; Capp, *Cromwell's Navy*, pp. 55, 72, 144; Abbott, IV, p. 173.

Deposition of Nicholas Cantiro (or Quintero) of Seville, 29 April 1656[28]

fo. 23^{v}

Extract of an examination of Nicolas Cantiro of Civil[29] in the kingdom of Spain, aged 24 years or thereabouts, taken upon oath before the judges of the <High Court of>[30] Admiralty of Scotland the 29th of April 1656.

The said Nicholas Cantiro saith he came from the Texel in the ship the Amsterdam about the latter end of March last, the said ship carrying 21[31] guns and 39 men. Remembereth not the captain's name, but believes he is a Hollander etc.[32] Saith[33] was now going a[34] passenger in this ship, the Amsterdam, for Cadiz in Spain. Saith the said ship came out of the Texel but 4 days before she was cast away, being the latter end of March, and that the said ship was bound for Cadiz in Spain, this deponent being present at the loading of all the goods. Saith there was loaden on board the said ship about one hundred great cables for the Spanish galleons, some of them as thick as a man's thigh, and containing from 120 to 150 fathoms in length. And saith farther that there was also loaden on board[35] the said ship about 120[36] barrels of powder, several barrels of shot; that the rest of her lading[37] consisted of tammies, fustians, etc.[38] Saith the said [. . .][39] were loaden at Amsterdam by one Juan Tullien who speaks divers languages, but believes he is a Hollander. This deponent further saith he heard many people in Amsterdam say that the cables and rope were for the use of the Spanish armado, but knows not to whom the goods were consigned etc.[40] They went about <the north>[41] Scotland with this ship for fear

[28] There is a closely similar version of this document in *TSP*, IV, p. 745.
[29] i.e. Seville.
[30] Interlined.
[31] *Ibid.*, p. 745 reads 'one and twenty' for '21'.
[32] *Ibid.* omits 'etc'.
[33] *Ibid.* inserts 'he the said deponent, being coming from Porto Rico, and bound for Spain, was taken by an English man of war off the Canary islands and'.
[34] *Ibid.* reads 'a-going' for 'going a'.
[35] *Ibid.* reads 'aboard' for 'on board'.
[36] *Ibid.* reads 'one hundred' for '120'.
[37] *Ibid.* reads 'loading' for 'lading'.
[38] *Ibid.* supplies 'taffaty, bays, hats, linnen, and woollen cloth' for 'etc.'.
[39] *Ibid.* reads 'goods'.
[40] *Ibid.* substitutes 'Saith, there was but four passengers in the ship, one whereof hath been a pilot at Amsterdam. Saith they came out of the Texell with near two hundred sail of ships with several convoys bound for several places but saith [they]' for 'etc'.
[41] Interlineated. *Ibid.* inserts 'of'.

of English men of war. Saith the captain of the ship[42] and divers others told this deponent and others that the cables were[43] for the use of the armado of Spain. And saith the commander *Juan Tullien* is now freighting another ship at Amsterdam with the like commodities to go [for] Spain. Says[44] the[45] ship was cast away upon Tuesday the 1st[46] of April about 4 of the clock in the afternoon, near unto a castle, that most of the upper good[s] were cast on shore the next morning, and that several of the[47] goods were taken up by the governor of the said castle. 4 cartloads whereof he sent to a marquis' house hard by the castle.[48] Saith further that he heard[49] that the[50] ship after her unloaden at Calis would[51] have been imployed in the Venetian service.[52]

News from W.R., London, 6 May 1656[53]

fo. 29^r

. . . . *There is a supply going to the Fleete which imports something*, but in regard all seems so close I am bound to be silent also. *His Highness & Councill sat on the Lord's day & very long in private yesterday being Munday which is nott usuall.* There is money going for Ireland because they have not returns

[42] According to a later newsbook report the captain was one 'Tyckie Jansen'; *Publick Intelligencer*, 38 (23–30 June 1656), p. 657.

[43] *TSP*, IV, p. 745 inserts 'fit'.

[44] *Ibid.* reads 'saith' for 'says'.

[45] *Ibid.* inserts 'said'.

[46] *Ibid.* inserts 'day'.

[47] *Ibid.* inserts 'said'.

[48] A letter written by Monck to Cromwell on 15 April 1656 identifies this as the ship wrecked 'upon a Rock neer Tayne' around 1 April 1656. The Tain referred to was that in Caithness, rather than the larger settlement of the same name on the Dornoch Firth. There was a garrison at nearby Thurso Castle and Col Morgan was ordered to secure what goods could be salvaged. The 'marquis' house' may be that occupied by the marquis of Montrose in 1650, still remembered as such in 1798. A detailed inventory of the cargo of the salvaged cables, hawsers, and ropes was later published; BL, Additional MS 38848, fo. 51^r; *Publick Intelligencer* 30 (21–28 Apr. 1656), p. 511; 38 (23–30 June 1656), p. 657; Firth and Davies, II, p. 478; *Originales Parochiales Scotiae: The Antiquities Ecclesiastical of the Parishes of Scotland* (Edinburgh, 1853), II, pt ii, p. 837.

[49] *TSP*, IV, P. 745 inserts 'it reported'.

[50] *Ibid.* inserts 'said'.

[51] *Ibid.* reads 'was to' for 'would'.

[52] *Ibid.* adds 'Nicoulus Quintero [i.e. 'Cantiro'], Examined William Welch, Thomas Fleetwood, interpreter.'

[53] These two brief passages in shorthand appear at the end of a longhand newsletter carrying naval news.

enough of exchange, and I hear when that arrives the army there is like to be [randevouzed].[54]

W.R.[55]

William Clarke, marginal annotation, 6 May 1656

fo. 29^{v}

<Master Drummond, intelligence. The copy sent in a letter to the Protector.>[56]

John Mayer, Berwick, to General George Monck, 9 June 1656[57]

fo. 38^{r}

My Lord

This morning there was a fight at sea betwixt a frigot of ours (as it is supposed) and 5 of the enemy, but after a long and hot dispute one of them were blown up which sunk down right (which is thought is ours), but the 5 remain still upon our coasts. Something to that[58] effect I received even now from the lieutenant that commands at the island fort with this addition that the other 5 are much tottered[59] in pieces in their masts and sayles. The fight was within sight of the town. I thought it my duty to give your Lordship an account of it lest there may come some ships out from you which cannot come with safety.

[54] On 1 April 1656 the Council ordered the war treasurers to send £35,000 to the forces in Ireland. It was conveyed there later in the month by Capt. Robert Vessey in the *Nightingale*; *CSPD 1655–1656*, pp. 246, 538.

[55] Probably either William Ross, an occasional provider of news to the Scottish headquarters (e.g. Worc. MS XXVIII, fo. 44^{r}), or William Rowe, another regular correspondent.

[56] Marginated. The longhand document to which this note refers is headed, 'The Contents of the last Lettre from overseas of the Date the 15th of April 1656 the last being of the Date the 10th April 1656'. The informant was most probably David Drummond, for whom see Dow, *Cromwellian Scotland*, pp. 189–190.

[57] On 10 June 1656 Monck sent a copy of this deposition, together with a covering letter to Cromwell; *TSP*, V, pp. 102–103.

[58] *Ibid.*, p. 102 reads 'this' for 'that'.

[59] Meaning 'battered and shaken', of a building or ship (*OED*). *TSP*, V, p. 102 reads 'shattered'.

This is the best account at present from

my Lord
your very humble servant
John Mayer[60]

Berwick June 9 at 11 a clock at night

For the right honourable General Monck commander-in-chief of all the forces in Scotland these, Scotland.[61]

The ship was the Greyhound frigot, Captain[62] commander and had 26 brass guns.[63]

William Clarke, memorandum, 30 June 1656

fo. [49]ʳ

The 1st news came to Dalkeith of the <resolution for>[64] calling of a Parliament in *7bris* in a letter from Master Thurloe to my Lord General.[65]

William Clarke, memorandum, 16 July 1656

fo. [51]ᵛ

This day the writs for the electing of parliament members in Scotland came by an express messenger to Edinburgh, but before that there were letters sent from the Lord General and others of the Council to several parts of Scotland for the election of several persons mentioned in their letters.[66]

[60] John Mayer, Mayor or Mears was deputy governor of Berwick; F&D, II, p. 522.
[61] The version in *TSP*, V, p. 102 ends here.
[62] Blank.
[63] In his covering letter to Cromwell, Monck identifies the frigate as the *Greyhound*. The ship was severely disabled in the fight and when the Ostenders went aboard to ransack her the crew fired the ship's powder in the captain's cabin, killing all hands, including the boarders; *ibid.*, p. 103; *Publick Intelligencer*, 39 (30 June–7 July 1656), p. 672.
[64] Marginated.
[65] It was not until the following day that Gilbert Mabbott sent out this important news, or that Thurloe wrote to inform Henry Cromwell in Ireland. The decision had been taken in strict secrecy; *CP*, III, p. 68; *TSP*, V, p. 176. We may take Clarke's date as being reliable. Monck acknowledged the news on 1 July; *ibid.*, p. 175.
[66] The writs were dated 10 July and Parliament assembled on 17 September 1656; *CSPD 1656–1657*, p. 9; *CJ*, VII, p. 423. It was of course no accident that the majority of MPs for

News from John Thurloe, 16 July 1656[67]

fo. [51]ᵛ

... *Col. Brayne is dispatched & began his Journey for Scotland yesterday. The shippes appointed to carry the men for Jamaica have lyen a great while in the downes for a Winde.* If it please God to send a wind they will soon be with you. It's his Highness' fear that Brayne's business will keep him in Scotland too long and that the ships will stay for him and therefore desires you very earnestly to hasten him away with all possible speed. His stay may be the loss of the islands and the lives of all the men and therefore I again beg of you that you will post him away.[68]

The success of the Spaniards against the French at Valenchien is confirmed by our letters yesterday.[69]

J.T.

[Secretary] John Thurloe

William Clarke, memorandum, 22 August 1656

fo. [65a]ʳ

This day the Lord Broghill with his lady and family went from Edinburgh to Berwick.[70] The Lord General and the rest of the Council brought him a good part of the way. The Lord General, ~~Judge Swinton~~ and he were nobly entertained at *Broxmouth* the earl of Roxburgh's house.[71]

Scotland (listed in Terry, pp. lxii–lxiv) were English. Monck's letter to Thurloe of 30 August 1656 suggests, like this document, that he had a large part in their election; *TSP*, V, p. 366. But see also P.J. Pinckney, 'The Scottish representation in the Cromwellian parliament of 1656', *Scottish History Review*, 46 (1967), pp. 95–114.

[67] I have not included the first paragraph of this letter (in longhand), which contains foreign news.

[68] It was not until October that the regiment raised in Scotland for the West Indies under Brayne's command was able to sail on its ill-fated expedition to Jamaica, where it arrived on 14 December 1656; F&D, II, pp. 704–706.

[69] The news that the Spanish army had broken through the French siege at Valenciennes on 6 July reached Paris on 8 July, a considerable blow to the Anglo-French coalition against Spain, probably reached Cromwell on 11 July; *TSP*, V, p. 190; *Mercurius Politicus*, 318 (10–17 July 1656), p. 7104; Abbott, IV, p. 204; *CSPV 1655–1656*, p. 193.

[70] Broghill, newly-elected MP for Edinburgh, was travelling to London for the opening of Parliament on 17 September 1656. As president of the Council in Scotland he had been held in high regard; before his departure he was lavishly entertained at Parliament House in Edinburgh; Terry, p. lxiii; *TSP*, V, p. 322; J. Nicoll, *A Diary of Public Transactions and other Occurrences* ... (Edinburgh, 1836). p. 183; *Publick Intelligencer*, 47 (25 Aug.–1 Sept. 1656), p. 801.

[71] During the battle of Dunbar (3 September 1650) Cromwell had established his headquarters in the grounds of Broxmouth House (*C&P*, I, p. 328).

Jeremiah Smith, The Downs, to General Monck, 25 August 1656

fo. 66v

Right Honourable

All our ships are still [continued] before Dunkirk and Ostend.[72] They will not have them draw off as yet, the weather beginning to grow very bad. It is a great adventure to keep so many there that are of such a great draught of waters. I have now on board of me one Sir John [. . .] who came from Flushing in a fisherboat to one of our men of war. He pretends that he is going to his Highness to acquaint him with several state occurrences that have passed lately in France betwixt Charles Stuart and the king of Spain.[73] I did detain him here till I did[74] here from Whitehall upon [our/his] arrival. I despatched away to the commissioners of the Admiralty and to secretary Thurloe. He informs me that it is agreed on betwixt the king of Spain and Charles Stuart that the Romish religion shall be established in England with all [courts] belonging to the same, and that the treaty twixt Spain and France doth go on very amicably. The king of France is to marry the infantess of Spain and have with her in dower all the provinces belonging to Flanders and convert all [his] property and title in them to the crown of France.[75] The pope is to make Don Jon of Austria, who is the king of Spain's bastard son, legitimate. I am confident there is some plot a-hatching in England, that the old malignant begins to be so high, and the cavaliers that are in /Flanders

fo. 67r

Flanders read it with the greatest confidence. On Saturday last I intercepted 40 libels that were to be delivered to several commanders

[72] English ships were continuing to blockade these two ports; see above, p. 248; *Publick Intelligencer*, 32 (5–12 May 1656), p. 537; 42 (21–28 July 1656), pp. 707–708; *CSPV 1655–1656*, pp. 200–201. Earlier in August, when eleven English ships were involved, Gilbert Mabbott wrote that 'not one of those Rogueish Piratts dare peep out'; *CSPD 1656–1657*, p. 54; Hull CRO, BRL 621.

[73] In April 1656 a secret treaty had been signed between the exiled Charles Stuart and Philip IV of Spain, to be ratified within three months. Predictably, any negotiations between the two caused great uneasiness in England; *CClarSP*, III, pp. 109–110; *CSPV 1655–1656*, pp. 202–204. Charles visited the Spanish commander. Don John of Austria, some time in late August; *Publick Intelligencer*, 48 (1–8 Sept. 1656), p. 809.

[74] Clearly part of the verb is missing here.

[75] The marriage took place under the Treaty of the Pyrenees in November 1659, Louis XIV thereby acquiring, *inter alia*, considerable property in Flanders; R. Lockyer, *Habsburg and Bourbon Europe* (Harlow, 1974), p. 420.

of ships and have secured all letters going to any seamen. I sent the libels to Whitehall[76] one whereof I have inclosed sent your honour to think of as you see cause. The king of Spain is using all his indeavours possible with the Hollander for their breach of peace with us. They alledge that their treasure is so exhausted and their debts not yet satisfied, and the people so discontented through their late losses, that they cannot do it.[77] But the king of Spain does promise them to satisfy their charge and make all loss good. He desires not to be known to any, only I intimate this to your honour of whom I beg excuse for the present trouble and remain

your ever faithful and obedient servant

Jeremiah Smith

Dunbar in the Downs August 25th 1656

For the Right Honourable General Monck, commander-in-chief of all the forces in Scotland these, Scotland.

Newsletter from Jeremiah Smith, The Downs, 20 [September] 1656

fo. 74^{r}

Dunbarre in the Downs 8bris 20 1656[78]

Since my last are arrived from the Downs in the western seas the [Dover] and the [Colchester] frigots. 3 more are expected every day. They lost their company in bad weather. They bring little news, but say that the seamen generally are in good health and are very cheerful to take their turns to cruze about the Havana and ply where the Spanish ships [must/most] pass, and though they have not yet met with any are still in hopes they shall at some time make prize of Spanish merchant

[76] Smith wrote to the Admiralty Commissioners on 23 August 1656; *CSPD 1656–1657*, p. 82. His enclosure to Monck may have been the pamphlet *Englands Remembrancers* (London, 1656), which George Thomason noted was scattered round the London streets on 1 August; Capp, *Cromwell's Navy*, pp. 145–146; G.K. Fortescue, *Catalogue of the Pamphlets, Books and Manuscripts*. . . , 2 vols (London, 1908), II, p. 156. The tract is not found among Clarke's surviving collection at Worcester College.

[77] The United Provinces were reported still to be resisting these overtures in a newsletter of 22 September 1656; *TSP*, V, p. 437.

[78] From its position in Clarke's notebook, and from the news this letter contains, the month should read '7bris'.

men or of the king's great plate ships and men of war.[79] It seems [from] them the Spaniard is very fearful and wary and skulks betwixt port and port as he observes our ships clear [of/off] his coasts. Upon such an opportunity belike the late Spanish fleet that our ships met withall near Cadiz[80] and which we expect daily to be brought in the Channel, but have not lately heard of their coming by reason of cross winds, got away from thence under [. . . .] of ours, who being [reached] 20 days before the harbour mouth of Havana took a small bark who informed them so much whereupon these 5 frigots were fled for England. I perceive there were not left of the land soldiers upon Jamaica above 1,500 [. . . .] some dying before being over-run with a spirit of laziness that they have not wrought anything in way of a plantation.

Jeremiah Smith

Paper concerning the proposed Act of Union, undated[81]

fo. 97^r

Concerning the clause intended to be added to the Act of Union between England and Scotland for confirmation of the laws, practises or customs of Scotland, or proposing them to be made as the rules for the administration of justice to the people in Scotland, whether such a clause may not admit of these insuing objections or queries:

<1.>[82] Whether it may not be necessary to [. . .] and set down in particular which laws, practises or customs should be confirmed are fit to be made rules of administration of justice to the people in Scotland [is] because many of the laws of Scotland *vizt.*, their acts of Parliament which are only their *Jus scriptum et que habent authoritatum juris in fero* are antiquated and obsolete and no doubt some of them contrary to and inconsistent with the interest of the present government.

<2.>[83] For the contract words though in many of them (there is much of equity, justice and reason) yet are they not any of them singly or

[79] Vice-Admiral Goodson was cruising off Havana in late July, but learned that the Spanish silver fleet had sailed for home four days before his arrival, on 14 July 1656; C.H. Firth, *The Last Years of the Protectorate*, 2 vols (London, 1909), I, p. 50.

[80] Capt. Richard Stayner had recently scored a notable success near Cadiz when he captured two of the returning Spanish galleons sinking two others; Vaughan, *Protectorate of Oliver Cromwell*, II, pp. 26–29; Capp, *Cromwell's Navy*, p. 98. The captured booty was landed at Portsmouth and transferred to the Tower of London two months later; *CP*, III, p. 81.

[81] This document is discussed in the introduction to this chapter, pp. 247–248.

[82] Marginated.

[83] Marginated.

per se or all of them together (under a strict and legal consideration) to be accounted *a jus scriptum*, as that which has the face of public authority upon it, so as to make [them] to have *authoritatem juris in fero* as daily experience shews, being often slighted and denied in *foro* and they are very often contradicted, and further,

<3.>[84] As to their customs, although some may be good, yet since the present government many of them have been taken away and deemed as wholly tyrannical and oppressive.[85]

<2. *Quere*>[86] Whether or no under the general as (*Dolus versatur in qualitate*) there may not be something intended (amongst many others) to follow *in consequentiam*, *vizt.* that the acts made by his Highness and Council in relation to the nation in the intervals of Parliament (as in particular that concerning debtors and creditors) as also other transactions of State here should become null and voyd, the commission for administration of justice [. . .] letters of [. . .] upon excommunications or pass [condemnations] as heretofore, and that interest become as high and absolute in power and tyranny over the people as ever.

<3. *Quere*>[87] Whether this may not be a subtil and tacit way to [strike off] and in a short time obliterate the authority and [memorial] of the present interest and government and to give a fair way that all things may return into the old channel of bribery, oppression, injustice and iniquity. Lastly it may be considered whether the [imposition] of laws mentioned in the model or Instrument of Government, may not suffice this nation [( ][88] without a special confirmation by act of parliament etc as well as the others of England and Ireland but that there lies some special design in this etc.

[84] Marginated.

[85] The distinction between the uses of 'custom' in English and in Scots law is discussed in Levack, 'The proposed union of English law and Scots law', p. 100. In Scotland the word denoted a precedent versed in the law and in its judicial interpretation.

[86] Marginated.

[87] Marginated.

[88] This outline resembles an opening round bracket, but there is no matching closing one.

9. NOTEBOOK XXIX

[May]–15 December 1657[1]

Introduction

In London and elsewhere the first half of 1657 was marked by uncertainty over whether Cromwell would now accept the title of king. Clarke's shorthand provides further corroboration of the traditionally accepted reasons for Cromwell's final rejection of kingship in May 1657.[2] One newsletter confirms that at the last minute Fleetwood and Desborough applied pressure on the Protector to turn down the title, but that neither of them would associate himself with the army petition to be brought before Parliament on 8 May in a last-ditch effort to prevent Cromwell from accepting. While it is already known that both Fleetwood and Desborough had advance knowledge of the petition, we learn from the same newsletter that they were able to show it to Cromwell in person before it reached the House,[3] where Fleetwood was just in time to prevent it from being presented. MPs immediately adjourned to the Banqueting House, where the Protector made his decision known to them.[4]

Cromwell's refusal of the kingship did not appease John Lambert. His implacable opposition to the oaths imposed on MPs, privy counsellors, and the Protector himself by the Additional Humble Petition and Advice of 26 June 1657 caused a final rift between the two men.[5] A newsletter from London, probably from Gilbert Mabbott, describes the extent and nature of the personal differences between them, and reveals that Cromwell's well-documented generosity to Lambert on this occasion did not extend to granting his request for the lucrative position of Clerk of the Hanaper.[6]

[1] Worc. MS XXIX.

[2] *LYP*, I, pp. 190–191; p. 261 below.

[3] *Ibid.*

[4] *LYP*, I, pp. 192–193.

[5] S.R. Gardiner (ed.), *The Constitutional Documents of the Puritan Revolution 1625–1660* (3rd edn, Oxford, 1903), pp. 461–464; *LYP*, II, pp. 3–6.

[6] P. 262. The holder of this office for the last ten years, Sir William Allanson of York, had died there on 6 December 1656; M.F. Keeler, *The Long Parliament 1640–1641*, pp. 83–84.

News from [G.M.], [London], [May 1657][7]

fo. 60[v]

It is related that both the Lord Fleetwood <and Major-General Disbrowe>[8] a day or 2 before his Highness's refusal of the kingly government[9] did very earnestly press him against it, and the Lord Disbrowe told him that [—] <he had and>[10] he would fight against kingship in any person [whatsoever] that should accept it or that to that purpose.[11]

It is observable that though the Lord Fleetwood and Major-General Disbrowe did both disown the [knowledge] of the petition in the House yet they both perused it and saw it and shewed it my Lord Protector before ever that it was presented to the House etc.[12]

News from [G.M.], [London], [18 July 1657][13]

fo. 99[v]

The discourse the Protector had with the Lord Lambert was to this effect. He told him that he was informed that the Lord Lambert was not satisfied with the present government. His Lordship told him that he knew not that he had given any occasion for such a report. His

[7] In Clarke's notebook this document comes immediately after the newsletter of 9 May 1657 from G.M. (probably Gilbert Mabbott) partly reproduced in *CP*, III, pp. 107–108, and is probably a postscript to it.

[8] Marginated.

[9] The latest of a series of proposals that Cromwell should assume the crown was presented to Parliament by Sir Christopher Packe on 23 February 1657; Firth, 'Cromwell and the crown', pp. 429–442; *LYP*, I, chs V–VI.

[10] Interlined.

[11] Cromwell had apparently decided to accept the crown, but was dissuaded at the last moment by an ultimatum from Desborough. Sir Charles Firth deduced that Fleetwood (and Lambert too) may also have forced Cromwell's hand; *ibid.*, pp. 190–191.

[12] Presumably the petition presented to Parliament by army officers on 8 May; *ibid.*, pp. 191–192. Although later circulated in print with the addition of a postscript of 'very bad and dangerous consequence', no copy is known to have survived. Cromwell wrote to Monck ordering its immediate suppression in Scotland; *S&P*, pp. 354–355. Ludlow also implicates Desborough, although not Fleetwood, in its preparation; Ludlow, *Memoirs*, II, p. 25.

[13] This is apparently the postscript to a longhand letter from G.M. (probably Gilbert Mabbott) the first eight lines of which are printed in *CP*, III, pp. 113–114. It enlarges considerably upon the first sentence of that letter, which reports a 'private conference' between Cromwell and Lambert on 11 July 1657. I have discussed this above. The 'Memorandum' appears to be a continuation of the same document, and I have treated it as such.

Highness [retorted] that he would not take the oath of a Council. His Lordship answered that he knew not how people came to divine such things, it being more than ever he declared as yet.[14] His Highness said that he did not affect his person. The Lord Lambert returned that he wished he could love him now as well as he did 12 months since. His Highness alledged that some said there was some [competing] with their families. The Lord Lambert said he knew nothing of any ground there was for it. His Highness demanded of him if he were willing, to arrest further jealousies, to lay down his commission. He said he would not turn his back upon the good cause he had so long owned, but if his Highness would command it from him under his hand and seal he should have it.[15] Thereupon they departed and his Highness sent an order under his hand and seal for him to deliver it to Master Scobell,[16] and after a few days the Lord Lambert coming to Whitehall he invited him to be no stranger there and ordered him 3,000*l* and 2,000*l* a year and added that he would take care he might leave in a good condition notwithstanding his taking away his commission.[17]

Memorandum. The discourse the Lord Lambert and Protector had about the Clerk of the Hamper[18] which the Major-General desired of him and he went out and asked the Lord Claypole[19] if his father would accept of it, who said he thought he would and then he came in again and asked my Lord Lambert what that was that he spoke to him about, and he told him and then he told him it was disposed of.[20]

[14] Lambert had, however, spoken out against the oaths on 24 June 1657; Burton, *Diary*, II, p. 295.

[15] Contemporary reports agree that Lambert surrendered his commission 'very calmly'; *CSPD 1657–1658*, p. 41; *CSPV 1657–1659*, p. 88; *TSP*, VI, p. 427.

[16] It was to William Jessop, Clerk of the Privy Council, and not Henry Scobell, Clerk of Parliament, that Lambert was ordered to surrender his commission; *CP*, III, pp. 113–114; Abbott, IV, p. 577; *CSPV 1657–1659*, p. 88.

[17] The amount of £2,000 is confirmed by both Ludlow and Nieupoort; Ludlow, *Memoirs*, II, p. 30; Abbott, IV, p. 578. The arrangement was to continue until a committee of the Privy Council had advised upon a suitable settlement on Lambert, whose salary before handing over his official positions was later calculated to have been over £6,500; *CP*, III, pp. 119–120; *A Narrative of the late Parliament, (so called) Their Election and Appearing, The Seclusion of a great part of them* ([London, 1658]), p. 9.

[18] i.e. Hanaper, the department of the Chancery into which fees were paid for the sealing and enrolment of charters and other documents. The office was abolished in 1832; *OED*.

[19] John Claypole, the Protector's son-in-law, was elevated to Cromwell's Other House in December 1657; *Mercurius Politicus*, 394 (10–17 Dec. 1657), p. [165].

[20] In 1620 the office, which was held for three years, was valued at £2,400, or £800 annually; G.E. Aylmer, *The King's Servants* (London, 1961), p. 222.

Newsletter from G.M.,[21] [London], marginal comment, 3 November 1657

fo. 122r

<False>[22]

John Thurloe, [London], to [George Monck], 15 December 1657[23]

fo. 137r

Wee are still alarum'd with the Cavaleers, & truly the Symptomes of an insurrection are great, & of a generall disposition of the Cavaleer partie thereunto besides the Intelligence which wee have which is certaine, & their Designe is as well uppon Scotland as England & Middleton is sent for from Dantzick & those partes for that end. There is one Sinclair who was prisoner in Chester that is escaped who before his escape had means of communicating with his confederates in Lancashire and Cheshire and it's thought he is gone for Scotland.[24] It [were exceeding well] that he [were] [. . .] for in case he be known. *The Enemy in Flanders doth very much threaten Mardyke but hath yett made noe attempt if they come they are not well prepared for them in the Fort. There is a Marshall of France in itt to defend itt & neere 3,000 Souldiers. Itt is certaine that Sir John Reynolds & Colonel White are cast away at Sea coming from Mardyke which is a very great blowe to us.*

J.T.

John Thurloe

[21] Probably Gilbert Mabbott.

[22] Marginated. The letter is printed in *CP*, III, p. 123. The comment appears to relate to the first sentence (from 'The late' to 'President thereof'), which has been underlined in the manuscript.

[23] Monck's reply to this letter, dated 24 December 1657 at Dalkeith, is printed in *TSP*, VI, pp. 703–704.

[24] By the date of his reply Monck had received intelligence that Sinclair was expected to reach Edinburgh in three days' time. Monck was unable to identify which particular Sinclair this was (*ibid.*, p. 704), as am I.

10. NOTEBOOK XXX

23 March–6 September 1658[1]

Introduction

In March 1658, Clarke's old colleague George Bilton, Deputy Treasurer for the army in Scotland, came under investigation for serious embezzlement.[2] The two men had a close working relationship and Clarke must, however groundlessly, have had fears that he would be implicated in the affair.[3] The two accomplices named in Thurloe's letter to Monck about the case,[4] Short and Drywood, were sent to Scotland to answer for their conduct, although Monck was forced eventually to release Short through lack of evidence.[5] Bilton was later imprisoned and his estates in Scotland sequestered.[6]

In April, encouraged by recent reports that Monck had refused to obey orders from the Protector to return to England, royalists on the Continent made an unsuccessful attempt to convert Monck to their cause.[7] Their letter to him, written in Rotterdam on 18 April and now found also in Clarke's shorthand, reached Monck three months later and was immediately forwarded by him to John Thurloe.[8] A covering letter which was not apparently sent to Thurloe directed that Monck's letter was to be delivered to William Clarke to ensure its safe passage to the general's own hands.[9] There is nothing to indicate whether Clarke himself kept this second letter from Monck, or whether it was Monck's

[1] Worc. MS XXX.

[2] Bilton's career, and subseqent disgrace in Scotland, are traced in *SS*, p. 145. Suspicions about him had been raised in January 1657 by a colleague, Charles Zinzan; Worc. MS LI, fo. 45^{r}. The amount involved ran into some tens of thousands of pounds; *ibid.*, fo. 48^{v}.

[3] Pp. 77, 95, 162, 174, Although in an earlier letter Clarke had addressed Bilton as 'Father' (p. 96 above), by February 1654 he appears to have been distancing himself somewhat from him; p. 153.

[4] Pp. 265–266.

[5] Worc. MS XXX, fo. 86^{r}; *CSPD 1657–1658*, p. 320; *CSPD 1658–1659*, pp. 12, 157; *TSP*, VII, p. 19.

[6] *CSPD 1658–1659*, p. 126; *S&P*, pp. 412, 414.

[7] *CSPD 1657–1658*, pp. 324, 333, 357–358; *CSPV 1657–1659*, p. 177. The reports later turned out to be a ploy to flush out Royalists in Scotland; *CSPD 1657–1658*, p. 324; *CSPV 1657–1659*, p. 188.

[8] P. 269; *TSP*, VII, pp. 232–233.

[9] P. 268.

decision not to send it on to the authorities in London.[10] A marginal note discloses that the bearer of the letter was arrested in Edinburgh two days later, taken to Dalkeith for questioning, and later detained in Edinburgh.[11] Although Monck was careful to send the letter to Thurloe immediately, he played down the episode, explaining that he 'did nott thinke fitt to trouble his highnesse with itt' on the grounds that it was simply a 'knavish trick of some Scotchman or other' for which he would 'make them smart'.[12] Nonetheless, according to Clarke's notes, he was fully aware of its true origin.

The termination of the second Protectorate Parliament in February 1658 resulted in renewed serious financial difficulties for the government. For both this and another pressing reason, the nomination of the Protector's successor, there were by the summer expectations that another parliament would soon be called.[13]

All such preoccupations were soon overshadowed by the news of Cromwell's death on 3 September 1658. His dying moments are vividly described in an anonymous personal account, written in shorthand immediately under the longhand copy of the Council's official notification of the death.[14] The letter confirms what is usually accepted – that shortly before he died, and as forecast by Dorothy Clarke in her letter of 27 August,[15] Cromwell nominated his son Richard to succeed him. Among his last preoccupations was his concern for persecuted Protestants in Europe.

John Thurloe, Whitehall, to George Monck, 23 March 1658

fo. [62]^{r}

Sir

We can get little out of Short and Drywood touching Bilton's business, save what their papers will tell us, which have been seized whereof the

[10] Monck claimed that the letter which he did send to Thurloe had been 'left with the officer of the guard'; *TSP*, VII, p. 232.

[11] P. 268; *TSP*, VII, p. 268.

[12] *Ibid.*, p. 232.

[13] P. 271, the second from Clarke's wife Dorothy, presumably visiting London from Scotland, where she had recently suffered the loss of an infant son; Worc. MS XXX, fo. [17]^{r}, in shorthand.

[14] P. 272; Worc. MS XXX, fos 155^{v}–156^{r}. Clarke also made a longhand copy of the account, probably after the Restoration. Apart from one brief quotation I have not found that it has been used in modern accounts, perhaps because it lies among Clarke's previously less accessible unbound papers, which have only recently been catalogued; Worc. MS CLXXXI, fo. 413^{v}; Sherwood, *Court of Oliver Cromwell*, p. 111.

[15] P. 271.

best use will be ~~paid~~ made[16] towards a further discovery, and when we are gone as far as we have, any [light] to give us both the persons and papers shall be sent to you.[17] Serjeant, who dwells at Northampton, was also sent for, but he is not able to make such a journey.[18] His papers were also seized and tomorrow morning the committee will peruse them. It's intended that with these men one of the Treasurers shall be sent down to you that the whole business may be before you, the better to inable you to state things clearly.

All our time here is taken up in attending the motions of the enemy who do still alarum us with invasions and insurrections.[19] They have written from France to their party here that they may certainly expect them so soon as the wind comes any point southerly.[20]

I [do/did] perceive that they [do/did] more rely upon another party of men of their [regard] and clear discoveries are come to our hands in [that/time], and upon this account Major Robert Harley was committed to the Tower and Sir William Waller confined.[21] The city of London continues very hearty to his Highness and the present government.

I rest
your most humble and faithful servant

John Thurloe

Whitehall, March 23 1657/8

For the Right Honourable the Lord General Monck, commander-in-chief of all the forces in Scotland.

[16] Superimposed on 'paid'.

[17] Financial statements to assess the extent of Bilton's fraud were immediately prepared in Scotland and in England; Worc. MS LI, fos 45^r–48^v; *CSPD 1657–1658*, pp. 320, 356, 370.

[18] A month later the Council ordered that if Joseph Serjeant was not fit to travel to London, he was to be examined in Northampton, along with the seizure of any money belonging to Bilton in his possession; *ibid.*, p. 371.

[19] The threat from the royalists and their decision to postpone an invasion until the following winter are discussed in *LYP*, II, pp. 53–69.

[20] According to Sir Edward Walker, writing from Brussels on 11 March 1658, the royalist force was too weak to attempt an invasion at this time; *CSPD 1657–1658*, p. 325.

[21] Implicated in the latest royalist plot, both men were arrested, examined by Cromwell and imprisoned. One report stated that Waller was allowed to remain in his house on parole; Worc. MS XXX, fos [62]^v; 64^v; *TSP*, VII, p. 20; *CSPD 1657–1658*, p. 357.

Newsletter from G.M., marginal annotation, 24 April 1658[22]

fo. 84r

The Commission for a Hihg-Court [sic] of Justice is sealed and the Court will sit very suddainly. Mr Stapeley (a Member of the late parliament) hath a pardon for life and Estate (upon his ingenuous confession of the whole Businesse). Dr Hewet (Lecturer at St Gregories neere Paules) will be the first man tryed (Mr Stapeley haveing confest that he had not accepted of a Commission from Charles Stuart but through the importunity of the said Doctor). The next will be the persons that treated two Captaines of Hull for the betraying of that Guarrison . . . <Sir Henry Slingsby drinking a cup of piss and slaver said that they might be hanged if they would know Major Waterhouse and Captain Overton>.[23]

News from G.M.,[24] [London], 8 May 1658

fo. 88v

. . . . A Commission sent from Charles Stuart <to Major Waterhouse>[25] *to bee Governor of the Castle, North & South blockhouses in Hull, uppon his Compliance with Sr Henry Slingsby for delivering uppe the South block-house* whenas he was governour.[26]

[22] As the longhand passage to which this shorthand note is attached is not available in printed form I have provided it in full.

[23] Marginated. Sir Henry Slingsby attempted in vain to suborn two officers of the garrison at Hull, Maj. Ralph Waterhouse (deputy governor) and Capt. John Overton, to the royalist cause (see also below). The port would have provided a valuable toehold in the event of a royalist landing. He was found guilty by a High Court of Justice on 25 May and executed on 8 June 1658; *Mercurius Politicus*, 417 (20–27 May 1654), p. [555]; *LYP*, II, pp. 76–77; F&D, II, p. 555. The newsletter continues in longhand; a second copy does not bear this annotation; Worc. MS CLXXXI, fo. 401r.

[24] Probably Gilbert Mabbott.

[25] Interlined.

[26] This short phrase in shorthand comes at the end of a longhand letter which begins on fo. 88r. There is a fair copy of the letter in Worc. MS. CLXXXI, fo. 404r in which, unusually, the phrase is again written in shorthand. According to one newsbook, Waterhouse was also offered £5,000. The commission was immediately sent to Cromwell; *Publick Intelligencer*, 127 (24–31 May 1658), p. [548]; Worc. MS XXX, fo. [77]r.

Mark Richson, Rotterdam, to George Monck, 18 April 1658[27]

fo. 118ᵛ

<This, with the insuing letter,[28] was brought out of Holland by one Alexander [Bissert] a merchant in Rotterdam, who was found out at[29] when he lay in Edinburgh the Monday following being the 5th instant, and committed 1st to Dalkeith in the church for that night and the next day sent to the marshall general at Edinburgh.>[30]

Honest Andrew

I am bound to desire this courtesy of me to get this letter conveyed to General Monck. It is from a very good friend and an old acquaintance of his which has desired me to send it to him and I know no body more fitter to send it to then to yourself, who live so near him. Send it by anybody to Master Clarke his secretary that it may come safe to his hands.[31] I have nothing more at present but to assure you that I am

your most loving friend

Mark Richson

Rotterdam, April 18/28 1658

For my loving friend Andrew Watson
dwelling at the sign of the Hart in Dalkeith
Scotland

The following letter was inclosed

[27] Although this letter is dated 18 April 1658, I have retained the order in which both it and its enclosure (below) appears in Clarke's notebook, under the date of its receipt at Dalkeith.

[28] See below.

[29] Blank.

[30] Marginated. It was not until 13 July that Monck reported to Thurloe that he had arrested the bearer of this letter and its enclosure. Monck may have delayed his report while attempting to persuade the prisoner to break his silence; *TSP*, VII, p. 268. There is no evidence to show that this covering letter which, unlike its enclosure, implicated Clarke directly, was sent to Thurloe.

[31] As Clarke records below, the letter reached him on 3 July 1658.

John Johnson, Rotterdam, to George Monck, 18 April 1658[32]

fo. 119ʳ

<*3 July 1658* This letter was brought to Dalkeith this day, delivered to Andrew Watson at the White Hart and from [thence] to Henry and so to me.>[33]

Sir

Here was a general report of late that you and your whole army had declared for King Charles, your lawful sovereign, which made all good and honest hearts rejoice and myself as much as any, or rather more, having some relation to you.[34] I hope it is a presage of what God will put in your heart to do, and truly sir you cannot do any thing that will more advance your salvation nor bring greater honour to yourself and family, for you may be any thing as great as you desire, and what any wise man should study more then that I know not. And this I know, that if the king be restored to his undoubted rights by your means, as I know he may if you do that which is in your power to do, you may, I say, make yourself and family what you desire which is more then you can hope for from that tyrant who keeps faith with none. For when his own turn is served he cares not if his instruments were hanged, nay he very often hangs them himself. And this I believe you are not ignorant of. Look upon Lambert and several others of his creatures how he has served them. Think it may be your own turn next. Therefore to prevent it let me beseech you to lay this my advice to heart and be a glorious instrument of re-establishing[35] our good and lawful prince who I am sure never disobliged you, or if he have he will make you a large amends. And this I will tell you, if you do not do it you will not be long safe in that government. If you were of a morose ill disposition I would spare this pains but knowing you to be of a good, sweet and honest nature I cannot but promise to myself good return of this my friendly advice which if you follow you shall live happy and honourable in this world and injoy everlasting happiness in the world to come.

[32] Although this letter is dated 18 April 1658, I have retained the order in which it appears in Clarke's notebook, under the date of its receipt at Dalkeith.

[33] Marginated. Monck immediately forwarded a copy of this letter, written in Clarke's hand, to Thurloe; BL, Additional MS 4156, fos 52ʳ–53ᵛ. With his covering letter of 3 July, it is printed in *TSP*, VII, pp. 232–233.

[34] I have discussed this deliberately circulated rumour above, p. 264n.

[35] *Ibid.*, p. 232, inserts 'of'.

If you knew the gallantry and the sweet and good disposition of the king, you would[36] need no other [...] <motive>[37] to stir you up to restore him to his crown, for you cannot demand anything of him for your own good and your family's but he will grant you. Therefore let me beseech you as a friend to think of it in time before it be too late. And what you do, do it suddenly, for your time will not be long in that government else, for that great monster is plotting how to remove you. If you knew who I were that writes you this advice you would easily give credit to it. I have ever loved and honoured your family and it would much rejoice me to see you to be the raiser of it, as you may do to what heighth or dignity you please. Therefore if I may but know what it is you desire to have, and it shall be granted and sent you signed and sealed under the king's own hand. Therefore let me receive your answer as soon as possibly you can and direct your letter thus, for Master John Johnston to be left at Thomas Martin's at the Arms of Scotland upon the Scidam[38] Head at Rotterdam. You must be sudden for there are forces arising to send down against you, but if you declare for the king you will have friends enough to 2d you. I beseech the Lord to put it into your heart and then I doubt not but God will bless and prosper you. I must conclude and rest, sir,

your most affectionate friend and servant

John Johnson[39]

Rotterdam

April 18/28 1658

Sir, you need not fear or doubt anything from whence this comes, for be assured it comes[40] from one that wishes you much happiness and has had the honour to be well known to you here in Holland. And if this advice of mine may take any good effect, I shall soon discover myself to you.

[41]For General Monck at Dalkeith in Scotland.[42]

[36] *Ibid.* reads 'will' for 'would'.

[37] Interlined.

[38] *Ibid.*, p. 233 reads 'Schedam'.

[39] The name of Johnson was frequently used by the royalists as a pseudonym; see, for example, G.F. Warner (ed.), *The Nicholas Papers: correspondence of Sir Edward Nicholas*, 4 vols (London, 1886–1920), II, p. 249; III, pp. 172, 174–176; IV, pp. 86, 102, 124, 130, 149.

[40] *TSP*, VII, p. 233 reads 'cometh' for 'comes'.

[41] *Ibid.* inserts 'superscribed'.

[42] *Ibid.* adds, 'Vera copia Ex William Clarke'.

News from T.C.,[43] London, 5 August 1658

fo. [141]ʳ

The calling of a Parliament is very variously discoursed and sometimes it is resolved to be again in good [. . .] and [then] laid aside, but certainly there will be great want of money without some supply or other.[44]

My Lord Richard is very diligent in Council and [disposes] himself much to business and is very obliging to all people and much in the esteem of his Highness.[45]

Dorothy Clarke, [London], to [William Clarke], 27 August 1658[46]

fo. [151]ᵛ

The Protector is sick of an ague and has fits that destroy him 18 hours together. He sent this last night for the Lord Richard and the Speaker of the last Parliament with some others to consult about proclaiming of his son, but they could not agree about it.[47] Some think it [should/must] be done by a Parliament, but for certain there is something in agitation for I had this from very good hands.

Dorothy Clarke

43 Possibly Monck's brother-in-law, Thomas Clarges.

44 After increasing financial difficulties, the State's debt at this time has been calculated to be about £1.5 million. Cromwell had terminated his short-lived second Protectorate Parliament in February 1658, and proposals for its successor were at a standstill; *CJ*, VII, pp. 578, 592; *LYP*, II, pp. 258–266, 274–280.

45 After a trip to 'Western parts' Richard was warmly received by his parents at Hampton Court on 17 July, after which he attended every session of the Privy Council from 20 July to 26 August; *Mercurius Politicus*, 425 (15–22 July 1658), p. 686; *CSPD 1658–1659*, p. xxiii.

46 The letter is placed above another from G.D. (probably George Downing) of the same date. Another copy (in longhand) omits Dorothy Clarke's name, leaving the impression that it forms the first paragraph of the letter from G.D. It omits the final sentence, 'Some think . . . '; Worc. MS CLXXXI, fo. 409ʳ.

47 Thurloe wrote to Henry Cromwell on 24 August 1658 that the fits associated with Cromwell's tertian ague were 'somewhat longe and sharp'. On 24 August ('this being the intervall day') the doctors brought Cromwell from Hampton Court to Whitehall where the air was considered to be better. Here he intended to nominate his successor; *TSP*, VII, pp. 354–356; *CSPV 1657–1659*, p. 238; *CP*, III, p. 161.

Newsletter from London, [3 September 1658][48]

fo. 156^{r}

Dr Bates watched with his Highness the night before he died and Master Manton prayed with him that morning.[49] Some few hours before he died he was distracted and in those fits would cry out, 'What will they do with the poor Protestants in Piedmont, in Poland[50] and other places?' and such kind of discourses.[51] He did not declare the Lord Richard[52] to be his successor till about 2 days before he died. Master Secretary Thurloe and Master Thomas Goodwin were witnesses to it. There was some debate in the Council before they would pass the vote for <the Lord Richard>[53] his being Protector, etc.[54]

Thomas Poole, Whitehall, to George Monck, 6 September 1658[55]

fo. 156^{v}

Itt is a Mercy worth all good mens observation to see all Men thankfull in this change, except Mr Feake & such as hee is for I think he knows not God that cannot obey those that God has set over them in authority.[56] *For hee did raile against the good choice which is published Lord Protector, and said if they had brought a Devill out of Whitehall in the Shape of a Man they would have made publication for him. This hee said in the pulpitt,* but wicked men make lies their [ammunition] and speak here as though your honour

[48] There is another copy of this newsletter in longhand at Worc. MS CLXXXI, fo. 413^{v}.

[49] Cromwell died at about 3 pm on 3 September 1658; *Mercurius Politicus*, 432 (2–9 Sept. 1658), p. 802.

[50] In Worc. MS CLXXXI, fo. 413^{v} 'in Poland' is omitted.

[51] Cromwell's groom of the bedchamber also recorded Cromwell's concern for 'the afflicted condition of God's People under persecution in other parts of the World' in his last hours; [Charles Harvey], *A Collection of Several Passages concerning his late Highness in the time of his sickness* (London, 1659), p. 16.

[52] i.e. his eldest surviving son, Richard Cromwell.

[53] Interlined.

[54] This supports Edward Phillips's statement about Goodwin's presence when Cromwell named his successor; Sir Richard Baker, *Chronicle of the Kings of England . . .*, (London, 5th edn, 1670) pp. 652–653; see also *LYP*, II, p. 305n.

[55] The longhand passages of this letter are printed in *CP*, III, p. 163, where the shorthand is signalled as '[cypher]'.

[56] Christopher Feake was briefly imprisoned for preaching against Cromwell earlier in 1658; *ibid.*, p. 146; *Publick Intelligencer*, 118 (29 Mar.–4 Apr. 1658), p. [420]; 119 (5–12 Apr. 1658), p. 446.

were discontented but the liars' portion is in the lake of brimstone.[57] So praying for your honour's health and long life I rest, giving you hearty thanks for all your good favours to your poor servant, and leave your honour in the arms of the true vine and am

your faithful servant
Thomas Poole[58]

Whitehall 6 September 1658

Lord General Monck

[57] '[A]nd all liars shall have their part in the lake which burneth with fire and brimstone', Revelation, XXI. 8.

[58] This was presumably the same Cornet Thomas Poole who received a grant of land in Scotland in April 1653; pp. 76, 79–80 above. In June 1655 Monck requested that he be promoted to lieutenant; *S&P*, pp. 288–289. Poole remained loyal to Monck in the crisis of October/December 1659; *CP*, IV, p. 129.

11. NOTEBOOK XXXI

4 January–29 September 1659[1]

Introduction

The year 1659 was a particularly turbulent one in the political life of the country. After more than usually acrimonious elections[2] Richard Cromwell's first and only parliament assembled on 27 January. It lasted less than three months and was brought down finally, amid increasingly strident appeals for a return to the principles of the 'Good Old Cause',[3] by the combined efforts of a minority group of republican MPs (the 'commonwealthsmen') and the 'Wallingford House' group, leaders of the army based in England.[4] As well as several new written accounts of the Parliament's collapse, there are records of two conversations with messengers from London, one bearing a letter from Richard Cromwell's brother-in-law, the Earl Fauconberg, and the other from Richard himself.[5]

There is no indication of the content of Fauconberg's letter, but it is possible that he was sounding Monck out to see whether he would join the royalist cause. In December 1658 Charles Stuart had already considered approaching Monck and was shortly to do so again. A letter of 8 July 1659 from Sir John Grenville to Edward Hyde which refers to 'the late correspondence' between Monck and Fauconberg may indeed be a reference to the meeting described here.[6] If, as seems

[1] Worc. MS XXXI.

[2] P. 277; R. Hutton, *The Restoration: A Political and Religious History of England and Wales 1658–1667* (Oxford, 1985), p. 28.

[3] P. 282.

[4] For the complex groupings and political manoeuvres in Richard's parliament see A.H. Woolrych, 'The Good Old Cause and the fall of the Protectorate', *Cambridge Historical Journal*, 13 (1957), pp. 133–161; I. Roots, 'The tactics of the Commonwealthsmen in Richard Cromwell's parliament', in D. Pennington and K. Thomas (eds), *Puritans and Revolutionaries* (Oxford, 1982 edn), pp. 283–309; D. Hirst, 'Concord and discord in Richard Cromwell's House of Commons', *English Historical Review*, 103 (1988), pp. 339–358.

[5] Pp. 285–288, 290–293.

[6] A. Bryant (ed.), *The Letters Speeches and Declarations of King Charles II* (London, 1935), p. 65; *CClarSP*, IV, pp. 263, 268. Grenville's letter makes it clear that Monck's brother was to visit Fauconbridge before paying a visit to Monck in Scotland.

likely, the letter did contain some kind of royalist overture, it is clear that – as during the summer of 1658 – Monck did not respond to it.[7]

Clarke's brief record of his own conversation with a personal messenger from Richard Cromwell to Monck answers questions about whether or not Richard attempted to contact Monck in Scotland.[8] We learn that Richard's motives were not to ask Monck for military assistance; to the contrary, he did not 'desire any to answer another for him further than might consist with the peace of the nations' and was now 'resolved to sit still and look on'.[9] Monck had already made up his mind that he could not adhere to Richard, but must endorse the new regime.[10] A few days after receiving Richard's messenger he sent a warm letter of support to Charles Fleetwood and the other grandees at Wallingford House.[11]

For two volatile weeks between Richard's downfall on 22 April and 7 May, when the General Council of the Army recalled the remaining members of the Rump to act as a Parliament, the country was in the hands of the army. It was to remain a pivotal force in English politics for the remainder of 1659, although increasingly the armies in Scotland and Ireland would distance themselves from the policies and actions of the Wallingford House group.

Tension and difficulties continued on all sides under the new regime.[12] Senior army officers increasingly resented the restrictive measures imposed by the Rump and as the quarrel worsened there was talk in army circles of placing the government again in the hands of a single person, and even of reinstating Richard Cromwell.[13]

Early in the year we are given the curious story of Richard's dealings with two Quakers arrested for passing themselves off as members of the watch.[14] The Protector's light-hearted dismissal of the incident and his decision to order their release, in spite of the widespread alarm currently surrounding all Quaker activities,[15] are in keeping with his Privy Council's lenient response to an appeal on the behalf of imprisoned Quakers in the preceding September. Nevertheless, only

[7] Pp. 268–270.

[8] Hutton, *Restoration*, p. 40.

[9] Pp. 292–293.

[10] P. 292.

[11] *TSP*, VII, pp. 669–670.

[12] See, for example, pp. 295, 296, 298–300, 307, 309.

[13] Pp. 297, 298–300, 305–307, 308, 309.

[14] P. 280.

[15] There were, for example, large numbers of Quakers meeting in London and even in Westminster itself around this time; Hutton, *Restoration*, p. 26.

a month after the incident described here some 144 Quakers were still held in custody around the country.[16]

By mid-June the Protectorate was at an end and Richard had become a public laughing-stock.[17]

News from [T.C.], London, 4 January 1659[18]

fo. [5]r

3 queries proposed to be debated on by the members of the insuing Parliament or at least [talked] on to be done: 1. whether or no that the authority of the late Parliament wherein the petition of advice and present government was [settled] are sufficient for the establishment of the government; 2. whether or no that the late Protector's will for declaring his successor be valid or no; 3. whether that it is fit for the Members sent from the ~~Parliament~~ Scotland[19] and Ireland should be fit to sit with those that are the free-born people of England in Parliament, being not allowed by their constitutions.

Memorandum, [Dalkeith], [11 January 1659]

fo. [9]v

Hague 11/21 January 1658/9

A letter [attached] from Master Downing wherein are the great preparations in Holland for the Sound.[20]

[16] G. Davies, *The Restoration of Charles II 1658–1660* (San Marino, 1955), pp. 27–28; Hutton, *Restoration*, pp. 36–37.

[17] P. 301.

[18] Apparently the postscript to a newsletter (in longhand) from 'T.C.' (possibly Thomas Clarges).

[19] 'Scotland' superimposed on 'Parliament'.

[20] There is no surviving copy of Downing's letter among Clarke's papers. Clarke must have intended to copy it into his notebook and, following his usual practice, entered this memorandum under the date on which the letter was written. Downing enlarged upon the information in a further letter to Monck dated 21/31 January 1659; *CP*, III, p. 175. His intelligence formed the basis of the report on the current situation with regard to the Sound which John Thurloe presented to the Commons on 21 February 1659; *CJ*, VII, p. 606; Burton, *Diary*, III, pp. 376–403, esp. p. 380; *TSP*, VII, pp. 619–620.

Newsletter from Francis Childe, Exeter, 15 January 1659

fo. [13]ʳ

We are in these parts most terrible enemies to an army man and not one of them should be chosen if we have all other interest. Some[21] a gallant [beat too as] the crows, jackdaws, and magpies play together.[22] *Colonel Robert Rolles & Sir John Northcott are our Shire Knights, & Mr Richard Forde of London & Major Gibbons our 2 Burgesses. The first was hang'd att the Exchange by his wooden image*, and the other a [fiery] Sir John.[23]

Francis Childe

News from J.R., Westminster, 27 January 1659[24]

fo. 17ʳ

Itt is a Commonwealthes interest doth oppose them but if you will have my opinion (and I think I take a right measure of men) *there will bee two to one for confirming of the present Settlement by a protector & two Houses against a Standing Commonwealth Councill (for Standing Pooles doe Corrupt)* . . .'.

News from Thomas Morgan, 3 February 1659[25]

fo. 23ʳ

By Lettres from Flanders itt is informed that it was the Lord Lockharts pleasure to command five Companies of Colonel Lillingtons Regiment from their winter quarters at Amiens in order to the Strengthening of Dunkirke <(although in myself's judgment it will much [. . .] them that some men desire an army in a garrison)>[26] *which was obeyed* . . . .[27]

T.M.

Thomas Morgan

[21] Blank.

[22] Three main groups contested the elections – supporters of the Protectorate, republicans, and crypto-royalists. There were many irregularities in the elections; G. Davies, 'The election of Richard Cromwell's Parliament', *English Historical Review*, 63 (1948), pp. 488–501.

[23] The two Members returned for Exeter were Thomas Bampfield and Major Gibbons; *Publick Intelligencer*, 161 (24–31 Jan. 1659), p. 180.

[24] This newsletter, probably from John Rushworth, is printed in *CP*, III, p. 176. This single shorthand phrase joins what are given there as paras 2 and 3.

[25] Printed in full in *ibid.*, pp. 179–180, where the writer is identified as 'G.M.' (p. 180n).

[26] Interlined.

[27] The document then continues in longhand.

Newsletter from G.M., London, 15 February 1659[28]

fo. 31^{v}

Sir Arthur Hesilrige upon the passing of the vote for the recognition of his Highness made a [~~. . .~~] speech to the effect following:

Master Speaker,

Now you have passed this vote I have but one word to say as an old Briton and an English knight. You have at one blow given away our liberties and set up a family that we must maintain at a vast charge. Here is a [structure] of brick to be made but where is the straw? It is such a burthen that the people [~~cannot~~] will not be able to bear. My motion is that the House may adjourn and go to prayers to seek deliverance from these burthens.[29]

The 14 instant a Committee of Officers were appointed to draw uppe some Heads to bee framed into a Petition & presented to the parliament in the name of the Army. His Highnesse was lately with the Officers att the Lord Fleetwoods and admonished them to bee prudent & carefull in the Draught of this intended Petition, which itt's well hop't will bee carefully observ'd.[30]

G.M.

A Member of Parliament answered Sir Arthur Haslerig that he wondered not that Sir Arthur Haslerig should be so much troubled at the alteration of the government from a commonwealth, but if he had got 8,000*l* a year by it as well as he, <~~8,000*l* per annum~~>[31] he thought he should be unwilling to part with it.

A Member of Parliament that mourned for his late Highness speaking in the House, he that replied to him, called him the gentleman of the long robe.[32]

There being one Master Freeman[33] that urging in the House that they should [establish] my Lord Protector who had an army that would back him, my Lord Fairfax moved he might be brought to the bar that should mention such things in the House and accordingly he was called to the bar.

[28] Probably from Gilbert Mabbott.

[29] The vote was passed on 14 February. There is no confirmation in Burton's *Diary* of the speeches quoted in this newsletter. Hesilrige's verbosity and filibustering tactics are described in Roots, 'Tactics of the Commonwealthsmen in Richard Cromwell's parliament', esp. pp. 306–309.

[30] This paragraph is printed in *CP*, III, p. 182.

[31] Interlined.

[32] For the reputed bias of the 'gentlemen of the long robe' towards Richard Cromwell, see Burton, *Diary*, III, p. 32n.

[33] Edward Freeman, MP for Leominster.

News from London, 17 February 1659

fo. [32]v

Master Neville questioned in the House for atheism, his denying the Scriptures etc.[34]

The 2 main things now in debate are the negative voice and militia.

News from G.D., The Hague, 18 February 1659[35]

fo. [33]v

Since the writing hereof is the post arrived from England and the whole town is full of nothing but talk of the confusions at London in the Parliament and presaging what the consequences thereof should be, to the disrepute of your affairs, discouraging your friends and heating your enemies.[36]

News from [G.M.], [London], 19 February 1659[37]

fo. 34v

The names of those appointed by the Parliament as a committee for receiving the whole [accounts] of the present revenue of England, Scotland and Ireland and of the whole forces by sea and land belonging to this Commonwealth, and who are impowered to call before them any person for making out the true revenue and condition of the armies and of the shipping at home and abroad, before which committee the Muster-Master General is appointed to predicate muster rolls of the whole commission officers, together with the particular number and strength of the regiments:

Sir Henry Vane
Sir John Carter
Mr Peter Middleton
Colonel Birch
Colonel Thompson
Joseph Jackson
Mr Scott
Lambert Godfrey

[34] *Ibid.*, pp. 296–305. Neville was acquitted; *CClarSP*, IV, p. 152.

[35] Postscript to a letter from 'G.D.', probably George Downing.

[36] i.e. the Royalists, who were hoping that divisions within Parliament and with the army would provide an opportunity for another attempt to restore the monarchy.

[37] Postscript to a newsletter from 'G.M.', probably Gilbert Mabbott.

Mr Scawen *Mr Biddolph*
Mr Bampfeild *Major Generall Browne*[38]

Which 12, or any five of them, are to meet the 18th instant by 2 of the clock in the afternoon and so forth, every sitting day until they be able and furnished to make a secret[39] report to the Parliament of the above trust.

News from W.R., Westminster, 21 February 1659[40]

fo. [36]^r

It is observable that in the debate about the Other House[41] there was a dissent between the protectoral party among themselfs whether they should have the old lords or those new ones lately named. During all which debate the commonwealth's party sat still and said nothing, but left them to dispute it among themselfs.[42]

Newsletter from [London], 1 March 1659

fo. 40^r

Some few days since a Quaker constable being upon the watch in London, he and his watchmen met with 2 troopers going the round, whom they disarmed and sent to prison, whereon the constable being questioned before his Highness came with his hat on his head and being demanded wherefore he committed the trooper, he made this defence, to wit:

Thou Richard Cromwell, thou master, thank thy servant Robert Tichborne for this.[43] For thy servant Robert Tichborne set thy servants

[38] This list corresponds with that in *CJ*, VII, p. 605, but not that given by Burton (*Diary*, III, p. 311), which provides only ten names, and includes John Lambert.

[39] Presumably 'secret' is used in its seventeenth-century sense of confidential or non-public. The report was presented to the House on 7 April; for its text see *CJ*, VII, pp. 627–631.

[40] Postscript to a newsletter, probably from William Ross.

[41] The debate began on 19 February 1659; *ibid.*, p. 605.

[42] All this is confirmed by Burton, *Diary*, III, pp. 349–369. The debate was continued on 22 February (*ibid.*, pp. 403–424), and the Commons finally voted in favour of transacting business with the Other House on 8 March 1659; *CJ*, VII, p. 611.

[43] The regicide Robert Tichborne, at this time colonel of the yellow regiment of the London trained bands, was a staunch supporter of both Oliver and Richard Cromwell (*DNB*, 'Tichborne').

to watch upon the high gates of the city about the 10th hour or 1st watch of the night and <lo [besides]>[44] about the 12th hour or 2nd watch of the night there appeared to thy servants, 2 sons of men on horseback, and thy servants ~~asked who are~~ said unto them, who are you? And they answered and said, We are the watch. And thy servants <said>,[45] Nay, but we are the watch. And it came to pass that they resisted, so thy servants fell upon them and smote them hip and thigh[46] and took them and bound them and cast them into prison, at which his Highness particularly laughed at and dismissed them, giving the authority to be discharged.[47]

Newsletter from Westminster, 17 March 1659[48]

fo. [54]^{r}

Our affairs [above] at Westminster are very perplexed. God only can disintangle them to whom it is our duty seriously to commend them, there never being such a time of hazard upon all accounts. *You will heare how the Chaire has sent one Speaker sick & another has left itt by death, Sir Lislebone Longe who died yesterday, Mr Bampfeild is now in itt* to whom I wish better success. *Yesterday Colonel Overton was released & his imprisonment voted illegall & unjust, & Major General Boteler was before the House for some actions in the Major Generall-shippe which was referr'd. Doctor Hewett's lady has petitioned the House for the Murther (as shee termes itt) of her husband, & is to have an hearing on Wednesday sennight. The Scotch Members sitting was in debate this day.* Master Weaver this day told the Speaker that they had suffered the Scotch gentlemen to sit in the House only to see [. . .], and now they expected to continue. By this you may see the strain of the rest, he being as moderate as any.[49]

[44] Interlined.

[45] Interlined.

[46] Judges, XV. 8.

[47] I have discussed Richard's response to this case above (pp. 275–276).

[48] As shorthand and longhand are interspersed, I have reproduced this newsletter in full.

[49] Although Burton, who arrived in the House after this debate had started, records a speech by the staunchly republican John Weaver on this day, it does not contain these phrases; Burton, *Diary*, IV, pp. 164–165. The debate on the right of the Scottish MPs to sit in the House (of which Weaver was one of the instigators) ran from 11–21 March; *ibid.*, p. 76; *CJ*, VII, pp. 613–616. On the day on which the resolution was passed, 21 March, Weaver was one of those sent by the House to visit the dying former Speaker Challenor Chute at his home in the country; *ibid.*, p. 615.

News from [London], 24 March 1659[50]

fo. 61ʳ

After the vote was passed for the [sitting] of the Scotch and Irish Members,[51] Master Sadler told the Speaker in his speech that what was once made in an epitaph upon the earl of Strafford he might invert else. It was

Here lies vile[52] and valiant dust
Huddled up twixt fit and just.

and might now say

The Scotch commissioners here must sit
Huddled up twixt just and fit.

Newsletter from Robert Lilburne, 29 March 1659[53]

fo. 65ʳ

All things here look with a sadder countenance at present than they have done these many years. Many give the good old cause for lost, but our God is still the same and I hope will not leave us in this [wilderness] condition. It is said here that there will be a general meeting of officers, but at this distance I must not tell you when.[54] I think my great fear is the designs for *Ch[arles] St[uart]* under other vizards.

R. L.[55]

Robert Lilburne

[50] Possibly the postscript to a newsletter from J.C.

[51] The vote for retaining Irish members in the House was passed on 23 March 1659, two days after the lengthy debates on the rights of Scottish MPs to sit; *CJ*, VII, p. 619.

[52] The original, quoted in Burton's *Diary* (IV, pp. 156, 227), and taken from the 'Epitaph on the Earle of Strafford' by John Cleveland (*Poems by J.C. with Additions* (London, 1651), p. 47), reads 'wise' for 'vile'.

[53] Robert Lilburne, now governor of York, had been elected MP for New Malton in Richard's Parliament but lost the seat on 7 March; *CJ*, VII, p. 611.

[54] Presumably Lilburne is referring here to the meeting of the General Council of Officers which Richard Cromwell was persuaded to allow to go ahead on 2 April 1659; A. Woolrych, Introduction to *Complete Prose Works of John Milton*, VII, revised edn (New Haven and London, 1980), p. 62.

[55] These initials are written in shorthand rather than the longhand characters by which Clarke usually identified correspondents.

News from [G.M.], 29 March 1659[56]

fo. 68v

The marquis of Argyle[57] made a long speech in the House concerning religion and against sectaries and 5th Monarchy-men, which was [freely] answered by Sir Henry Vane.

Upon the vote for transacting with the Other House, a motion being made that one[58] Grove, a member of the Commons, should carry up the vote to the Other House, Master Sadler stood up and said he had spoken once before upon that business[59] but had now one word to add, that when the children of Israel were delivered out of Egypt they returned again to [. . .] worshipped Baal and set up a grove.[60]

News from [London], [8] April 1659

fo. [75]r

There was much debate in Parliament about passing this declaration[61] for the fast [as] things debated were, 1st because that liberty in religion is therein laid down as a ground of humiliation, 2. the imposing the fast upon all sorts.[62]

News from G.M., London, 14 April, 1659[63]

fo. 80v

The Newes concerning the Agreement betweene France & Spaine continues. An Expresse was sent from hence on Tuesday last into France to know the Certainty therof & to Returne with all Speede.

Major-General Boteler's business was debated in the House. He carries it very high which, if [he/it] persists in, the House will go

56 Probably the postscript to a newsletter from G.M., (Gilbert Mabbott?).

57 Argyle was MP for Aberdeenshire in Richard's parliament.

58 Blank.

59 Sadler's earlier remarks were recorded by Thomas Burton; Burton, *Diary*, IV, p. 279.

60 I Kings, XVI. 31–33.

61 Clarke added this note to a longhand transcription of the draft declaration; Worc. MS XXXI, fos 73r–[75]r), for which see also *CJ*, VII, pp. 623–624.

62 Thomas Burton's lengthy account of this debate (*Diary*, IV, pp. 300–345) is discussed in Hirst 'Concord and discord in Richard Cromwell's House of Commons', pp. 339–358.

63 Postscript to the letter printed in *CP*, III, pp. 189–190, most probably from Gilbert Mabbott.

near to deprive him of being capable hereafter of any trust, civil or military.[64]

Yesterday Mr Challenor Chute late Speaker in the Commons died.

Newsletter from A.J., [London], 19 April 1659[65]

fo. 84v

The inclosed votes came uppe to the House with Mr Stephen's this Morning & tooke uppe our House in Debate till 2 of the Clock whether wee should now take them into Consideration or delay it till after the Declaration of the fast was passed and the Malignants by proclamation removed from London. It was carryed by one voyce to consider them to morrow morning, and indeed their will be much debate upon them.[66] I pray the Lord God to dispel this cloud and to prevent the breaches and divisions which threateneth us so sadly.

fo. 85r

Wee heare alsoe the Officers are to meete alsoe amongst themselves to morrow morning. The Lord send a spirit of soberness and unity and amity both on the House and on the officers that their adversaries make not advantage of any mistakes and jealousies may arise amongst them.[67]

A.J.

The Lord Disbrowe and the Protector had very high words about the officers going from London.

[64] For this debate see *CJ*, VII, pp. 636–637; Burton, *Diary*, IV, pp. 403–412; *TSP*, VII, p. 653. The action of the Commons in prosecuting Boteler for offences against royalists caused offence and alarm in army circles; Hutton, *Restoration*, p. 36.

[65] Almost certainly from Archibald Johnston of Wariston, who attended the Other House on that day; Historical Manuscripts Commission, *The Manuscripts of the House of Lord*, IV NS (London, 1908), p. 563. I have reproduced the entire document, in which longhand alternates with shorthand.

[66] *Ibid*, pp. 562–563. The resolutions concerned the prohibition of unauthorized meetings of the General Council of Officers, and other restrictive measures to be imposed upon the army. A longhand copy of them precedes this letter – presumably taken from the enclosure referred to in line 1; Worc. MS XXXI, fo. 84r–v; *CJ*, VII, p. 641; *The Parliamentary or Constitutional History of England*. . . , 24 vols (London, 1751–1762), XXI, p. 348.

[67] On 18 April the House of Commons had prohibited meetings of the General Council of Officers held without the express permission of the Protector and of Parliament. They had also voted that every officer, on pain of dismissal, must sign a declaration against the forcible coercion of Parliament; *CJ*, VII, p. 1. The proposed meeting to be held on the 20th did not take place; Hutton, *Restoration*, p. 37. On 18 April, before the measure could be passed, Richard disbanded the General Council and ordered the officers to return to their regiments.

Colonel Ashfield told the Protector that he had surprized them <to [order] them to their charges so suddenly>.[68] His Highness answered that he could not be surprised that had not been with his regiment for 2 years.[69]
The militia troops sent for by the Lord Fleetwood to London.

Newsletter from London, 23 April 1659[70]

fo. 87v

Major-General Browne offered to raise 40,000 men for the securing and guarding of his Highness and Parliament, and he would see whether the army would oppose them, and he would have them ready in 24 hours' time. Some of the regiments of the army are also [there on].[71]

Some letters say that the Protector has lost both himself and friends.

The design laid by the commonwealthsmen in Parliament because they could not carry it against the Protector's establishment, and Sir Henry Vane and Sir Arthur Hesilrige met in council with the Lord Fleetwood and Lord Disbrowe, and there it was agreed that Fleetwood should be General of the Army, but the Parliament to grant commissions, the Long Parliament being to be returned though they [are/were] divided [two and two]. One insisted that he should grant commissions, the other considers not.[72]

It is said that the Lord Broghill persuaded his Highness to sign the commission for dissolution of the Parliament.[73]

[68] Interlined. The position of this insertion is not indicated in the original.

[69] A similar version of this exchange is quoted in Davies, *Restoration*, p. 81.

[70] Although it is just possible that this newsletter is a postscript to the immediately preceding letter, identified in shorthand as coming from Thomas Fitch (Appendix A below, p. 370) and printed in *CP*, III, p. 193, I have treated it as a separate document.

[71] Browne, already a royalist supporter (*CClar.SP*, IV, pp. 176, 178), would be involved in the royalist rising later that summer and promoted the restoration of Charles II in 1660 (*OxDNB* 'Sir Richard Browne'). Other offers of military backing to Richard at this time are described by J.A. Butler, *A Biography of Richard Cromwell*, (Lewiston, NY, 1994), p. 117.

[72] This meeting considerably antedates previously recorded contacts between the army leaders and the republican MPs. Hitherto it has been supposed that the officers procrastinated until early May before contacting. Hesilrige and Vane; Davies, *Restoration*, p. 88; Hutton, *Restoration*, pp. 39–40.

[73] Although it is usually believed that Richard yielded immediately to pressure from the army officers, this report may be authentic. Broghill, who left for Ireland on 29 April (according to Ludlow to get Henry Cromwell's support) was one of Richard's closest advisers; *TSP*, VII, p. 665; Ludlow, *Memoirs*, II, p. 61. Bulstrode Whitelocke, who was among those who advised Richard on this matter, recorded that Broghill was also consulted and that 'most were for the dissolving of the parliament' (Whitelock, *Memorials*, IV, p. 343), while Ludlow (*Memoirs*, II, p. 69) wrote that Richard had 'taken a little time to consider of it'.

Some debate amongst the officers that those that were put out of their commands by Oliver late Protector, or the Richard Protector without a court martial might be restored to their commands.

John Swinton,[74] [London], to [George Monck], 23 April 1659

fo. 88r

My Lord

It will appear to your Lordship from the inclosed declaration what is become of the Parliament.[75] I know your Lordship has an account from better hands what the late transactions have been these 2 or 3 days past. I have been so great a stranger to the particular managements of things as I dare not upon hearsay undertake to give your Lordship a particular account of them, only suppose the account I gave your Lordship some weeks ago doth by this time appear not to have been altogether groundless. We do now seem to be launched again into the depth. Where we shall land can hardly be foreseen. We are mighty still at present and things have been carried with a [structure] of [calmness] which considering the present juncture of affairs is no small happiness, for in such courses [confusion] above all things is to be diverted.

J.S.

John Swinton

William Ross, [London], to [George Monck], 23 April 1659

fo. 88r

May it please your Lordship

Since my last there hath nothing proceeded in the House butt a vote of Adjournement which past yesterday in the forenoone, whereby the House is adjourned till Munday next butt I suppose the Adjournement may prove longer because of the inclosed whereunto I shall not add anything but commit you and your affairs to the directing of the Almighty, wishing heartily that He may furnish your Lordship with direction in these difficult times that you may be

74 MP for Berwickshire in Richard's parliament.

75 Probably [Richard Cromwell], *By the Lord Protector. A Proclamation About Dissolving the Parliament* (London, 1659). Clarke's copy, perhaps that referred to here, survives at Worcester College.

able to distinguish and know your friends from others, and that all of us may lament for our sins and provocations which justly occasioned these symptoms of the Lord's rath thus threatened against us and these poor nations whose condition requires the prayers of all honest men. As for particulars I offer them to the relation of the more intelligent.[76]

William Ross

Newsletter from [London], 23 April 1659

fo. 88r

Upon the Thursday night as Colonel Ingoldsby's troop came marching to Whitehall, Captain [Merriman][77] meets them and asks the Captain-Lieutenant <[. . .]>[78] who he was for. He answered, for the Protector, and he said he was for the good old cause and the Commonwealth, and then dismissed him and then addressed himself to the troop and cried, Gentlemen all you that are for the good old cause and Commonwealth follow me and march to Whitehall according to my Lord Fleetwood's orders. The like was done by a lieutenant of the same regiment to Major Duckett who was marching upon the Lord Protector's orders to Whitehall[79] and Major[80] did the like and carried away 5 companies of Colonel Goffe's regiment who was marching by the Lord Protector's orders to Whitehall, telling them that he had something to do with them as [well did he] and desired all those that were for the good old cause to follow him.

Sir Charles [Wolseley][81] and Captain John Garner governour of Dunottar Castle died this week at London.

Newsletter from [London], 25 April 1659

fo. [90]r

This day being Monday, the time to which the House of Commons had adjourned themselfs, Sir Arthur Hesilrige went through Westminster Hall, and going up to the lobby to go into the House found the door shut and guarded with soldiers, and demanding entrance he was

[76] 'Intelligent' in the sense of being well-informed.

[77] Probably Capt. John Merriman of Col Ingoldsby's regiment.

[78] Interlined.

[79] Blank.

[80] Blank.

[81] The shorthand is somewhat unclear but appears to read 'Wolseley'. If so, this is an unfounded rumour. Wolseley, a member of Richard's Council, did not die until 1714 (*OxDNB*). Gardiner had been cashiered in May 1654; F&D, II, p. 538.

denied by some of the soldiers, whereupon he told them he came to do his duty to his country, to sit in Parliament, but they told him that they had orders that he must not enter. Whereupon he said, then, soldiers, you will have no Parliament, and they said no. To which he replied, then you must expect no money, and so went down. Sir Henry Vane was coming up the stairs with him but, hearing he was repulsed, went no further.

News from [London], 26 April 1659[82]

fo. 91v

[godly][83] new lords

Lord Fleetwood
Lord Disbrow
Lord Barkestead
Lord Cooper
Lord Hughson
Lord Sydenham
Colonel Lilburne
Colonel Ashfeild
Major General Kelsey
Colonel Clarke
Lord Berry

Newsletter from London, 29 April 1659

fo. 95v

The Treaty betwixt the 2 Crownes of France & Spaine is asserted by Letters to divers Merchants though nott fully owned by Politicus.[84] *A Decemvirate must sitt at Whitehall under the Notion of a Committee* whereof the Lord Bradshaw and Sir Henry Vane they say must be 2. The Fifth Monarchy men are now very active for the Kingdom of Christ and [here is a very choice] at this present, but we cannot discern who may probably produce the

[82] It is just possible that this is the postscript to the letter of 26 April from John Thurloe which is printed in *CP*, III, p. 195. Thurloe is identified in shorthand as the sender of that letter; Appendix A, p. 370.

[83] In a small sample of three words it is impossible to be sure which of several possible equivalents, for example the figure 9, is intended here. The outline most closely resembles that for 'godly', but is not quite typical.

[84] Marchamont Nedham (dismissed on 13 May 1659) was still the editor of the official newsbook *Mercurius Politicus*; Davies, *Restoration*, p. 3n.

[least] good out of that heap of [evil]. The Lord Protector, 'tis likely, will be laid aside, and Fleetwood is already addressed unto by the title of Excellency. Ambition it seems will acknowledge no kindred, or any former favours put a lasting obligation upon thankless spirits. Many here stand at a gaze and wonder when the Israelites can be able to settle, in regard they have no basis to bottom on but the pretence of the good old cause, and the removal of the old Parliament. Here is talk of a new Lieutenant of the Tower, but little can be resolved on till Monck, Mountagu, and the Lord Henry declare themselfs.[85]

Major Babington suspend[ed] and Colonel Grosvenor confined to his chambers, who it seems were active against the officers in their late actings.[86]

Sir James MacDowall to Colonels Syler and Lytcott, 30 April 1659

fo. 96^{r}

London, last April

Much Honoured

I understand from Master Clarke that he has been interceding with you for offering Francis [Steer/Steel/Stell] in his place, and with all desired me to consent unto it. He seems to undertake much for his faithfulness wherefore knowing he would be very unwilling that any person unworthy or unfaithful should be owned by you, I am very apt to have charitable thoughts of Master [Steer/Steel/Stell] as being no wise known to me but by report, and therefore if you think fit to [confer] or restore him I shall be satisfied. This being all for present, I am

your most humble servant

James MacDowall[87]

For the much honoured Colonel Syler
and Colonel Lydcott[88] at Leith

[85] Just over one month later Col John Barkstead was arrested and on 10 June 1659 was replaced as Lieutenant of the Tower by 'Haslerigge's creature', Col Thomas Fitch; *Mercurius Politicus*, 570 (2–9 June 1659) p. [496]; Whitelock, *Memorials*, IV, p. 351.

[86] See Davies, *Restoration*, p. 86.

[87] Sir James MacDowall of Garthland was MP for Wigtonshire in Richard's parliament. By July 1659 he was at Leith; Worc. MS LI, fo. 82^{r-v}. See also Dow, *Cromwellian Scotland*, esp. p. 288n.

[88] i.e. Col Leonard Lytcott.

News from G.M., [London], 30 April 1659[89]

fo. 96v

Captain Elsmore putt out of imployment about the business of Mistress Green, by whom it is said he had 2 children etc.[90]

Colonel Lilburne, Colonel Hacker, Colonel Salmon and Colonel Ashfield for the returning of the Long Parliament, Fleetwood and Desbrowe said to be against it.

Conversation with Major Goodrick, 2 May 1659

fo. [97]v

Discourse with Major Goodrick[91]

That he came away from London the day after the dissolving of the Parliament, that Sir Arthur Hesilrige, Sir Henry Vane and others of the commonwealth party did in several speeches in the House exclaim against the proceedings of the officers in [drawing up] a force to Whitehall to inforce the Lord Protector, and so to dissolve the Parliament. And that the Lord Fairfax was much of the same mind, and that the Lord Lambert spoke most moderately of the business but at last concluded that it was not to be excused.

That being at the meeting of the officers when Lieutenant-Colonel Moss brought in the paper from the late Lord Pride's regiment he asked who stood next him [when] the common soldiers [...] for the good old cause for that most of them are cavaliers and for Charles Stuart's party, that thereupon Major Farley overhearing them was ready to draw upon him.[92]

89 Postscript to a newsletter, probably from Gilbert Mabbott; the letter and first few words of this excerpt are found in *CP*, III, p. 196.

90 Elsmore was to be arrested for his involvement in the abortive Royalist uprisings planned for the beginning of the following August; *ibid.*, IV, p. 37; *Publick Intelligencer*, 188 (1–8 Aug. 1659), pp. 629–630.

91 Presumably Maj. William Goodrick, a staunch supporter of Richard Cromwell, who had served in Cromwell's Scottish campaign of 1650–1651 and had remained there under Monck. He would therefore have been known to both Monck and Clarke; Worc. MS XXXI, fo. [12]r; Ludlow, *Memoirs*, II, pp. 61–62; F&D, I, pp. 256, 259–260, 263; C.A. Goodricke, *History of the Goodricke Family* (London, 1885), p. 47. The conversation recorded here apparently took place between Goodrick and Monck, Clarke himself also being present. Monck may well by this time have already learnt of the fall of the Parliament by a letter from Charles Fleetwood dated 23 April 1659; *L-P*, pp. 115–116.

92 The 'paper' was probably *To His Excellency the Lord Fleetwood, and the General Council of Officers: The humble Address of the Inferiour Officers and Souldiers of the Late Lord Pride's Regiment* (London, 1659), written and printed on 7 or 8 April; Burton, *Diary*, IV, pp. 388–389n. It appears that there had been a meeting of officers on the same day. The General Council

That he could never observe there was above 40 voices in the House of Commons for the old Commonwealth's way and that when the commonwealthsmen saw that the young gentlemen of estates would not accept of the new [~~. . . .~~] in expectation to bring in the old peers they would not go any further in that business but left it, but all the while before they got them to joyn with them.

That only himself and the Lord Chancellor Disbrowe were of the negatives in the business of Portman's or Colonel Overton['s] imprisonment by the late Protector to be illegal and [unjust] being he was General and that it might question all commands of soldiers.[93]

That they intend to have a committee of inspections to put a black mark upon all those that are not of some gathered church.

That upon the occasion of the [. . .] of officers of the Lord Lambert, Colonel Sanders, Colonel Okey etc., he said that his major should be removed as well as he.[94] And when I spoke of their regiments coming in he said he could not tell whether it would be my Lord Falconbridge's and my Lord Lambert's and that it may be they might think of [Colonel] Lilburne to command in Scotland in case they should remove the Lord General and then he would let the Scots beat him out of the castle as he did formerly.[95]

That he could not tell what would be the occasion of the dissolving of this late Parliament unless it were the questioning of some men about the act for the propagation of the gospel in south Wales. Also upon the pretence of raising money for that had gained estates of 500*l* a year out of nothing.

That ~~the Parliament might have raised~~ there was 150,000*l* in the hands of the excise men about London which the Parliament were in a way of getting in and now he thought they would not [give] 20,000*l*.

fo. [98]ʳ

That he could never observe any of the commonwealthsmen in the House to speak anything against the choice of the present Protector but that Sir Arthur Hesilrige himself said in a speech that he was a person without gall and without guile.[96]

had sent a petition to Richard on the 6th which was referred by him to both Houses on the 8th. Both Moss and Farley were supporters of the commonwealth faction; Farley was major in Goffe's regiment at this time, while Moss had assumed command of Col Pride's regiment sometime after Pride died in October 1658; Davies, *Restoration*, p. 74; F&D, I, pp. 333, 371.

[93] For these debates see Burton's *Diary*, III, pp. 494–498; IV, pp. 150–161.

[94] Goodrick had served in Lambert's regiment; F&D, I, p. 259.

[95] Lilburne acted as commander-in-chief in Scotland from March 1653 to April 1654 (*SS*, p. 38).

[96] Burton, *Diary*, III, pp. 104, 112.

Major Goodrick came with a letter from the Lord Fauconbridge to the Lord General that he shall give credence unto him and that what he should ingage he would make good with his life.[97]

His Lordship answered him that his Highness having dissolved the Parliament he could not adhere to him, declaring that himself and most of the officers here are for returning the old <Long>[98] Parliament and to keep things in peace.[99]

He said that when the vote came for the proclaiming of <papists and>[100] cavaliers to remove from London or 20 miles off that there was not one negative voice, whereas in former Parliaments there had been some debates that they might have their freedoms as well as others, being that they had paid for it and were brought into the same capacity with others.[101]

Memorandum, 7 May 1659

fo. 104^{v}

This day Master Underwood, one of the gentlemen belonging to his Highness, came with a letter from his Highness to General Monck at Dalkeith.[102] The purport was to give him a brief account of affairs and to advice [*sic*] him that[103] would not desire any to answer another for him further than might consist with the peace of the nations.[104]

Upon discourse with Master Underwood, I find that his Highness condescended to these and the commission for dissolving the late Parliament upon the importunity of the Lord Fleetwood, Lord Disbrowe etc., who told him that it was the advice of his father's best friends and that it should not be any prejudice to him, that otherwise all would be lost, that thereupon his Highness chose rather to adhere to the army, his father's old friends, then the Parliament and

[97] I have discussed the possible contents of Fauconberg's letter in my introduction to this chapter, pp. 274–275.

[98] Interlined.

[99] Hitherto there has been no evidence to suggest that Monck knew about the imminent collapse of the Protectorate until the day after this conversation, 3 May; Dow, *Cromwellian Scotland*, p. 240.

[100] Interlined.

[101] *CJ*, VII, p. 642.

[102] This was not the first time that Underwood, a gentleman of the bedchamber to both Richard and Oliver Cromwell, had been employed by Richard as a trusted personal messenger; Sherwood, *Court of Oliver Cromwell*, pp. 70–72.

[103] The word 'he' is omitted but clearly intended.

[104] Some three and a half lines left blank here.

all the new friends in the several parts of the nation which had made addresses to him.

That now he was resolved to sit still and look on.

Marginal annotation [7] May 1659[105]

fo. 107ᵛ

. . . *They have passed a Declaration to set forth the reasons of their Convening, and to assert the Government of the Nation to be in a free State and Commonwealth and have ordered Letters to be sent to all their Members that are qualifyed to invite them to attend the service of the house* . . . .

<Like a [warren] of witches amongst the [. . .] supreme [. . .] so [. . .] is the single [person].>[106]

Army officers in Scotland to the General Council of Officers, London, 9 May 1659[107]

fo. 106ʳ

Answer of the Lord General's, Colonel Talbot's and Colonel Wilkes' regiments to the letter from his Excellency the Lord Fleetwood and the Council of the Officers at Wallingford House dated 3rd May 1659.

Right Honourable and Worthy Friends

Yours of
the 3rd instant with the inclosed papers directed to Colonel Wilkes to be communicated to the Lord General's his own and Colonel Talbot's regiments was sent unto us by the right honourable[108] the Lord General Monck with his desire to be communicated as directed, which was performed accordingly. By which together with your actions have evidenced the[109] sense of the late declining state of the good old cause and of the reviving it now seems to have in your spirits with your

[105] The longhand newsletter to which this poorly written marginal note is attached, probably from Thomas Clarges, begins with a report of the reinstatement by the army of the Rump Parliament. I have reproduced only the sentence to which it refers.

[106] Marginated.

[107] This letter is printed in *Mercurius Politicus*, 568 (19–26 May 1659), pp. 461–462, where its date is given as 10 May. It pre-dates the letter from Monck to Fleetwood which is printed in *TSP*, VII, pp. 669–670. The letter from the General Council of Officers to which it is a reply is printed in *CP*, IV, pp. 4–6.

[108] *Mercurius Politicus*, 568, p. 461, omits 'the right honourable'.

[109] *Ibid.* reads 'your' for 'the'.

declared resolutions to pursue it in which our hearts are mutually knit unto you as to those who of necessity and love to your country (as we hope) and not novelty or faction have ingaged to expose your all and the whole army to jeopardy for the recovery of that almost lost cause which had many seals of divine presence with it of old, when it was witnessed unto by much blood and the expense of much treasure, but sithence[110] near wholly involved into a particular, and not (as intended) the interest of the publike. And that you have appeared at this season when no ways[111] else was left for the securing the interest of that cause and[112] good people of these nations from utter ruin. Whereby (we trust) you have frustrated the plots of the common enemy and their accomplices.[113] How ever they are reputed as friends or have laid their designs, is esteemed a mercy. All which have wrought the like sense in us in some measure as in you and ingaged us to inquire what have been the causes the nations in all their intended settlements have met with such disappointments in their counsels and actions at home and abroad as by the loss of that presence formerly found in both has for some years past been sadly experienced. And now having taken notice of your prudent and friendly advice to lay these proceedings[114] to heart and to indeavour love and union amongst ourselfs towards you which[115] brotherly counsel we accept with thankfulness, and resolve by the assistance of God to be found unanimously practical therein, desiring that you with us will really prosecute those things you have now once more declared for. And that you go on to improve the opportunity now in your hands, that so the nations and the good interest thereof may be secured upon that foundation of Parliamentary government which you and we have avowed so often to stand for. And as an expedient for the effecting thereof we humbly advise that the Long Parliament dissolved the[116] 20th of April 1653 be readmitted to assemble and exercise their legal authority as the probable way left after all our wanderings for the establishing of truth and peace in this Commonwealth to us and our posterity, with all just rights and privileges in matters essential to our well-being as men and Christians, and that God may direct and prosper you in all your good undertakings shall be the prayers of

your loving friends[117] and fellow soldiers

[110] *Ibid.*, 'since'.
[111] *Ibid.*, 'way'.
[112] *Ibid.* inserts 'the'.
[113] *Ibid.*, 'Complices'.
[114] *Ibid.*, p. 462 reads 'providences' for 'proceedings'.
[115] *Ibid.* reads 'that with' for 'which'.
[116] *Ibid.* omits 'the'.
[117] *Ibid.* reads 'Your humble and faithful Servants and fellow Soldiers'.

News from G.M., [London], 12 May 1659[118]

*fo. 119^r^*

Sir George Booth, Colonel Rossiter, Mr Prynne, Members of the old parliament attempted to goe into the House butt were Turn'd back by Adjutant Generall Allen.[119] Divers of the old Protector's ministers prayed that God would return the banished.

News from G.D., The Hague, 13 May 1659[120]

*fo. 121^v^*

If I had a [charger] I could let you know that our common enemy is now might and main at work. I pray God we may enough apprehend it.

News from G.M., Westminster, 17 May 1659[121]

*fo. 122^v^*

The Councill of State was yesterday perfected – consisting of 31 – 21 whereof were of the House & ten out of itt, and amongst others my Lord Warston is nominated a Councellour. Swinton was in competition with him and some say Argyle, but the old man carried it.[122]

News from T.C., [London], 19 May 1659[123]

*fo. 124^r^*

A petition on foot by some troopers for the increase of their pay from 2*s* 6*d* a day to be presented to the Parliament, which occasioned the Parliament to sit till 12 a clock at night to debate about some way for payment of the arrears in the army.[124]

118 Postscript to a longhand newsletter from G.M. (probably Gilbert Mabbott).

119 See Hutton, *Restoration*, pp. 43–44.

120 Postscript to a longhand letter from G.D., probably George Downing.

121 Postscript to a longhand letter, probably from Gilbert Mabbott.

122 Wariston claimed that he had tried to have the marquis of Argyle elected as the member for Scotland; J.D. Ogilvie (ed.), *Diary of Sir Archibald Johnston of Wariston 1655–1660*, III (Scottish History Society, 3rd ser., XXXIV, 1940), p. 113.

123 Postscript to a longhand newsletter, probably from Thomas Clarges.

124 *CJ*, VII, pp. 658–661.

Newsletter from [London], 2 June 1659

fo. [135][v]

There are jealousies in the house of the high, their speaking of Sir Henry Vane, Sir Arthur Hesilrige [are] grown already to that heighth as reported that what is moved by them is looked on as an opposing and so opposed, at best suspected, in the army. The Lord Lambert's growing greatness narrowly observed by Fleetwood[125] and Disbrowe, and those jealousies heated by bringing in Sir Henry Vane's eldest son to be a cornet in the army and the [new/now] intended alliance twixt him and Lord Lambert's daughter. But whether there be any certain grounds for this last I cannot aver. The army it self is in no good posture as having seen too much of their own strenth and by too busy hands, a little over much concerning themselfs with what is [beyond] their [sphere] but they have not been of late overprudently managed in the judgement of some, which gives them [new/now] occasion to be extravagant. The reins of discipline has been so much slacked that they have got the bit between their teeth and thereby become not so easily guided. The form of civil government is as hotly and highly debated amongst them in several juntos as by whom it should properly belong to debate those things, so that what the result of these debates may be God only knows. Under the act of indemnity some of them have offered unto the House several exceptions wherein they have appeared very partial, which much impairs the spirit of their justice and at the best brings matters to this unhappy issue, that if what they offer be accepted the world will look on the Parliament as acting under a force.[126] If [in reason rejected] it may lessen the good understanding that may be betwixt them and the Parliament. For all men are apt naturally to magnify their own results and to be angry with those that joyn not issue with them therein. This city more highly malignant than ever, the Presbyterian ministers neither prudent nor discreet, nor as some say good Christians, and they may in time see it and sorrow for it, though at present not taken notice of. Colonel Lockhart is expected this night from Dunkirk.[127] 3 commissioners for Ireland are also coming. The Dutch press us to a peace, in order

[125] Parliament appointed Fleetwood commander-in-chief of the army on 7 June 1659, (*ibid.*, p. 674).

[126] After passing its first and second readings on 23 May the act of indemnity was finally passed, after many postponements and delays, on 12 July 1659; Davies, *Restoration*, pp. 112–113; *CJ*, VII, p. 714.

[127] On 27 May the Council of State had acceded to Lockhart's request of 17 May that he might return to London on condition that he did so immediately; *TSP*, VII, p. 671; *CSPD 1658–1659*, p. 359; his arrival was widely reported, for example by *Mercurius Politicus*, 570 (2–9 June 1659), pp. 487–488.

whereunto Lord Whitelocke, Colonel Sidney and Colonel Berry are appointed plenipotentiaries to go to the Sound to meet with the Dutch ambassadour and so determine on all things there, the treaty betwixt France and Spain being equally dangerous to Holland as Portugal.[128] And who knows but that they are both agreed that the French shall not assist the Portugal against Spain, or Spain the Provinces against France, which perhaps makes the Dutch crave our alliance. But be it what it will, it's hoped we shall not reject it if it be to be had upon good terms. Yesterday the earl of [. . .] petition was read and laid aside, and perhaps he will stir no more in it.

The Common Council of London attended the House this day with an address.[129] Their (16) keep good correspondence with Sir Henry Vane and Lord Lambert, old friends, as well as Lord Fleetwood and Disbrowe. Captain Smith's business will breed some debate though he has many very good friends seriously ingaged for him. Colonel Whetham not yet returned from Portsmouth or there settled. Nothing done in Scotch business towards settlement of that nation [and/no] [we/true] wonder seeing so little is yet done towards settlement of ourselfs in England and charity begins at home. Tomorrow is the 1st day of the term, and the courts of Westminster not yet settled.

News from G.M., [London], 11 June 1659[130]

*fo. 142^v^*

Colonel Talbot had been outed had it not been for my Lord General's letter to the Speaker[131] which kept in him and some other officers in Scotland, though 2 of the captains of my Lord General's regiment of horse were accused as tipplers particularly Captain Johnston, as was mentioned in my Lord Lambert's letter.[132]

[128] *Ibid.*, pp. 485–486, reports that the commissioners had not yet been appointed by 4 June, two days after this letter was written. Whitelocke excused himself, and the three who were appointed were Sidney, Honeywood, and Thomas Boone; Whitelock, *Memorials*, IV, pp. 351–352; *CJ*, VII, pp. 677, 695, 700. The treaty between France and Spain would be signed on 28 October 1659.

[129] *Mercurius Politicus*, 569 (26 May–2 June 1659), p. 485.

[130] Postscript to the newsletter, most probably from Gilbert Mabbott, printed in *CP*, IV, pp. 19–20.

[131] For Monck's letter to the Speaker see *ibid.*, pp. 16–17. It was not until 27 September 1659 that the composition of Talbot's regiment was finally approved; *CJ*, VII, p. 787.

[132] On the changes made to Monck's regiment at this time see F&D, II, pp. 539–540.

News from [Neason], London, 14 June 1659[133]

fo. 144r

I received a letter written with your own hand dated the 7th of June instant subscribed by a person whom I much honour and render my humble thanks to him for his good acceptance of that mentioned in your letter. I will not take the boldness to write to him. You may if you please communicate what followeth unto him but to none else, and then dispose the letter to the fire for these times are jealous, and though a man give a plain narrative of matter of fact yet offence may be taken though none intended. Besides many of that person's letters have been opened at Theobalds at the post house there which made me at that time though upon a great and sudden change forbear to give you a brief account of affairs, but since I perceive by your letter it will be acceptable, take in good part this insuing narrative:

As soon as the Army had obtayned his last Highness' consent That noe Officer should be putt out of his Command butt by a Councill of Warre They then fell uppon matter of agitation a Parliament sitting which in few dayes after produced a Representacion from the Army to to [*sic*] *his Highnesse subscribed by many that never read itt & others that* did not know of your action in it. *Itt was communicated to the parliament & did hold forth to the World* that they were resolved to pluck out of places of trust etc. a *phrase practically knowne in the Army by pulling of Members formerly out, soe that from that time the Parliament concluded the Army will bee att the old Trade againe.*[134] *Butt to wipe the shame off themselves they pressed one night till 3 of the Clock in the Morning soe hard uppon the Protector that att last hee was constrayned to signe a Commission to dissolve the Parliament much against his minde, for that hee as well as the Nation knew they were a Parliament of as gallant Spiritts to preserve the Rights, Liberties, and properties of the people, as ever satt in Parliament yett the House of Commons, hearing the commission was come to dissolve them, & Troopes of Horse brought before both Houses which they looked uppon as a force uppon them as had bin that night before uppon the Protector and being exceedingly dissatisfied with some Grand Lords of the other House Members of the Army who procured that Commission to dissolve the Parliament they did scorne to owne their Lordshippe, though sent for, butt in a great fury adjourned till Munday following on which day the Commons came againe, butt a Company of Red-Coates* commonly called the keepers

[133] The longhand portions of this newsletter which appear in *CP*, IV, pp. 20–22, are interspersed throughout with shorthand and I have reproduced it in its entirety. From the first paragraph it appears to be addressed to an intermediary acting for Monck, possibly Clarke himself.

[134] Sir Charles Firth (*ibid.*, p. 20n) noted that 'in the Army's petition they speak of "plucking the wicked out of their places"' (quoting from *OPH*, XXI, p. 338).

of the liberties of England *were placed att the Parliament doore, and would nott lett the Members goe in, and now the Word was given through the Army by the Grandees of the Army before mentioned. That they should stand to the Good Old Cause, and the Good Peticion & Advice, which had setled 1,500,000li. per annum to maintaine the Army, and to limitt a Single Person in nature of a duke of Venice. Butt these Army Grandees who had thus forced the Protector and dissolved a Gallant Parliament were Trapanned, and that deservedly by the Inferiour Officers of the Army, who kept their Councill apart att St James's, with whom the Churches did att that time Confederate, and Swayed downe the Designe of those Grandees, & cryed uppe the Setting up of a Governement in nature of an Oligarchy of 70 wise/good*

fo. 144[v]

good men, which was backed by Colonel Titchborne (now nott so famous as then), and from divers of the Congregated Churches; butt the Cry was great against itt, as a thinge the people of England would nott bee bound by, soe att last the Churches were wrought over (by the persuasion as it is thought of Sir Henry Vane on whom they chiefly depend) *to restore the Longe Parliament which tooke Effect, and they mett accordingly* and are labouring hard for a being in order to a wellbeing, but they have a hard game to play, taking upon them a debt by taking upon them to be a Parliament of 2,400,000*l* yet should be inforced to lay a great tax upon the 3 nations when people are already so sufficiently discontented besides the press being at liberty without comptrol. *Desperate Bookes and other thinges are writt & published* exclaiming against the Parliament and their proceedings and [possessing] the people that this nation can never be settled in a firm peace till some of the old family be restored, as Master Prynne and others have publicly owned, *who have stated another Good old Cause as hee calls itt* upon the royal account contrary to the good old cause stated by the army *and these thinges are suffered to goe abroad without Question.*[135] *Itt is nott fitt for a private pen to reprove a Parliament otherwise one might with Submission say. They suffer by such permission.* That which adds to the greatest discontent of the army is that *about 160 Officers, Colonells, Lieutenant Colonells, Majors, Captains, Lieutenants, Cornetts, Ensignes, & Quartermasters are putt out of their Commands without hearing, without charge, without Tryall* and those (7) of the army who are imployed upon that unacceptable service are under that secrecy that they must not let a man know whether he is in or out till another comes in his place and be appointed of and put in and the Parliament is kept blindfold therein, not knowing who they put out

[135] A month earlier *The Faithfull Scout* had reported that 'Mr Prin hath declared some dislike against the present Government, terming the Good Cause, to be an Instant Cause, and the Government of King, Lords and Commons, to be the Good Old Cause'; *Faithfull Scout*, 3 (6–13 May 1659), p. 241.

so that this unexamined way of proceedings gives high and mighty discontent.[136] *The Parliament have Setled Commissioners for the management of the businesse of the Navy* but General Mountagu is not named in the act for that business, so it is supposed he is not intended to be confirmed to be a commander at sea and his regiment at land is disposed of to another who is still in the Sound. *Noe newes from Ireland butt that Commissioners are going thither to command that Nation, & a lettre is to bee sent on purpose for the Lord Harry to come over* in what posture he [is turns but] not certainly here. *Wee take itt for granted That the peace is concluded betweene Spaine & France.* My Lord Fairfax sits neither at the Parliament house nor at the Council. The letter he lately received from your friend in Scotland he communicated to some Members to observe your friend's desire therein, but I believe same course will be taken with them in Scotland as here in England when they think fit to fall upon business, for the letter to the Parliament concerning the 3 regiments therein marched did not procure an answer suitable to the request. In brief there is an evil councillor called necessity <(which of necessity)>[137] some say should be made use of at this time which lords all over all rule and order.

14 June 1659, London
[Neason][138]

News from G.M., [London], 16 June 1659[139]

fo. [144a]r

It is observable that the greatest countenancers of the petitioners against tithes and those who brought them into the House is Sir Henry Blunt who is reputed to arrest one that said that the Kingdom was only meant [to consider people in [two/zeal]].[140]

Lieutenant-General Ludlow

[136] For the seven commissioners for the nomination of officers appointed by Parliament on 12 May see below, p. 306.

[137] Interlined.

[138] Unfortunately this important signature is blurred in the original. It may in any case, in view of the cryptic tone of the letter, be a *nom de guerre*.

[139] Postscript to a longhand newsletter, probably from Gilbert Mabbott.

[140] Blunt was one of those who presented such a petition from the county of Hertfordshire on 21 June 1659; *CJ*, VII, p. 690.

William Cary, [London], to [William Clarke], 22 June 1659

fo. [146]v

It is a great shame that his Highness should be so much abused, for openly in the streets do women cry his Highness' picture which is in this manner, an owl in a fowl's coat sitting on a horse.[141]

W.C.

William Cary

Satirical pamphlet, [28] June 1659[142]

fo. 159v

Several resolves prepared by the commanding junto to pass the House

Resolved

That the Warr with Spaine bee continued in regard it multiplies the number of beggars in the Nation, and consequently wee shall have good souldiers cheape to advance the work of reformation being it was[143] received as an orthodox tradition that broken merchants make excellent sword men.

<Resolved>[144] that since we can produce no more wise men then what is in[145] Parliament and Council of State or[146] no other militia than 4,000 horse and foot in London that all the rest of the nation be declared carnal and guilty of sequestrations.[147]

<Resolved>[148] that since the present militia are so accustomed to unhouse parliaments, we establish a country militia under pretence

[141] William Clarke's unique copy of this print showing Richard Cromwell, now in Worcester College library, was reproduced as the frontispiece to *CP*, III. See also Sheila O'Connell, *The Popular Print in England 1550–1850* (London, 1999), pp. 122, 168 and colour plate III. I am very grateful to Kate Colleran and Sheila O'Connell for discussions about the print.

[142] This is a copy of the anonymous satirical pamphlet *Several Resolves prepared by the Commanding Junto to pass the House*, provisionally dated by Thomason to 14 June 1659; Fortescue, II, p. 241. There is no copy of the printed version at Worcester College. See Hutton, *Restoration*, pp. 48, 307n.

[143] *Several Resolves*. . . , 'is'.

[144] Marginated.

[145] *Ibid.* inserts 'the'.

[146] *Ibid.*, 'nor'.

[147] *Ibid.* omits the final 's'.

[148] Marginated.

of suppressing the cavaliers and shuffle them out or force them upon some desperate outlandish design and so their arrears shall be paid by their ruin.

Resolved that in regard those water Christians of the fleet are a kind of giddy headed fellows and possibly for want of pay may be apt to return to the obedience of Charles Stuart, that there be forthwith an order made to pay them out of the excise and customs[149] of the Jamaica commodities and in the interim that Lawson be presently sent to divide the navy and shave[150] them off their pay with Parson Peters' old cheats.

Resolved that whereas[151] whimsy buzzes in the brains[152] of the officers it be adjudged the sense of the private soldiery though they never be consulted with in the business.

Resolved that all such officers as can pretend to be gentlemen be turned off in regard they may retain some dregs of the old English honour and liberty which is destructive to the present work.

Resolved that the army (except that in Scotland and Ireland and in the fleet at sea) for their good and faithful service to the good old cause be rewarded with the House's livery *vizt* blue coats and that that mark of the beast and abomination of the land[153] their old red coats with black buttons of the gift of the late tyrant be taken off and hung up by the Scots colours in Westminster Hall in token of victory and in the 1st year of[154] restoration of[155] liberty.

Resolved that the soldiers be new shoed at the Commonwealth's charges[156] and that my lord Hewson, that experienced artificer be intrusted with the sale of their old commodities to the end the Commonwealth may not be defrauded or deceived and that the money arising from the sale of them do go towards the satisfaction of their arrears.

fo. 160r

Resolved that if the army do not unhouse, molest or disturb us that we assume our former authority and make them our slaves to fight our battles as formerly while we injoy the fat of the land, for it is a

149 *Ibid.*, p. 4, 'custom'.

150 *Ibid.*, 'stave'.

151 *Ibid.*, 'whatsoever'.

152 Indistinguishable from 'veins' in Clarke's shorthand, but confirmed by the printed version.

153 *Ibid.*, 'lord'.

154 *Ibid.* inserts 'the'.

155 *Ibid.* inserts 'our'.

156 *Ibid.*, 'charge'.

great grief of heart to us and a quenching of the spirit to be awed as servants that formerly ruled as princes.

Resolved that if the city will once more give down their milk for the promoting of the good old cause (which in the heat of their zeal they so[157] extolled, set up, preached, prayed and fought for, though to their great loss and repentance) that Master Peters (after [our/his][158] long and illegal divorce made betwixt them and us by the late tyrant Oliver) do again marry and unite us the Parliament of England and the city, that the wedding be kept in[159] Guildhall, that a banquet be provided at the Commonwealth's charge and that all committee men, sequestrators and excise men, informers, and our[160] self-seeking saints of the race of Judas (our good and faithful servants) be there and assisting[161] us in the carrying on of that great work.

Resolved that there be a restraint upon presbytery as well as popery and prelacy because it some what resembles Christianity.

Resolved that there be a collection of the several addresses to the late tyrant and his son and placed amongst Tredeskin's monsters[162] to perpetuate the infamy of all the powers both ecclesiastick and civil and military[163] that have governed England these[164] 5 years.

Resolved that Master William Prynne (provided he will forbear to set his and our sins before us) be restored to his seat[165] in the House and[166] to his recordership of the city of Bath.

Resolved that Henry Cromwell, Lord Lieutenant[167] of Ireland and son of the late tyrant, do continue his absolute power and command until the House can take it from him and dispose of it other ways.[168]

Resolved that the late Lord Protector's[169] relations or kindred that did any ways[170] act against his interest in the promotion of the good old cause be rewarded and to that purpose Sir[171] Whimsy Mildmay

[157] *Ibid.*, p. 5 inserts 'highly'.
[158] Replaced in *ibid.* by 'this'.
[159] *Ibid.* inserts 'the'.
[160] *Ibid.* reads 'other' for 'our'.
[161] *Ibid.*, 'assist'.
[162] A reference to John Tradescant (1608–1662), traveller, collector, and gardener, for whom see *OxDNB*.
[163] *Several Resolves*. . . , p. 6, 'ecclesiastical, civil and military'.
[164] *Ibid.*, 'this'.
[165] *Ibid.* reads 'do sit' for 'be restored to his seat'.
[166] *Ibid.* inserts 'return'.
[167] *Ibid.* reads 'Lord Deputy' for 'Lord Lieutenant'.
[168] *Ibid.* reads 'otherwise' for 'other ways'.
[169] *Ibid.* omits 'Lord'.
[170] *Ibid.*, 'way'.
[171] *Ibid.* reads 'Mr' for 'Sir'.

the bauble keeper is to consult with the remains of Archee for such a distinguishable habit as may be suitable to their merit.

Resolved that when the city marshall and the sheriffs' beagles go a whore-hunting they pass over the seraglio[172] of Henry Marten and Master Scot, our fellow members, as two qualified nunneries to cool the concupiscence of the saints.

fo. 160v

Resolved that the 5,000*l* which the city appointed for feasting his late highness and new house of peers be distributed in Bedlam and Bridewell as most[173] indigent fools and knaves.

Resolved that money[174] addresses be voted neither fast or loose.

Resolved that if their Catholike and Christian majesties shall[175] after this general peace enterprise a croysada and begin with England as the most[176] adjacent infidels that Master Manton (the Presbyterian) who is so large a benefactor of the devils be appointed to excommunicate them as malignants and enemies to tender consciences.

Resolved that the tyrant's design in helping the Swede our fellow labourer in all[177] villainous oppression be still supported with the expence of English blood and treasure.

Resolved that there be no support or[178] supplies sent to the poor English soldiers at Jamaica that are rotting there until they send a considerable parcel of pineapples, *Tartufolij*,[179] eringoes,[180] to fortify the decayed concupiscence of the decayed lecheries.[181]

Resolved that the House[182] take it into their consideration whether our present government may not be thought like that of the Romans under Nero and Heliogabulus when Henry[183] Neville sometime an eminent bardash[184] in Italy is now so great a favourite to[185] the state.

[172] *Ibid.*, 'seraglios'.

[173] *Ibid.* substitutes 'at more' for 'as most'.

[174] *Ibid.* reads 'Monck's addresses'.

[175] *Ibid.*, p. 7 places 'shall' after 'general peace'.

[176] *Ibid.* inserts 'near'.

[177] *Ibid.* omits 'all'.

[178] *Ibid.* reads 'sort of' for 'support or'.

[179] From the Italian 'tartuffo', truffle, implying concealment or hypocrisy (*OED*). *Several Resolves* . . ., p. 7 reads 'Gartuffoli and'.

[180] Eryngo, the candied root of the sea-holly, once used as a sweetmeat and regarded as an aphrodisiac (*OED*).

[181] *Ibid.*, 'of the famous state lechers'.

[182] *Ibid.* adds 'do'.

[183] *Ibid.* reads 'Harry Neville'.

[184] *Ibid.*, 'Burdash'.

[185] *Ibid.* reads 'of' for 'to'.

Resolved that these resolves[186] be forthwith printed that the nation may see the glorious result of all their blood and treasure that has been spent since they betrayed their liberties to their slaves.

Advertisement to the soldiery:

Take notice that there is no way left in this hard[187] dispensation of tyranny to the whole nation of England to represent their grievances both[188] with the hazard of their lives to throw them about in a clandestine way and the tyrants fearing that these discoveries[189] in the end may cause[190] the generous thoughts of forlorn English souls amongst you (having[191] imitation of Mehomet who forbade all sort of learning lest the wickedness of his law should be found out) made an act that you should[192] not pry into those papers that display the groans of their afflicted country and intend to continue you still the instruments of their lusts which how glorious it is to have the infamous titles of executioners and hangmen of your fellow brethren I leave to the [worst][193] of you all to judge.

[News] from [London], [28 June] 1659

fo. 161^r

Alterations *in Col: Saunder's Regt*[194]

Captain Hope is out and Captain Izod has his troop.[195]
Captain Wright out and Captain Pretty to have his troop.
Captain Dendy out and Cornet Hacker to be captain-lieutenant.
Lieutenant Franks, lieutenant to Captain Hope, is out and one Captain [Digby/Diggory Barton] is for his place.
Lieutenant Brightman is out [to] Captain Coulson and one Captain Hodgson to have his place.
Cornet Davis, Captain Hope's cornet and Cornet Morton, Quartermaster Pinegar and Quartermaster [Paul] are out, but of

[186] *Ibid.* reads 'Acts' for 'resolves'.
[187] *Ibid.*, p. 8 reads 'sad' for 'hard'.
[188] *Ibid.* reads 'but' for 'both'.
[189] *Ibid.* reads 'discoverers' for 'discoveries'.
[190] *Ibid.*, 'rouze up' for 'cause'.
[191] *Ibid.* reads 'have in'.
[192] *Ibid.* reads 'shall' for 'should'.
[193] *Ibid.* 'meanest'.
[194] The changes in this regiment are summarized in F&D, I, p. 288.
[195] The committee for the nomination of officers had appointed Hope but he may have resigned his commission to be replaced by Thomas Izod; *ibid.*, p. 288.

these there is Captain Hope, Lieutenant Brightman, Cornet [Davis] and Cornet Morton and Quartermaster [Paul] are provided for in other regiments, the rest totally out. Barton is moved for to be major.[196]

Newsletter from [London], [29 June] 1659

fo. 161r

The Committee for Nomination of Officers

[acknowledging] the 7 wise men

Lord Fleetwood	*Sir Arthur Heslerigge*
Lord Lambert	*Sir Henry Vane*
Major General Disbrow	*Colonel Algernoun Sydney*
Colonel James Berry	

News from G.M., [London], 7 July 1659[197]

fo. [166]r

Colonel Smyth late Governor of Hull to have Colonel Fitches Regiment.

Colonel Daniel the 6th instant out of his regiment. Lieutenant-Colonel Pearson to have the regiment and Major Holmes said to be his lieutenant-colonel.[198]

The plenipotentiaries are gone for the Sound. The Lord Lockhart made extraordinary Ambassadour to goe to Bayonne.

The Citty Militia setled.

A new design about a single person.[199]

[196] This was Nathaniel Barton; *CJ*, VII, p. 723.

[197] Postscript to a newsletter, probably from Gilbert Mabbott.

[198] In fact Holmes was appointed to Sawrey's regiment, while it was Clement Keane who became lieutenant-colonel of Pearson's regiment; F&D, II, pp. 479, 494.

[199] For a similar report, see below, p. 309. Around this time one of Hyde's informants reported, 'The Army is divided, some for the Parliament, and some for themselves and a single person, they say for Lambert'; *CClarSP*, IV, p. 286. In April the soldiers' demands had included 'A Comanwealth and noe single person'; *CP*, III, p. 213.

News from G.M., [London], 14 July 1659[200]

fo. 170r

The act for the militia of London yesterday passed.[201] All is stable yet great jealousies amongst great persons.[202] A few days will shew the end. Their great militia is raising which gives some cause of fear to the army and great burthen and discontent to the country.[203] Our affairs in Denmark stands pretty well. English and Swedes lie before Copenhagen, the Hollanders in the Belt.

A. Johnston [of Wariston], [London], to George Monck, 14 July 1659[204]

fo. 170r

My Lord

There is such throng of business that with very great difficulty I got your letters read and answered by the Council, the intelligences cometh so thick of the designs of the malignants to rise in many places at once upon expectation or assurance of Charles Stuart and what he can do to be with them.[205] The Council are very diligent to use all means of prevention. We are are [*sic*] sending Major-General Disbrowe to the west. The Forest of Dean, Coventry and Chester[206] are places designed by the adversaries. The Council have taken[207] the roll of all those who have given bond to the Lieutenant of the Tower[208]

[200] Postscript to a newsletter, probably from Gilbert Mabbott.

[201] *CJ*, VII, p. 716.

[202] 'Our present affayres are very odd, the grandees and commonwealthsmen striving for superiority', wrote an unknown correspondent in an intercepted letter of 22 July 1659; *TSP*, VII, p. 704.

[203] *CSPD 1659–1660*, pp. 15–16, 24.

[204] Much of this letter is printed (from another copy, now apparently lost) in *L-P*, p. 118. Variations have been noted as footnotes. Its tone is markedly different from another written by Johnston to Monck on the same date by order of the Council of State; Worc. MS LI, fo. 78r.

[205] See also the intercepted letter of 22 July 1659 in *TSP*, VII, p. 704. On 14 July 1659 the Council of State instructed Johnston and Col James Berry to prepare a letter to Monck ordering him to secure the paroles of 'dangerous persons', i.e. royalists who had been bound over to keep the peace; Bodl., MS Rawlinson C. 179, p. 177r; *CSPD 1659–1660*, p. 27. For more evidence of Johnston's concerns about such rumours at this time, see Wariston, *Diary*, III, pp. 124–125.

[206] *L-P*, p. 118 reads 'Chichester'.

[207] *Ibid.* reads 'will take'.

[208] Col Thomas Fitch, appointed Lieutenant of the Tower on 10 June 1659; *CP*, IV, p. 19.

and demand personal assurance of them. They desire that you do the like in Scotland and Lieutenant-General Ludlow in Ireland.[209] All excepted persons are to go out of London either tomorrow or be under hazard of execution. The business anent[210] sending commissioners in Scotland will be taken into consideration with the act of union and grace.[211] They have laid on me this night to despatch a packet to the Lord Lockhart and so I must cut short but shall rest

your Lordship's humble servant

A. Johnston

14 July

Your Lordship will do well to look to MacNaughton and some other highlanders who are speaking strange language as some writes.[212]

News from [London], [15] July 1659

fo. [171]r

Persons like to be put out of *Colonel Michells late Regiment now Major Generall Overtons.*[213]

Newsletter from [London], 19 July 1659

fo. [171]v

Yesterday Lieutenant Generall Ludlow went for Ireland. It's whispered that the Parliament will adjourn the next week. *The king of Spaine hath drawne out his Army butt Dunkirke is in noe Danger.*

[209] See *CSPD 1659–1660*, p. 27. After this sentence *L-P*, p. 118 inserts, 'Mr Reynolds did give me the enclosed ticket to be sent to you'.

[210] 'Anent', Scots, meaning 'concerning, about'; M. Robinson (ed.), *Concise Scots Dictionary*, (Aberdeen, 1985). See Sir Charles Firth's comment, *CP*, III, p. 189n.

[211] Johnston records that he 'spak freely' to Fleetwood about sending commissioners to Scotland two days after writing this letter; Wariston, *Diary*, III, p. 125. The next sentence is omitted in *L-P*, p. 118. Bulstrode Whitelocke was very much involved in measures to resuscitate the act for union with Scotland; Whitelock, *Memorials*, IV, pp. 349, 355, 362.

[212] *L-P*, p. 118, reads 'write'.

[213] There follows in longhand a list of the affected officers. When changes were made to Overton's regiment on 27 July, the name of only one of these, Lt Laverock, appears as having been retained in the regiment. Mitchell himself took over Thomas Fitch's regiment in Scotland; *CSPD 1659–1660*, pp. 31, 45.

There has been a great debate in the Parliament about a Member of Parliament <Major Harley>[214] who gave out that the Lord Fleetwood should send for the late Protector to come to London and that he would set him up again into his place and dissolve the Parliament, and the Lord Fleetwood being examined about it said that he had sent to one of the brothers, but not about any such business.[215] Yet it's said that [Disbrowe] said openly that they would set up the Protector again so that there is great divisions about the business.

Memorandum, [Dalkeith], 5 August 1659

fo. 178r

This day there came an express from Captain John Mason from Carlisle informing that there was a rising in Lancashire and that there were 500 marched with colours who, being met by our scouts and asked who they were for, fired at them.[216]

News from [London], 29 September 1659

fo. 225v

Sir Arthur Hesilrige and the Lord Lambert reconciled.[217]

The Lord Howard committed close prisoner to the Tower.[218]

Charles Stuart to be assisted both by France and Spain to marry Cardinal Mazarin his niece and in case he recover his kingdom to declare himself Catholike, to see the king of France *incognito* before he goes to Brussels.[219]

[214] Marginated.

[215] Word of this incident was sent to Monck three days later by another correspondent; *CP*, IV, pp. 24–25.

[216] Capt. Mason was deputy governor of Carlisle, and is not to be confused with the colonel of the same name. He appears to have been responsible for establishing post stages in the area; *CSPD 1659–1660*, p. 94. The express and its enclosures are to be found in *CP*, IV, p. 31 (where its sender is tentatively identified as John Mayer), and pp. 32–33 (Col West to [Col Birch]).

[217] On the deteriorating relations between Hesilrige and Lambert, see *CClarSP*, IV, p. 294; Davies, *Restoration*, pp. 146, 148. See also Hutton, *Restoration*, p. 65.

[218] On 21 September 1659 Col Charles Howard was ordered to be sent to the Tower for high treason; *CSPD 1659–1660*, pp. 217–218.

[219] Earlier in the month the Venetian resident in London had reported to the Doge and Senate that 'The government has been disturbed and alarmed by a report . . . of negotiations for a marriage between the king of Scotland and a niece of Cardinal Mazarini and that French and Spanish forces will assist his Majesty to return to his country. This is much discussed at Whitehall'; *CSPV 1659–1661*, p. 71.

12. NOTEBOOK XXXII

4 October 1659–17 February 1660[1]

Introduction

In the autumn of 1659 relations between army and Parliament reached breaking point. On 13 October the Rump was ousted by a military coup,[2] and the heightened tension in London is reflected in the large number of documents which Clarke recorded in shorthand.[3] Some republican MPs, foremost among them Sir Arthur Hesilrige and Thomas Scot, refused point-blank to have any dealings with the new regime while others, notably Henry Neville and Sir Henry Vane, co-operated with the army leaders at Wallingford House in the hope that some political stability might be restored.[4]

News of the coup reached Monck on 17 or (more probably) 18 October 1659.[5] In contrast to his support for the officers after Richard's downfall earlier in the year, Monck consistently refused to back the army leaders in London, informing both them and members of the deposed Council of State that he and the substantial force which he commanded in Scotland wished the Parliament to be reinstated.[6] He was, however, powerless to act for the former Council before receiving word that they wished him to do so. In November, in the absence of such a message, he attempted to heal the breach by sending

[1] Worc. MS XXXII.

[2] Thomas Clarges warned Monck that his position under the new regime was at risk (p. 317, 318).

[3] There are sixty-four relevant documents in shorthand and only ten in longhand in this volume. I have discussed Clarke's increased use of shorthand during times of heightened political tension in the Introduction (p. 6) and in Appendix C.

[4] These events are described in detail in Hutton, *Restoration*; Woolrych, Introduction to *Complete Prose Works of John Milton*, VII; A. Woolrych, 'Last quests for a settlement 1657–1660, in G.E. Aylmer (ed.), *The Interregnum, The Quest for Settlement 1646–1660* (London and Basingstoke, 1974), pp. 183–204.

[5] F.M.S. McDonald, 'The timing of General George Monck's march into England, 1 January 1660', *English Historical Review*, 105 (1990), p. 365.

[6] Pp. 319, 321–323, 325–329, 332–333. In order that his position should be clear, his letters both to the army officers and to the Council were printed in Scotland for immediate distribution in England; [George Monck, duke of Albemarle], *Three letters from the Lord Generall Monck*... (Edinburgh, 1659). Members of his army who refused to endorse this ultimatum were quickly disposed of (p. 336 below).

representatives to London for discussions with the army leaders. To his considerable dismay these came to nothing.[7]

Early in the confrontation Clarke's former commander, Robert Lilburne, made an attempt to win him over to the Wallingford House officers.[8] While Clarke's reply was a model of tact and moderation, he made it unequivocally clear that he would remain loyal to Monck. It was this loyalty which was to earn him rich rewards after the Restoration of Charles II.

We now know that it was not until early December that the former Speaker and Council managed to get word to Monck that they would welcome his intervention.[9] Immediately, despite a considerable military presence on the English side of the border under the command of John Lambert and Robert Lilburne, Monck began final preparations for a full-scale invasion.[10] By synchronizing his campaign with armed support orchestrated by Lord Fairfax in Yorkshire to the south of Lambert and Lilburne, Monck was able to lead his army across the border on 1–2 January 1660 and march virtually unopposed to London.[11]

Here, after a further clash with both leading civilians and army officers,[12] he restored the old Long Parliament, thus paving the way for the restoration in May 1660 of the Stuart dynasty. Almost the last document in my transcript[13] is an unheaded, undated collection of vitriolic comments against Monck, apparently the record of some sort of meeting, and apparently written around 14–15 February 1660. The remarks have an air of authenticity, and their content is plausible, but I have been unable to identify any meeting around this time which involved all those named, some of them MPs, others members of the Council of State. The comments may have been made at a gathering of secluded and non-secluded MPs held by Monck in the City on 14 February at which we are told a 'free and civill discourse' took place.[14] Clarke may indeed have recorded them as proof of the plots which

[7] Pp. 331, 334–336, 337–338.

[8] P. 319. The incident is described in Baker's *Chronicle*, p. 688, but only now do we have the text of both Lilburne's letter and Clarke's reply to it (p. 000).

[9] Pp. 343–346. I have discussed in detail the significance of Monck's exchange of letters with Lenthall and the members of the deposed Council of State in McDonald, 'The timing of General George Monck's march into England', pp. 363–376.

[10] Pp. 347–348.

[11] Pp. 354, 356–357, 358–359, 360–361. These events are fully described in A.H. Woolrych, 'Yorkshire and the Restoration', *Yorkshire Archological Journal*, 39 (1956–1958), pp. 483–507.

[12] Pp. 361, 362–363. Fleetwood had again been appointed commander-in-chief.

[13] P. 362.

[14] *CP*, IV, p. 264.

were being hatched against Monck even before he reached London,[15] or they may relate to a hostile meeting by a narrower group. Whatever the answer, they remind us that Monck's arrival in a silent city,[16] on 3 February 1660 was not welcomed by all who witnessed it.

Newsletter from [London], 4 October 1659

fo. [3]ᵛ

At the meeting of the Council of Officers when Sir Arthur Haslerig urged [to/upon] them that the making up of these <persons>[17] general officers which they desired would bring in a single person, it was answered that their danger is no man will turn out himself and that if he came in he would [drive] more furiously than ever Oliver did.[18]

Major [Hubbert/Hubbard], Major [Brigham/Brigman], Major Evelyn and Major Barton were against the last address agreed upon by the officers in Somerset House chapel.[19]

General Council of Officers, Whitehall, to George Monck, 5 October 1659[20]

fo. 4ᵛ

Right Honourable

We do by command from the General Council of Officers of the army now in London transmit the inclosed to you being a true

[15] W.D. Christie, *Life of Anthony Ashley Cooper*, 2 vols (London, 1871), I, pp. 214–215.

[16] P. 361.

[17] Marginated.

[18] Parliament had sent some of its members to the officers' daily meetings 'to learn their plans and the motives for such conventicles'. According to the Venetian resident there was some support in the army for Lambert's reputed aspirations to become Protector; *CSPV 1659–1661*, pp. 72, 74.

[19] On this day another London correspondent (probably Gilbert Mabbott) also reported the Somerset House meeting. According to a London newsletter of 6 October, the dissenting officers were Cols Alured, Saunders, and Moss, Lt-Col Nicholas Andrews, and Majors Evelyn and Breaman; Worc. MS XXXII, fos 4ʳ, [5]ᵛ.

[20] This letter appeared in print, with minor differences, in [J. Lambert], *A Letter from The Lord Lambert And other Officers To General Monck* (London, 1659), pp. 3–4; *Weekly Intelligencer of the Common-wealth*, 25 (18–25 Oct. 1659), p. 194; *Weekly Post*, 25 (18–25 Oct. 1659), p. 201. Variations from the shorthand text which are common to all of these are given without attribution; for variations which do not occur throughout, the relevant titles are provided.

copy of the representation and petition[21] which was this day by them humbly presented to the Parliament and the votes of the House passed thereupon and are further to signify as[22] their desire[23] that the same may be communicated to all the[24] commission[25] officers of that part of the army under your command and[26] the subscriptions of all[27] taken to the representation and petition that are free to sign the same, which being so signed it is desired you will be pleased to cause them[28] close sealed up and returned to Thomas Sandford esquire, secretary to his Excellency the Lord Fleetwood, who is to give an account thereof.[29] As we have thus fulfilled the General Council's pleasure, we are well assured you will be pleased to comply with their request which is all at present from

your humble servants

John Lambert

Richard Creed John Disbrow

Robert Barrow John Mason William Packer

Whitehall 5th 8bris 1659

For the right honourable General Monck
at Dalkeith, Scotland

[21] *The humble Representation and Petition of the Officers of The Army, To the Parliament of the Commonwealth of England* (London, 1659) was presented to Parliament on 5 October 1659 and printed on the same day; *CJ*, VII, p. 792. Monck received advance notice that the officers intended to present the petition from Thomas Clarges; Baker, *Chronicle*, 1670, p. 681.

[22] '[A]s' is omitted.

[23] '[D]esires' replaces 'desire'.

[24] '[T]he' is omitted.

[25] *Weekly Intelligencer of the Common-wealth* and *Weekly Post* read 'commissioned' for 'commission'.

[26] '[T]hat' is inserted after 'and'.

[27] '[M]ay be' is inserted.

[28] '[T]o be' inserted here.

[29] As Monck pointed out in answer to this letter (see below), a major impediment was the officers' request for signatures to be added to their petition retrospectively.

George Monck to the General Council of Officers, Whitehall, 13 October 1659[30]

fo. [16]r

Right Honourable

I received a letter directed to me[31] from yourself and others of the 5th of this instant with the inclosed[32] in pursuance of an order from[33] the General Council of Officers, as you are pleased to intimate, and must humbly beg your excuse that I am not able to satisfy your commands in that particular. Indeed our force is very small and our enemies[34] very numerous,[35] and I should[36] be unwilling to set anything on foot that might[37] breed jealousies[38] among[39] us. And finding many officers resolved to[40] decline the signing all papers of that nature and rather propense to bear[41] their testimony to the Parliament's authority and declare[42] their absolute adherence thereunto, I have thought it my duty to suspend the execution of your desires lest it might[43] make a breach of affection among[44] us. And I further humbly offer it[45] to your thoughts that the petition having already been presented and in part answered by the Parliament, our concurrence therein cannot be any ways advantageous.[46] I shall not interpose mine own judgement

[30] This letter appeared in print, with small but significant differences, in [Lambert], *A Letter from The Lord Lambert And other Officers*, pp. 5–7; *A True Narrative of the Proceedings in Parliament, Councell of State, General Councell of the Army, and Committee of Safetie; from the 22. of Septemb. untill this present*... (London, 1659), pp. 14–15; *Weekly Intelligencer of the Commonwealth*, 25 (18–25 Oct. 1659), pp. 194–195; *Weekly Post*, 25 (18–25 October 1659), pp. 201–202. Variations from the shorthand text which are common to all of these are given without attribution; for variations which occur in only one or some of these, the relevant titles are provided.

[31] '[T]o me' is omitted.

[32] 'Papers' inserted here.

[33] '[O]f' replaces 'from'.

[34] 'Enemy' replaces 'enemies'.

[35] '[G]reat' replaces 'numerous'.

[36] *A True Narrative*..., *Weekly Post*, and *Weekly Intelligencer* all read 'shall' for 'should'.

[37] '[M]ay' replaces 'might'.

[38] '[J]ealousie' replaces 'jealousies'.

[39] '[A]mongst' replaces 'among'.

[40] '[R]esolved to' is omitted.

[41] '[D]eclare' replaces 'bear'.

[42] '[D]eclare' is omitted.

[43] '[M]ight' is omitted in *Weekly Intelligencer* and elsewhere replaced by 'may'.

[44] Both *Weekly Post* and *Weekly Intelligencer* read 'affections' for 'affection among us'. *A True Narrative* reads 'affections amongst us'.

[45] '[I]t' is omitted.

[46] By the time that Monck received it, army officers, led by John Desborough, had already presented the petition to Parliament, on 5 October 1659; *CJ*, VII, p. 792; p. 313

concerning it, but do earnestly desire that matters of such great weight might[47] not be imposed upon us who were not present at the debates or[48] privy to ~~your~~ the[49] counsels[50] by which your resolutions may be governed and led to such actions. I shall not further trouble you but only represent to your thoughts the great necessity we have to labour for unity in this day of our fears. I shall not need to tell you that misunderstandings between the Parliament and army are the great hopes of our adversaries and there is no other way to gratify their design.[51] I bless the Lord for those great[52] evidences that I see of a peaceable spirit in your address. I do and I hope[53] I shall always indeavour and pray that God would not break the staff of our beauty or the staff of our bands[54] that he would make all good men (though of different[55] judgments) one in his hand that we may arrive at that blessed settlement for which we have expended so much blood and treasure.[56] And as I have always indeavoured to manifest[57] my obedience in acquiescing [in/his][58] wisdom of those that God places[59] over me, so I shall continue and ever be

your Lordship's[60]

Dalkeith 13th 8bris 1659

To the Right Honourable the Lord Lambert and the rest of the General Council of Officers at Whitehall.[61]

above. Monck gave direct orders to all the regiments under his command that they were not to sign it; Baker's *Chronicle*, p. 681.

47 '[M]ay' replaces 'might'.

48 '[N]or' replaces 'or'.

49 '[T]he' is superimposed upon 'your'.

50 The printed sources read 'Councils' for 'counsels'.

51 *A True Narrative*... reads 'designs' for 'design'.

52 *A True Narrative*..., *Weekly Intelligencer*, and *Weekly Post* all omit 'great'.

53 'I hope' is omitted.

54 Zechariah, XI. 7–14. *A True Narrative*..., *Weekly Intelligencer*, and *Weekly Post* all read 'the staff of our Beauty, or staff of Bands'.

55 *Weekly Intelligencer* inserts 'in' after 'different'.

56 *Weekly Post* reads 'treasures' for 'treasure'.

57 '[E]xpress' replaces 'manifest'.

58 This word is replaced by 'the'.

59 '[P]laceth' replaces 'places'.

60 All the printed versions add 'very humble Servant George Monck'.

61 *A True Narrative*... is addressed 'For the Right Honourable, the Lord Lambert, To be Communicated to the Council of Officers'.

George Monck to Speaker Lenthall, Westminster, 13 October 1659[62]

fo. [61]^{v}

Right Honourable

I received yours of the 7th of this[63] instant and cannot but with thankfulness acknowledge the great grace and favour the Parliament are pleased to vouchsafe to me in taking notice of my weak and worthless indeavours in their service.[64] I confess such incouragement is sufficient to reward the highest merits. I hope I shall make such use of it not only to satisfy my self as the best recompense for my former[65] poor services[66] but as a motive to future obedience and[67] loyalty to them. I bless the Lord I have a witness in mine own heart that my designs tend not to any other end then my country's good and I shall with more cheerfulness return the sword into your hands then ever I received it with, and desire to attend your pleasure. If you shall have no further use of my service,[68] I shall give you the best account I can of the forces here and indeavour to[69] keep them in due obedience to you (but I cannot undertake for men of some spirits). I shall not trouble your counsels with my impertinences[70] any further but intreat you to give me leave to mind you (which[71] I know is much upon your hearts already) that you would be pleased to hasten the settlement of the government of these nations into[72] a commonwealth way[73] in

[62] This letter is printed in [George Monck, duke of Albemarle], *A Letter from General Monck. From Dalkeith, 13 October 1659* (London, 1659); *A True Narrative*..., pp. 22–23; *Weekly Post*, 25 (18–25 Oct. 1659). pp. 199–200. Variations from the shorthand text which are common to all of these are given without attribution; for variations which occur in only one or some of these, the relevant titles are provided.

[63] [Monck], *A Letter from General Monck*... reads 'the' for 'this'.

[64] The letter to which this is a reply (for which see *CP*, IV, pp. 59–60) was written on 7 October 1659 by order of Parliament; *CJ*, VII, p. 792. The order was made on 5 October, the same day as, but immediately after, the delivery of the officers' petition; Worc MS XXXII, fo. [5]^{v}. By the time Monck's reply reached the Speaker Parliament had already been prevented from sitting; *Weekly Post*, 25 (18–25 Oct. 1659), p. 200; Baker, *Chronicle*, p. 681.

[65] *Weekly Post* omits 'former'.

[66] *A True Narrative*... reads 'service' for 'services'.

[67] *Weekly Post* reads 'in' for 'and'.

[68] *Ibid.* attaches the phrase, 'If you shall... service' to the previous sentence, Worc. MS LII does not.

[69] *A True Narrative*... omits 'indeavour to'.

[70] [Monck], *A Letter from General Monck*... reads 'impertinencies' for 'impertinences'.

[71] *Weekly Post* reads 'what' for 'which'.

[72] *Ibid.* reads 'in' for 'into'.

[73] *A True Narrative*... reads 'in the way of a Commonwealth' for 'into a Commonwealth way'.

successive parliaments so to be regulated in elections as you shall think fit, and that you will[74] increase[75] your favour upon[76] the ministers of the gospel and the sober professors thereof. And God will be in the midst of you and bless you, and you need not doubt but the hearts and hands of all good men will be with you. And for myself I desire that you would be assured that I do not think my life too precious to hazard in the defence of the supreme authority, the Parliament of England. The Lord bless your counsels[77] with peace and success and make you a terror to the nations round about, which is the earnest prayer of him who is

your Lordship's most faithful and humble servant,

George Monck

Dalkeith 13th 8bris 1659

For the Right Honourable William Lenthall Esquire, Speaker to the Parliament of England at Westminster.

Thomas Clarges, [London], to George Monck, 19 October 1659[78]

fo. [22]v

Yesterday the Council of Officers met and they have voted the Lord Fleetwood shall be commander-in-chief of the army and Lambert major-general and Disbrowe commissary-general, and that no commissions shall be granted but to such as shall be approved on by a committee of nomination who are Fleetwood, Lambert, Disbrowe, Berry, Ludlow, and Sir Henry Vane.[79] Colonel Clarke desired one more might be added and it was thought you were the man he meant, but Berry was against it and this day there was one told me that you had been nominated to be major-general of the foot,[80] but it is doubted that you are not free to act. I never observed so universal a discontent amongst all men as at this time and I believe the officers themselfs can

74 *Ibid.*, reads 'would' for 'will'.

75 *Weekly Post* reads 'intreat' for 'increase'.

76 [Monck], *A Letter from General Monck*... and *Weekly Post* read 'favours to' for 'favour upon'.

77 *Weekly Post* reads 'councils'.

78 During the political crises of 1659, Monck was particularly dependent on the information and help of his brother-in-law, Thomas Clarges. Clarges had already alerted Monck to the officers' proceedings in London; Baker, *Chronicle* (1670), pp. 681, 685.

79 All this is confirmed by Ludlow himself in his *Memoirs*. II, pp. 130–131.

80 Ludlow also heard this report on about the same date (*ibid.*, p. 130).

scarce tell which way to move. The inclosed act of Parliament puts a stop to all collections of money and the Treasury is very low at present. At the meeting yesterday when they were pressing on to nominate the above-said officers there was a colonel moved that they would not be so hasty in the actions but stay till they had heard out of Scotland and Ireland, but nothing could stop the carrier. Many say the Parliament was ill advised in voting those 9 officers out of their places.[81] But they say in answer that they were necessitated to do it to assert their own freedom that it might be known whether the army or the Parliament are to govern the nations, and they suspected these officers had some design against them because after their petition was delivered to the Parliament and answered they sent to get subscriptions to it. There be about 8 of the Council who have already declined to act with the rest till the 1st of 10bris. Their names are Sir Arthur Hesilrige, the Lord Bradshaw, Colonel Thomson, Master Dixwell, Colonel Morley, Master Nevile, Colonel Walton, Master Josiah Berners, and it is believed many others also refuse, as Master Scot, Sir Anthony Ashley Cooper and others. Cobbett and one Brown that had been an ensign went on the last Sabboth day towards you.[82] I hope you will be careful of your person. Sir Arthur Hesilrige goes into the country to morrow and Colonel Hacker and Colonel Morley are gone already.

October 19 1659

Letter from Doctor Clarges to the General.

Memorandum, [Linlithgow], 21 October 1659

*fo. [27]*v

Present[83]

[81] The nine signatories of the army petition of 5 October were stripped of their commissions on 12 October 1659. Government of the army was then placed in the hands of seven commissioners, of whom Monck was one; *CJ*, VII, p. 796. The Venetian Resident commented that '[the Parliament's] behaviour was too severe, injurious and haughty, condemned by everyone and generally disgusting to all'; *CSPV 1659–1661*, p. 83.

[82] According to another correspondent, who confirms the date of their departure from London, Browne had formerly belonged to the Excise at Leith; *CP*, IV, p. 69. Cobbett had sided with the army against the Rump and was sent by the others to present their case to Monck, who promptly arrested him and imprisoned him in Edinburgh Castle; *DBR*, 'Cobbett'.

[83] This heads a longhand list of those present at the meeting of Monck's council of officers at Linlithgow on 21 October 1659.

Memorandum, Edinburgh, 27 October 1659

fo. [48]^{v}

This day the general and officers of the army met at Edinburgh and after some debate and obstruction made by Captain Samuel Poole of Colonel Fairfax's regiment,[84] agreed upon the ensuing letters[85] in answer to those from the officers at Whitehall. They ordered that Colonel Wilkes[86] should thank Master Collins and Master Gumble for their pains in the sermon preached yesterday before them at their fast in the Tron Church.[87]

Robert Lilburne, York, to William Clarke, 27 October 1659[88]

fo. [61]^{r}

Master Clarke

I could wish you a better imployment than dispersing of such rash proceedings as in your last you acquainted me with, although perhaps you may think otherwise of it.[89] But truly it's looked upon here, as the common phrase is, a pig of the same sow that was lately in Lancashire and Cheshire,[90] and I am confident if the Lord do not continue you in Scotland on your strange forewarning he will infeeble and [waste/blast] you as he did those late pretenders. The course you take is at the best to play Charles Stuart's game, and whether you have dealt Christianly with your brethren or not, that will shew. I remember an old maxim of Machiavel, divide and conquer. I wish it

[84] Poole's objections are fully described in F&D, II, p. 504. The incident was trivialized in *The Faithfull Intelligencer From the Parliaments Army in Scotland*, unnumb. [N&S 146.1B] (29 Nov.–3 Dec. 1659), p. 9.

[85] The letter, which follows in longhand (Worc. MS XXXII, fos 49^{v}–[52]^{r}), is printed in John Toland's edition of [George Monck, duke of Albemarle], *A Collection of Letters Written by His Excellency* (London, 1714), pp. 9–13.

[86] Blank.

[87] Monck's order for this day of fasting and humiliation is found in the same volume; Worc. MS XXXII, fo. 33^{r}.

[88] The wording of Lilburne's attempt to suborn Clarke (described in Baker's *Chronicle*, p. 688) is recorded here for the first time (above, p. 311). For Clarke's considerably briefer and considered reply see below (p. 324).

[89] This probably refers to *A Letter of the Officers of the Army in Scotland, under the Commander in Chief there, to the Officers of the Army in England* (Edinburgh, 1659), issued from Linlithgow on 22 October 1659 under Clarke's signature as secretary. It is found in draft in Worc. MS XXXII, fos 30^{r}–[32]^{r}.

[90] i.e. the abortive Royalist rising of the preceding July–August.

be not the design of some amongst you. If it were not, why are there such practises as are now exercised amongst you, rather [resembling] the great Sultan and his janizaries at Constantinople then otherwise.[91] [These are same] things which proclaim a [war] [blood/wound] and imprison good men and prefer men of loose conversation. Before you [reason] the matter, is there either Christianity or humanity therein? Methinks it looks so like the [passages] and evil spirit in those that passed sentence upon our dear friends before they heard them, nay if I be not mistaken, for that which but 2 or 3 days before they gave them thanks for. If there be any fear of God before your eyes consider what you do before you ingage to [wound/blood] and raise up that evil spirit which you cannot easily conjure down and then repent of your doings when it's too late. Will you please to tell our dear friends amongst you of these things and let us not take advantage of one another's [haltings]. For my own part I had no hand in these late divisions and I hope my indeavours shall be to reconcile rather than to wound, which I take to be the duty of all of us that fear of the name of the Lord. And let our friends remember that good saying, study peace with all men but especially with brethren; if they be fallen restore them with the spirit of meekness and think not by [club law] to beat them out of their principles. It would rejoice me to hear of this Christian-like spirit amongst you. I do not altogether despond of it. I believe the Lord will suffer the spirit of division to get no such power. As to our so dear and loving to one another [hold] each one's [side] to the inclosed[92] [in/his requital] with yours wherein I hope you may understand more harmony then [otherwise] seems to be amongst you in Scotland. If it be the will of God [let] that evil spirit depart from you.

Your loving friend, Robert Lilburne

York. 27th 8bris 1659

For William Clarke Esquire, secretary to General Monck at Dalkeith, in Scotland.

Robert Lilburne

[91] 'All honest men are much grieved that the Officers of the Army, that have professed to much for God, should set up a Sword-government, which is not endured by any nation but the Turks, and those under them'; *Faithfull Intelligencer from the Parliaments Army in Scotland*, unnumb. (29 Nov.–3 Dec. 1659), p. 2.

[92] Blank.

Charles Fleetwood, London, to Colonels Wilkes, Reade and Sawrey, [Leith], 27 October 1659[93]

fo. 70r

Gentlemen

I have lately seen the copies of the declaration which is under the name of the Declaration of the Officers of the Army in Scotland, a [principal] whereof are such that for the most part of them I hope we are one in heart with you therein, and if there can be no other way for the speedy settlement of these nations then by a return of the Parliament I think it will be out of dispute with us to consent thereunto.[94] But if after 5 months' experience of them[95] there has been no more effected in you [to/upon] a settlement than what we have experienced, that you should now threaten us with the sword into the same opinion with your selfs seems very strange. And if those things be [really/openly] [upon/from] your hearts then it's the way of Christ so to deal with your fellow brethren who have equally laboured in those hardships in what the [duty/doubts] of the day have called for with your selfs that before you have indeavoured to know the grounds of our proceedings and what the intentions of our designs are, that we should be declared to the world as your enemy. It is a practice very unsuitable to the principles you pretend unto in your paper and indeed to that ancient kindness and love I had hoped had been in you to this army. We would not, nay we durst not, have so dealt with you when occasion have you given hereby to have the precious name the Lord to be reproached that now (as it were) a staff of beauty and bonds should be broken.[96] For let me say though we may be as unworthy as you can imagine us to be in what we have done, yet surely you should have cast upon us a mantle of love to have covered our nakedness instead of making us as the shame of nations, which you have done as much as in you lieth. I hope your principles you profess are real, and if so I am sure they will judge your practice to profess yourselves to be friends to the church of Christ. And to [design] the purity and power thereof and yet put yourselfs in a posture of opposition against many precious members thereof is very strange, nay gives me leave to say your action is like to indanger the churches and liberties of the [people]

93 Several documents in this volume are not placed in strictly chronological sequence in Clarke's notebook. I have rearranged them in order of date.

94 Like Lilburne in the previous document, Fleetwood is here presumably referring to the *Letter of the Officers of the army in Scotland* (see above, p. 319n).

95 i.e. the restored Rump, which held office from 7 May–13 October 1659.

96 This quotation from Zechariah, XI. 7–14 echoes Monck's letter of 13 October 1659 (p. 315 above). Presumably 'bonds' should read 'bands'.

throughout these nations. For what can this action of yours tend unto but to give Charles Stuart and his party the advantage to inthrone that interest again? And though I trust you have an obedience to the thing yet no majesty universal but will easily conclude that should be the issue. The late insurrections could not in any measure conduce so much to that design as now you do if the Lord prevent [not].[97] Who can you think to joyn with in this action but those of that spirit and principle (let men deceive you as they will). You will have no other for your companions in the way you are in. You are ingaging (I believe) the most of the precious saints of this nation throughout against you in their prayers. I know we are strangely represented to you as persons against magistracy and ministry and wholly given up to vain opinions. These [discourses] are but snares to intrap you and not truths to lead you. The Lord has a precious seed amongst us whom he has [given] and will own, who make it their business to worship a Lord/in

*fo. 70^v^*

in spirit and in truth, prize and [regard] the ordinances of Christ as their choice food, and cannot part with a gospel ministry or with gospel administrations, who would rejoice in such a magistracy as might execute justice and righteousness in the land and hold it their duty to submit thereunto as an ordinance of God. But under a specious pretence of obedience would be unwilling to be abused out of all our interest in this cause for which we have so long [contended]. And when we see authority breaking in upon us blame us not if we labour to prevent such an inundation as may hazard all we [reap/help]. I am tender of the spirit of those who in their day have been serviceable and were it not for that I could easily demonstrate you [are/were] grossly abused in those representations which [are/were] made unto you. Send any in your number to us and you will find it true. Although I am unworthy of such a command yet give me leave to say I have a command of you, and out of love to you I require your subjection to it and that before you ingage further in this business. You, Colonel Wilkes and Colonel Reade, my old aquaintance[s], I expect it [from you] that some of your number who have a real love [to/upon] the interest of this cause, may come up hither and understand these matters lest you be found [fighters] against the Lord and have the blood of saints as well as of men to answer for. I am confident your persuasion in this way you have begun will be witnessed against by

[97] It is unclear whether the phrase, 'if the Lord prevent [not]' belongs to the preceding or following sentence.

the Lord when jealousy will be [provoked]. I dearly love and tender your welfare and therefore am the more passionate in what I write. I have at least discharged my duty and remain

your affectionate friend and servant

Charles Fleetwood

Wallingford House 8bris 27 1659

For the honourable Colonel Wilkes, Colonel Reade and Colonel Sawrey, to be communicated to the several commission officers of the army in Scotland.

Newsletter from Ralph Knight, Kelso, 28 October 1659

fo. 60r

I understand That they att Newcastle will nott lett any Troope or Companie into the Towne that they are not sure of. However if your Lordship please to send me a regiment of foot I make no question of getting the town, but what your Lordship intends should be done with all possible speed.[98] *Colonel Lilburne hath staid all Disbrowes Regiment in the Byshoprick, & the North parte of Yorkshire & hath sent for all the Officers to signe the Agreement of the Army as they call it, which being done I suppose hee will send them all to Newcastle.*

I intend to be at Alnwick upon Sunday at night and on Monday at Morpeth, when I shall expect your Lordship's commands.

Ralph Knight

Kelso 28 8bris 1659

[98] One of Monck's most trusted officers, Knight's movements around this time are traced in F&D, I, pp. 138–139. His unsuccessful attempt to seize Newcastle for Monck is described, but not dated, in Baker's *Chronicle*, p. 688; this newsletter suggests that he set out from the headquarters on 26 or 27 October 1659. Lambert appears to have been well entrenched at Newcastle by 5 November; *Mercurius Politicus*, 593 (3–10 Nov. 1659), p. 859.

William Clarke to Robert Lilburne, York, 3 November 1659[99]

fo. [61]v

Honoured Sir

I received yours of the 27th of 8bris but not any other since the late sufferings, though I suppose you have sent more because I had some inkling of one that was kept from me. I shall not presume to answer any particulars of your last. It should widen the dissent which now seems to be [. . .] and I would not add oil to the flame but rather bring water to quench the fire of civil dissensions. For this day upon letters from my Lord Fleetwood and my Lord Lambert (brought by Colonel Talbot and Dr Clarges) my Lord General and the officers here have made choice of Colonel Wilkes, Lieutenant-Colonel Clobery and Major Knight to go to the officers at London and indeavour a right understanding to whom and all lovers of truth and peace I shall pray for good success.[100] And that after so many and hazardous shipwrecks these poor nations may injoy a realm of prosperity in the settlement both of the privileges of Parliament and liberties of the people, and that there may be no more complaining in our streets. For all which I know your indeavours will not be wanting.

William Clarke

Edinburgh 3th 9bris 1659

For the Right Honourable Major-General Robert Lilburne these at York

[99] Clarke's reply to the letter of 27 October 1659 from his former commander-in-chief (p. 319 above) is a model of diplomacy and restraint.

[100] According to Baker's *Chronicle* (p. 689), Monck first appointed Clobery and Knight, asking them to nominate the third commissioner. Wilkes, who was 'reputed to be a good Religious man, and acceptable to Fleetwood, and the Officers in England', was to incur Monck's displeasure for disclosing his instructions; *CP*, IV, pp. 97–99, 197n. Clobery may have had royalist contacts; *CClarSP*, IV, pp. 451, 476.

[George Monck] to Charles Fleetwood, London, 3 November 1659[101]

fo. [62]^{r}

My Lord,

I had the favour yesterday to receive your Lordship's of the 25th of 8bris by Colonel Talbot and Dr Clarges and am obliged to your Lordship for the great respect manifested to me in it, of which the sending[102] 2 such friends in this occasion is not the least.[103] I have very seriously considered all your Lordship writ and have discoursed with Colonel Talbot about the whole matter, but am sorry to find your Lordship so much mistaken in your[104] apprehensions of things. As to what Sir Arthur Hesilrige, Colonel Walton and Colonel Morley acted in drawing regiments to Westminster Hall it was but their duty, they being trusted by the Parliament (in whom the militia was asserted by the blood of many precious saints [)] to manage and dispose[105] their forces in defence thereof and those soldiers that were produced[106] to oppose them were the proper deluders[107] of the army. But truly my Lord I was much distracted at my 1st hearing of the practices of our brethren at London who did not only to the great scandal of the army interrupt the Parliament but began immediately to form themselfs into such a posture as denounced a war to all that condescended not to them. As 1st they assembled some officers together that called themselfs a general council and these chose a commander-in-chief, a major-general and commissary-general in direct opposition to the Parliament's authority who had before by act of Parliament repealed your Lordship's commission and[108] not only

[101] The arrival of this letter in London was reported in *Mercurius Politicus* 593 (3–10 Nov. 1659), p. 860. This version shows small but significant differences, here noted as footnotes, from that printed in *CP*, IV, pp. 85–87, which is taken from Worc. MS LII, fo. 5^{v}. Except where these sources differ from each other no reference is given.

[102] '[O]f' inserted here.

[103] The letters from Fleetwood and Lambert, both dated 25 October 1659, were read out to a council of war at Edinburgh on this day, 3 November; *CP*, IV, pp. 70–74, 77–78, 97. Clarges, who had been despatched at very short notice from London, and arrived at Edinburgh on 2 November, may have been chosen as a messenger in the hope that he would return with inside information about Monck's plans. Conversely he used this opportunity to encourage Monck in his stand for Parliament, and was to prove a valuable ally after his return to London; Baker, *Chronicle*, pp. 685, 688.

[104] *CP*, IV substitutes 'the' for 'your'.

[105] *Ibid.* omits 'dispose'. *CP*, IV replaces 'and dispose' with 'all'.

[106] '[I]nduced' replaces 'produced'.

[107] '[D]eviders' replaces 'deluders'.

[108] The phrase, 'before by act of Parliament repealed your lordship's commission and' is omitted.

declared against such officers but settled the government of the army in 7 commissioners. And since that (if our ordinary letters are true [)] they have[109] constituted [to/upon] themselfs the[110] legislative authority of[111] these nations and appointed committees or councils for the raising monies and making war and peace which at once divest[112] the people of such essential and undoubted rights as the greatest tyrants amongst us never openly pretended to and against which even themselfs and your Lordship have often solemnly witnessed. I beseech your Lordship what does this signify but a dividing the army and[113] make the most glorious cause that ever men ingaged in a personal contest? And if your Lordship and those with you oppose the Parliament's army (which the Lord has so often and so eminently owned), let the Lord judge betwixt[114] you and us where the guilt will rest. And although your Lordship is so confident of the justice of your[115] actings as to tell me you believe not 2 of the church[116] approved[117] of my faithfulness to the cause I prosecute, I must tell your Lordship without vanity I believe[118] there is not any truly godly professor uninterested[119] that denies us his prayers and best wishes and in the distinction of godly persons, I desire your Lordship not to conclude them godly that say they are so except they act[120] righteously, wherefore to use your Lordship's own words, I beg you to refuse and decline everything which may cause further differences and divisions amongst us. Certainly if we sought[121] ourselfs we have as good a title as our brethren at London to impose upon the people and set up general councils and councils of state if we affected arbitrary exercise of government, which notwithstanding that your Lordship says[122] is not in your[123] intentions all unbiased men may[124] read the contrary in these actions. As to what your Lordship mentions of blame in[125] the authority I exercise in this army as a commissioner

109 '[D]one little less then' is inserted.
110 '[[T]o/upon] themselfs the' is omitted.
111 '[O]ver' replaces 'of'.
112 '[D]ivests'.
113 *CP*, IV inserts '[to]'.
114 '[B]etweene' replaces 'betwixt'.
115 *CP*, IV substitutes 'the' for 'your'.
116 '[C]hurches'.
117 '[A]pprove' replaces 'approved'.
118 '[T]hat' inserted after 'believe'.
119 '[U]nprejudiced' replaces 'uninterested'.
120 '[A]re' replaces 'act'.
121 Worc. MS LII reads 'fought' for 'sought', given in *CP*, IV as 'sought'.
122 *CP*, IV, inserts '[it]'.
123 *Ibid.* reads 'the[ir]' for 'your'.
124 '[R]unn and' is inserted here.
125 *CP*, IV reads 'blameing' for 'blame in'.

of Parliament, I may say thus[126] much, that since by the force upon the Parliament the commissioners are hindered from the execution of their trust,

fo. [62]v

I may make use of such of their forces as are under my charge to restore them and when the Lord pleases to return the Parliament to their trust I will submit my actings therein to their judgment.

Thus I have hastily given your Lordship an account of things and to testify unto you how unwilling I am to[127] decline any overtures of mediation, I do freely accept of your Lordship's invitation thereunto and if your Lordship please to appoint 2 or[128] 3 of those with you to meet[129] the like number from hence in[130] behalf of the Parliament's[131] army in some convenient place,[132] I shall not despair of an happy issue from their indeavours[133] and till your Lordship returns an answer to this I shall desire Colonel Talbot to stay here, that if anything in order to this may be further desired from me I may discourse with him about it. I must not omit to acquaint your Lordship that Colonel Lilburne as it were manages an open war against us here by procuring subscriptions of ingagements and drawing horse and foot in more then ordinary or usual numbers towards our borders and guarding all our armies and stopping or[134] searching all our letters, so that if I send some men to prevent a surprize upon us[135] I presume[136] your Lordship will put no ill interpretation upon my duty in it, being confident your Lordship does not intend by the offer of this mediation[137] to insnare us. I am

my Lord
your Lordship's[138]

Edinburgh 3th 9bris 1659

For the Right Honourable the Lord Fleetwood these at Wallingford House.[139]

[126] In *CP*, IV, 'this'.
[127] Omitted in Worc. MS LII; *CP*, IV inserts '[to]'.
[128] '2 or' is omitted.
[129] '[T]reate w[i]th' replaces 'meet'.
[130] '[T]he' is inserted.
[131] '[T]his' replaces 'the Parliament's'.
[132] '[I]n some convenient place' is omitted.
[133] The rest of this sentence is omitted.
[134] '[A]nd' replaces 'or'.
[135] Worc. MS LII reads 'ours'; *CP*, IV reads 'ous'.
[136] '[H]ope' replaces 'presume'.
[137] '[M]editation' replaces 'mediation'.
[138] *CP*, IV inserts '[very humble servant, George Monck]'.
[139] The direction is omitted.

[George Monck] to John Lambert, [London] 3 November 1659[140]

fo. [65]^{r}

My Lord

I have received your Lordship's from Whitehall of the 25th of 8bris and should have been glad to have found that satisfaction from Colonel Talbot of the forces at London in their late actings as your Lordship gave me hopes of in it. My principle is to love the worst order better than the best confusion and[141] it is much upon my spirit that this poor Commonwealth can never be happy if the army make itself a divided interest from the rest of the nation, which must bring us into such a slavery as will not be long indured and at last when all means fayle, if ever we are settled, the Parliament must do it. I have in my station here always avoided designs of divisions and could heartily wish[142] your Lordship and[143] that part of the forces at London had not made that unhappy rent by their late violent acting; and for the love and friendship I ever bore[144] your Lordship I shall joyn with you in all good means to preserve you[145] from the[146] consequences of the effects[147] that must ensue if the breaches are made wider. And in order hereunto I have heartily and freely accepted my Lord Fleetwood's tender of mediation for a good understanding and unity betwixt us[148] and refer your Lordship to my letter to his Lordship to which I shall only add that I am,

my Lord,

your Lordship's very humble servant

Edinburgh 3th 9bris 1659

To the Right Honourable the Lord Lambert

[140] Monck's reply to Lambert's letter from Whitehall of 25 October 1659 (printed in *CP*, IV, pp. 77–78) was written on the day upon which Lambert began his march north; *Particular Advice*, 35 (28 Oct.–4 Nov. 1659), p. 432. This version shows small but significant differences, here noted as footnotes, from that printed in *CP*, IV, pp. 87–88, which is taken from Worc. MS LII, fos 6^{v}–7^{r}. Except where these two sources vary, I have not given specific references.

[141] 'My principle ... best confusion and' is omitted.

[142] *CP*, IV substitutes '[desire]' for 'wish'. Worc. MS LII omits this word altogether.

[143] '[Y]our lordship and' is omitted.

[144] 'I have ever borne' is substituted for 'I ever bore'.

[145] '[T]hese nations and your selfe' replaces 'you'.

[146] Here 'sad' is inserted.

[147] *CP*, IV omits 'of the effects'.

[148] '[B]etweene us' replaces 'betwixt us' and the sentence continues, 'and have sent upp Colonel Wilkes, Lieut. Colonel Clobury, and Major Knight from my selfe and the rest of the officers heere to treate with your Lordshipp and officers above for that purpose, and hope that their endeavoures may produce an happy reconciliation of these differences, which is the hearty desire of'. This concludes the letter.

Charles Fleetwood and John Desborough, London, to Major-General Thomas Morgan, 5 November 1659[149]

fo. [91]v

Sir

Having perused your letter sent by Major Cobbett to my Lord Lambert and thereupon finding your ready and cheerful compliance to [renew] your interest with our old friend Major-General Monck for a right understanding in order to peace, we give you our hearty thanks for your readiness therein and desire that you would please to use your goodest indeavour for the begetting a peacable composure in order to the healing these wounds, and if you upon conference find him any ways inclinable to terms, that you would cause him to express them, and if they be such as we shall be satisfied may stand with [reason] and honour to grant, you may be assured they shall be condescended to. We are your

very affectionate friends and servants

Charles Fleetwood

John Disbrowe

Wallingford House, *November* 5 1659

For the Honourable Major-General Morgan Morgan [*sic*] at the headquarters in Scotland. Charles Fleetwood

[149] Morgan, who had been laid up at York with gout for some time, feigned disapproval of Monck's stand. As this letter demonstrates, the army leaders hoped that by allowing him to return to Scotland on the pretext of rejoining his regiment he would persuade Monck to change his mind. Morgan, however, carried out a double bluff by taking with him a message received from Lord Fairfax via the York minister Edmund Bowles. Travelling with Dr Troutbeck, Morgan arrived at Monck's headquarters on 7 November (p. 330 below). Thomas Clarges, who took part in the ensuing discussions, then delivered Monck's reply to Fairfax in Yorkshire, while at the same time reassuring Lambert, who had understandably been 'much troubled when he heard that Morgan had deserted him'; Baker, *Chronicle*, pp. 688, 689, 690, 691. I have rearranged the original sequence of the documents on pp. 329–340 in order to reflect their chronological order.

John [Humfries], London, to Lieutenant-Colonel John Mayer, Berwick, 5 November 1659[150]

fo. [93]^v

John [Humfries]

Sir,

If this letter should come to your hand send me an answer directed to me John [Humfries] of London, England, to be left at the post office, London, where I shall call for it; and write no news but that mine of the 5th of *9br* is well received so I may continue my advice to you [. . .].

Unto the Honourable Lieutenant-Colonel Mears, Governor of Berwick, these delivered with care and speedy post.[151]

Memorandum, Edinburgh, 7 November 1659

fo. 81^r

This day Captain Deane returned towards London with the aforementioned answer.[152] He lay that night at Judge Swinton's where were divers Scotch gentlemen.

Major General Morgan and Doctor Troutbeck came to Edinburgh.[153]

[150] This excerpt comes at the end of the letter printed in *CP*, IV, pp. 101–103.

[151] Lt-Col Mears, or Mayer, had managed to secure Berwick for Monck despite the opposition of part of the garrison; F&D, I, p. 138; II, p. 523.

[152] This was 'A Returne of the Generall & Officers in Scotland to the Answer of the Officers at Whitehall', dated at Edinburgh 7 November 1659; Worc. MS XXXII, fo. 81^r; printed, with an addition, in [Monck], *A Collection of Letters*, pp. 24–29. Deane, sent to Scotland in his capacity as a Treasurer at War, used the opportunity to attempt to suborn Monck's troops. Monck refused the offer which he brought of advancement in return for cooperation with the officers at Wallingford House; *CP*, IV, pp. 105, 174.

[153] See p. 329n above. On the day after their arrival Monck sent Morgan to Linlithgow, Stirling, and Fife to secure the allegiance of members of the army serving in those areas, and shortly afterwards on the same errand to the area east of Edinburgh; p. 336 below; *CP*, IV, p. 108.

Robert Lilburne, Newcastle, to George Monck, 7 November 1659

fo. 90v

My Lord

I am glad you have replied [to] my Lord Fleetwood's overture as you mention in your last[154] for I am of opinion neither our honest brethren in Scotland or those here would (at the long run) have been gainers by these divisions, and certainly as we love the peace and happiness of this Commonwealth we notwithstanding [care] rather to reason the matter and condescend to one another as brethren and friends and bear with one another's infirmities (if anything of dissatisfaction arise amongst us) then to take advantage and run precipitately into extremes and the [oldest] of all remedies. As I am confident God would not suffer this spirit to grow to any great heights, so I doubt not even in spite of all enemies that he will bring forth thereby and fix a happy compliance in the hearts of all the members thereof that truly fear him. And therefore I am willing to do my part as you have done yours in [forbidding] the advance of these forces under my charge beyond their quarters they are now in, and am ready to serve you as there shall be a further opportunity. Give me leave only to speak 2 or 3 words more in behalf of those at London whom you say made the [breach]. I am confident they did not design or [. . .] upon that which happened, but it's generally believed (if I may tell it you without offence) you did. But whether it be so or not as peradventure it is not, I dare say if the case had been others' as yours, they would never have dealt so with you as you have with them. And whatever may prove the issue of the [intended] mediation, I am [. . .] to believe they will so far aquit themselfs as they may with comfort appeal both to God and all good men to judge of their actions and whether they or others (I will not say yourself) gave the [1st/best] occasion of confidence. Since I wrote this, Colonel Wilkes and the rest have been with me whom I have satisfied as to my own [particular/principle] in those instructions you gave them, but because my Lord Lambert commands in chief and is come (I think) by this time as far as York, I have referred them to him for further assurance and remain

your humble servant

Robert Lilburne

Newcastle 7th 9bris

For the Right Honourable General Monck these, Edinburgh.

[154] This presumably refers to Monck's letter of 3 November 1659 (p. 325 above).

Memorandum, [Edinburgh], 7 November 1659

*fo. 94^v^*

This day about 40 of Captain Deane's troop of Colonel Twisleton's regiment with their colour[s] went away from him from Drunfriez[155] into England refused to sign the ingagement. They would have had him to have gone away with them.[156]

George Monck to Robert Lilburne, Newcastle, 10 November 1659

*fo. [91]^r^*

Sir

I received yours of the 7th instant[157] and can assure you that there is no man living can with more cheerfulness imbrace the proposals of an accommodation than myself. So it may be accompanied with the asserting and establishing those righteous ends for which we have ingaged the liberty of our consciences as Christians and of our persons and estates as men, which cannot be otherwise secured then in a Commonwealth government by successive Parliaments and this present Parliament to have a legal period, but must needs resent those reproaches that I have borne for my indeavours in this work. And I could heartily wish that yourself had not helped and assisted in this ingrateful [office]. I thank God that my conscience beareth me witness that this is the only purpose of my heart to answer the mercies of God and keep the vows and ingagements that I have taken. I will not boast of what it has pleased the Lord through mercy to assist me in, but I may express it without vanity that I opposed the interest of the late king's family almost in my person alone in Ireland and was there serviceable to secure that nation from his tyranny. And I think you are not ignorant what my indeavours both at sea and land have been against the common enemy. Yet to be traduced as a cavalier and in the presence of yourself and others without the least [occasion] makes me wonder what can be the intent of that calumny. Can it be a cavalier design to restore that Parliament which voted the late king to the block? And that I have no further design, I take God to witness. It doth as much afflict me that you confidently affirm in your letter that I 1st made the breach. I beseech you to remember that I dissolved not

155 Dumfries.

156 Capt. Thomas Deane's adherence to Monck and the defection of his troop are described in F&D, I, p. 169.

157 See p. 331 above.

the parliament, that I did not at 1st suspend the officers of the army from their commands, which was done in England, and such who were eminently godly in their own judgements and had appeared for the cause of God even [under bonds] in the late Protector's time. I desire you to consider whether against my commission and conscience I could have declared against the Parliament to whom I had so lately ingaged obedience and faithfulness, but I shall offer myself and those whom you pleaded for to the great God who is a righteous judge and to His pleasure, resolving not to desert a good cause, and leave you to peruse the inclosed[158] having no further but to let you know I am

your very humble servant

George Monck

Edinburgh, 10th 9bris 1659

For the Right Honourable Major-General Lilburne these at Newcastle.

Memorandum, [Edinburgh], 15 November 1659[159]

fo. [98]ʳ

My Lord General did in a Speech breifly sett forth to them the grounds of the present undertaking.

Memorandum, [Edinburgh], 16 November 1659

fo. 99ᵛ

Captain Williams came to Dunbar and secured Captain James Thompson, drew the soldiers out of town upon pretence of [orders from] Lord General Monck.[160]

[158] There is no indication in Clarke's notebook of what this enclosure might have been.

[159] There is one phrase in shorthand in the note on 'General Monck's Proceedings with the Commissioners of Scotland' printed in *CP*, IV, pp. 113–114. It comes between the end of the first sentence on p. 114 and the beginning of Monck's address.

[160] See F&D, II, p. 496.

Marginal notation, 16 November 1659[161]

fo. 100[r]

<Agreed. Presented to [the] General the 17th in the morning.>[162]

Colonel Timothy Wilkes to Lieutenant-Colonel Robert [Reade], Leith, 16 November 1659[163]

fo. [127][v]

Lieutenant-Colonel

I salute you in the Lord desiring your earliest welfare.[164] I have inclosed sent you a copy of our agreement which at present the Lord, I trust, has led us unto with our dear brethren in this nation. Indeed, I do not find but that we do mutually mind the same thing and indeed we have found that our brethren had mistakes of us and we of them from false reports. We have sat day and night since we came hither, only the Lord's day excepted. We have sent the agreement signed by his Excellency the Lord Fleetwood by consent and in behalf of himself, the General Council and army here, with purpose to perform the same we have done the like to them. Indeed our divisions here have occasioned the common enemy to lift up his head, nay in many parts of this nation [now] offer to put themselfs in a condition to rise which they were resolved on if our [rift] had increased. I hope the Lord has his care also to these poor nations and the good interest therein [guided/granted]. As to this composure, hoping that it is not in the hearts of our brethren the officers in Scotland to desire blood but rather to condescend as far as possible we could for peace sake, not going beyond our instructions. Pray present my love to all my fellow

[161] This note refers to the 'Answer of the Commissioners to General Monck'; *CP*, IV, pp. 115–116.

[162] Marginated.

[163] The surname of the officer to whom this letter is addressed is left blank in Clarke's notes, but he was most probably Robert Reade, based at Leith (for whom see M. Tolmie, *The Triumph of the Saints* (Cambridge, 1977) p. 158; *S&P*, p. 242n). Reade was one of those appointed on 3 November to draw up the commissioners' instructions; Worc. MS XXXII, fo. 53[r]; *CP*, IV, pp. 97, 99. Still with Monck on 7 December 1659, he may have been displaced shortly afterwards; *ibid.*, p. 178; F&D, I, p. 396. Monck's commissioners also wrote from Charing Cross to Monck and to his General Council of Officers on the same day; *CP*, IV, pp. 116–118.

[164] It is unclear whether the phrase, 'desiring your earliest welfare', belongs to the previous or the following sentence.

officers, my love to my wife and also to yours.[165] I do not doubt but what we have done will be cheerfully owned by you all. We have found great opposition in getting that we have done. We did very much insist upon the return of the Parliament but not only the officers of the army but the good people generally against the same as apprehending the same would be destructive to the good interest of the honest people of these nations (after the business). Pray present my service to my Lord General. Indeed what you have intrusted us with all has layn very heavy upon us. We have sometimes in our debates been ready to leave all and return, which if we had done according to reason would have been ruin [. . .] both to the army and nations. In haste I commend you to the Lord and am

your real friend and servant

Timothy Wilkes[166]

Near Wallingford House
this 16th of 9bris 1659

For Lieutenant-Colonel Robert[167], Leith, these.

Newsletter from Robert Andrew, Newcastle, 18 November 1659

*fo. [104]*r

This night at 11 there was news come hither that all differences are settled between those in Scotland and England.[168] 1. That there shall be a government without king, a single person or House of Lords. *2ly* That a godly preaching ministry shall be maintained and incouraged. 3. That schools of learning and universities shall be maintained and incouraged. *4ly* that there shall be an indemnity for all people. 5. That 7 officers from Scotland and 7 in England shall meet to do the [considering] of these officers turned out by the late Parliament and are deserving men. Lastly that 3 officers in England, 3 from Ireland and 3 from Scotland shall constantly attend in London for ordering the affairs of the army there, maintaining discipline and a

[165] It was Reade's wife who clandestinely circulated Anabaptist pamphlets round Leith citadel at the end of December 1659; *ibid*, pp. 229–230 (where Col Thomas Hughes's letter is assigned to October 1659), pp. 231–232.

[166] Monck's commissioners wrote from Charing Cross to the General Council of Officers in Scotland and to George Monck on the same day in much the same vein (*ibid.*, pp. 116–118).

[167] Blank.

[168] Monck probably received the news on the same day; McDonald, 'Timing of General George Monck's march', p. 365.

good understanding amongst all. The Lord Lambert is comed hither with his own regiment [etc.].

Robert Andrew

Memorandum, [Edinburgh], 19 November 1659

fo. [103]^{v}

This day Major-General Morgan & Adjutant-General Smyth being sent the day before to Haddington to tender the declaration to be subscribed by Captain Ashby's troop, they generally refused it except only his trumpet and 2 more whereupon there was 33 of them, but most [subscribed] at Haddington and dismounted when they came near Edinburgh and their horses taken from them and discharges given them.[169]

John Williamson, London, to [Havelock Trent], Leith, 19 November 1659[170]

fo. [128]^{r}

London 19 9bris 1659

Brother [Trent]

I have this day received yours by way of John Douglas with the inclosed from *G.M.*,[171] which I do not intend to deliver in respect I find it is agreed, for your 3 commissioners made very short work. They began on Monday the 14th and Tuesday the 15th all was done. They lay at Colonel Salmon's quarters and spake with few of any judgement but their own[172] and who alarumed them with *C.S.* coming and new plots intended. That night they came to town Colonel Whetham, governor of Portsmouth and the governor of Hurst Castle sent a remonstrance to Lord Fleetwood that they could not adhere to the army but must declare for the Parliament, and Colonel Overton finding himself like

169 Capt. Richard Ashby's was one of three troops in Col Twisleton's regiment disarmed and dismounted by Monck at this time. Another was that of Capt. Thomas Deane; p. 332 above; F&D, I, pp. 169–170.

170 Given the nature of the news which this letter contains, its phraseology and its references to interception of post, the names of these correspondents (neither of whom I have been able to trace) may well be *noms de guerre*.

171 George, or General, Monck.

172 The commissioners had been expected to stay at the house of William Clarke's brother-in-law, the London goldsmith William Cary; *CP*, IV, p. 109.

to be betrayed at Hull by 2 of his officers who were seizing on 2 of the blockhouses for the army, for that the army dares not trust him, whereby he clapped them both in prison.[173] These things and city and country being ready to rise, and they fearing their own army would rather joyne with *G.M.*[174] then fight against him, those I say [are/were] the cause. They followed them so close with pretences of Charles Stewart and I know not what, and scarce any man ever spake a word to them of the Parliament's party till all was done, for they were carried to Colonel Salmon's quarters and in 2 days the main business was done and ['fore 2] on Wednesday the guns shot off from the Tower. Pray let not *Will W.*[175] know anything of my letters, or as few as you can, for 2 may keep council, but hardly 3. Colonel Wilkes is now right for the army and most free of them all, and is for a synod or any thing [when/what] they please etc. Clobery is the wisest of them. However it may prove for the best. There is 10 months' pay for the army arrears to be paid and none of the officers secluded either in England or Scotland to be readmitted but by a committee of 14 to be chosen [out of] the army in England and [out of] the army in Scotland, who are to meet at Newcastle the 1st of 10bris next. So if [Holmes and . . .] etc. come in, then Hacker, Okey, Alured and Saunders will come into the army here. Present my humble service to my Lord General and his lady. I am in haste. Your loving friend

John Williamson

The last letters were not opened. They have done now opening letters.[176]

I pray inquire if [. . . .] had not a letter from John Lewin and whether it was carried to *G.M.*, and send me word at large how all things are carried. For this [. . .] they intend to lay on searches and will not hold within the Parliament's [. . . .]

For Master [Havelock Trent] merchant in Leith in Scotland.

173 Overton strove, somewhat unrealistically to remain neutral in the controversy between the two armies (*ibid.*, p. 244n).

174 General, or George, Monck.

175 Possibly William Welch, clerk or secretary to the Admiralty judges at Leith, who on 19 November 1659 was issued with a pass to go 'with his horses, servants, swords and necessaries' into England; Worc. MS XLIX, fo. [108]^{v}; *S&P*, p. 390. Some arms were seized at Welch's house in Leith in December 1659, around which time he wrote to his wife that he feared imprisonment if he returned to Leith; *CP*, IV, pp. 229–230, where the month should read 'December' 1659. A newsletter from London, written on 3 November 1659, which reports that 'W.W.' had written a long letter either from Edinburgh or from Leith, stirring up feelings against Monck among the London militia, may refer to the same man (*ibid.*, p. 92).

176 Despite an undertaking to the contrary, John Lambert was known to be intercepting packets both to and from Scotland; *ibid.*, pp. 109–110, 132–133, 172–173.

John Banks, London, to John Williamson, [London], 22 November 1659

fo. 138r

London the 22 9bris 1659

Loving Friends

I have not had one line from you since the [receipt of that formerly] and [. . . .] if you and the 9 officers of the army who rather then they would lay down their commissions would hazard the destroying of 3 nations and throw down all powers to set up themselfs; and we had no hopes left but that now all our liberties, [privileges/pledges] of Parliament and what ever else was dear unto us would be devolved under the domination of the sword until your declaration came from the north and [renewed/revived/relieved] us, during which I did, by all the means I could, send you intelligence how affairs stood and of the dissatisfaction in city and country, but fear most of my letters were intercepted. But now all things look with another face, for your plenipotentiaries arrived here Saturday night and after a visit to my Lord Fleetwood, away they went to Colonel Salmon's quarters. The next day was not for business, so on Monday they began their treaty and on Tuesday the 15th they agreed upon our articles by which the peace was concluded, and ['fore 2] the great guns went off from the Tower, which sudden clapping up of the business <for they [feared] on Monday their army with Lambert would [not ingage]>[177] before that any of the Parliament party had speech with them, only my Lord Fleetwood and the officers, which doth amaze all men. The truth is they had notice that Colonel Overton had imprisoned 2 of his officers that went about to secure the blockhouses doth stand out, and Colonel Whetham sends them on Monday a declaration from the officers of his garrison that they dissented from them and desired the Parliament might be permitted to sit. Also Hurst Castle in the west did the like and all the rest being ready to take fire, they followed them day and night telling them they[178] 100 thousand in arms. That if they would not agree they [. . . .] it would be the sword speedily, and also persuaded them Charles Stewart was raising men and the like so that the business was done. But for what I can perceive they have agreed to such things as can never [stand] for they can never lay a right foundation without turning in the Parliament, and they know [here] themselfs and have been labouring to get 40 of the old Members to sit again, and do some drudgery for them as to pass the act for 100,000*l* per mensem

[177] Interlined.

[178] Presumably 'had' is omitted here.

cessment etc. But it's thought they cannot get so many but they have about 22 that have consented to sit and Timothy Wilkes is now as zealous an army man as I am a parliamentary, and is for a senate of 70 whatever they be for. I assure you he is, for I have been told <by>[179] several Parliament men that if they could would send down some of their House and assist

fo. 138^v

the strength of my Lord General Monck with their councils etc. he would be forced to treat. They cried, still if he do but keep Scotland he will do [his/our] work and that all passages being stopped they could not get to him, and they were now about sending to him, but I fear it's now too late. We are like to have strange [. . .] when such persons are a quorum for it's thought not a man of those 5 chosen by the commissioners except Wariston (who is for any change[)] will meddle [up] with the business. The Lord knows our liberties and freedoms as men or Christians do now stand but on very weak sandy foundations except they keep their oaths, promises and ingagements better than yet they have done. However they are surer in a parliament than in 90,000 of them. I pray assure *G.M.*[180] that there are letters on the way to him and care is taken to clothe him with power and instructions to act.[181] Sir Arthur Hesilrige is in town and remembers his words to him, and many thanks are returned to him for [his] courage in this good cause by the Parliament. *Vale.*

John Banks

Master John Williamson Esq ([. . . .])

I wrote to him last post
The letter to my Lord Maior will be delivered tomorrow. A Common Council being called already it was judged meet to deliver it [from] several Members of Parliament.[182]
Both letters came safe and one will be delivered tomorrow. The judges break not the Term on Saturday and will not sit by this power. All things are worse and worse.

[179] Interlined.

[180] General, or George, Monck.

[181] Letters endorsing Monck's support written a few days previously by the deposed Council of State and Speaker did not reach him until early in December (pp. 343, 344 below).

[182] Monck's letter of 12 November 1659 was delivered to the Common Council of London on the evening of 23 November by Cols Markham and Atkins, who were immediately imprisoned by the Committee of Safety. Monck's three commissioners in London disclaimed the letter, saying it was a forgery; *CP*, IV, pp. 134–137; Baker, *Chronicle*, pp. 694–695; *Mercurius Politicus*, 595 (17–24 Nov. 1659), p. 908.

Send your answer to this as before directed or to Master John Banks, merchant, London, to be left at the post office.

George Monck to the Ministers of the Congregated Churches about London, 23 November 1659[183]

fo. 96r

Honoured and Dear Friends

I received yours and am very sensible of your great[184] kindness which you have expressed to the army in Scotland in sending down such honourable and revered persons[185] so long [and] tedious a journey whom we have received with thankfulness and great joy as the messengers of the churches and ministers of Christ; and have taken notice of this office of love and of your care of these 3 nations. I do promise for myself[186] and the rest of the officers here that your interest, liberty and incouragement shall be very dear to us and we shall take this as a renewed obligation to assert to the uttermost what we have already declared for the churches of Jesus Christ. I doubt not but you have received satisfaction of our inclinations to a peacable accommodation, and do hope that some difficulties being obviated[187] we shall obtain a fair composure. I do assure you that the great things which have been upon my heart to secure and provide for and[188] our liberties and freedom[189] as[190] the subjects and servants of Jesus Christ which are conveyed to us in the covenant of grace assured in the promises purchased for us by the blood of our Saviour and given as his great legacy to[191] his churches and people, in comparison of which[192] we esteem all other things as dung[193] and dross but as they have relation to and dependence on this most noble end. The other are our laws and rights as men which must have their estate in the 2d place and for which many members of the churches have been eminent instruments to labour in sweat and blood for these 18 years last past and our

[183] Printed in full in [Monck], *A Collection of Letters*, pp. 32–34. Differences between the two versions are given as footnotes. The letter to which this is a reply is printed in *CP*, IV, pp. 81–82, and the ministers' reply is found in Worc. MS XXXII fo. [168]v.

[184] *A Collection of Letters* omits 'great'.

[185] These emissaries are identified in *CP*, IV, p. 82n.

[186] *A Collection of Letters* reads 'my trust' for 'myself'.

[187] *Ibid.* substitutes 'united' for 'obviated'.

[188] *Ibid.* substitutes 'are' for 'and'.

[189] *Ibid.*, 'freedoms'.

[190] *Ibid.*, inserts 'we are'.

[191] *Ibid.* substitutes 'of' for 'to'.

[192] *Ibid.* reads 'what' for 'which'.

[193] Philippians, III.8.

ancestors for many hundred years before. The substance of which may be reduced to Parliamentary government, and the people's's[194] consenting to the laws by which they are to be governed. That this privilege of the nations may be so bounded that the churches may have both security and incouragement is my great desire and of those with me. So that I hope you will own those just things and give us that assistance that becomes[195] the churches of Christ in pursuance of this work. And we do assure you that we shall comply as far as possible with respect had to the[196] security and safety of these nations and the preservation of our ancient birthrights and liberties. And we shall pray that we may be kept from going out of God's way under pretence of doing his[197] work. I do in the name of the whole army and for myself give you all our affectionate thanks for this your work of love, and though we are not able to make such returns as are in our hearts and desires to do, yet we shall indeavour by all ways and means to express our care and love to the churches and shall leave the reward to Him who is the God of peace and has[198] in especial[199] assured a blessing to the peace makers. And conclude with the words of David, 1 Sam[uel] 25.32, 'blessed be the Lord God of Israel and blessed be your advice and blessed be you all'. Now the Lord be a wall of fire round about you and let his presence be in his churches and they filled with his glory. I have no more but to intreat your prayers for an happy issue to these unhappy differences. Which is the prayer of him who is

revered sirs and dear friends

your very affectionate friend and[200] servant

Edinburgh 23 9bris 1659

<To[201] Dr Owen, Master Hooke and Master Greenhill, to be communicated to the churches in and about London.>[202]

[194] *A Collection of Letters*, 'people'.
[195] *Ibid.*, 'which becometh'.
[196] *Ibid.* substitutes 'your' for 'the'.
[197] *Ibid.* reads 'God's' for 'his'.
[198] *Ibid.* substitutes 'truth' for 'has'.
[199] *Ibid.*, 'special'.
[200] *Ibid.* omits 'friend and'.
[201] *Ibid.* substitutes 'For my Reverend Friends' for 'To'.
[202] Marginated.

Newsletter from [London], undated[203]

fo. [146]ʳ

It is here rumoured that General Monck intends his advance speedily into England which is a design that his best friends here think not advantageous to him considering the season and the considerable force he is like to meet with. We do understand that most the northern parts are generally indisposed to assist the Lord Lambert or the army's design and so on the contrary both he and it conceived generally. All others are well disposed and much desire of a free Parliament as the only remedy left us for avoiding the destruction of the 3 nations.

It is [observable] that when Sir Arthur[204] had first put his army against the Lambertians he said he cared not if they took and hanged him so his arse were against Wallingford House.

Memorandum, Haddington, 2 December 1659

fo. [147]ʳ

This night the Lord General Monck came to Haddington where an express met him from the commissioners at London.[205]

Major Farmer and the forces drawn from Alnwick, the foot into Berwick and the horse into Scotland. They drew off in the night about 7 of the clock and got to Berwick in the morning. 24 miles.[206]

Memorandum, Dunbar, 3 December 1659

fo. [147]ᵛ

This night the General came to Dunbar and lay there the night and on Sunday.[207]

[203] From its position in Clarke's letter-book this was probably written about 1 December. This attribution is supported by a letter from Newcastle of that date which also reports that Monck was marching towards Berwick; *Mercurius Politicus*, 597 (1–8 Dec. 1659), p. 938.

[204] i.e. Sir Arthur Hesilrige, whose regiment was stationed in several key northern garrisons in late 1659. Its cooperation with Monck was a vital factor in his confrontation with Lambert; F&D, II, pp. 522–523.

[205] This probably refers to the letter of 26 November 1659 which is found in *CP*, IV, pp. 139–140.

[206] Farmer had been ordered to Alnwick on 8 November 1659, but was withdrawn when Lambert's forces were nearing Morpeth in order to prevent any unplanned skirmishes; *ibid.*, p. 108; F&D, I, p. 140.

[207] i.e. 4 December.

The deposed Council of State, London, to George Monck, received 4 December 1659[208]

fo. 148r

This day Captain Elms came to Berwick, and with him Master Horton, servant to Sir Arthur Haslerig, who brought the following letters:[209]

Sir

We have been too long silent, but this opportunity offering itself we cannot but let you understand the principles of our hearts since[210] your faithful actings in discharge of your trust and duty to this Parliament, and for the good of the 3 nations and posterity in these times of so great hypocrisy and defection is most gratiously acknowledged by us, and we can assure you exceedingly well resented by all sober and interested persons that love a Commonwealth. And you may be confident that we shall adhere to you, and shall to our utmost promote the good cause which you have hereto with so much wisdom and courage highly owned, and that it is our resolution to stand or fall with you in defence thereof, and that we shall as occasion offers itself, the Lord inabling, be assisting to you according to your declaration for removing the force from this Parliament that so they may sit with freedom and by God's blessing lay a foundation for an happy and lasting settlement of these great extremity so eminently to assist.

We are, Sir,

your most faithful and real servants

London 19 November 1659

Anthony Ashley Cooper
Robert Wallop
Thomas Scot, President
Arthur Haslerig

[208] Because the date of receipt of this and the following document is crucially important I have followed Clarke in allocating them to the day of their arrival rather than to that on which they were written – a departure from his normal practice. The delay was critical, as I have suggested in McDonald, 'Timing of General George Monck's march', pp. 363–376. The letter is paraphrased in Baker's *Chronicle*, p. 695. Two of its signatories, Ashley Cooper and Hesilrige, had held a 'fruitless conference' with Monck's commissioners at the Fleece Tavern three days before it was written; Christie, *Life of Anthony Ashley Cooper*, I, pp. 199–200.

[209] Elms may have been related by marriage to Hesilrige, and Horton was possibly the son of Col Thomas Horton; McDonald, 'Timing of General George Monck's march', p. 371n. Monck was already on his way to Berwick, where they awaited his arrival. Here, on the same day, he also received letters from Lambert and his officers; below, p. 347; *CP*, IV, p. 171.

[210] Baker's *Chronicle* begins the letter at this point.

Josiah Berners
Henry Neville
[Henry] Morley[211]
Valentine Walton
Robert Reynolds

For the Right Honourable General Monck, commander-in-chief of all the forces in Scotland

William Lenthall, London, to George Monck, received 4 December 1659

fo. 148r

Sir

Soon after the late interrupting of the Parliament I received one from you and no more, and should have returned an answer to the same before this but that the ways and passages were obstructed.[212] But having now this safe hand I thought it high time to let you know that your seasonable [remedy] for restoring this present Parliament in order to their settling of a glorious Commonwealth is not only exceeding resented by myself and the rest of the Members of Parliament in general, but universally appreciated (as far as I can gather) by all sober men of what judgement [. . .][213] who I do verily believe will be as ready to assist you in what they may. Thus humbly beseeching the God of truth and faithfulness to be your shield and buckler, I think it my honour that I can subscribe,

your very affectionate friend to serve you

William Lenthall, Speaker

London 9bris 21 1659

For General Monck these

[211] Apparently 'Herbert Morley' is intended here.

[212] Another reference to Lambert's interception of post both to and from Monck (as reported, for example, by one of Monck's commissioners on 24 November 1659, and in Monck's reply to that letter of [28] November 1659; *CP*, IV, pp. 134, 141).

[213] I have revised my reading of this phrase from that given in McDonald, 'Timing of General George Monck's march', p. 370, which read 'by all sober men of action [. . .]'.

George Monck to the deposed Council of State, London, 5 December 1659

fo. 148v

<5 *December* from Dunbar. Letter from General Monck to the Council of State>[214]

Right Honourables

Yours of 9bris the 19th came safe to my hands.[215] They came indeed in relation to our expectation here late but in respect to our desires welcome. We could not have thought that after we had so fully declared and so freely and [fair/far] ingaged for the parliament we could have been so long without incouragement from our friends in England especially from your Lordships whose interest was so nearly concerned with ours. And we did nevertheless think that it was for want of that some persons have deserted us who otherwise would have stood by us but it has pleased God that the fearfulness and perfidiousness of those persons has not so much weakened our hands as united our hearts. And we are now not only unanimous and courageous, but of sufficient [incouragement] through the assistance of God if not to go through with the business alone yet to defend ourselves and divert so great a part of their strength as that they shall not be able to hinder you from raising forces in the south, as we do not question but you will with all your might attempt. And if other intelligence be true will not be difficult for you to do.

However in the meantime we earnestly intreat you to send us some eminent persons from amongst you to assist our councils and countenance our actings and some horse officers if they can find any way by land. Yet the passage by sea is easy and open.[216]

We hope the late agreement made by our commissioners has given you no occasion to alter your resolution and that you have by this time even from common fame received sufficient satisfaction in that point. Your Lordships may assure yourselfs we shall make no agreement that shall be so contrary to your declarations or prejudicial to the privileges of Parliament. I could wish that there might some way be found out for a better and more frequent correspondence between your Lordships and us here which may be done best by sea. It would very much promote our common business and would be to me very

[214] Marginated.

[215] Monck used the same phrase, 'came safe to my hands', when writing to his commissioners on [28] November 1659; *CP*, IV, p. 140.

[216] Baker's *Chronicle* relates that around this time Monck 'sent an express to Clarges, to provide him some good Horse-Officers, and send them by Sea in a nimble Bark' (p. 697).

acceptable if it were but for the opportunity I should have thereby [proven] to subscribe myself what I am always have resolved to be

your Lordship's most humble servant

George Monck

Dunbar 5th 10bris 1659

For my very loving friends these

George Monck to William Lenthall, London, 5 December 1659

fo. 148ᵛ

<Letter to the Speaker>[217]

Right Honourable

I have received yours of 9bris 21 which was very welcome, though it came very late. We expected ere this not only to have heard from you, but to have heard you had been acting something for us which in the time of this directing of their army towards us had not been difficult. But we hope there is yet no time lost and if you please yet <not>[218] to appear for us, we shall be able to give you opportunity to do what you please. In the meantime, we intreat you to send us some considerable persons to assist and countenance our councils and some horse officers which will not be hard for you to do either by sea or land. Fear not but we will stand to our declarations and think not that we will live in the isle of Great Britain any longer then it may be governed by Parliament. I shall commit no more particulars to paper but expect an opportunity by a more frequent correspondence. In the meantime I commit you to the protection of the Almighty and remain

your very humble servant

George Monck

Dunbar 5th 10bris 1659

[217] Marginated.
[218] Interlined.

Memorandum, Berwick, 5 December 1659

fo. [149]^{r}

This day the General came to Berwick.

Colonel Zanchy came to him and presented him the letter from the officers at Newcastle.[219]

Newsletter, London, to [George Monck], 8 December 1659

fo. [155]^{r}

Sir

Since the declaring of Portsmouth, the people of [. . .] and Plymouth, Arundel and Bristol and [Colchester], Chester and [. . .], and many strong places are for you, and the city of London in 2 or 3 days will be in a posture which puts those here to their wits' ends, and they are in consultation to cheat you upon pretences of a free parliament, but you should not be roused by them, and if you keep your ground until January your business will be done without striking a stroke, for here are not a thousand men, and all in distractions.[220]

Memorandum, [Coldstream], 10 December 1659[221]

fo. [151]^{v}

This day Major Ogle Return'd from Newcastle with a Lettre from the Lord Lambert who he left very malevolent with Colonel Lilburne and the rest. *They would nott permitt him to speake with his owne Sister nor any other nor to lie alone. ~~Capt.~~ Cornett Caithnesse lay with him. Hee told him that they had*

[219] Zanchy left Newcastle on 1 December, arriving two days later at Berwick where he was held in custody until Monck's arrival. His detention was used by Lambert as a pretext for sending troops towards the Scottish border; *Mercurius Politicus*, 597 (1–8 Dec. 1659), p. 938; 598 (8–15 Dec. 1659), p. 944; *CP*, IV, p. 183. Monck then retaliated by detaining Zanchy, who was to have returned immediately with Monck's reply of 7 December; Worc. MS XXXII, fo. 150^{r}; Baker, *Chronicle*, p. 696.

[220] The governor of Portsmouth, Col Whetham, had declared for a Parliament on 3 December 1659, and news reached London on 6 December that Bristol and parts of Devonshire had followed suit; Davies, *Restoration*, p. 181; *CP*, IV, p. 168.

[221] The longhand sections of this document are printed in *ibid.*, pp. 181–182. Clarke appears to have been at Coldstream from 9–16 December; Worc. MS XXXII, fos 151^{r}, 165^{r}.

30,000 men uppe in Armes for them in severall places in England, besides those att Newcastle and London, that there was none but drunkards and swearers in General Monck's army and that he was an [. . . .] and cavalier. *That there were Scotchmen entertayned in every Troope & company & serve to Command them*, that Tinptallon, Dunnottar and other places were delivered to the Scots.[222]

Memoranda, [Coldstream], [10 December 1659][223]

fo. [152]^r

Intelligence

That Colonel Smith abused Captain Durdoe's men, pulling them by the hair of the head in the streets at Newcastle.[224]

The commissioners come in to Newcastle.[225]

5 troops gone towards [Carlisle].

There came in 5 troops to Morpeth and 4 troops lay up and down in the country and 10 companies of foot in the town, that they intended to march this day to Alnwick.[226]

That the Lord Fleetwood sent to the Lord Lambert to march southward which he refused. 5,000 apprentices up in London under several commanders who are not known, the apprentices and boys bearing off Sir Henry Vane's colours, selling them by the yard, and trampling them in the kennel.[227]

[222] Monck's commissioners in London had heard on 26 November 1659 the unfounded rumour that Monck had delivered Dumbarton and Dunnottar Castles over to the Scots; *CP*, IV, pp. 140, 143. Officers deemed untrustworthy had been transferred from Tantallon to the Bass Rock at the beginning of November; *True Narrative of the Proceedings in Parliament*, p. 66.

[223] These undated notes occur around 10 December in Clarke's notebook. At least some of them have come from Newcastle. Thomas Gumble emphasized its importance in Monck's intelligence system; *Life of General Monck*, p. 170.

[224] Probably Col Henry Smith, whose movements at this time are described in F&D, II, pp. 515–516. During December Monck wrote at least twice to Lambert requesting Durdoe's release; *CP*, IV, pp. 196, 224.

[225] Lambert informed Monck that the commissioners had arrived on 'Thursday att night', i.e. 8 December 1659.

[226] These movements of troops were ordered by Lambert upon hearing of the detention of Col Zanchy; p. 347n above; *CP*, IV, pp. 182–183.

[227] i.e. 'canal', or gutter; *OED*. The apprentices' riots in London were widely reported; *CP*, IV, pp. 164–166, 168; *Mercurius Politicus*, 597 (1–8 Dec. 1659), p. 939; *The Publick Intelligencer*, 206 (5–12 Dec. 1659), p. 930. There are eyewitness accounts in Bodl., MS Carte LXXIII, fos 333, 335 (Samuel Pepys), and W.L. Sachse (ed.), *The Diary of Thomas Rugg 1659–1661* (London, 1961), pp. 14–15. Sir Henry Vane had collaborated with the military regime and

Newsletter from London, 10 December 1659

fo. 163v

Att Norgate on Wednesday last Colonel Hewson, Colonell of the Souldiers that kill'd the Aprentices was found guilty of Murther, and were interrupted by the Committee of Safety. There hath bin all this weeke debates about the City & the Committee of Safety. Hull has declared for Par[liament]. *There came Newes this weeke of the King of Sweden's having* an [irrecoverable] loss in Funen and most of his nobles killed, and one of his nobles escaped.[228]

A. Johnston [of Wariston], London, to Sir James Stewart, Edinburgh, 10 December, 1659[229]

fo. 163v

[230]The General Council of Officers have[231] resolved that a Parliament be called and sit in or before February, and that it consist of 2 assemblies.[232] They are much inclined to use all possible means to prevent war, blood and mischief so far as they can. The city is much calmed since at their desire the grenadoes[233] are removed. There are 2 regiments of foot and 2 of horse lying about Portsmouth. The Lord who is the God and Prince of Peace and can command,[234] create

opposed the return of the Rump; V.A. Rowe, *Sir Henry Vane the Younger* (London, 1970), pp. 228–230. There follows a final memorandum in longhand.

[228] The great defeat inflicted on Charles X on the island of Fünen (mod. Fyn) by the combined armies of Holland, Poland, Austria, and Denmark in November 1659 was reported in several English newsbooks, one wryly commenting that 'The victory of the Danish and other forces got in Funen's represented every day greater'; *Mercurius Politicus*, 599 (15–22 Dec. 1659), p. 957.

[229] This letter is substantially the same as that headed 'Lord Wariston to his brother, Sir James Stewart, Lord Provost of Edinburgh' (the Remonstrant, Sir James Stewart of Coltness) in *L-P*, pp. 132–133 (from another copy, now apparently lost). Presumably it was intercepted by Monck, who was extremely hostile to Wariston; J. Buckroyd, 'Bridging the gap: Scotland 1659–1660', *The Scottish Historical Review*, 66 (1987), pp. 6–7, 9.

[230] *L-P*, p. 132, begins 'This is to show you that'.

[231] *Ibid.* reads 'has' for 'have'.

[232] In a letter to Fleetwood of 16 December 1659, some members of the displaced Council of State condemned the 'strange new parliament' which had been declared by the Council of Officers on 10 December 1659; Davies, *Restoration*, p. 183.

[233] *L-P*, p. 132 reads 'Grenadiers' for 'grenadoes'. However, the outline in Clarke's shorthand is clear and is confirmed by two newsletters which report the placing of 'Granadoes' (grenades) around St Pauls and elsewhere in the City after the apprentices' riots of 5 December 1659; Bodl., MS Carte LXXIII, fos 333, 335 (Samuel Pepys to Edward Mountagu); *CP*, IV, p. 187. 'Grenadier' is in any case a late seventeenth-century word (*OED*).

[234] *L-P*, p. 132 inserts 'and'.

peace, restore it and preserve it in the[235] nations and move the heart of every one to contribute to it in their relations and stations. I send you Doctor Owen's answer to the 2 grand questions of the time about magistrates' power in matters of religion and the other about tithes.[236] I desire you to communicate it to Master Stirling and Sir John.[237] I wish it were imprinted. So praying the Lord to send us good news from one another, I rest

your loving brother and servant

A. Johnston

10 10bris

For the Right Honourable Sir James Stewart, Provost of Edinburgh, Scotland.

Robert Andrews, Newcastle, to Margaret Stewart, Tarvet,[238] 11 December 1659[239]

fo. [156]^r

My Dear,

I wonder I do not hear from thee. If thy [soul] be [gaining] anything in this ends that I care the less, thy being kind to Jesus will easily persuade me to dispense with all unkindness. For it is impossible not to be kind to me if thou be kind to Him. Let us at present together before Him frequently, not only in behalf of our [own souls], our little babies and interests, but in behalf of all who love Him and cleave to his institutions and ordinances. These times turn us to double our deliverance. If we do so they will blow over. Be not discouraged for anything that can fall out. There is a prize at the stake that is of very much value though our treacheries and ingratitudes have been many.

[235] *Ibid.*, p. 133 reads 'these' for 'the'.

[236] The extract printed in *L-P* ends here.

[237] Wariston was in close touch with his fellow Protesters John Stirling and Sir John Christie at this time; Buckroyd, 'Bridging the gap', p. 5.

[238] i.e. Tarbet?

[239] The inclusion of this letter in Clarke's letter-book probably indicates that it had been intercepted by Monck's excellent intelligence system, probably along with the preceding document. It is possible to interpret it as an encoded message from Newcastle, where Lambert was based at this point. On 22 December 1659 Stewart wrote to Monck strongly rejecting claims that he had received any letter from Lambert; *CP*, IV, pp. 211–212. An important newsletter addressed to an unidentified correspondent came from the same well-informed source during the previous month (above, p. 335). I have altered the original order of documents on pp. 350–354 to reflect their chronological sequence.

Yet the same Almighty will do for His great name's sake, and for my part I do not yet apprehend but that our old enemies are those for whom this rope is intended. Remember me to the children, to both our neighbours and to all friends. I am thy loving husband,

Robert Andrews

Newcastle 10bris 11. 1659

For Margaret Stewart at Tarvet, to be sent to Sir James Stuart, Provost of Edinburgh, to send her these.

News from J.B., London, 13 December 1659[240]

fo. 164r

like to bee a perfect [. . .] war therefore consider of it and prepare. One writes from Newcastle that there was a design to have murthered *G.M.*[241] but his headquarters being at Berwick it's prevented. /Pray

fo. 164v

Pray take notice John Banks[242] is gone for Holland and therefore direct your letters to *Mr Jo: Brookes-head* merchant in London. Remember my most humble service to my *L.G.*[243] We are much rejoyced to here [*sic*] he stands for the present Parliament without which no foundation can be laid. The letter to Ireland shall be printed. Another letter to the Lord Mayor and Common Council concerning the former letter and that you intend this old Parliament shall meet to lay a foundation for to call a free Parliament that you cannot question that a Parliament should be brought in by the sword and another House to secure them in their wicked actings and that you still offer your resolutions and direct as is above to Master John Brookeshead. When the wind is west[244] expect good news

Your humble servant

J.B.

[240] This is a continuation of the longhand newsletter printed in *CP*, IV, pp. 186–187, which also reproduces the first sentence of its postscript.

[241] George, or General, Monck.

[242] For John Banks, see p. 338 above. The instruction to write instead to John Brookeshead may indicate a change of code-name.

[243] Lord General, i.e. Monck.

[244] It is not clear whether this phrase belongs to this or the preceding sentence.

London 13 10bris 1659

Colonel Atkins & Colonel Markham are still in prison butt goe out as I heare with their Messenger.[245] Write how strong you are horse and foot etc.

News from B.H., London, 15 December 1659[246]

fo. [187]r

<Intelligence that came to my Lord General out of England.>[247]

Though I am debarred of the privilege of your good company, yet I cannot omit to give you the trouble of this to shew how things are ordered [here/through/though] the [west/haste] they are very much [put off/out of] your [. . .][248]

This is only with the tender of my compliments to yourself. I am

your kinsman and servant

B.H.

Newsletter from Leonard Lytcott, Coldstream, 16 December 1659[249]

fo. [165]r

My Honoured Friends

According to my promise I have sent you a 2nd diurnall for other intelligence. Your hundred [. . .] government is laid aside. Your friends in the south, I hear, are [falling upon] Sir George Booth's free Parliament, the [spirit/honour] of the nation so much declaimed against by you all. Sir Henry Vane's loose foot with Charles [Cary/Carew]. It is such

[245] On 10 December Fleetwood had offered to release Atkins and Markham in exchange for some of the officers held at Portsmouth; [A. Hesilrige], *The True Copys of several Letters from Portsmouth* (London, 1659), p. 5.

[246] These brief passages in shorthand begin and end this newsletter, the longhand section of which appears in *CP*, IV, p. 194.

[247] Marginated.

[248] Then follows the longhand extract reproduced in *ibid.*

[249] Leonard Lytcott, one of Monck's most trusted officers, was John Thurloe's nephew; Baker, *Chronicle*, p. 694; F&D, II, p. 475. He appears to have provided a clearing station for information between England and Monck; see, for example, *CP*, IV, pp. 216–217.

a [diversion/direction] to obstruct our friends who rises unanimous for us in all parts of England. The great antisectarian Wariston and Lord Whitelocke are for anything for nothing and everything for money, now at their wits' end.[250] No hobgoblin nor spirit can be conjured up to get a penny from the people. [Their spirit is] their cause and the malignant interest may as soon work upon the belief in the moon, and moonshine in the water take as much impression as these new fangles upon the people of England. The rotation of the wheels of state begin to run right. The apprentice boys of London drive the cart in the right channel that neither Charles' Wain nor the new State waggoners can either lead or drive the chariot horses for this Commonwealth. The Turks trade by a sword. Government declines so fast that the [ghosts] of [. . .] is layd and [long jacket] [. . .] act to slow down the frantick undertaking of our Parliament drivers. Pardon my merriness. The sprightliness of the 2 elements of air and water we converse with makes us [. . .]. Be pleased to up-end all your discontented Quakers in Scotland, for here our ministers ride upon the best horses. Having filled my papers [. . .] with the service of all your friends here presented your names. My Lord General, Colonel Fairfax, Colonel [Rich], Major [Drew/Freere] etc, and lastly the least of your most humble servants,

Leonard Lytcott

Newsletter from [London], 23 December 1659

fo. 175^r

Vice-Admirall Lawson declaring for the parliament Two Troopes of Colonel Berrie's Regiment are gone into Portsmouth, Three Troopes of Colonel Lilburne's Regiment, Smythson's, Margary's, Wilkinson's. Fears for you. This day Lambert offended at Creed for opening his letters at Morpeth without order.[251]

The Council is blamed [. . . .] of their march. It is [quit] of Yorkshire. Fears for you.

Disbrowe's Regiment march't back into Herefordshire. Ludlow of Ireland now in England, declared for the Parliament, with Colonel Rich.[252]

250 An Edinburgh newsbook described Wariston as 'that changeing Warriston'; *Mercurius Britanicus*, 2 (8–15 Dec. 1659), p. 15.

251 Thomas Lilburne, writing to Sir Arthur Hesilrige from York on 3 January 1660, reported that Lambert wished to 'make his peace with Maj. Creed and others'; *CSPD 1659–1660*, p. 295. Information originating from Creed about Lambert's movements at this time was being passed to the royalists; *CClarSP*, IV, p. 500.

252 Sent to retake Portsmouth for the army, Rich was one of those who changed sides by entering the garrison; F&D, I, p. 156.

Generally [. . .] and believed here Lambert could be content with his own peace.

4 troops of Colonel Swallow's also gone back.[253]

Newsletter from [Newcastle], 23 December 1659

fo. 175r

Sir

Yesterday till 11 of the clock the Council of Officers sat. The result was to march, but the day is not absolutely determined, but on Monday it is generally supposed they will march, though I writ it not yesterday, which Captain Banister[254] has that they would not march. But they are grieved that you would not treat and say they have lost their opportunity. They cannot march that I can hear above 4,000 foot and 2,400 horse. I am confident that utmost Lilburne's regiment will do them little good, Strangeways' troop but 8 men with their colours, and Smithson's troop will not ingage, not one man of them.[255] But if they march, draw them but in Scotland, and you are sure of a strong party of Yorkshire. Fear not. Be of good courage. Prayers are here for you. God bless you.

Atkinson,[256] one of your soldiers, was with us yesterday and on Saturday morning will be again. I shall tell him what I know.

Sir George Booth dead in the Tower.[257]

[253] Robert Swallow had been given Whalley's regiment earlier in 1659, and had supported the army in its recent termination of Parliament; *ibid.*, pp. 193, 228–229.

[254] Capt. Peter Banister was sent by Monck to Newcastle with a request for safe conduct for letters to the rebels in Portsmouth. Lambert refused and sent Banister back to Berwick, where he was no doubt able to relay valuable information about Lambert's position; *Mercurius Politicus*, 600 (22–29 Dec. 1659), p. 987; Baker, *Chronicle*, p. 698; F&D, II, p. 525.

[255] On Monck's recommendation both Strangeways and Smithson received the thanks of the Council of State on 8 February 1660; *ibid.*, I, p. 276. Lilburne marched south to York with only two troops on the day on which this newsletter was written; *Parliamentary Intelligencer*, 2 (26 Dec.–2 Jan. 1660), p. 16.

[256] Presumably Capt. Thomas Atkinson of Col Hewson's regiment; F&D, II, p. 409.

[257] An unfounded rumour. Booth, imprisoned after the abortive royalist rising of July–August 1659, did not die until 1684; *OxDNB*.

Samuel Atkins, London, to [George Monck], 24 December 1659[258]

fo. 205ᵛ

Mr Speaker, Mr Scott, Mr Weaver, Sir Anthony Ashley Cooper, Mr Josiah Berners, and many more present[259] their service to your Excellency. I have Colonel Mears'[260] letters of the 16th instant which is well understood that you will leave all the rebels to the mercy of the Parliament.

Lawson is still with his fleete att Gravesend and all unanimous for the Parliament but there will be [no] more

fo. [206]ʳ

need of them in this particular. The Lord make us all truly thankful to God and your Excellency whom he has made an instrument to redeem these nations from the worst of slavery. My service to yourself, your lady and to Major-General Morgan, Colonel Mayers, Colonel Lytcott and all that have been faithful under you. I have written several letters and given you [. . .] advice from time to time but fear they have not half come to hand. However I have discharged my duty [to] your Excellency. Craving pardon for my [boldness]

I remain

your very humble servant

Samuel Atkins[261]

Ireland have all declared for the Parliament and have secured Colonel Jones[262] as letters to Fleetwood yesterday affirm. I was released of my imprisonment last Saturday after 21 days close imprisonment for delivering your letter to my Lord Maior etc, but the case is now altered.

[258] This is a continuation of the newsletter printed in *CP*, IV, p. 220. Parts of the shorthand version are duplicated in *L-P*, pp. 136–137, which adds a postscript not found in shorthand.

[259] The shorthand outline for 'present' has been read as the longhand 'to' in *CP*, IV, p. 220, which omits the rest as '[*cypher*]'.

[260] John Mayer, governor of Berwick, was an important link in Monck's communications network (p. 330 above). This phrase rules him out as the intended recipient of this letter, as suggested in *L-P*, p. 136.

[261] Samuel Atkins, an English merchant and farmer of salt imports into Scotland based at Leith, had been imprisoned immediately after delivering Monck's letter of 12 November 1659 to the Lord Mayor and Common Council of London; F&D, I, p. 391; *CP*, IV, p. 301; *Mercurius Politicus*, 595 (17–24 Nov. 1659), p. 908; p. 339n above. He was sometimes given the title of colonel, although he does not appear to have held this rank either during or after the Civil War; *S&C*, p. 317; F&D, I, pp. 391–392. In 1670 his part in promoting 'our Restoration' was recognized by Charles II; *CSPD Additional 1660–1670*, p. 292.

[262] Col John Jones, regicide, was arrested at Dublin on 13 December 1659; Davies, *Restoration*, p. 248.

The Anabaptists are all as tame as asses and as mute as fishes, the Lord make us thankful.

Memorandum, Whittingham, 3 January 1660

fo. 215[v]

I dined at Chillingham. Saw the place in [a] stone where a toad was taken out, being now part of a chimney piece, upon the slitting of the stone.[263]

Memorandum, [Northallerton], 9 January 1660

fo. [225][r]

The Lord Generall march't from Darlington to Northallerton. Master Harrison, the last year sheriff of Yorkshire, met him at the end of the town.[264]

Memorandum, Topcliffe, 10 January 1660

fo. 226[r]

The Lord Generall march't from Northallerton [to] Topliffe 8 miles. Colonel Waters met him at the town.

Memorandum, [York], 11 January 1660

fo. [227][v]

The Lord General marched with the army *from Topliffe to Yorke where hee stay'd till Munday following the 16th instant.*[265]

[263] Chillingham Castle, belonging to Lord Grey of Wark, had been briefly occupied by a party of Lambert's horse about 9 December 1659, forcing Monck to withdraw; *CP*, IV, p. 179. It lies some four miles south-east of Wooler (Monck's headquarters on 3 January). Clarke had an informant there; Appendix A, p. 372. The 'toad-stone' is described in M.H. Dodds (ed.), *A History of Northumberland*, XIV (Newcastle-upon-Tyne, 1935), pp. 335, 344, and in more detail in W.W. Tomlinson, *Tomlinson's Comprehensive Guide to the County of Northumberland*, 11th edn (Newcastle-upon-Tyne, n.d.), pp. 492–493. I owe this last reference to the kindness of Richard Sharp.

[264] It was from Northallerton that Monck sent word to London of Lambert's capitulation; *Occurrences from Forraigne Parts*, 54 (2–10 Jan. 1660), p. 581. *Mercurius Politicus* reported that Monck did not reach Northallerton until Tuesday 10 January; 603 (12–19 Jan. 1660), p. 1016.

[265] York had been delivered up to Fairfax's army by Lilburne without a struggle on 2 January; *Occurrences from Forraigne Parts*, 54 (2–10 Jan. 1660), p. 582. There follow three lines of longhand.

The Lord Fairfax came to him [Thursday] and he dined with him on Saturday at *Nun Appleton.*[266]

William Lenthall, Westminster, to Major-General Morgan, 13 January 1660[267]

fo. [229]^r

Sir

The Parliament of the Commonwealth of England receiving information from General Monck of your readiness and cheerfulness to joyn with him in indeavouring the restoration of the Parliament to the exercise of the trust reposed in them, this so signal testimony of your publike spirit and faithfulness has put a new lustre upon your former services, and has occasioned a command to me in the name of the Parliament to give you thanks for your faithfulness and good services, which you may assure yourself will at all times be answered with a return of favour answerable to the merit thereof. This being all I have in command to say to you, I rest

your assured friend,

William Lenthall, Speaker

Westminster, January 13, 1659

For his much respected friend, Major-General Morgan at his quarters in Scotland.[268]

[266] Evidently written in retrospect. The 12th was a Thursday and so the date of Monck's visit to Nun Appleton, reported by *The Parliamentary Intelligencer*, 6 (23–30 Jan. 1660), p. 65, would have been the 14th. Baker's *Chronicle* (p. 700) confirms that Fairfax had a meeting with Monck at York, and the *Parliamentary Intelligencer* wrote that 'The Lord Fairfax gave his Excellency the Lord General Monck a very noble entertainment at his house, about seven miles distant from this place'; 6 (23–30 Jan. 1660), p. 65.

[267] Parliament gave order for this letter to be written on 12 January 1660; *CJ*, VII, p. 808. I have reversed the original order of this and the following document, in order to reflect their chronological sequence.

[268] On 16 January Morgan received orders from Monck to remain at York with three regiments. He did not return to Scotland until 17 February 1660; *Parliamentary Intelligencer*, 6 (23–30 Jan. 1660), p. 66; *L-P*, p. 153.

George Monck, York, to Sir Arthur Hesilrige, Whitehall, 14 January 1660

fo. [227]^{r}

Right Honourable

Master Gilbert Mabbott having during the late interrupting of the Parliament been very serviceable to the publike not only by his usual correspondence, but other private intelligence to myself and the army in Scotland, I make bold to recommend him unto you for some suitable imployment, being there will be divers [vacancies] upon occasion of the late [. . .] and defections, and such men who appear in unseasonable times deserve all fitting incouragement,[269] and your respect herein I will take as a service done to

your very humble servant

George Monck

York, 14 January 1659

For the Honourable Sir Arthur Hesilrige, one of the ~~commissioners for the government of the army these at Whitehall~~

Council of State at Whitehall

Memorandum, [Ferrybridge], 16 January 1660

fo. [231]^{r}

This day the Lord Generall Monck came from Yorke to Ferribrigs where he lay that night.[270]

Memorandum, [Langold], 17th January 1660

fo. [231]^{v}

This day the Lord Generall went from Ferribrigs to Langold, Colonel Knight's house, where he lay that night.[271]

[269] On 27 January 1660 it was reported that Mabbott was to be constituted Advocate of the Army in Ireland; *CJ*, VII, p. 825.

[270] Monck's arrival with his army at Ferrybridge on the 16th was seen in London as final confirmation that he would be able to place his troops entirely at Parliament's disposal; *Exact Accompt*, 57 (13–20 Jan. 1660), p. 6; *Parliamentary Intelligencer*, 5 (16–23 Jan. 1660), p. 57.

[271] Col Ralph Knight, a former major in Monck's own regiment, replaced Col Saunders on 23 December 1659. His regiment of horse, together with Monck's own, formed Monck's

Sir Thomas Osborne,[272] Sir Thomas[273], Captain Weston and other gentlemen met my Lord General at Major Knights's house.

Samuel Atkins, London, to [William Clarke?], 17 January 1660[274]

fo. 233r

All our Eyes and Expectations are uppon his Excellency waiting what further good thinges hee will doe for these distressed Nations and the rewarding the militia and the settling Newcastle, Tynemouth and other places in such faithful hands doth wonderfully [rejoice] all sober honest men not only hear [*sic*] but in all other parts though there are another sort of people not so well satisfied, but that I hope will signify little.

This oath of Abjuration keepes out very many, nay the Major parte of the Councill of State from acting in that capacity. Master Gumble will inform his Excellency of this at large.[275] *Doctor Clarges, and Colonel Whetham sett out to meet you this Morning, Mr Scott & Luke Robinson are alsoe this afternoone gone in a Coach to doe the like: This day the House have secluded Colonel Sidenham & Major Sallaway. The last is alsoe committed to the Tower: The Gentlemen of Devonshire have sent a Letter to the Parliament by Mr Bamphfield that was Speaker to the last parliament to desire that the Secluded Members may bee admitted to sitt without any oaths or Engagements imposed uppon them with some other thinges tending to the setling the Nation: Heere is much talke of a New Plott some say by the Anabaptists and 5th Monarchy men to rise, others say a Cavaleere Designe is on Foote, but this I doe assure you the Guardes are all doubled about the Citty & many forces brought uppe to London (to secure the Citty & peace thereof) this day.* His Excellency is [called long] for here. I pray you direct him for that now you are at [the harbour's mouth] that he may so steer as to secure himself to all that are affirmed with him which are all the honest sober men in these nations.

Samuel Atkins

first division on his march into England. Knighted in 1660, he was made lieutenant-colonel of Buckingham's regiment of foot in 1673; F&D, I, pp. 139, 140, 290.

[272] Osborne, the future earl of Danby, was a client of the duke of Buckingham, possibly as early as this; A. Browning, *Thomas Osborne, Earl of Danby and Duke of Leeds 1632–1712*, 3 vols (Glasgow, 1951), I, p. 23. Osborne's seat was at Kiveton, some six miles west of Worksop.

[273] Blank.

[274] Clarke would have known Atkins (for whom see above, p. 355n) at Leith where Atkins was based and Clarke had a house.

[275] Gumble delivered Monck's letter of 6 January from Newcastle to Parliament on 12 January 1660, returning on the 18th; *CJ*, VII, p. 808; Davies, *Restoration*, p. 268.

Memorandum, [Mansfield], 18th January 1660

fo. [232][r]

This day the Lord Generall came from Langold to Mansfeild where he quartered that night.

The Lord Mansfield met my Lord General on the way near his house and afterwards Master Pierrepont near ~~Worksop~~ Carlton,[276] and went with him in his coach within a mile of Mansfield.

Satirical verse, 19 January 1660

fo. [235][r]

Till it be understood
Who under Monck's hood[277]
  [Enter] a city and puts out his horns
Till the 10 days be out
The Speaker has the [gout]
  And the Rump doth sit upon thorns.

Memorandum, [Nottingham], 19 January 1660[278]

fo. [235][r]

This day the Lord Generall march't from Mansfeild to Nottingham.

The Lord Chesterfield[279] came to his Lordship. Next day the Lord Chaworth[280] and other gentlemen of the country.

[276] Carlton in Lindrick, Notts. Presumably this was a member of the family of the 2nd earl of Kingston, whose seat was at Thoresby, also near Worksop, and quite possibly Oliver Cromwell's friend William Pierrepont MP. The Lordship of Carlton was later jointly in the hands of the earl of Chesterfield and Charles Medows Pierrepont Esq.; R. Thoroton, *The Antiquities of Nottinghamshire*, III (Wakefield, 1796), p. 13.

[277] There were many punning references to 'Monck's hood'. This example is a variation on the 1st verse of *The Rump Dock't* ([London], 1660); for another, see Sachse, *Diary of Thomas Rugg*, p. 30. The same phrase was used to begin Ludlow's account of the Restoration; A.B. Worden (ed.), *A Voyce from the Watch Tower*, (London, 1978), p. 85.

[278] Here Monck had a secret meeting with Clarges, who brought the latest information about the military and political situation in London; Baker, *Chronicle*, p. 701.

[279] Philip Stanhope, 2nd earl of Chesterfield.

[280] Patrick Chaworth, 3rd Viscount Chaworth of Armagh.

Memorandum, [Stony Stratford], 26 January 1660

fo. 239v

My Lord Generall march't from Northampton to Stony Stratford. The commissioners of Parliament went with him. Those of the city went before to Fenny Stratford.

Memorandum, [London], 3 February 1660

fo. 245r

The Lord Generall came from Barnett to Whitehall. No [jubilations] of the people or ringing of bells.[281] Only those that cried out were for a free Parliament.[282]

The Speaker met his Lordship in the Strand and saluted him.[283]

Memorandum, [London], 10 February 1660

fo. 248r

According to yesterdayes Resolves of Parliament the Officers & Souldiers were imployed in ~~breaking~~ that odious and barbarous act *of braking & destroying the Gates of the Citty of London.*[284]

[281] This was in marked contrast to Monck's reception elsewhere; *CSPV 1659–1661*, p. 114; *Parliamentary Intelligencer*, 5 (16–23 Jan. 1660), p. 57. Sir Anthony Ashley Cooper recorded only that 'there was no apparent opposition' to Monck on his entry into London (Christie, *Life of Anthony Ashley Cooper*, I, p. 205), while according to Baker's *Chronicle* 'all both within and without [was] in a great Calm' (p. 704).

[282] Samuel Pepys recorded that 'in his passage through the town [Monck] had many cry out to him for a free Parliament; but little other welcome', while in his diary for January Thomas Rugg wrote, 'Now the citizans of London are indeffrent quiet and have hopes of Lord Generall Moncks cominge to towne and side with them upon the score of a full and free Parliment'; R.C. Latham and W. Matthews (eds), *The Diary of Samuel Pepys*, 11 vols (London, 1970–1983), I, p. 40; Sachse, *Diary of Thomas Rugg*, p. 30.

[283] Monck quartered at Whitehall, 'receiving visits from members of parliament and others' on the following two days, Saturday and Sunday; *CSPV 1659–1661*, p. 115. On 6 February he was officially received, with great ceremony, by Parliament; *CJ*, VII, pp. 834–835; *Occurrences from Forraigne Parts*, 62 (31 Jan.–7 Feb. 1660), p. 648.

[284] Monck was reluctant to carry out this order, but turned it to his advantage by quartering in the City and placing his army in Finsbury; *Parliamentary Intelligencer*, 8 (6–13 Feb. 1660), p. 112.

Memorandum, [London], undated[285]

fo. [250]ʳ

<Colonel [Walton]>:[286] ~~Colonel~~ observing of the general and [. . .] [calling] him General Monck (about a week since) answered General Monck, General Turd.

< Master Scot's eldest son>:[287] As soon as he came to London on telling them that General Monck had done good service for them and desiring to know what they would do for him, he said that they should clip, nay, they should cut his wings.

<Another member>:[288] That the[289].

<Ludlow *14 February*>:[290] That now they had shewed their [false] general a trick.[291]

<Henry Marten>:[292] That if ever they got him in their power they would make him know that that was not a letter fit to be sent to a Parliament of England.[293]

<Master Thomas Scot>:[294] Now we have set the fool on horseback to ride to his own destruction and I think there has not been the [wiser] Secretary of State a good while.

[295] and Master [Raly[296]/Cary].

<Major[297] (~~for Colonel Morley~~)>[298] Could any cavalier have done more than the General [by his letter] for [he ties] the Parliament to break and dissolve on the 7th of May[299] and then [they] will be any interregnum and then they will dissolve themselves. Captain Stearns.[300]

[285] I have discussed this puzzling memorandum above (pp. 311–312).

[286] Marginated. The regicide Col Valentine Walton was deprived of his command by Monck in February 1660 (*DBR*, 'Walton').

[287] Marginated.

[288] Marginated. Presumably meaning another MP.

[289] Blank.

[290] Marginated.

[291] Ludlow had visited Monck on the preceding day, 13 February, a meeting which is described in detail in Ludlow's *Memoirs*, II, pp. 225–227.

[292] Marginated.

[293] This is apparently a reference to Monck's letter of 11 February 1660; *OPH*, XXII, pp. 98–103.

[294] Marginated. Presumably, as earlier, Thomas Scott the younger, referring to his father who was acting as Secretary of State at this time.

[295] Blank.

[296] The two names are indistinguishable in Clarke's shorthand. If the former, this would be 'Raileigh' (as in *CP*, IV, p. 264), or Rawleigh.

[297] Blank.

[298] Marginated.

[299] Davies, *Restoration*, p. 283.

[300] Probably Capt. Robert Stearne, a member of the Irish brigade which had been sent to England at the time of Booth's rising in August 1659.

<[Marten's]>:[301] After that a servant of Marten's that set up in the city spoke to him and wondered that he did prefer such [. . .] which he knew is to [relish] the Lord General and his officers. He answered that he had no mind to do it but that if Master Scot was so earnest for it that he would not let him alone till he had delivered it.

Memorandum, [London], 17 February 1660[302]

fo. 252v

After several hours' discourse to no purpose Master Knightley went away discontented being he could not be agreed that secluded Members[303] should come in.

[301] Marginated.

[302] This comment appears below the record of the meeting held on this day, at which the following were present: Oliver St John, Sir Anthony Ashley Cooper, Sir Arthur Hesilrige, Col Hutchinson, Mr Weaver, Col Morley, Carew Rawleigh, Col Birch, Col Harlow, Mr Knightley, and Sir John Temple. Knightley was one of the secluded MPs ([W. Prynne], *The Curtaine Drawne, Or the Parliament exposed to view* . . . (London, 1659), p. 3), and was elected to the new Council of State on 23 February 1660; *CJ*, VII, p. 849.

[303] i.e. Members of the old Long Parliament excluded in Pride's Purge, 6 December 1648.

APPENDICES

APPENDIX A

Identification of correspondents

In several instances where writers (and occasionally recipients) of letters copied into Clarke's notebooks in longhand are not named, or are identified only by their initials, Clarke has identified them in shorthand. These are listed below, together with dates and geographical locations. References are provided for those which appear in Sir Charles Firth's edition of *The Clarke Papers*.

Notebook XXV[1]

fo. 59^{v} From Gabriel *Weire*, [London], 28 May 1653.

Notebook XXVI[2]

fo. 171^{r} From George Downing, Westminster, 6 December 1654.

Notebook XXVIII[3]

fo.[48]^{v} From Stephen Winthrop, London, 27 June 1656.

fo.75^{r} From Jeremiah Smith, on board the *Dunbar* in The Downs, 22 September 1656.

fo.75^{r} From Lord Broghill, [Westminster], 22 September 1656.[4]

[1] Worc. MS XXV.
[2] Worc. MS XXVI.
[3] Worc. MS XXVIII.
[4] *CP*, III, p. 74.

Notebook XXIX[5]

fo. [60a]^v From Jeremiah Smith, London, 14 May 1657.

fo. 107^r From William Rowe, [London], 18 August 1657.[6]

fo. 110^v From Sir John Reynolds, St Quentin, 21 August 1657.[7]

fo. [111]^r From Richard Ward, [London], 1 September 1657.

fo. 117^v From Joachim Hane, road before Dunkirk, 3 October, 1657.[8]

fo. 118^v From William Goodson, on board the *Dover* in Mardyke Pitts, 8 October 1657.[9]

fo. 123^r From William Rowe, [London], 5 November 1657.[10]

fo. 124^v From Richard Hughes, 4 November 1657.[11]

fo. 131^v From Joachim Hane, Mardyke, 30 November 1657.[12]

fo. 134^v From William Rowe, [London], 10 December 1657.

fo. 136^v From J. Thurloe, [London], undated, but probably written between 10 and 14 December 1657.

Notebook XXX[13]

fo. [1]^r From John Drummond, London, 1 January 1658.[14]

fo. 14^r From Major-General Morgan, Mardyke, 28 January 1658.[15]

fo. [77]^r From William Cary, London, 6 April 1658.[16]

fo. 85^v From Lieutenant-Colonel Hughes, London, 27 April 1658.

[5] Worc. MS XXIX.

[6] *CP*, III, p. 115, where only the first part of this newsletter is reproduced.

[7] Old Style. The letter provides the date in both Old Style and New Style (2 September). Sir John Reynolds, governor of Mardyke, was drowned in the English Channel on 5 December 1657; *LYP*, I, p. 297.

[8] *CP*, III, p. 120, where the writer is correctly identified.

[9] *Ibid.*, p. 121, where the writer is correctly identified.

[10] *Ibid.*, pp. 125–126, where the date is given as 7 November 1657.

[11] *Ibid.*, pp. 124–125.

[12] *Ibid.*, pp. 128–129.

[13] Worc. MS XXX.

[14] *CP*, III, p. 131.

[15] *Ibid.*, pp. 134–135.

[16] *Ibid.*, p. 146, where only the second part of this letter is printed.

*fo. [90]^r^* From John Thurloe, [Westminster], 12 May 1658.[17]

*fo. 117^r^* From John Harper, London, 29 June 1658.

*fo. [121]^r^* From John [Crossen], 6 July 1658.

*fo. 123^r^* From William Lowther, York, 10 July 1658.

*fo. [157]^r^* From William Lowther, Copmanthorpe, Yorks, 7 September 1658.[18]

*fo. [174]^r^* From Nicholas Ashwell, London, 7 October 1658.

Notebook XXXI[19]

*fo. [19]^r^* From John Northant, Westminster, 29 January 1659.

*fo. [19]^v^* From Samuel Desborough, Westminster, 29 January 1659.

*fo. 22^v^* From Henry Whalley, [London], 3 February 1659.

*fo. 22^v^* From Sir James MacDowall, [London], 3 February 1659.[20]

*fo. 23^v^* From John Thomson, London, 5 February 1659.

*fo. 23^v^* From Sir James MacDowall, [London], 5 February 1659.

*fo. 26^v^* From Archibald Johnston, Westminster, 10 February 1659.

*fo. 26^r^* From John Toppin, Tynemouth Castle, 11 February 1659.[21]

*fo. 30^v^* From Edward Scotton, Westminster, 15 February 1659.[22]

*fo. [33]^r^* From John Northant, London, 17 February 1659.[23]

*fo. [42]^r^* From Judge Swinton, Westminster, 5 March 1659.

*fo. 50^v^* From Henry Whalley, [London], 12 March 1659.

[17] *Ibid.*, p. 149.

[18] There is another copy of this letter at Worc. MS CLXXXI, fo. 414^r^.

[19] Worc. MS XXXI.

[20] *CP*, III, p. 179, letter beginning, 'Though this parliament consists'.

[21] Maj. John Topping, governor of Tynemouth, declared for the Parliament in January 1660; F&D, II, p. 524.

[22] *CP*, III, pp. 181–182. This identification supports that tentatively made by Sir Charles Firth of Scotton, MP for Devizes in Richard's parliament, as the author of a letter of 19 March 1659, signed simply 'E.S.'; *ibid.*, III, p. 186. Scotton was to be appointed captain in John Disbrowe's regiment on 4 July 1659; *CJ*, VII, pp. 704, 706.

[23] *CP*, III, pp. 182–183, where this correspondent's initials are transcribed as 'G.M.'.

fo. [54][v] From Archibald Johnston [of Wariston], [London], 17 March 1659.[24]

fo. 72[v] From John Mayer, [London], 7 April 1659.[25]

fo. 76[r] From John Thomson, [London], 9 April 1659.

fo. 77[r] From Thomas Margetts, Westminster, 9 April 1659.

fo. 78[v] From William Ross, Westminster, 12 April 1659.[26]

fo. 80[r] From Archibald Johnston of Wariston, [London], 14 April 1659.[27]

fo. 81[r] From the marquis of Argyle, [London], 14 April 1659.

fo. 81[v] From William Ross, [London], 16 April 1659.

fo. 84[r] From William Ross, [London], 19 April 1659.

fo. 86[v] From William Ross, [London], 21 April 1659.[28]

fo. 87[v] From Thomas Fitch, [London], 23 April 1659.[29]

fo. 91[r] From John Thurloe, [London], 26 April 1659.[30]

fo. 95[v] From John Mason, [London], 29 April 1659.[31]

fo. 103[r] From Thomas Margetts, [London], 3 May 1659.[32]

fo. 105[r] From Thomas Clarges, [London], 5 May 1659.

fo. 105[v] From Edward Raddon, [London], 5 May 1659.[33]

[24] *Ibid.*, p. 185, where this correspondent's initials are given as 'E.S.'.

[25] *Ibid.*, pp. 187–188. Lt-Col John Mayer was actively involved in drawing up the petition presented by the army to Richard Cromwell on 6 April 1659; *CP*, III, p. 187; see Hutton, *Restoration*, pp. 35–36 for the framing of the petition.

[26] Commissary William Ross, MP for Berwickshire in Richard's parliament. He seems to have been particularly trusted by Monck; *TSP*, VII, p. 633.

[27] *CP*, III, pp. 188–189, where the writer is correctly identified.

[28] *Ibid.*, pp. 190–191, where the writer is correctly identified.

[29] *Ibid.*, p. 193.

[30] *Ibid.*, p. 195, where the writer is correctly identified.

[31] *Ibid.*, where its possible writer is given as Capt. John Miller. Mason, a radical and General Baptist, opposed Richard's Protectorate and after Richard's fall was appointed an adviser to the seven army commissioners on the Scottish regiments (*DBR*, 'Mason'). His identification as author of the letter greatly helps to clarify its tone and meaning, and its possible effect on its recipient, Monck. His subsequent activity in weakening Monck's army is noted in Baker, *Chronicle*, p. 670. Miller remained loyal to Monck throughout 1659; *CP*, IV, pp. 6, 128, 178.

[32] *Ibid.*, p. 3. In Davies, *Restoration*, p. 118, this newsletter is attributed to 'Thomas Mabbott'.

[33] *CP*, IV, p. 8. Edward Raddon was among those ordered to return to England on a charge of high treason in April 1666; Ludlow, *Memoirs*, II, p. 490.

fo. 108^v From Thomas Fitch, [London], 7 May 1659.[34]

fo. 120^v From Bernard Gilpin, on board the *Nantwich* off Elsinore, 8 May 1659.

fo. [132]^v From Henry Monck, Dublin, 29 May 1659.[35]

fo. 134^r From Roger Sawrey, [London], 31 May 1659.

fo. 141^r From Thomas Savage, London, 9 June 1659.[36]

fo. [146]^v From Gilbert Mabbott, [London], 21 June 1659.

fo. 161^v From Henry Monck, Dublin, 29 June 1659.[37]

fo. [171]^r From 'Judge Swinton or Jo. Swinton', London, 18 July 1659.[38]

fo. [196]^r From William Goodson, on board the *Swiftsure* in the Sound, 31 July 1659.

fo. 186^v From Richard Ward, [London], 6 August 1659.[39]

fo. 203^v From Richard Ward, [London], 31 August 1659.[40]

Notebook XXXII[41]

fo. [13]^v From Clement Nedham, [London], [10–11 October 1659].[42]

fo. 94^r From Henry Monck, Dublin, 3 November 1659.[43]

fo. [74]^v From Benjamin [Martin], Alnwick, 5 November 1659.

fo. [161]^v From John Banks, London, 6 December 1659.

34 *CP*, IV, pp. 8–9.

35 *Ibid.*, p. 11, where the writer is correctly identified.

36 *Ibid.*, pp. 18–19.

37 *Ibid.*, p. 23, where the writer is correctly identified.

38 *Ibid.*, p. 24. The alternative equivalents given by Clarke for the initials 'J.S.' may be an illustration of his fondness for play on words, or may be a wry comment on Swinton's 'uncertain status as a judge', for which see Dow, *Cromwellian Scotland* p. 325n.

39 *CP*, IV, p. 37.

40 *Ibid.*, p. 49.

41 Worc. MS XXXII.

42 Signatory of a lengthy, undated letter copied in longhand, *ibid.*, fos 10–[13]^v. It directly precedes another newsletter dated 11 October 1659 and is likely to have been written around that date.

43 *CP*, IV, p. 95, where the writer is correctly identified.

fo. 162^{r-v} To Master Trent, London, from John [Doe], London, 6 December 1659.[44]

fo. [165]^{v} To Captain William Newman, Leith, 13 December 1659.[45]

fo. [201]^{v} From Thomas Morgan, Kelso, 27 December 1659.

fo. 210^{r} From William Warren, Chillingham Castle, 30 December 1659.

[44] *Ibid.*, pp. 167–168.
[45] *Ibid.*, p. 187.

APPENDIX B

The court martial of Colonel Edward Sexby

I have not normally provided transcriptions of longhand documents from Clarke's papers which have special relevance to those which appear in shorthand. However, I reproduce below the longhand account which until now has been our only source for Colonel Edward Sexby's court martial in June 1650, with which the reader may wish to compare the much more detailed shorthand record.[1]

Notebook XIX[2]

fo. 26^{r}

<Edinburgh June 14 1651>[3]

On Wednesday last Colonel Sexby came againe to his Triall, the proceedings of that day were cheiflie uppon the 2 last Articles (vizt) about the execution of the souldier at Morpeth & the mustering of some men in Captain Somners Company which were absent. The Colonel [proved] the Heighth of the distemper of his Regiment at Newcastle etc. and particularly of Captain Gosnells Company who cried, noe mony noe march, soe that he was necessitated to [. . .] the Souldier that was Condemned of Sir A. Haslerigg for an example. The Court came not to Issue but adjorned till Friday. Friday the Court met againe. Lieutenant Colonel Pike (who was sick before) was examined upon the 1st article & severall other particulars & after some further answer made by the Colonel to the 2 last articles he addressed himselfe to the Court declaring that he had divers thinges objected against him which were not shewen to him or any officer told him of any dislike they had to his proceedings till they were drawen into articles that he was satisfyed in his Conscience that he had done nothing wilfully but if hee had transgressed through weakness with an intention for the publique good he hoped the Court would make a favourable

[1] Pp. 26–36.
[2] Worc. MS XIX.
[3] Marginated.

fo. 26^v

Construction of his actions.

Colonel Sexby being withdrawen a Lettre was read from Sir A. Haslrigg wherein he cleered the Colonel as to the Hanging of the man that he [. . .] the Souldier to him either to <bee carried>[4] to the Headquarters or to execute by the way as he should see cause.

After this the Court had some debate on the whole matter but adjorned till the next day.[5]

This day <after 7 or 8 houres debate>[6] by the Court Marshall of the articles against Colonel Sexby they have voted him to be put by his Command cheefly upon the accompt of the 2d article which was for the detayning of pay from 7 or 8 souldiers belonging to him at Portland

fo. 27^r

Who would not goe with him for Ireland which (although as to his owne intentions he did for the advancement of the publique Service) yet now proves to bee the greatest crime, coming under an Article of Warre.

[4] Interlined.

[5] The rest of this paragraph, not reproduced here, does not relate to Sexby's case.

[6] Interlined.

APPENDIX C

A note on William Clarke's shorthand

There are no transcriptions of Clarke's surviving shorthand notes in the several published editions of his papers, although the occurrence of brief shorthand phrases in lengthier passages written *en clair* is sometimes, although not invariably, signalled.[1] Despite considerable scholarly interest in shorthand methods and history during the 1880s and 1890s, when the existence of Clarke's manuscripts first became generally known, his shorthand notes appear to have escaped any attempt at decipherment.[2] A comparison with the shorthand of Samuel Pepys (first transcribed some sixty years previously) would have proved fruitful. While superficially the two men's notes do not look much alike – the precise and orderly penmanship of Pepys, written as he reflected at leisure on his day, contrasting markedly with Clarke's fluent and rapid hand – we now know that they both used the same shorthand system.[3]

C.L. Stainer, who examined the Clarke manuscripts for his 1901 edition of Cromwell's speeches, came close to the truth when he commented at length on the use of shorthand by Clarke and others, speculating that the method used 'may have been Mr Shelton's or Mr Riche's'.[4] But it was only in 1973 that Clarke's shorthand was identified by Dr Eric Sams as being written in Shelton's *Tachygraphy*, the system used by Pepys and one of the most popular of the seventeenth century.[5]

[1] For example in *CP*, I, p. 24n, where they are described as 'an unintelligible cypher', and *S&P*, p. 241. I have discussed the technical difficulties of transcribing Clarke's shorthand above, pp. 11–12.

[2] I have discussed possible reasons for this in Henderson, 'The hidden hand of William Clarke', pp. 70–73.

[3] Pepys wrote very slowly, probably about twelve words per minute; Matthews (ed.), T. Shelton, *Tutor to Tachygraphy*, p. vii. Although his diary was first published under the editorship of Richard, Lord Braybrooke in 1825, it was not until the 1870s, and a six-volume edition by the Revd Mynors Bright, that Pepys's shorthand method was identified as Shelton's *Tachygraphy*; Latham and Matthews, *Diary of Samuel Pepys*, I, pp. lxxvi–lxxxvii On Pepys's love of neatness as reflected in his shorthand see *ibid.*, pp. xxviii, xlviii n.

[4] C.L. Stainer, *Speeches of Oliver Cromwell 1644–1658*, pp. vii–xi. Jeremiah Rich's *Charactery. Or, a most easie and exact method of short and swift writing* (London), did not appear until 1646, making it a less likely candidate.

[5] E. Sams, 'Sir William Clarke's shorthand', in Aylmer, *Sir William Clarke Manuscripts 1640–1664*, pp. 29–34. See also *OxDNB*, 'Shelton'. The many editions of both this and

Consequently the documents presented in this edition appear for the first time. In the evaluation of any documentary material which has been transmitted through the medium of shorthand, it is important to understand its limitations in comparison with ordinary longhand. It may be useful to consider here some aspects of the use and reliability of seventeenth-century shorthand in general, and Clarke's in particular.

After the publication of the first modern shorthand schemes in England towards the end of the sixteenth century there are few known instances of personal shorthand systems, and most practitioners (whether in the seventeenth or the twenty-first century) have usually found it more convenient to learn a ready-made method than to invent their own. Our enquiry can perhaps most appropriately begin by asking to what extent early shorthand systems were able to satisfy the expectations and demands of those who used them.

The first schemes to appear in print, invented by Timothy Bright and Peter Bales respectively, were cumbersome, complicated and impractical.[6] However, significant progress was soon made with the invention of a part-alphabetic, part-phonetic system published anonymously by John Willis in 1602, and the further refinements introduced by his namesake Edmond Willis some sixteen years later.[7] Together these two paved the way for a spate of new methods, most derived from them to some extent, over the next two centuries. Nevertheless, although they made appreciable progress towards solving earlier difficulties with speed and ease of memorizing, even these were slow and cumbersome in comparison to the considerably more streamlined methods of today.

Whatever their limitations, the new abbreviated writing systems quickly became fashionable in seventeenth-century England, although they were not adopted in Europe until the middle of the century. They made a considerable impression upon visitors from abroad, for example the Polish scholar Jan Comenius, who in 1641 described them in a letter to friends at home.[8] Many years later John Wilkins compared shorthand to logarithms which 'took a considerable

Shelton's later method, *Zeiglographia or a new art of Short-writing* (London, 1650), are listed in R.C. Alston, *A Bibliography of the English Language . . . , VIII, Treatises on Short-hand* (Leeds, 1966).

[6] T. Bright, *Characterie. An arte of short, swifte and secrete writing by Character . . .* (London, 1588); P. Bales, *The Writing Schoolemaster: Conteining three Bookes in one: the first teaching Swift writing; the second, True-writing, The third, Faire writing . . .* (London, [1590]); F.M.S. McDonald, 'Timothy Bright', in H. Stammerjohann (ed.), *Lexicon Grammaticorum*, 2 vols (Tübingen, 1996).

[7] [J. Willis], *The Art of Stenographie* (London, 1602), was published anonymously, probably because the patent granted to Timothy Bright on 13 July 1588 (Signet Bill 1588 July A Elizabeth) still had one year to run; E. Willis, *An Abreviation of Writing by Character* (London, 1618).

[8] R.F. Young, *Comenius in England* (Oxford and London, 1932), p. 65.

time, before the Learned Men in other parts, did so farr take notice of them as to bring them into use', adding that 'tis not to this day . . . brought into common practice in any other Nation'.[9]

When William Clarke learnt Shelton's *Tachygraphy*, probably as a boy, he chose one of the most popular shorthands of his day, although he could as easily have selected any one of half a dozen rival systems.[10] Like other extra-curricular subjects, they were taught in schools, in the university towns, in London around the Inns of Court, and elsewhere in the country; many (although not all) were also available in printed form. In the editions of Shelton's *Tachygraphy* printed by the university press at Cambridge in 1635, 1641, and 1647, the title page states that the method had been 'approved by both Unyversities', and on one copy a seventeenth-century owner has written 'and espesially at Cambridge'.[11] There are no copies of any of Shelton's primers in Clarke's library at Worcester College, and we do not know whether he was self-taught or learnt his shorthand directly from a writing-master.

Even the earliest schemes offered some genuine advantages in comparison to longhand. The conciseness of shorthand made it ideal for marginal and other annotations, as can be seen in many seventeenth-century libraries, Clarke's being no exception. For example, he noted the birth of his son George in a printed almanac, and he annotated copies of both the Old and New Testaments. He jotted down a *risqué* ballad about Ann Hyde, duchess of York, on the back of a printed advertisement, and wrote an English translation in the margins of Richard Brathwait's Latin play, *Mercurius Britannicus*, all in shorthand.[12]

It was also ideal for personal notes and reminders, and Clarke frequently used it for private memoranda in official record books. For example, in 1648–1649 this was how he recorded the payments which he and his superior, John Rushworth, appear to have received for official warrants and passes, as well as comments about those to whom they were issued.[13] In longhand copies of letters where correspondents

[9] J. Wilkins, *An Essay Towards a Real Character And a Philosophical Language* (London, 1668), p. 13.

[10] These are listed in Alston's *Bibliography*.

[11] W.J. Carlton, *Bibliotheca Pepysiana. A Descriptive Catalogue of the Library of Samuel Pepys. IV. Shorthand Books* (London, 1940), p. vii.

[12] Sir George Wharton, *Calendarium Carolinum* (London, 1661); K. [Anderson], *Katherin Alderson, widdow of the disceased James Alderson, Barber-Chirurgion* . . . , ([London, 1661]), s.sh., verso ; [R. Brathwait], *Mercurius Britannicus. Judicialis Censura: Curialis Cura* ([–], [1641]), *passim* (all now at Worcester College).

[13] Worc. MS LXIX, *passim.*

were identified by their initials only, he often recorded their full names in shorthand marginalia.[14]

From its earliest days one of shorthand's most successful applications was in concealing private or confidential information, as the pioneer inventor Timothy Bright had pointed out in *Characterie*.[15] In his *Tutor to Tachygraphy* Thomas Shelton wrote that many of his pupils learnt his system with this advantage specifically in mind, particularly 'divers Merchants and Factors, who have in forraigne parts used Bibles and Testaments, written in this hand, where they durst not make use of those that are Printed'.[16]

Samuel Pepys was not alone in protecting his diary entries by writing them in shorthand; others who did so included Samuel Jeake, Elias Ashmole, and John Locke.[17] Locke wrote that it was worth learning shorthand for 'concealment of what [men] would not have lie open to every eye', adding that the writer could introduce variations of his own for greater privacy.[18] On occasion William Clarke used the pages of his working notebooks as a diary to record events which were particularly important in his private life. Such entries were always written in shorthand, as were most copies of his personal correspondence.[19] But he most often employed it to camouflage sensitive official information, often in the form of newsletters, which he copied into his notebooks and then presumably destroyed the longhand originals, of which very few survive. Confidential information about matters within the headquarters was similarly protected. For example, one notebook which records orders, warrants and passes issued by General Monck during the period 1654–1655, is written mainly *en clair*; the few shorthand entries all relate to local intelligence gathering, to the Overton plot, and to secret arrangements to capture leading Scottish noblemen.[20]

[14] These are listed in Appendix A above.

[15] Bright, *Characterie*, sig. A3[r]; J. Knowlson, *Universal Language Schemes in England and France* (Toronto and Buffalo, 1975), p. 19.

[16] Shelton, *A Tutor to Tachygraphy, or, Short-writing* (London, 1642), sig. A3[r].

[17] M. Hunter and A. Gregory (eds), *An Astrological Diary of the Seventeenth Century, Samuel Jeake of Rye, 1652–1699* (Oxford, 1988), pp. 25, 279; W. Matthews, *British Diaries* (London, 1950), pp. 14, 29, 36.

[18] 'Of Education' in [J. Locke], *The Works of John Locke* (10th edn, 1801), IX, p. 151.

[19] For example, on 12 February 1657 he recorded the birth of a son and, just under a year later, the little boy's death 'and with him dies my greatest hopes and joys'; Worc. MS XXIX, fo. [4][v]; XXX, fo. [17][r]. It is probable that his pre-1650 notebooks also contained such private material but that he eliminated it from his post-Restoration fair copies of official papers.

[20] Worc. MS XLVI, unfoliated, e.g. entries for 26 October 1654, 13 and 21 December 1654; for entries relating to the Overton plot, 29 December-15 March 1655. Much of the correspondence relating to the plot is similarly written in shorthand; pp. 231–241, 242–243, 244–245 above.

Although comparatively simple to decrypt, shorthand was used successfully as an informal and convenient cipher;[21] in some respects it may even have been more secure than conventional ciphers, since it did not require a prearranged key which could fall into the wrong hands.

Tachygraphy was the method favoured by most, if not all, of Clarke's working colleagues, including John Rushworth[22] and other so far unidentified members of the army secretariat.[23] Thomas Wragge also evidently used *Tachygraphy*, as Clarke could read his notes and implied that Rushworth could do so also.[24] In this way the secretaries were able to use it as a means of communicating privately with each other. In November 1650 Rushworth, writing from London to Clarke in Edinburgh, asked him to send letters often 'but write very cautiously unless you write in shorthand'.[25] Proceedings of the meeting of army officers at Saffron Walden on 7 May 1647 were protected by being sent to London in shorthand, when a member of the army secretariat (most likely Clarke himself, or possibly Thomas Wragge) wrote, perhaps to Rushworth, 'I was charged not to communicate it to any, and soe I have sent it in short hand for your own use'.[26] Technically, shorthand was not a cipher and so did not infringe the ordinance of April 1643 which made it an offence to send 'any Letters or Papers written with Cyphers, or any other unknowne Characters'.[27]

Where seventeenth-century shorthand was considerably less effective, despite its reputation to the contrary, was in recording speech verbatim. Early inventors often covered their claims in this respect by stipulating that such speech should be uttered 'treatably',[28] and there was a considerable amount of popular comment to the same effect. John Phillips, for example, wrote:

> There *Will* writes Short-hand with a pen of brasse,
> Oh how he's wonder'd at by many an asse
> That see him shake so fast his wartie fist

[21] J. F[alconer], *Cryptomenysis Patefacta* (London, 1685), p. 89; J. Davys, *An Essay on the Art of Decyphering, in which is inserted a Discourse of Dr Wallis*... (London, 1737), p. 16.

[22] F. Henderson, '"Posterity to judge" – John Rushworth and his "Historicall Collections"', *Bodleian Library Record*, 15 (1996), pp. 247–259.

[23] For example, see BL, Additional MS 21417, fo. 288v.

[24] *CP*, I, p. 31.

[25] *L-P*, p. 79. For another request for intelligence to be concealed in 'characters', or shorthand, see [Haselrig, Sir Arthur], *A Letter from [him] in Portsmouth*... (London, 1659), p. 6.

[26] *CP*, I, p. 28; see also *ibid.*, p. 31.

[27] *Mercurius Aulicus*, [42] (15–21. Oct. 1643), p. 598.

[28] P. Bales *The arte of brachygraphie: that is to write as fast as a man speaketh treatably*, ... (London, 1597); [J. Willis], *Art of Stenographie*, sig. A2v, 'he that is well practized in this Art may write Verbatim, as fast as a man can treateably speak'.

As if he'd write the Sermon 'fore the Priest
Has spoke it . . .
Nay I could see that many Short hand wrote,
Where listning well, I could not hear a jote;[29]

It was also customary to rely on more than one note-taker whenever possible; several versions could then be compared and a final edition agreed upon. The parliamentary diarist Thomas Burton, for instance, records that he compared his version of Cromwell's lengthy speech of 25 January 1658 with those taken by John Smythe, Clerk of the Commons, and John Rushworth.[30] Of three shorthand writers in attendance when Charles I was beheaded,[31] one was almost certainly William Clarke.[32] Depictions of the king's execution rarely feature a note-taker and then show only one, kneeling on one knee and resting a pad on the other.[33]

In the two months after his part in recording the proceedings of the High Court of Justice set up to try King Charles I, Clarke took notes at the trial and executions of James Hamilton, earl of Cambridge, the earls of Norwich and Holland, Sir Arthur Capel, and Sir John Owen.[34] As in the case of the king's trial and execution, he supplied transcripts to his brother-in-law, the official licenser Gilbert Mabbott;[35] the printing was then put in hand by another close contact, John Playford, who may have been related to Clarke.[36] Official note-takers present at earlier state trials such as that of Archbishop Laud

[29] [J. Phillips], *A Satyre against Hypocrites* (London, 1655), pp. 5, 9, quoted in E. M. Simpson, *A Study of the Prose Works of John Donne* (Oxford, 1924), pp. 268–269. I owe this reference to the kindness of Dr Geri McIntosh. William Clarke's copy of the pamphlet survives in Worcester College library.

[30] Burton, *Diary*, II, p. 351. Burton did not use a conventional shorthand scheme, but relied on a personal system of 'speedwriting'; BL, Additional MSS 15859–15864.

[31] *England's Black Tribunall* (London, 1660), p. 65.

[32] Lesley Le Claire first drew my attention to Clarke's copy of *King Charles His Speech Made upon the Scaffold at Whitehall-Gate* (London, 1649), where he twice placed an asterisk and 'W.C.' in the margin to indicate that he was not only present but was directly addressed by the king; the 1703 edition of *England's Black Tribunall* (p. 47) is more specific: at the same point it adds '(Mr Clark, who wrote)'. Its publisher, Henry Playford, was descended from Clarke's friend John Playford, and presumably added this from personal knowledge.

[33] Ashmolean Museum, Oxford (Sutherland Collection, C. 111. 198).

[34] For these proceedings see Worc. MS LXX; for Clarke's presence see, for example, *ibid.*, fo. 134^{v}.

[35] C.V. Wedgwood has written that 'The ultimate decision about publication [of the king's trial and execution] would rest with [Theodore] Jennings and Mabbott, and the shorthand writers had presumably been employed by either or both of them'; *The Trial of Charles I* (Harmondsworth, 1983), p. 195.

[36] C.W., *A Perfect Narrative of the whole Proceedings of the High Court of Iustice in the Tryall of the King . . .* (London, 1649); *King Charles his Tryal. Together with the speeches of Duke Hamilton, the Earl of Holland, and the Lord Capel, immediately before their execution, 9 March* (London, 1649). Clarke often referred to Playford as 'my brother Playford'.

in 1644 probably included not only Rushworth and Clarke but also John Hinde, known to contemporaries as the 'stenographer of the scaffold'.[37] Records of oral material rarely survive in Clarke's extant shorthand; in the present edition, notes on two conversations of 1659 have clearly been written in retrospect and are not verbatim accounts.[38]

Modern writers have tended to be somewhat dismissive about Clarke's effectiveness as a shorthand writer. Sir Charles Firth believed that Clarke was 'not a very skilful note-taker',[39] while A.S.P. Woodhouse in the introduction to his revised edition of Clarke's record of the Putney debates believed that its deficiencies were due to 'a frenzied effort on the part of the stenographer to catch up with the speaker', noting that 'No speech of any length is wholly free from . . . defect'.[40] In fact, considering the primitive techniques available at the time, the record of the debates is remarkably complete. More recently, attention has been drawn to the deficiencies of the 'crude shorthand' rather than those of the writer,[41] although the statement still requires some modification. In the fifty years or so which had elapsed since the earliest published methods of Bright and Bales, shorthand methods had made considerable advances, although still very primitive and cumbersome in comparison with the methods of today. Clarke was clearly an experienced note-taker by the autumn of 1647, and his shorthand skills must have been exceptional in order for him to have been entrusted with reporting many major events. It is, however, virtually impossible that one man acting alone, however skilled, could have recorded the three full days of debate at Putney using any shorthand system then available.[42] As with other such accounts, the record is almost certainly a composite text taken from more than one set of notes.[43] Thus it is clear that particular caution must be exercised in the interpretation of shorthand records of oral material.

[37] Worc. MS LXXI; W. Laud, *The Archbishop of Canterbury's Speech Or His Funerall Sermon* (London, 1645), which Hinde claimed was an accurate version of Laud's speech as spoken, not as in Laud's written notes. Hinde published accounts of many such events, for example Sir Henry Hyde, *A true Copy of [his] Speech on the Scaffold . . . Taken in Short-hand* (London, 1651).

[38] Pp. 290–293 above.

[39] *CP*, I, p. xiii.

[40] Woodhouse, *Puritanism and Liberty*, p. [*12*]. Woodhouse also observed the defectiveness of the punctuation, doubtless unaware that Clarke included virtually no punctuation marks when he was writing in shorthand.

[41] A. Woolrych, 'Looking back on the Levellers', *The Historian*, 34 (1992), p. 5.

[42] Clarke's longhand transcription of the Putney debates is found in Worc. MS LXV. The original shorthand notes have not survived.

[43] F. Henderson, 'Reading, and writing, the text of the Putney debates', in M. Mendle (ed.), *The Putney Debates of 1647: The Army, the Levellers and the English State* (Cambridge, 2001), pp. 36–50.

If, however, as in the present case, the purpose of the writer was convenience or secrecy, when he could normally proceed at his own pace, the original can be more safely relied upon as an authentic record. Moreover, as such material will most often have been written for the writer's personal use, deliberate distortion of the text by the writer can usually be ruled out, and the writer will have made what he or she believes to be an accurate record[44] – something the reader may wish to take into account when reading and assessing this fifth volume of *Clarke Papers* – recorded throughout by William Clarke in what is undoubtedly his own hand.

[44] See S.R. Gardiner's comments in a somewhat different context in *C&P*, III, p. 72n.

SELECT BIBLIOGRAPHY

Printed primary sources

Abbott, W.C., *The Writings and Speeches of Oliver Cromwell*, 4 vols (Oxford, 1937–1947).

Akerman, J.Y. (ed.), *Letters from Roundhead Officers written from Scotland and Chiefly Addressed to Captain Adam Baynes, July MDCL-June MDCLX* (Bannatyne Club, XIV, 1856).

Baker, Sir Richard, *A Chronicle of the Kings of England from the Time of the Romans Government unto the Death of King James . . . whereunto is now added the Reign of King Charles the I and the first thirteen years of King Charles the II* (London, 1670).

Birch, T. (ed.), *A Collection of the State Papers of John Thurloe Esq*, 7 vols (London, 1742).

Calendar of State Papers, Domestic Series

Calendar of State Papers, Venetian

A Declaration of the Armie to his Excellency The Lord Cromwel, for The dissolving of this present Parliament, and chusing of a new Representative (London, 1652).

Dunlop, R. (ed.), *Ireland under the Commonwealth, being a selection of documents relating to the government of Ireland from 1651 to 1659*, 2 vols (Manchester, 1913).

England's Black Tribunall (London, 1703).

Firth, C.H. and Rait, R.S. (eds), *Acts and Ordinances of the Interregnum 1642–1660*, 3 vols (London, 1911).

Firth, C.H. (ed.), *The Clarke Papers: Selections from the Papers of William Clarke*, 4 vols, (Camden Society, N.S. XLIX, LIV, LX, LXII, 1891–1901). Vols I–II reprinted with a new introduction by A. Woolrych, London, 1992.

Firth, C.H. (ed.), *The Memoirs of Edmund Ludlow Lieutenant-General of the Horse in the Army of the Commonwealth of England, 1625–1672*, 2 vols (Oxford, 1894).

Firth, C.H. (ed.), *The Narrative of General Venables* (Camden Society, N.S. LXI, 1900).

Firth, C.H. (ed.), *Scotland and the Commonwealth* (Scottish History Society, XVIII, 1895).

Firth, C.H. (ed.), *Scotland and the Protectorate* (Scottish History Society, XXXI, 1899).

Gardiner, S.R. and Atkinson, C.T. (eds), *Letters and Papers relating to the First Dutch War 1652–1654*, 6 vols (London, 1899–1930).

Historical Manuscripts Commission, *Report on the Manuscripts of F.W. Leyborne-Popham, Esq. of Littlecote, Co. Wilts* (Norwich, 1899).

Journals of the House of Commons, VI (London, 1803), VII (London, 1813).

Joyce, G., *A True Narrative of the Occasions and Causes of the late Lord Gen. Cromwell's anger and indignation against Col George Joyce and his proceedings against him* ([London], 1659).

Kitson, E. and Clark, E.K., 'Some Civil War Accounts, 1647–1650' (Thoresby Society, XI, 1904), pp. 137–235.

Latham, R.C. and Matthews, W. (eds), *The Diary of Samuel Pepys*, 11 vols (London, 1970–1983).

Macray, W.D. and Coxe, H.O. (eds), *Calendar of the Clarendon State Papers preserved in the Bodleian Library*, 6 vols (Oxford, 1869–1976).

[Monck, George, duke of Albemarle], *A Collection of Letters Written by his Excellency General George Monck, Afterwards Duke of Albemarle, Relating to the Restoration of the Royal Family* (London, 1714).

Ogilvie, J.D. (ed.), *Diary of Sir Archibald Johnston of Wariston*, III, 1655–1660 (Scottish History Society, 3rd ser., XXXIV, 1940).

The Parliamentary or Constitutional History of England; Being a Faithful Account Of all the Most remarkable Transactions In Parliament, From the earliest Times, to the Restoration of King Charles II, 24 vols (London, 1751–1762).

Reeve, H. (ed.), *A Journal of the Swedish Embassy in the years 1653 and 1654 impartially written by the Ambassador Bulstrode Whitelocke*, 2 vols (London, 1828).

Rutt, J.T. (ed.), *The Diary of Thomas Burton Esq. Member in the Parliaments of Oliver and Richard Cromwell, from 1656–1659 . . .*, 4 vols (London, 1828).

Sachse, W.L. (ed.), *The Diary of Thomas Rugg 1659–1661* (London, 1961).

Stainer, C.L. (ed.), *Speeches of Oliver Cromwell 1644–1658* (London and New York, 1901).

Terry, C.S. (ed.), *The Cromwellian Union* (Scottish History Society, XL, 1902).

To the Supreame Authoritie the Parliament of the Common-Wealth of England, The humble Petition of the Officers of the Army ([London], 1652).

A True Narrative of the Proceedings in Parliament, Councell of State, General Councell of the Army, and Committee of Safetie; from the 22. of Septemb. untill this present... (London, 1659).

Vaughan, R. (ed.), *The Protectorate of Oliver Cromwell and the state of Europe... illustrated in a series of letters between Dr John Pell..., Sir Samuel Morland, Sir William Lockhart, Mr Secretary Thurloe*, 2 vols (London, 1839).

Whitelock, Bulstrode, *Memorials of the English Affairs from the Beginning of the Reign of Charles the First to the Happy Restoration of King Charles the Second*, 4 vols (Oxford, 1853).

Woodhouse, A.S.P. (ed.), *Puritanism and Liberty. Being the Army Debates (1647–9) from the Clarke Manuscripts with Supplementary Documents*, 2nd edn (London, 1974).

Secondary sources

Aylmer, G.E., *Sir William Clarke Manuscripts 1640–1664* (Brighton, 1979).

Aylmer, G.E., *The State's Servants: The Civil Service of the English Republic 1649–1660* (London and Boston, 1973).

Bayley, A.R., *The Great Civil War in Dorset 1642–1664* (Taunton, 1910).

von Bischoffshausen, S.F., *Des Politik des Protectors Oliver Cromwell in der Auffassung und Thatigkeit seines ministers des Staatssecretars John Thurloe* (Innsbruck, 1899).

Buckroyd, J., 'Bridging the gap: Scotland 1659–1660', *The Scottish Historical Review*, 66 (1987), pp. 1–25.

Capp, B., *Cromwell's Navy* (Oxford, 1989).

Capp, B., *The Fifth Monarchy Men* (London, 1972).

Christie, W.D., *Life of Anthony Ashley Cooper*, 2 vols (London and New York, 1871).

Davies, G., *The Restoration of Charles II 1658–1660* (San Marino, 1955).

Dictionary of National Biography, 63 vols (London, 1885–1900).

Dow, F.D., *Cromwellian Scotland 1651–1660* (Edinburgh, 1979).

Firth, C.H., 'Cromwell and the crown', *English Historical Review*, 17 (1902), pp. 429–442.

Firth, C.H., *The Last Years of the Protectorate 1656–1658*, 2 vols (London, 1909).

Firth, Sir Charles and Davies, G., *The Regimental History of Cromwell's Army*, 2 vols (Oxford, 1940).

Gardiner, S.R., *History of the Commonwealth and Protectorate 1649–1660*, 3rd edn, 3 vols (London etc., 1901).

Greaves, R.L. and Zaller, R. (eds), *Biographical Dictionary of British Radicals in the Seventeenth-Century*, 3 vols (Brighton, 1982–1984).

Gregg, P., *Free-born John: A Biography of John Lilburne* (London etc., 1961).

Henderson, F., 'The hidden hand of William Clarke', *Worcester College Record* (1998), pp. 70–73.

Henderson, F., '"Posterity to judge" – John Rushworth and his "Historicall Collections"', *The Bodleian Library Record*, 15 (1996), pp. 247–259.

Henderson, F., 'Reading, and writing, the text of the Putney debates' in M. Mendle (ed.), *The Putney Debates of 1647: The Army the Levellers and the English State* (Cambridge, 2001), pp. 36–50.

Hirst, D., 'Concord and discord in Richard Cromwell's House of Commons', *English Historical Review*, 103 (1988), pp. 339–358.

Hutton, R., *The Restoration: A Political and Religious History of England and Wales 1658–1667* (Oxford, 1985).

Israel, J., *The Dutch Republic: Its Rise, Greatness, and Fall* (Oxford, 1995).

Levack, B.P., 'The proposed union of English law and Scots law in the seventeenth century', *Juridical Review*, (1975), pp. 97–115.

McDonald, F.M.S., 'The timing of General George Monck's march into England, 1 January 1660', *English Historical Review*, 105 (1990), pp. 363–376.

Nelson, C. and Seccombe, M. (comps), *British Newspapers and Periodicals 1641–1700* (New York, 1987).

Oxford Dictionary of National Biography, 60 vols (Oxford, 2004).

Oxford English Dictionary, 2nd edn, 20 vols (Oxford, 1989).

Pincus, S.C.A., *Protestantism and Patriotism: Ideologies and the Making of English Foreign Policy, 1650–1668* (Cambridge, 1996).

Roots, I., 'Cromwell's ordinances: the early legislation of the Protectorate', in G.E. Aylmer (ed.), *The Interregnum: The Quest for Settlement* (London and Basingstoke, 1974 edn), pp. 43–64.

Roots, I., 'The tactics of the Commonwealthsmen in Richard Cromwell's parliament', in D. Pennington and K. Thomas (eds), *Puritans and Revolutionaries: Essays in Seventeenth-Century History Presented to Christopher Hill* (Oxford, 1982).

Sherwood, R., *The Court of Oliver Cromwell* (London, 1977).

Taft, B., '*The Humble Petition of several Colonels of the Army*: causes, character and results of military opposition to Cromwell's Protectorate', *Huntington Library Quarterly*, 42 (1978), pp. 15–41.

Taft, B., '"They that pursew perfaction on earth . . .", the political progress of Robert Overton', in I. Gentles, J. Morrill, and B. Worden (eds), *Soldiers, Writers and Statesmen of the English Revolution* (Cambridge, 1998), pp. 286–303.

Venning, T., *Cromwellian Foreign Policy* (Basingstoke, 1995).

Woolrych, A., *Commonwealth to Protectorate* (Oxford, 1982).

Woolrych, A., Introduction to *Complete Prose Works of John Milton*, VII, revised edn (New Haven and London, 1980).

Worden, Blair, *The Rump Parliament 1648–1653* (Cambridge, 1977 edn).

INDEX OF CORRESPONDENTS

GENERAL INDEX